This book is to be ret ned   r bef e
the last date   r   w.

16-BIT MICROPROCESSORS
Architecture, Software, and Interface Techniques

WALTER A. TRIEBEL
Intel Corporation

AVTAR SINGH
Anderson Jacobson Inc.

Prentice-Hall, Inc.
Englewood Cliffs, New Jersey 07632

Library of Congress Cataloging in Publication Data

Triebel, Walter A.
  16-bit microprocessors.

  Bibliography: p.
  Includes index.
  1. Intel 8086 (Microprocessor) 2. Motorola 68000
(Microprocessor) 3. Microcomputers. I. Singh, Avtar,
1947–   . II. Title. III. Title: Sixteen-bit
microprocessors.
QA76.8.I292T75 1984   001.64   84–13472
ISBN 0–13–811407–2

Cover design: George Cornell
Manufacturing buyer: Gordon Osbourne

Walter A. Triebel
  To my mother, Marie F. Triebel

Avtar Singh
  To my son, Jasbir
  To my daughter, Harjeet

Printed in the United States of America

10 9 8 7 6 5 4 3 2 1

ISBN 0-13-811407-2 01

Prentice-Hall International, Inc., *London*
Prentice-Hall of Australia Pty. Limited, *Sydney*
Editora Prentice-Hall do Brasil, Ltda., *Rio de Janeiro*
Prentice-Hall Canada Inc., *Toronto*
Prentice-Hall of India Private Limited, *New Delhi*
Prentice-Hall of Japan, Inc., *Tokyo*
Prentice-Hall of Southeast Asia Pte. Ltd., *Singapore*
Whitehall Books Limited, *Wellington, New Zealand*

Contents

Preface

Today, people involved in the design of electronic systems involving microprocessors and microcomputers must have a thorough knowledge of three primary areas: microcomputer architecture, microcomputer software, and hardware interfacing techniques. However, most of the books presently available on the subject stress the architecture of microprocessors, their instruction sets, and programming techniques. Typically, very little information is provided on hardware design and interfacing techniques. This leaves a gap in a person's understanding of how a microprocessor interacts and interfaces with its memory and I/O subsystems. This information is the key to successful application of microcomputer systems.

In this book we have attempted to close this gap between the study of microprocessors and microcomputer systems by putting equal emphasis on the subjects of microprocessor architecture, programming, and hardware interfacing techniques. The book is for use in electrical engineering and electrical engineering technology curricula offered at universities and community colleges. However, the wealth of practical information and applications that are included make the book a valuable reference for practicing engineers and technicians.

A large number of books are already available on microprocessors. However, most of these books deal with the older 8-bit microprocessors, such as the 8080, 6800, and Z-80. Currently, much of the activity in the semiconductor industry is focused on the development and introduction of second- and third-generation 16-bit microprocessor families, such as the 99000, 8086, 68000, Z-8000, and 16000. In our book we have elected to address the educational needs of these newer 16-bit microprocessors and their microcomputer systems.

Instead of presenting the general concepts of all 16-bit microprocessors and microcomputers at an overview level, we have elected to present in detail just two of the most popular device families, the 8086 by Intel Corporation and the 68000 by Motorola Incorporated. Each of these devices is covered in a similar way and at essentially the same depth.

The material presented in the book represents the state-of-the-art of 16-bit microcomputer system technology. It includes topics common to 8-bit microprocessor technology, such as microprocessor internal architecture, microcomputer system architecture, instruction execution, addressing modes, instruction set, programming techniques, program and data storage memory subsystems, input/output circuitry, and interrupt and exception processing.

Moreover, the advent of 16-bit microprocessor technology has led to the introduction of newer system concepts, such as pipelining, instruction prefetch, microcoding, illegal instruction detection, macroinstruction emulation, user and supervisor modes of operation, bus cycles, bus demultiplexing, bus arbitration, memory segmentation, and LSI peripheral controllers. We have also included detailed coverage of these more modern topics.

Use of the book does require some prior knowledge of basic digital electronics. This background is at a level consistent with but not necessarily as extensive as the material covered in the senior author's earlier Prentice-Hall books: Walter A. Triebel, *Integrated Digital Electronics,* 1979, and Walter A. Triebel and Alfred E. Chu, *Handbook of Semiconductor and Bubble Memories*, 1982.

We would like to express special appreciation to Donald Mushinsky for his technical verification and many worthwhile comments on the material covering the 8086 microprocessor.

Every effort has been made to provide up-to-date information on the devices we introduce. However, it is recommended that the reader check with the manufacturer for the most recent data.

WALTER A. TRIEBEL
AVTAR SINGH

1

Introduction to Microprocessors and Microcomputers

1.1 INTRODUCTION

The most recent advances in computer system technology have been closely related to the development of high-performance 16-bit microprocessors and their microcomputer systems. During the last three years, the 16-bit microprocessor market has matured significantly. Today, several complete 16-bit microprocessor families are available. They include support products such as large-scale integrated (LSI) peripheral devices, development systems, emulators, and high-level software languages. Over the same period of time, these higher-performance microprocessors have become more widely used in the design of new electronic equipment and computers.

This book presents a detailed study of two of the most popular 16-bit microprocessors, the 8086 by Intel Corporation and the 68000 by Motorola Incorporated.

In this chapter we begin our study of 16-bit microprocessors. The following topics are discussed:

1. The digital computer
2. Mainframe computers, minicomputers, and microcomputers
3. Hardware elements of the digital computer system
4. General architecture of a microcomputer system
5. Types of microprocessors and single-chip microcomputers

1.2 THE DIGITAL COMPUTER

As a starting point, let us consider what a *computer* is, what it can do, and how it does it. A computer is a digital electronic data processing system. Data are input to the computer in one form, processed within the computer, and the information that results is either output or stored for later use. Figure 1.1 shows a modern computer system.

Computers cannot think about how to process the data that were input. Instead, the user must tell the computer exactly what to do. The procedure by which a computer is told how to work is called *programming* and the person who writes programs for a computer is known as a *programmer*. The result of the programmer's work is a set of instructions for the computer to follow. This is the computer's *program*. When the computer is operating, the instructions of the program guide it step by step through the task that is to be performed.

For example, a large department store can use a computer to take care of bookkeeping for its customer charge accounts. In this application, data about items purchased by the customers, such as price and department, are entered into the computer by an operator. These data are stored in the computer under the customer's account number. On the next billing date, the data are processed and a tabular record of each customer's account is output by the computer. These statements are mailed to the customers as a bill.

In a computer, the program controls the operation of a large amount of electronic circuitry. It is this circuitry that actually does the processing of data. Electronic computers first became available in the 1940s. These early computers were built with vacuum-tube electronic circuits. In the 1950s, a second generation of computers was built. During this period, transistor electronic circuitry, instead of tubes, was used to produce more compact and more reliable computer systems. When the *integrated circuit* (IC) came into the electronic market during the 1960s, a third generation of computers appeared. With ICs, industry could manufacture more complex, higher-speed, and very reliable computers.

Today, the computer industry is continuing to be revolutionized by the advances made in integrated-circuit technology. It is now possible to manufacture *large-scale integrated circuits* (LSI) that can form a computer with just a small group of ICs. In fact, in some cases, a single IC can be used. These new technologies are rapidly advancing the low-performance, low-cost part of the computer marketplace by permitting simpler and more cost-effective designs.

1.3 MAINFRAME COMPUTERS, MINICOMPUTERS, AND MICROCOMPUTERS

For many years the computer manufacturers' aim was to develop larger and more powerful computer systems. These are what we call *large-scale* or *mainframe computers*. Mainframes are always *general-purpose computers*. That is, they are designed

Figure 1.1 Modern large-scale computer (International Business Machines Corp.).

with the ability to run a large number of different types of programs. For this reason, they can solve a wide variety of problems.

For instance, one user can apply the computer in an assortment of scientific applications where the primary function of the computer is to solve complex mathematical problems. A second user can apply the same basic computer system to perform business tasks such as accounting and inventory control. The only difference between the computer systems used in these two applications could be their programs. In fact, today many companies use a single general-purpose computer to resolve both their scientific and business needs.

Figure 1.1 is an example of a mainframe computer manufactured by International Business Machines Corporation (IBM). Because of their high cost, mainframes find use only in central computing facilities of large businesses and institutions.

The many advances that have taken place in the field of electronics over the past two decades have led to rapid advances in computer system technology. For instance, the introduction of *small-scale integrated* (SSI) *circuits*, followed by *medium-scale integrated* (MSI) *circuits*, and *large-scale integrated* (LSI) *circuits*, has led the way in expanding the capacity and performance of the large mainframe computers. But at the same time, these advances have also permitted the introduction of smaller, lower-performance, and lower-cost computer systems.

As computer use grew, it was recognized that the powerful computing capability of a mainframe was not needed by many customers. Instead, they desired easier access to a machine with smaller capacity. It was to satisfy this requirement that the *minicomputer* was developed. Minicomputers, such as that shown in Fig. 1.2, are also digital computers and are capable of performing the same basic operations as the earlier, larger systems. However, they are designed to provide a smaller functional capability. The processor section of this type of computer is typically manufactured using SSI and MSI electronic circuitry.

Minicomputers have found wide use as several-purpose computers, but their lower cost also allows their use in dedicated applications. A computer used in a dedicated application represents what is known as a *special-purpose computer*. By ''special-purpose computer'' we mean a system that has been tailored to meet the needs of a specific application. Examples are process control computers for industrial facilities, data processing systems for retail stores, and medical analysis systems for patient care. Figure 1.3 shows a minicomputer-based retail store data processing system.

The newest development in the computer industry is the *microcomputer*. Today, the microcomputer represents the next step in the evolution of the computer world. It is a computer that has been designed to provide reduced size and capability from that of a minicomputer, with a much lower cost.

The heart of the microcomputer system is the *microprocessor*. A microprocessor is a general-purpose processor built into a single IC. It is an example of an LSI device. Through the use of LSI circuitry in the microcomputer have come the benefits of smaller size, lighter weight, lower cost, reduced power requirements, and higher reliability.

Figure 1.2   Minicomputer system (Digital Equipment Corp.).

Figure 1.3   Retail store data processing system (Sweda International Incorporated).

Figure 1.4   Calculator (Texas Instruments, Incorporated).

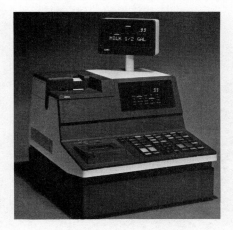

Figure 1.5 Point-of-sale terminal (NCR Corporation).

Figure 1.6 Electronic toy (Texas Instruments, Incorporated).

The low cost of microprocessors, which can be as low as $1, has opened the use of computer electronics to a much broader range of products. Figures 1.4 through 1.6 show some typical systems in which a microcomputer is used as a special-purpose computer.

Microcomputers are also finding wide use as general-purpose computers. Figure 1.7 is an example of a personal computer system. In fact, microcomputer systems designed for the high-performance end of the microcomputer market are rivaling the

Figure 1.7 Personal computer (International Business Machines Corporation).

performance of the lower-performance minicomputers and at a much lower cost to the user.

1.4 HARDWARE ELEMENTS OF THE DIGITAL COMPUTER SYSTEM

The hardware of a digital computer system is divided into four functional sections. The block diagram of Fig. 1.8 shows the four basic units of a simplified computer: the *input unit, central processing unit, memory unit,* and *output unit.* Each section has a special function in terms of overall computer operation.

The *central processing unit* (CPU) is the heart of the computer system. It is responsible for performing all arithmetic operations and logic decisions initiated by the program. In addition to arithmetic and logic functions, the CPU controls overall system operation.

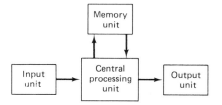

Figure 1.8   Block diagram of a digital computer (Walter A. Triebel, *Integrated Digital Electronics,* © 1979. Adapted by permission of Prentice-Hall, Inc., Englewood Cliffs, N.J.).

On the other hand, the input and output units are the means by which the CPU communicates with the outside world. The *input unit* is used to input information and commands to the CPU for processing. For instance, a Teletype terminal can be used by the programmer to input a new program.

After processing, the information that results must be output. This output of data from the system is performed under control of the *output unit.* Examples of ways of outputting information are as printed pages produced by a high-speed printer or displayed on the screen of a video display terminal.

The *memory unit* of the computer is used to store information such as numbers, names, and addresses. By "store," we mean that memory has the ability to hold this information for processing or for outputting at a later time. The programs that define how the computer is to process data also reside in memory.

In computer systems, memory is divided into two different sections, known as *primary storage* and *secondary storage.* They are also sometimes called *internal memory* and *external memory,* respectively. *External memory* is used for long-term storage of information that is not in use. For instance, it holds programs, files of data, and files of information. In most computers, this part of memory employs storage on magnetic media such as magnetic tapes, magnetic disks, and magnetic drums. This is because they have the ability to store large amounts of data.

Internal memory is a smaller segment of memory used for temporary storage of programs, data, and information. For instance, when a program is to be executed, its instructions are first brought from external memory into internal memory together with the files of data and information that it will affect. After this, the program is executed and its files updated while they are held in internal memory. When the processing defined by the program is complete, the updated files are returned to external memory. Here the program and files are retained for use at a later time.

The internal memory of a computer system uses electronic memory devices instead of storage on a magnetic media memory. In most modern computer systems, semiconductor read-only memory (ROM) and random access read/write memory (RAM) are in use. These devices make internal memory much faster-operating than external memory.

Neither semiconductor memory nor magnetic media memory alone can satisfy the requirements of most general-purpose computer systems. Because of this fact, both types are normally present in the system. For instance, in a personal computer system, working storage is typically provided with RAM, while long-term storage is provided with floppy disk memory. On the other hand, in special-purpose computer systems, such as a video game, semiconductor memory is used. That is, the program that determines how the game is played is stored in ROM, and data storage, such as for graphic patterns, is in RAM.

1.5 GENERAL ARCHITECTURE OF A MICROCOMPUTER SYSTEM

Now that we have introduced the *general architecture* of a digital computer, let us look at how a microcomputer fits this model. Looking at Fig. 1.9, we find that the architecture of the microcomputer is essentially the same as that of the digital computer in Fig. 1.8. It has the same function elements: input unit, output unit, memory unit, and in place of the CPU, a *microprocessor unit* (MPU). Moreover, each element serves the same basic function relative to overall system operation.

The difference between minicomputers, mainframe computers, and microcomputers does not lie in the fundamental blocks used to build the computer; instead, it relates to the capacity and performance of the electronics used to implement their blocks and the resulting overall system capacity and performance. As indicated earlier, microcomputers are designed with smaller capacity and lower performance than either minicomputers or mainframes.

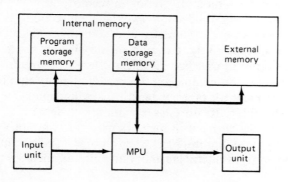

Figure 1.9 General microcomputer system architecture.

Unlike the mainframe and minicomputer, a microcomputer can be implemented with a small group of components. Again the heart of the computer system is the MPU (CPU) and it performs all arithmetic, logic, and control operations. However, in a microcomputer the MPU is implemented with a single microprocessor chip instead of a large assortment of SSI and MSI logic functions such as in minicomputers and mainframes. Notice that correct use of the term "microprocessor" restricts its use to the central processing unit in a microcomputer system.

Notice that we have partitioned the memory unit into an internal memory section for storage of active data and instructions and an external memory section for long-term storage. As in minicomputers, the long-term storage medium in a microcomputer is frequently a floppy disk. However, Winchester rigid disk drives are becoming popular when storage requirements are higher than those provided by floppy disks. In industrial applications, where the environment for the equipment is rugged, bubble memories are also employed as long-term storage devices.

Internal memory of the microcomputer is further subdivided into *program storage memory* and *data storage memory*. Typically, internal memory is implemented with both ROM and RAM ICs. Data, whether they are to be interpreted as numbers, characters, or instructions, can be stored in either ROM or RAM. But in most microcomputer systems, instructions of the program and data such as lookup tables are stored in ROM. This is because this type of information does not normally change. By using ROM, its storage is made *nonvolatile*. That is, if power is lost, the information is retained.

On the other hand, the numerical and character data that are to be processed by the microprocessor change frequently. These data must be stored in a type of memory from which they can be read by the microprocessor, modified through processing, and written back for storage. For this reason, they are stored in RAM instead of ROM.

Depending on the application, the input and output sections can be implemented with something as simple as a few switches for inputs and a few light-emitting diodes (LEDs) for outputs. In other applications, for example in a personal computer, the input/output (I/O) device can be more sophisticated, such as video display terminals and printers, just like those employed in minicomputer systems.

Up to this point, we have been discussing what is known as a *multichip microcomputer system*, that is, a system implemented with a microprocessor and an assortment of support circuits, such as ROMs, RAMs, and I/O peripherals. This architecture makes for a very flexible system design. Its ROM, RAM, and I/O capacity can be easily expanded by just adding more devices. This is the circuit configuration used in most larger microcomputer systems. An example is the personal computer system shown in Fig. 1.10(a).

Devices are now being made that include all the functional blocks of a microcomputer in a single IC. This is called a *single-chip microcomputer*. Unlike the multichip microcomputer, single-chip microcomputers are limited in capacity and not as easy to expand. For example, a microcomputer device can have 4K bytes of ROM, 256 bytes of RAM, and 32 lines for use as inputs or outputs. Because of this limited

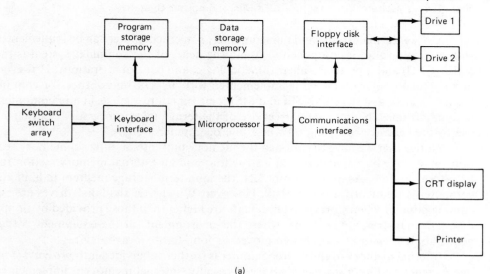

(a)

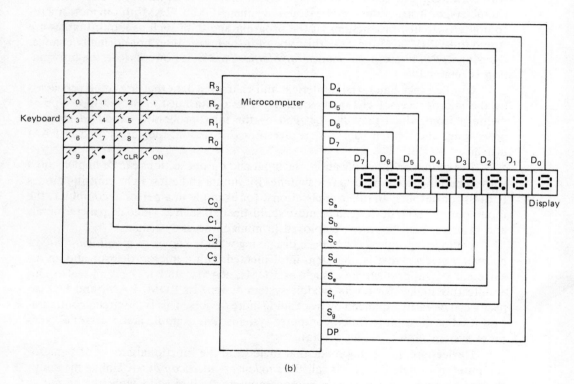

(b)

Figure 1.10   (a) Block diagram of a personal computer; (b) block diagram of a calculator.

capability, single-chip microcomputers find wide use in special-purpose computer applications. A block diagram of a calculator implemented with a single-chip microcomputer is shown in Fig. 1.10(b).

1.6 TYPES OF MICROPROCESSORS AND SINGLE-CHIP MICROCOMPUTERS

The principal way in which microprocessors and microcomputers are categorized is in terms of the number of binary bits in the data they process, that is, their word length. Figure 1.11 shows that the three standard organizations used in the design of microprocessors and microcomputers are 4-bit, 8-bit, and 16-bit data words.

The first microprocessors and microcomputers, which were introduced in the early 1970s, were all designed to process data that were arranged 4 bits wide. This organization is frequently referred to as a *nibble* of data. Many of the early 4-bit devices, such as the PPS-4 microprocessor made by Rockwell International Incorporated and the TMS1000 single-chip microcomputer made by Texas Instruments Incorporated, are still in wide use today.

The low performance and limited system capabilities of 4-bit microcomputers limit their use to simpler, special-purpose applications. Some common uses are in calculators and electronic toys. In this type of equipment, low cost, not high performance, is the overriding requirement in the selection of a processor.

In the 1973–1974 period, second-generation microprocessors were introduced. These devices, such as Intel Corporation's 8008 and 8080, were 8-bit microprocessors. That is, they were designed to process 8-bit (one-byte-wide) data instead of 4-bit data.

The newer 8-bit microprocessors exhibited higher-performance operation, larger system capabilities, and greater ease of programming. They were able to provide the system requirements for many applications that could not be satisfied by 4-bit microcomputers. These extended capabilities led to widespread acceptance of multichip

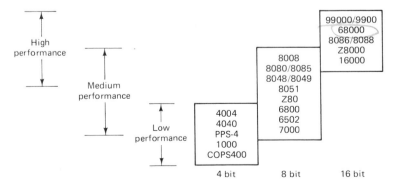

Figure 1.11 Microprocessor and single-chip microcomputer categories and relative performance.

8-bit microcomputers for special-purpose system designs. Examples of some of these dedicated applications are electronic instruments, cash registers, and printers.

Somewhat later, 8-bit microprocessors began to migrate into general-purpose microcomputer systems. In fact, the Z-80A is the host MPU in a number of today's most popular personal computers.

Late in the 1970s, 8-bit single-chip microcomputers, such as Intel's 8048, became available. The full microcomputer capability of this single chip further reduces the cost of implementing designs for smaller, dedicated digital systems. In fact, 8-bit microcomputers are still being designed for introduction into the marketplace. An example is Intel's new 8051 family of 8-bit microcomputers. Newer devices, such as the 8051, offer a one-order-of-magnitude-higher performance, more powerful instruction sets, and special on-chip functions such as interval/event timers and universal asynchronous receiver/transmitters (UARTs).

The plans for development of third-generation 16-bit microprocessors were announced by many of the leading semiconductor manufacturers in the mid-1970s. The 9900 was introduced in 1977, followed by a number of other key devices, such as the 9981, 8086, 8088, Z8000, 68000, 99000, and 16000. All these devices provide high performance and have the ability to satisfy a broad scope of special-purpose and general-purpose computer applications. All of the devices have the ability to handle 8-bit as well as 16-bit data words. Some can even process data organized as 32-bit words. Moreover, their powerful instruction sets are more in line with those provided by minicomputers instead of those by 8-bit microprocessors.

In terms of special-purpose applications, 16-bit microprocessors are replacing 8-bit processors in applications that require very high performance: for example, certain types of electronic instruments. A single-chip 16-bit microcomputer, the 9940, is also available for use in this type of application.

.16-bit microprocessors are also being used in applications that can benefit from some of their extended system capabilities. For instance, they are beginning to be used in word-processing systems. This type of system requires a large amount of character data to be temporarily active; therefore, it can benefit from the ability of a 16-bit microprocessor to access a much larger amount of internal data storage memory.

Most new personal computer designs are being done with 16-bit microprocessors. Actually, IBM's personal computer and Texas Instruments' home computer already use 16-bit microprocessors to implement their microcomputers. In this book we concentrate on two 16-bit microprocessors, the 8086 and 68000, and their microcomputer systems.

ASSIGNMENT

Section 1.2

1. What guides the computer as to how it is to process data?
2. What type of electronic devices are revolutionizing the low-performance, low-cost computer market today?

Section 1.3

3. What is the key difference between mainframe, mini-, and microcomputers?

4. What is meant by "general-purpose computer"?

5. What is meant by "special-purpose computer"?

Section 1.4

6. What are the building blocks of a general computer system?

7. What is the difference between primary and secondary storage?

Section 1.5

8. What are the basic building blocks of a microcomputer system?

9. What is the difference between program storage and data storage memory in a microcomputer?

10. What is the difference between internal and external storage memory in a microcomputer?

Section 1.6

11. What are the standard data word lengths of microprocessors and microcomputers available today?

12. What is the difference between a multichip microcomputer and a single-chip microcomputer?

13. Name five 16-bit microprocessor families.

2

The 8086 Microprocessor

2.1 INTRODUCTION

In Chapter 1 some general aspects of microprocessors and microcomputers were introduced. With the present chapter we begin our study of Intel's 8086 microprocessor and its microcomputer system, describing their general architectural aspects. The next five chapters are devoted to such aspects as instruction set, programming, memory interface, input/output interface, and interrupt handling. Specifically, this chapter deals with:

1. The 8086 microprocessor
2. Minimum- and maximum-mode systems and interfaces
3. Internal architecture of the 8086 microprocessor
4. The 8284 clock generator and 8086 bus cycle
5. Instruction execution in the 8086 system

2.2 THE 8086 MICROPROCESSOR

The 8086, first announced in 1978, was the first 16-bit microprocessor introduced by Intel Corporation. It has been followed by a steady stream of family components such as the 8088 microprocessor, the 8087 numeric processor, and the 8089 I/O processor.

The 8086 is manufactured using *high-performance metal-oxide-semiconductor* (HMOS) *technology* and the circuitry on its chip is equivalent to approximately 29,000

14

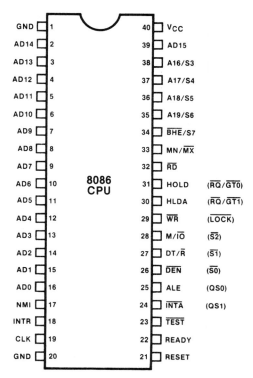

Figure 2.1 Pin layout of the 8086 microprocessor (Intel Corporation).

transistors. It is enclosed in a 40-pin package as shown in Fig. 2.1. Many of its pins have multiple functions. For example, in the pin layout we see that address lines A_0 through A_{15} and data bus lines D_0 through D_{15} are multiplexed. For this reason, these leads are labeled AD_0 through AD_{15}.

The 8086 is a true 16-bit microprocessor with 16-bit internal and external data paths. It has the ability to address up to 1M byte of memory via a 20-bit-wide address bus. Moreover, it can address up to 64K of byte-wide input/output ports or 32K of word-wide ports.

2.3 MINIMUM-MODE AND MAXIMUM-MODE SYSTEMS

The 8086 microprocessor can be configured to work in either of two modes. These modes are known as the *minimum system mode* and the *maximum system mode*. The minimum system mode is selected by applying logic 1 to the MN/$\overline{\text{MX}}$ input lead. Minimum 8086 systems are typically smaller and contain a single microprocessor. Changing MN/$\overline{\text{MX}}$ to logic 0 selects the maximum mode of operation. This configures the 8086 system for use with multiple processors. This mode-selection feature lets the 8086 better meet the needs of a wide variety of system requirements.

Depending on the mode of operation selected, the assignments for a number of the pins on the 8086's package are changed. As shown in Fig. 2.1, the pin functions specified in parentheses are those that pertain to a maximum mode system.

The signals that are common to both modes of operation, those unique to minimum mode, and those unique to maximum mode are listed in Fig. 2.2(a), (b), and (c), respectively. Here we find the name, function, and type for each signal. For example, the signal $\overline{RD}$ is in the common group. It functions as a read control output and is used to signal memory or I/O devices when the 8086's system bus is set up for input of data. Moreover, notice that the signals hold request (HOLD) and hold acknowledge (HLDA) are produced only in the minimum-mode system. If the 8086 is set up for maximum mode, they are replaced by the request/grant bus access control lines $\overline{RQ/GT}_0$ and $\overline{RQ/GT}_1$.

2.4 MINIMUM-SYSTEM-MODE INTERFACE

When the minimum system mode of operation is selected, the 8086 itself provides all the control signals needed to implement the memory and I/O interfaces. Figure 2.3 shows a block diagram of a minimum-mode configuration of the 8086. The minimum-mode signals can be divided into the following basic groups: address/data bus, status, control, interrupt, and DMA. For simplicity in the diagram, multiplexed signal lines are shown to be independent.

Address/Data Bus

Let us first look at the address/data bus. In an 8086-based system these lines serve two functions. As an *address bus*, they are used to carry address information to the memory and I/O ports. The address bus is 20 bits long and consists of signal lines A_0 through A_{19}. Of these, A_{19} represents the MSB and A_0 the LSB. A 20-bit address gives the 8086 a 1M-byte memory address space. Moreover, it has an independent I/O address space which is 64K bytes in length.

The 16 *data bus* lines D_0 through D_{15} are actually multiplexed with address lines A_0 through A_{15}, respectively. By "multiplexed" we mean that the bus works as an address bus during one period of time and as a data bus during another period. D_{15} is the MSB and D_0 the LSB. When acting as a data bus, they carry read/write data for memory, input/output data for I/O devices, and interrupt-type codes from an interrupt controller.

Status Signals

The four most significant address lines, A_{19} through A_{16}, are also multiplexed, but in this case with status signals S_6 through S_3. These status bits are output on the bus at the same time that data are transferred over the other bus lines. Bits S_4 and S_3 together form a 2-bit binary code that identifies which of the 8086's internal segment registers was used to generate the physical address that was output on the address bus during the current bus cycle. These four codes and the register they represent

Common Signals		
Name	Function	Type
AD15–AD0	Address/Data Bus	Bidirectional, 3-State
A19/S6–A16/S3	Address/Status	Output, 3-State
$\overline{BHE}$/S7	Bus High Enable/ Status	Output, 3-State
MN/$\overline{MX}$	Minimum/Maximum Mode Control	Input
$\overline{RD}$	Read Control	Output, 3-State
$\overline{TEST}$	Wait On Test Control	Input
READY	Wait State Control	Input
RESET	System Reset	Input
NMI	Non-Maskable Interrupt Request	Input
INTR	Interrupt Request	Input
CLK	System Clock	Input
Vcc	+5V	Input
GND	Ground	

Minimum Mode Signals (MN/MX = Vcc)		
Name	Function	Type
HOLD	Hold Request	Input
HLDA	Hold Acknowledge	Output
$\overline{WR}$	Write Control	Output, 3-State
M/$\overline{IO}$	Memory/IO Control	Output, 3-State
DT/$\overline{R}$	Data Transmit/ Receive	Output, 3-State
$\overline{DEN}$	Data Enable	Output, 3-State
ALE	Address Latch Enable	Output
$\overline{INTA}$	Interrupt Acknowledge	Output

Maximum Mode Signals (MN/MX = GND)		
Name	Function	Type
$\overline{RQ}$/$\overline{GT1, 0}$	Request/Grant Bus Access Control	Bidirectional
$\overline{LOCK}$	Bus Priority Lock Control	Output, 3-State
$\overline{S2}$–$\overline{S0}$	Bus Cycle Status	Output, 3-State
QS1, QS0	Instruction Queue Status	Output

(a)

(b)

(c)

Figure 2.2 (a) Signals common to both minimum and maximum modes (Intel Corporation); (b) unique minimum-mode signals (Intel Corporation); (c) unique maximum-mode signals (Intel Corporation).

17

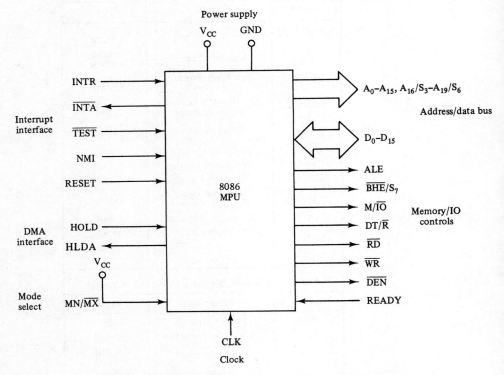

Figure 2.3 Block diagram of the minimum-mode 8086 MPU.

are shown in Fig. 2.4. Notice that the code $S_4 S_3 = 00$ identifies a register known as the *extra segment register* as the source of the segment address.

Status line S_5 reflects the status of another internal characteristic of the 8086. It is the logic level of the internal interrupt enable flag. The last status bit S_6 is always at the 0 logic level.

Control Signals

The *control signals* are provided to support the 8086's memory and I/O interfaces. They control functions such as when the bus is to carry a valid address, in which direction data are to be transferred over the bus, when valid write data are on the bus, and when to put read data on the system bus. For example, *address latch enable* (ALE) is a pulse to logic 1 that signals external circuitry when a valid address word is on the bus. This address must be latched in external circuitry on the 1-to-0 edge of the pulse at ALE.

Another control signal that is produced during the bus cycle is $\overline{\text{BHE}}$ (*bank high enable*). Logic 0 on this line is used as a memory enable signal for the most significant byte half of the data bus, D_8 through D_{15}. This line also serves a second function, which is as the S_7 status line.

S_4	S_3	Segment register
0	0	Extra
0	1	Stack
1	0	Code/none
1	1	Data

Figure 2.4   Memory segment status codes.

Using the M/$\overline{\text{IO}}$ (*memory/IO*) and DT/$\overline{\text{R}}$ (*data transmit/receive*) lines, the 8086 signals which type of bus cycle is in progress and in which direction data are to be transferred over the bus. The logic level of M/$\overline{\text{IO}}$ tells external circuitry whether a memory or I/O transfer is taking place over the bus. Logic 1 at this output signals a memory operation, and logic 0 an I/O operation. The direction of data transfer over the bus is signaled by the logic level output at DT/$\overline{\text{R}}$. When this line is logic 1 during the data transfer part of a bus cycle, the bus is in the transmit mode. Therefore, data are either written into memory or output to an I/O device. On the other hand, logic 0 at DT/$\overline{\text{R}}$ signals that the bus is in the receive mode. This corresponds to reading data from memory or input of data from an input port.

The signals *read* ($\overline{\text{RD}}$) and *write* ($\overline{\text{WR}}$), respectively, indicate that a read bus cycle or a write bus cycle is in progress. The 8086 switches $\overline{\text{WR}}$ to logic 0 to signal external devices that valid write or output data are on the bus. On the other hand, $\overline{\text{RD}}$ indicates that the 8086 is performing a read of data off the bus. During read operations, one other control signal is also supplied. This is $\overline{\text{DEN}}$ (*data enable*), and it signals external devices when they should put data on the bus.

There is one other control signal that is involved with the memory and I/O interface. This is the READY signal. It can be used to insert wait states into the bus cycle such that it is extended by a number of clock periods. This signal is provided by way of an external clock generator device and can be supplied by the memory or I/O subsystem to signal the 8086 when they are ready to permit the data transfer to be completed.

Interrupt Signals

The key interrupt interface signals are *interrupt request* (INTR) and *interrupt acknowledge* ($\overline{\text{INTA}}$). INTR is an input to the 8086 that can be used by an external device to signal that it needs to be serviced. This input is sampled during the final clock period of each *instruction acquisition cycle*. Logic 1 at INTR represents an active interrupt request. When an interrupt request has been recognized by the 8086, it indicates this fact to external circuits with pulses to logic 0 at the $\overline{\text{INTA}}$ output.

The $\overline{\text{TEST}}$ input is also related to the external interrupt interface. Execution of a WAIT instruction causes the 8086 to check the logic level at the $\overline{\text{TEST}}$ input. If logic 1 is found, the MPU suspends operation and goes into what is known as the *idle state*. The 8086 no longer executes instructions; instead, it repeatedly checks the logic level of the $\overline{\text{TEST}}$ input waiting for its transition back to logic 0. As $\overline{\text{TEST}}$ switches to 0, execution resumes with the next instruction in the program. This feature can be used to synchronize the operation of the 8086 to an event in external hardware.

There are two more inputs in the interrupt interface: the *nonmaskable interrupt* (NMI) and the *reset interrupt* (RESET). On the 0-to-1 transition of NMI, control is passed to a nonmaskable interrupt service routine. The RESET input is used to provide a hardware reset for the 8086. Switching RESET to logic 0 initializes the internal registers of the 8086 and initiates a reset service routine.

DMA Interface Signals

The *direct memory access* (DMA) interface of the 8086 minimum-mode system consists of the HOLD and HLDA signals. When an external device wants to take control of the system bus, it signals this fact to the 8086 by switching HOLD to the 1 logic level. At the completion of the current bus cycle, the 8086 enters the hold state. When in the hold state, signal lines AD_0 through AD_{15}, A_{16}/S_3 through A_{19}/S_6, $\overline{\text{BHE}}$, $M/\overline{\text{IO}}$, $DT/\overline{R}$, $\overline{\text{RD}}$, $\overline{\text{WR}}$, $\overline{\text{DEN}}$, and INTR are all in the high-Z state. The 8086 signals external devices that it is in this state by switching its HLDA ouput to the 1 logic level.

2.5 MAXIMUM-SYSTEM-MODE INTERFACE

When the 8086 is set for the maximum-mode configuration, it produces signals for implementing a *multiprocessor/coprocessor system environment*. By "multiprocessor environment" we mean that more than one microprocessor exists in the system and that each processor is executing its own program. Usually in this type of system environment, there are some system resources that are common to all processors. They are called *global resources*. There are also other resources that are assigned to specific processors. These dedicated resources are known as *local* or *private resources*.

Coprocessor also means that there is a second processor in the system. However, in this case, the two processors do not access the bus at the same time. One passes control of the system bus to the other and then may suspend its operation. In the maximum-mode 8086 system, facilities are provided for implementing allocation of global resources and passing bus control to other microcomputers or coprocessors.

8288 Bus Controller—Bus Commands and Control Signals

Looking at the maximum-mode block diagram in Fig. 2.5, we see that the 8086 does not directly provide all the signals that are required to control the memory, I/O, and interrupt interfaces. Specifically, the $\overline{\text{WR}}$, $M/\overline{\text{IO}}$, $DT/\overline{R}$, $\overline{\text{DEN}}$, $\overline{\text{ALE}}$, and $\overline{\text{INTA}}$ signals are no longer produced by the 8086. Instead, it outputs three status signals $\overline{S}_0$, $\overline{S}_1$, and $\overline{S}_2$ prior to the initiation of each bus cycle. This 3-bit *bus status code* identifies which type of bus cycle is to follow. $\overline{S}_2\overline{S}_1\overline{S}_0$ are input to the external *bus con-*

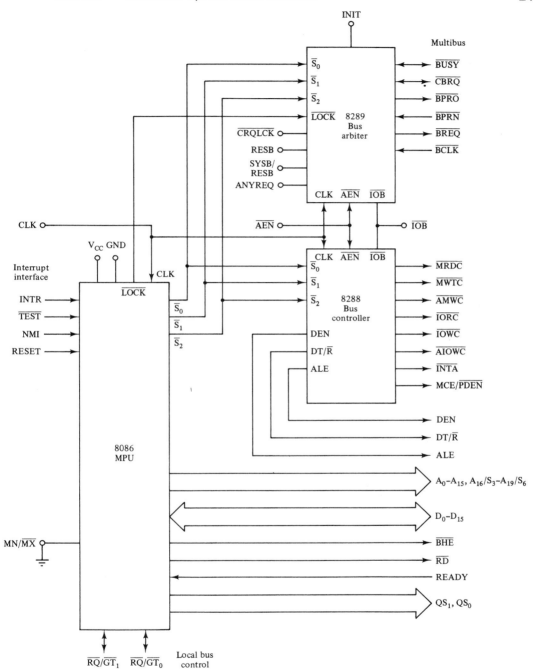

Figure 2.5   8086 maximum-mode block diagram.

troller device, the 8288, which decodes them to identify the type of MPU bus cycle. In response, the bus controller generates the appropriately timed command and control signals.

Figure 2.6 shows the relationship between the bus status codes and the types of bus cycles. Also shown are the output signals that are generated to tell external circuitry which type of bus cycle is taking place. These output signals are: *memory read command* ($\overline{MRDC}$), *memory write command* ($\overline{MWTC}$), *advanced memory write command* ($\overline{AMWC}$), *I/O read command* ($\overline{IORC}$), *I/O write command* ($\overline{IOWC}$), *advanced I/O write command* ($\overline{AIOWC}$), and *interrupt acknowledge command* ($\overline{INTA}$).

The 8288 produces one or two of these eight command signals for each bus cycle. For instance, when the 8086 outputs the code $\overline{S}_2\overline{S}_1\overline{S}_0$ equals 001, it indicates

Status Inputs			CPU Cycle	8288 Command
$\overline{S2}$	$\overline{S1}$	$\overline{S0}$		
0	0	0	Interrupt Acknowledge	$\overline{INTA}$
0	0	1	Read I/O Port	$\overline{IORC}$
0	1	0	Write I/O Port	$\overline{IOWC}$, $\overline{AIOWC}$
0	1	1	Halt	None
1	0	0	Instruction Fetch	$\overline{MRDC}$
1	0	1	Read Memory	$\overline{MRDC}$
1	1	0	Write Memory	$\overline{MWTC}$, $\overline{AMWC}$
1	1	1	Passive	None

Figure 2.6 Bus status codes (Intel Corporation).

that an I/O read cycle is to be performed. In turn, the 8288 makes its $\overline{IORC}$ output switch to logic 0. On the other hand, if the code 111 is output by the 8086, it is signaling that no bus activity is to take place.

The control outputs produced by the 8288 are DEN, DT/$\overline{R}$, and ALE. These three signals provide the same functions as those described for the minimum system mode. This set of bus commands and control signals is compatible with the *Multibus*, an industry standard for interfacing microprocessor systems.

The 8289 Bus Arbiter—Bus Arbitration and Lock Signals

Looking at Fig. 2.5, we see that an 8289 *bus arbiter* has also been added in the maximum-mode system. It is this device that permits multiple processors to reside on the system bus. It does this by implementing the *Multibus arbitration protocol* in an 8086-based system.

Addition of the 8288 bus controller and 8289 bus arbiter frees a number of the 8086's pins for use to produce control signals that are needed to support multiple processors. *Bus priority lock* ($\overline{LOCK}$) is one of these signals. It is input to the bus arbiter together with status signals $\overline{S}_0$ through $\overline{S}_2$. The outputs of the 8289 are bus arbitration signals: *bus busy* ($\overline{BUSY}$), *common bus request* ($\overline{CBRQ}$), *bus priority out* ($\overline{BPRO}$), *bus priority in* ($\overline{BPRN}$), *bus request* ($\overline{BREQ}$), and *bus clock* ($BCLK$).

They correspond to the *bus exchange* signals of the Multibus and are used to lock other processors off the system bus during the execution of an instruction by the 8086. In this way the processor can be assured of uninterrupted access to *common system resources* such as *global memory*.

Queue Status Signals

Two new signals that are produced by the 8086 in the maximum-mode system are queue status outputs QS_0 and QS_1. Together they form a 2-bit *queue status code*, QS_1QS_0. This code tells the external circuitry what type of information was removed from the queue during the previous clock cycle. Figure 2.7 shows the four different queue statuses. Notice that $QS_1QS_0 = 01$ indicates that the first byte of an instruction was taken off the queue. As shown, the next byte of the instruction that is fetched is identified by the code 11. Whenever the queue is reset due to a transfer of control, the reinitialization code 10 is output.

QS1	QS0	Queue Status
0 (low)	0	No Operation. During the last clock cycle, nothing was taken from the queue.
0	1	First Byte. The byte taken from the queue was the first byte of the instruction.
1 (high)	0	Queue Empty. The queue has been reinitialized as a result of the execution of a transfer instruction.
1	1	Subsequent Byte. The byte taken from the queue was a subsequent byte of the instruction.

Figure 2.7   Queue status codes (Intel Corporation).

Local Bus Control Signals—Request/Grant Signals

In a maximum-mode configuration, the minimum-mode HOLD, HLDA interface is also changed. These two signals are replaced by *request/grant lines* $\overline{RQ}/\overline{GT}_0$ and $\overline{RQ}/\overline{GT}_1$, respectively. They provide a prioritized bus access mechanism for accessing the *local bus*.

2.6 INTERNAL ARCHITECTURE OF THE 8086

The internal architecture of a microprocessor describes its functional components and their interaction. Figure 2.8 shows a block diagram of the internal architecture of the 8086 microprocessor.

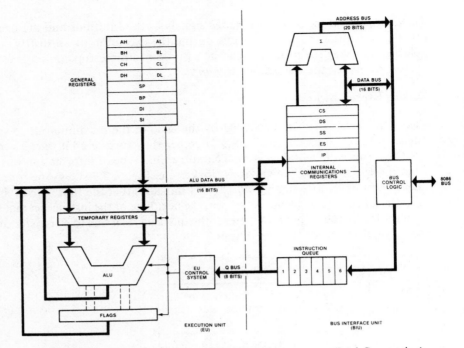

Figure 2.8 Internal architecture of the 8086 microprocessor (Intel Corporation).

Internal Blocks of the 8086

Within the 8086 microprocessor, the internal functions are divided between two separate processing units. They are the *bus interface unit* (BIU) and the *execution unit* (EU). In general, the BIU is responsible for performing all bus operations, such as instruction fetching, reading and writing operands for memory, and inputting or outputting of data for peripherals. On the other hand, the EU is responsible for executing instructions.

Both units operate asynchronously to give the 8086 an overlapping instruction fetch and instruction execution mechanism. In essence, this parallel processing of the BIU and EU eliminates the time needed to fetch many of the instructions. This results in efficient use of the system bus and significantly improved system performance.

Bus Interface Unit

The bus interface unit is the 8086's interface to the outside world. It provides a full 16-bit bidirectional data bus and 20-bit address bus. The bus interface unit is responsible for performing all external bus operations. Specifically, it has the following functions: *instruction fetch, instruction queueing, operand fetch and storage, address relo-*

cation, and *bus control*. To implement these functions, the BIU contains the *segment registers, internal communication registers, instruction pointer, instruction object code queue, address summer*, and *bus control logic*. These components are identified in Fig. 2.8.

The BIU uses a mechanism known as an *instruction stream queue* to implement a *pipeline architecture*. This queue permits prefetch of up to six bytes of instruction code. Whenever the queue of the BIU is not full, that is, it has room for at least two more bytes, and at the same time, the EU is not requesting it to read or write operands from memory, the BIU is free to look ahead in the program by prefetching the next sequential instruction. These prefetched instructions are held in its *first in, first out (FIFO) queue*. With its 16-bit data bus, the BIU fetches two instruction bytes in a single memory cycle. After a byte is loaded at the input end of the queue, it automatically shifts up through the FIFO to the empty location nearest the output. The EU accesses the queue from the output end. It reads one instruction byte after the other from the output of the queue.

If the queue is full and the EU is not requesting access to operands in memory, the BIU does not perform any bus cycles. These intervals of no bus activity, which may occur between bus cycles, are known as *idle states*. Moreover, if the BIU is already in the process of fetching an instruction when the EU requests it to read or write operands from memory or I/O, the BIU first completes the instruction fetch bus cycle before initiating the operand read/write cycle.

The BIU also contains a dedicated adder which is used to generate the 20-bit *physical address* that is output on the address bus. This address is formed by adding an appended 16-bit segment address and a 16-bit offset address. For example, the physical address of the next instruction to be fetched is formed by combining the current contents of the code segment (CS) register and the current contents of the instruction pointer (IP) register.

The BIU is also responsible for generating bus control signals such as those for memory read or write and I/O read or write. These signals are needed for control of the circuits in the memory and I/O subsystems.

Execution Unit

The execution unit is responsible for *decoding* and *executing* all instructions. Notice in Fig. 2.8 that it consists of an *ALU, status and control flags, eight general-purpose registers, temporary registers*, and *queue control logic*.

The EU extracts instructions from the top of the queue in the BIU, decodes them, generates operand addresses if necessary, passes them to the BIU and requests it to perform the read or write bus cycles to memory or I/O, and performs the operation specified by the instruction on the operands. During execution of the instruction, the EU tests the status and control flags and updates them based on the results of executing the instruction. If the queue is empty, the EU waits for the next instruction byte to be fetched and shifted to the top of the queue.

When the EU executes a branch or jump instruction, it transfers control to a location corresponding to another set of sequential instructions. Whenever this happens, the BIU automatically resets the queue and then begins to fetch instructions from this new location to refill the queue.

2.7 INTERNAL REGISTERS OF THE 8086

The 8086 has four groups of user-accessible internal registers. They are the *instruction pointer, four data registers, four pointer and index registers*, and *four segment registers*. They represent a total of thirteen 16-bit registers. In addition to these registers, there is another 16-bit register called the *status register*, with 9 of its bits implemented for *status* and *control flags*.

Instruction Pointer

The *instruction pointer* (IP) is a 16-bit register within the 8086 that identifies the location of the next instruction to be executed in the current code segment. It is similar to a program counter (PC); however, IP contains an offset pointer instead of the physical address of the next instruction. This is because the 8086 contains 16-bit registers and memory, but requires a 20-bit address. The offset must be combined with the contents of another register, in this case the code segment register (CS), to generate the physical address of the instruction. This register is physically located in the BIU.

Every time an instruction word is fetched from memory, the BIU updates the value in IP such that it points to the next sequential instruction word in memory.

Data Registers

As shown in Fig. 2.8, there are four general-purpose data registers that are located within the EU of the 8086. During program execution, they are used for temporary storage of frequently used intermediate results. The advantage of storing these data in internal registers instead of memory is that they can be accessed much faster.

The *data registers* are shown in more detail in Fig. 2.9(a). Here we see that the four data registers are referred to as the *accumulator register* (A), the *base register* (B), the *count register* (C), and the *data register* (D). Each register can be accessed either as a 16-bit word or as two 8-bit bytes. References to a register as a word are identified by an X after the register letter. For instance, the accumulator is referenced as AX. In a similar way, the other three registers are referred to as BX, CX, and DX.

On the other hand, when referencing one of these registers on a byte-wide basis, its high byte and low byte are identified by following the register name with the letter H or L, respectively. For the A register, the most significant byte is referred to as AH and the least significant byte as AL. The other byte-wide register pairs are BH and BL, CH and CL, and DH and DL.

Any of the general-purpose data registers can be used for arithmetic or logic operations such as add or AND. However, for some operations, such as those performed by string instructions, specific registers are used. In the case of a string in-

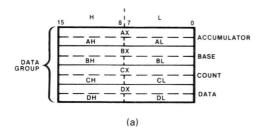

(a)

REGISTER	OPERATIONS
AX	Word Multiply, Word Divide, Word I/O
AL	Byte Multiply, Byte Divide, Byte I/O, Translate, Decimal Arithmetic
AH	Byte Multiply, Byte Divide
BX	Translate
CX	String Operations, Loops
CL	Variable Shift and Rotate
DX	Word Multiply, Word Divide, Indirect I/O

(b)

Figure 2.9 General-purpose registers (Intel Corporation); (b) dedicated register functions (Intel Corporation).

struction, register C is used to store a count representing the number of bytes to be moved. This is the reason it is given the name "count register."

Another example of dedicated use of data registers is that all I/O operations require the data that are to be input or output to be in the A register, while register D holds the address of the I/O port. Figure 2.9(b) summarizes the dedicated functions of the general-purpose data registers.

Pointer and Index Registers

There are four other general-purpose registers shown in Fig. 2.8, two *pointer registers* and two *index registers*. They are used to store offset addresses of memory locations relative to the segment registers. The values held in these registers can be loaded or modified through software. This is done prior to executing the instruction that references the register for address offset. In this way, the instruction simply specifies which register contains the offset address.

Figure 2.10 shows that the two pointer registers are the *stack pointer* (SP) and *base pointer* (BP). The stack pointer permits easy access to locations in the stack segment of memory. The value in SP represents the offset of the next stack location

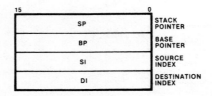

Figure 2.10 Pointer and index registers (Intel Corporation).

which can be accessed relative to the current address in the stack segment (SS) register; that is, it always points to the top of the stack.

BP also represents an offset from the SS register. However, it is used to access data within the stack segment.

The index registers are used to hold offset addresses for instructions that access data stored in the data segment of memory. For this reason, they are always referenced to the value in the data segment (DS) register. The *source index* (SI) register is used to store an offset address for a source operand and the *destination index* (DI) register is used for storage of an offset that identifies the location of a destination operand. For example, a string instruction that requires an offset to the location of a source or destination operand would use these registers.

Segment Registers

As we indicated earlier, the physical address of the 8086 is 20 bits wide, but its registers and memory locations which contain logical addresses are just 16 bits wide. This gives a 1M-byte address space. However, the address space is segmented into 64K-byte segments and just four segments can be active at a time. It is for selection of the four active segments that the 16-bit *segment registers* are provided within the BIU of the 8086.

These four registers are the *code segment* (CS) *register*, the *data segment* (DS) *register*, the *stack segment* (SS) *register*, and the *extra segment* (ES) *register*. These registers are shown in Fig. 2.11. They are loaded with 16-bit addresses that identify which segments of memory are active. For example, the value in CS identifies the starting address of the 64K-byte segment known as the code segment. By "starting address," we mean the lowest-addressed byte in the active code segment. The values held in these registers, for instance the current code segment address, are frequently referred to as the current segment register values.

Code segments of memory contain instructions of the program. The contents of CS identify the starting location of the current code segment in memory. To access the storage location of an instruction in the active code segment, the 8086 must

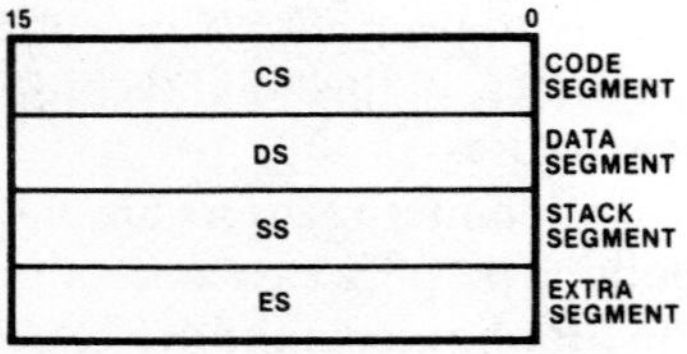

Figure 2.11 Segment registers (Intel Corporation).

generate its 20-bit physical address. To do this, it combines the contents of the instruction pointer (IP) register with the value in CS to produce the physical address that will be output on the address bus.

The active code segment can be changed by simply executing an instruction that loads a new value into the CS register. For this reason, we can use any of the 16 independent 64K-byte segments of memory for storage of code.

The contents of the data segment (DS) register identify the starting location of the current data segment in memory. This is a second active 64K segment that provides a read/write memory space in which data can be stored. Operands for most instructions are fetched from this segment. However, a prefix may be included with the instruction to obtain operands from any of the other segments. Values in the source index (SI) register or destination index (DI) register are combined with the value in DS to form the 20-bit physical address of the source or destination operand in the data segment.

The stack segment (SS) register contains a logical address that identifies the starting location of the current stack segment in memory. It is the 64K segment to which the values of the instruction pointer (IP), status flags, and other registers are pushed whenever a hardware interrupt, software interrupt, or subroutine call occurs. After the service routine or subroutine is complete, the original system status is restored from the stack by executing pop instructions and the return instruction. The next location to which a word is to be pushed or from which a word is to be popped is identified by combining the current value in SS with the stack pointer (SP).

The last segment register identifies the fourth active 64K-byte memory area. This area is called the *extra segment* (ES). The extra segment is usually used for data storage. For instance, the string instructions use the value in ES with the contents of DI as an offset to specify the destination address.

Flag Register

The *flag register* is a 16-bit register within the EU. However, as shown in Fig. 2.12, just 9 of its bits are implemented. Six of these bits represent status flags. They are the *carry flag* (CF), the *parity flag* (PF), the *auxiliary carry flag* (AF), the *zero flag* (ZF), the *sign flag* (SF), and the *overflow flag* (OF).

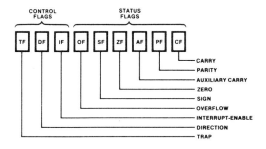

Figure 2.12 Status and control flags (Intel Corporation).

The *status flags* indicate conditions that are produced as the result of executing an arithmetic or logic instruction. That is, specific flag bits are reset (logic 0) or set (logic 1) at the completion of execution of the instruction.

Let us first summarize the operation of these status flags.

1. The *carry flag* (CF): CF is set if there is a carryout or a borrow in for the most significant bit of the result during the execution of an arithmetic instruction. Otherwise, CF is reset.

2. The *parity flag* (PF): PF is set if the result produced by the instruction has even parity, that is, if it contains an even number of bits at the 1 logic level. If parity is odd, PF is reset.

3. The *auxiliary carry flag* (AF): AF is set if there is a carryout from the low nibble into the high nibble or a borrow in from the high nibble into the low nibble of the lower byte in a 16-bit word. Otherwise, AF is reset.

4. The *zero flag* (ZF): ZF is set if the result of an operation is zero. Otherwise, ZF is reset.

5. The *sign flag* (SF): The MSB of the result is copied into SF. Thus SF is set if the result is a negative number or reset if it is positive.

6. The *overflow flag* (OF): When OF is set, it indicates that the signed result is out of range. If the result is not out of range, OF remains reset.

For example, at the completion of execution of a byte addition instruction, the carry flag (CF) could be set to indicate that the sum of the MSBs in the operands caused a carryout condition. The auxiliary carry flag (AF) could also set due to the execution of the instruction. This depends on whether or not a carryout occurred from the least significant nibble to the most significant nibble when the byte operands are added. The sign flag (SF) is also affected and it will reflect the logic level of the MSB of the result.

The status flags are read only; therefore, they can only be tested. The 8086 provides instructions within its instruction set which are able to use these flags to alter the sequence in which the program is executed. For instance, ZF equal to logic 1 could be tested as the condition that would initiate a jump to another part of the program.

The other three implemented flag bits are *control flags*. They are the *direction flag* (DF), the *interrupt enable flag* (IF), and the *trap flag* (TF). These three flags control functions of the 8086 as follows:

1. The *trap flag* (TF): If TF is set, the 8086 goes into the single-step mode. When in the single-step mode, it executes one instruction at a time. This type of operation is very useful for debugging programs.

2. The *interrupt flag* (IF): For the 8086 to recognize maskable interrupt requests at its INT input, the IF flag must be set. When IF is reset, requests at INT are ignored and the maskable interrupt interface is disabled.

3. The *direction flag* (DF): The logic level of DF determines the direction in which string operations will occur. When it is reset, the string instruction automatically decrements the address. Therefore, the string data transfers proceed from high address to low address. On the other hand, setting DF causes the string address to be incremented. In this way, transfers proceed from low address to high address.

Bits CF, DF, IF, and TF of the flag register can be modified at any point in the program through user software. That is, special instructions are provided in the instruction set of the 8086 such that they can be set or cleared. For instance, at the beginning of an interrupt service routine, IF could be reset. This locks out the occurrence of another maskable interrupt. At the end of the service routine, it could be set once again to enable the maskable interrupt interface.

2.8 SYSTEM CLOCK

The time base for synchronization of the internal and external operations of the 8086 microprocessor is provided by the CLK input signal. At present, the 8086 is available in two different speeds. The standard part operates at 5 MHz and the 8086-2 operates at 8 MHz. CLK is externally generated by the 8284 clock generator and driver IC. Figure 2.13 is a block diagram of this device.

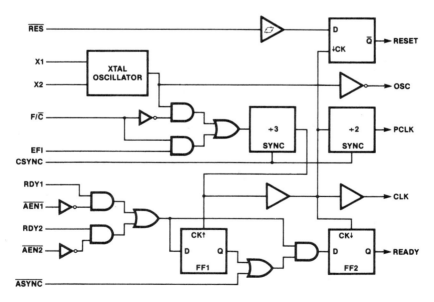

Figure 2.13   Block diagram of the 8284 clock generator (Intel Corporation).

The normal way in which this clock chip is used is to connect either a 15-MHz or a 24-MHz crystal between its X_1 and X_2 inputs. This circuit connection is shown in Fig. 2.14. Notice that a series capacitor C_L is also required. Its typical value when used with the 15-MHz crystal is 12 pF. The *fundamental crystal frequency* is divided by 3 within the 8284 to give either a 5-MHz or a 8-MHz clock signal. This signal is buffered and output at CLK. CLK can be directly connected to CLK of the 8086.

The waveform of CLK is shown in Fig. 2.15. Here we see that the signal is at *MOS-compatible voltage levels* and not TTL levels. Its minimum and maximum low logic levels are $V_{Lmin} = -0.5$ V and $V_{Lmax} = 0.6$ V, respectively. Moreover, the minimum and maximum high logic levels are $V_{Hmin} = 3.9$ V and $V_{Hmax} = V_{CC} + 1$ V, respectively. The *period* of the 5-MHz clock signal can range from a minimum of 200 ns to a maximum of 500 ns, and the maximum *rise* and *fall times* of its edges equal 10 ns.

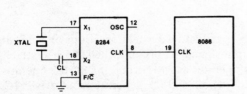

Figure 2.14   Connecting the 8284 to the 8086 (Intel Corporation).

Figure 2.15   CLK voltage and timing characteristics (Intel Corporation).

In Fig. 2.13 we see that there are two more clock outputs on the 8284. They are *peripheral clock* (PCLK) and *oscillator clock* (OSC). These signals are provided to drive peripheral ICs. The clock signal output at PCLK is always half the frequency of CLK. That is, it is either 2.5 MHz or 4 MHz. Also, it is at TTL-compatible levels rather than MOS levels. On the other hand, the OSC output is at the fundamental clock frequency, which is three times that of CLK. These relationships are illustrated in Fig. 2.16.

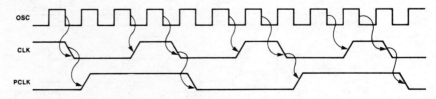

Figure 2.16   Relationship between CLK and PCLK (Intel Corporation).

2.9 BUS CYCLE

The *bus cycle* of the 8086 is used to access memory, I/O devices, or the interrupt controller. As shown in Fig. 2.17(a), it corresponds to a sequence of events that starts with an address being output on the system bus followed by a read or write data transfer. During these operations, a series of control signals are also produced by the 8086 to control the direction and timing of the bus.

The bus cycle of the 8086 processor consists of at least four clock periods. These four time states are called T_1, T_2, T_3, and T_4. During T_1, the BIU puts an address on the bus. For a write memory cycle, data are put on the bus during period T_2 and maintained through T_3 and T_4. When a read cycle is to be performed, the bus is first put in the high-Z state during T_2 and then the data to be read must be put on the bus during T_3 and T_4. These four clock states give a *bus cycle duration* of 125 ns × 4 = 500 ns in an 8-MHz 8086 system.

If no bus cycles are required, the BIU performs what are known as *idle states*. During these states no bus activity takes place. Each idle state is one clock period long and any number of them can be inserted between bus cycles. Figure 2.17(b) shows two bus cycles separated by idle states. Idle states are also performed if the queue is full and the EU does not require the BIU to read or write operands from memory.

Wait states can also be inserted into a bus cycle. This is done in response to a request by an event in external hardware instead of an internal event such as a full queue. In fact, the READY input of the 8086 is provided specifically for this purpose. Figure 2.17(c) shows that logic 0 at this input indicates that the current bus

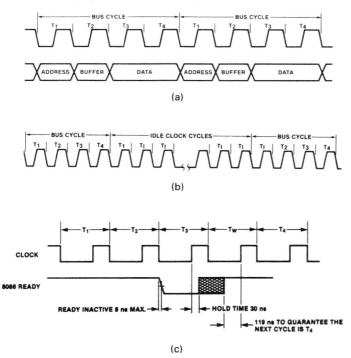

Figure 2.17   (a) Bus cycle clock periods (Intel Corporation); (b) bus cycle with idle states (Intel Corporation); (c) bus cycle with wait states (Intel Corporation).

cycle should not be completed. As long as READY is held at the 0 level, wait states are inserted between periods T_3 and T_4 of the current bus cycle and the data that were on the bus during T_3 are maintained. The bus cycle is not completed until the external hardware returns READY back to the 1 logic level. This extends the duration of the bus cycle, thereby permitting the use of slower memory devices in the system.

2.10 INSTRUCTION EXECUTION SEQUENCE

During normal system operation, the 8086 fetches instructions one after the other from program memory and executes them. After an instruction is fetched it must be decoded within the 8086 and if necessary its operands read from either data memory or from internal registers. The operation specified in the instruction is performed on the operands and the results written back to either an internal register or a location in data memory. The 8086 is now ready to execute the next instruction.

Figure 2.18 shows in detail the overlapping of instruction fetch and execution by the 8086. Notice that as the EU is executing the previously fetched first instruction, the BIU fetches the second sequential instruction over the system bus. After this, a third instruction is fetched and put in the queue. During the third period, the second instruction is available at the output of the queue. It is extracted from the queue by the EU and executed. At the same time, the BIU uses the bus to write the result of the first instruction into memory. In the next period, a fourth instruction is fetched by the BIU and put into its queue. During the fifth period, an operand required by the third instruction is read over the bus. Finally, the third instruction is executed and a fifth instruction fetched. Notice that during this interval of time four new instructions were fetched and loaded into the queue and three instructions were executed.

An assembly language program and its equivalent 8086 machine code are shown in Fig. 2.19(a). This program is a loop that executes repeatedly. Notice that the instructions are coded using one, two, three, or four bytes. For example, the instruction MOV AX,0F802 is represented with the three bytes $B8_{16}$, 02_{16}, and $F8_{16}$. On the other hand, PUSH AX takes up just one byte, which is 50_{16}.

The program is stored in the code segment of memory as consecutive bytes as shown in Fig. 2.19(b). Notice that it takes 16 byte addresses to hold the complete program.

Remember that the queue status and bus status are output signals of the maximum-mode 8086. QS_1QS_0 identifies the instruction queue status initiated by the EU during the previous clock period. Moreover, the code at $\overline{S}_2\overline{S}_1\overline{S}_0$ tells an external 8288 bus controller which type of bus cycle is currently in progress.

Also remember that the interaction between the BIU and EU is by way of the queue for prefetched instruction opcodes and immediate operands. On the other hand,

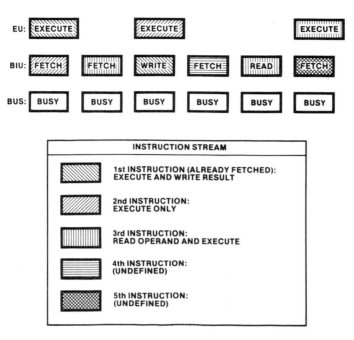

Figure 2.18 Overlapping instruction fetch and execution (Intel Corp.).

bus cycles must be requested of the BIU by the EU for accessing data operands in memory.

Figure 2.19(c) shows in detail the relationships between signals, bus activity, and internal queue status that are important to understand the instruction execution sequence of the 8086. This diagram includes the clock periods (CLK), bus status codes ($\overline{S}_2\overline{S}_1\overline{S}_0$), types of bus cycle (BIU activity), contents of the queue (QUEUE), queue status codes (QS_1QS_0), and instruction execution cycle (EU instruction execution).

Let us now trace the operation of the 8086 step by step through the execution of an instruction from the program in Fig. 2.1(a). In this example we will assume that the jump instruction JMP $-14 had already been read out of the queue by the EU. Therefore, during clock periods 1 through 7 the EU is performing this operation. At clock period 1 in Fig. 2.19(c), we see that the queue has been initialized and contains no valid opcodes. Therefore, during this period, queue status $QS_1QS_0 = 10$ is output. This indicates that the queue is empty. Moreover, the bus is idle (T_I) for clock periods 1 and 2.

The next four clock periods, 3 through 6, represent a code fetch bus cycle. Notice that the bus activity identifies the four clock periods T_1 through T_4 of a read bus cycle. During this bus cycle, $B802_{16}$ is fetched from program storage memory and loaded into the queue. The code fetch status code $\overline{S}_2\overline{S}_1\overline{S}_0 = 100$ is output by the 8086 during periods T_1 and T_2 of the bus cycle.

The next four clock periods, 7 through 10, represent another read bus cycle. This cycle corresponds to the fetch of $F850_{16}$ and its placement in the queue. But at the same time, the EU reads the first two bytes of the MOV instruction from the queue. The first byte, which is $B8_{16}$, is accompanied by the first byte queue status code, $QS_1QS_0 = 01$, and the second byte, 02_{16}, is accompanied by the $QS_1QS_0 = 11$ status code. Remember that this is a three-byte instruction and the last byte, which is $F8_{16}$, was just fetched into the queue. At the end of this second instruction fetch bus cycle, we find that just two bytes, $F8_{16}$ and 50_{16}, remain in the queue. They represent the last byte of the MOV instruction and the complete PUSH instruction.

During clock periods 11 through 14, another code fetch bus cycle takes place. Moreover, during the first half of the bus cycle, the EU removes the third byte of the MOV instruction from the queue. This completes execution of the MOV AX,0F802H instruction. Execution of the remaining instructions proceeds similarly.

ASSEMBLY LANGUAGE	MACHINE CODE
MOV AX, 0F802H	B802F8
PUSH AX	50
MOV CX, BX	8BCB
MOV DX, CX	8BD1
ADD AX, [SI]	0304
ADD SI, 8086H	81C68680
JMP $ −14	EBF0

(a)

B8
02
F8
50
8B
CB
8B
D1
03
04
81
C6
86
80
EB
F0

(b)

Figure 2.19 (a) Example program (Intel Corporation); (b) code storage in memory; (c) execution sequence (Intel Corporation).

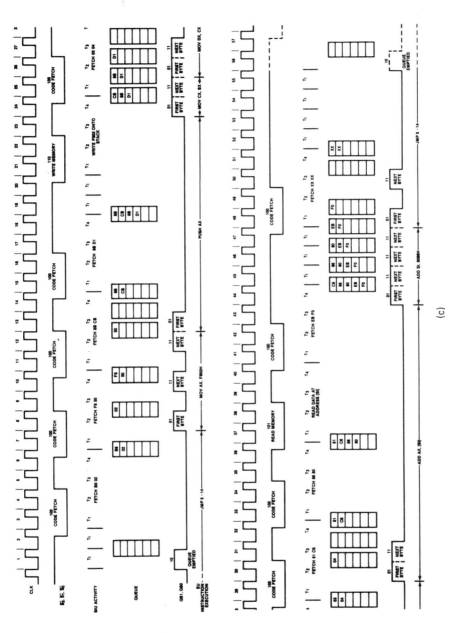

Figure 2.19 (continued)

(c)

37

ASSIGNMENT

Section 2.2

1. Name the technology used to fabricate the 8086 microprocessor.
2. What is the difference between the 8086 and 8088 MPUs?
3. How much memory can the 8086 directly address?
4. How large is the I/O address space of the 8086?

Section 2.3

5. How is the minimum or maximum mode of operation selected?
6. Describe the differences between the minimum-mode 8086 system and the maximum-mode 8086 system.

Section 2.4

7. What are the word lengths of the 8086's address bus and data bus?
8. What does "the status code $S_6S_5S_4S_3$ equals 0001" mean in terms of the memory segment that is being accessed and the interrupt enable/disable status?
9. What signal does the 8086 respond with when it acknowledges an active interrupt request?
10. List the signals that go to the high-Z state in response to a DMA request.

Section 2.5

11. Identify the signal lines of the 8086 that are different for the minimum-mode and maximum-mode interfaces.
12. What control signals are generated by the 8288 bus controller in a maximum-mode system? Which input signals does the 8288 accept from the 8086?
13. What function is served by the 8289 bus arbiter in a maximum-mode 8086 system?
14. If the 8086 executes a jump instruction, what queue status code would be output?
15. Which pins provide signals for local bus control in a maximum-mode 8086 system?

Section 2.6

16. Specify the basic functions served by the bus interface unit and execution unit of the 8086.
17. Describe the internal interface between the BIU and EU.

Section 2.7

18. Make a list of the general-purpose registers of the 8086 and specify their lengths.
19. What dedicated operations are assigned to the general-purpose register?
20. What is the difference between an instruction pointer and a program counter?
21. Identify the pointer and index registers of the 8086. In what way are they different from the general-purpose registers?
22. Why are segment registers provided in the 8086? State the function of each segment register.

23. What is the difference between the functions of status and control flags? Make a list of the status and control flags provided in the 8086. Describe the function of each of these flags.

Section 2.8

24. What is the primary function of the clock generator in an 8086 system? Which signals that are produced by the clock generator are applied to the 8086 MPU?
25. What are the voltage levels of the clock waveform supplied to the 8086 MPU?

Section 2.9

26. Whenever the 8086 reads from or writes to memory, what signal must be received before the bus cycle will run to completion?
27. What is the difference between an idle state and a wait state?

Section 2.10

28. Explain why and how the execution time of the current instruction will be affected by the previous instruction.

3

8086 Microprocessor
Programming 1

3.1 INTRODUCTION

Chapter 2 was devoted to the general architectural aspects of the 8086 microprocessor. In this chapter we introduce a large part of its instruction set. These instructions provide the ability to write simple straight-line programs. Chapter 4 covers the rest of the instruction set and some more sophisticated programming concepts. The following topics are presented in this chapter:

1. Software model of the 8086 microprocessor
2. Assembly language and machine language
3. The 8086 addressing modes
4. The 8086 instruction set
5. Data transfer instructions
6. Arithmetic instructions
7. Logic instructions
8. Shift instructions
9. Rotate instructions

3.2 SOFTWARE MODEL OF THE 8086 MICROPROCESSOR

The purpose of developing a *software model* is to aid the programmer in understanding the operation of the microcomputer system from a software point of view. To be able to program a microprocessor, one does not need to know all of its hardware

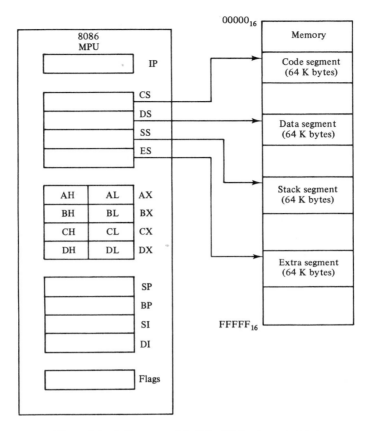

Figure 3.1 Software model of the 8086 microprocessor.

features. For instance, we do not necessarily need to know the function of the signals at its various pins, their electrical connections, or their switching characteristics. Moreover, the function, interconnection, and operation of the internal circuits of the microprocessor also need not normally be considered.

What is important to the programmer is to know the various registers within the device and to understand their purpose, functions, and operating capabilities and limitations. Furthermore, it is essential to know how external memory is organized and how it is addressed to obtain instructions and data.

The software architecture of the 8086 is illustrated with the model in Fig. 3.1. Looking at the model, we see that it includes the 13 internal registers and flags of the 8086 and 1M byte of external memory. Our concern here is with what can be done with this architecture and how to do it through software. For this purpose, let us review briefly the elements of the model. Moreover, this time we concentrate on their relationship to software.

Memory Structure and the Segment Registers

As shown in Fig. 3.1, the 8086 microprocessor supports 1M byte of external memory. This memory space is organized as bytes over the address range 00000_{16} to $FFFFF_{16}$. From an addressing point of view, even- or odd-addressed bytes of data can be independently accessed. Information in the form of 16-bit words can also be stored and accessed. For words of data, the most significant byte is stored at the higher byte address and the least significant byte at the lower byte address.

Notice in Fig. 3.1 that just four 64K-byte segments of memory are active at a time. These segments are called the *code segment, stack segment, data segment*, and *extra segment*. Instructions and data operands in these segments are referenced with the help of the 16-bit segment registers CS, SS, DS, and ES that are located within the microprocessor. Each of these registers contains a 16-bit base address that is used in the generation of the physical memory address that points to the start of the corresponding segment in memory. For example, the code segment register (CS) points to the lowest-addressed location in the current code segment. It is this segment of memory that contains instructions of the program.

The offset of the next instruction that is to be fetched from the current code segment is identified by instruction pointer IP. That is, the contents of CS and IP are combined to form the 20-bit address of the next instruction. After the instruction is fetched, IP is incremented such that it points to the next sequential instruction.

The data segment register (DS) points to the segment of memory in which data to be processed are typically stored. The locations of this segment can be accessed by instructions for use as source or destination operands.

The programmer has the ability to change the values in the segment registers under software control. For example, a new data segment can be established by simply changing the value in DS. This can be done by executing just one or two instructions.

The General-Purpose Registers

The general-purpose group of registers consists of four 16-bit registers called AX, BX, CX, and DX. Each of these registers is addressable as a whole for 16-bit operations or as two 8-bit registers to handle byte operations. For instance, the register AX is a 16-bit register for word operations. But for byte operations, it is considered as two separate 8-bit registers, AH for the high byte and AL for the low byte. In a similar way, word registers BX, CX, and DX are also addressable as byte-wide register pairs BH,BL, CH,CL, and DH,DL.

The registers in this group are known as the *accumulator register* (AX or AL,AH), *base register* (BX or BH,BL), *count register* (CX or CH,CL), and the *data register* (DX or DH,DL). These names imply special functions that are performed by each register.

Each of the four general-purpose registers can be used as the source or destination of an operand during an arithmetic, logic, shift, or rotate operation. The use of the accumulator register is also assumed by some instructions. For example, it is either the source or destination register for data during all I/O-mapped input and output operations. Furthermore, multiplication and division arithmetic operations, translate-table operations, and string operations also always use part of the AX register.

During the execution of instructions using what is called the *based addressing mode*, base register BX is used as a pointer to an operand in the current data segment. Thus it contains a memory offset address, not a source or destination operand.

The count register gets its name from the fact that it is used as a counter by some instructions. For instance, its lower byte, CL, contains the count of the number of bits by which the contents of the operand must be rotated or shifted by multiple-bit rotate or shift instructions. It is also used as a counter by string and loop instructions.

The data register, DX, is used in all multiplication and division operations. It must also contain an input/output port address for some types of input/output operations.

Pointer and Index Registers

The next group of four registers consists of two pointer and two index registers. The two pointer registers are the *stack pointer* (SP) and *base pointer* (BP).The contents of the stack pointer are used as an offset from the current value of SS during the execution of instructions that involve the stack segment in external memory. It identifies the location of the top of the stack in the current stack segment. The value in SP is automatically incremented or decremented, respectively, whenever a POP or a PUSH instruction is executed.

The base pointer also contains an offset address into the current stack segment. This offset address is employed when using the based addressing mode and is commonly used by instructions in a subroutine that reference parameters that were passed by way of the stack.

The *source index register* (SI) and the *destination index register* (DI) are used to hold offset addresses for use in indexed addressing of operands in memory. In instructions that use the indexed type of addressing, the source index is generally with reference to the current data segment, and the destination index is with reference to the current extra segment.

The index registers can also be used as source or destination registers in arithmetic and logical operations. Unlike the general-purpose registers, these registers must always be used for 16-bit information and cannot be accessed as two separate bytes.

Flags

The 8086 microprocessor also contains nine 1-bit flags. These flags, identified in Chapter 2, are CF, PF, AF, ZF, SF, TF, IF, DF, and OF. The states of most of these flags reflect the result of the instruction just executed. Specifically, these are the carry, auxiliary carry, zero, sign, parity, and overflow flags. These flag bits can be tested under software control to determine the sequence in which the program should be executed.

The rest of the flags control operating features of the 8086. For instance, the logic level of DF determines whether the contents of the count register are to be incremented or decremented during string operations. Similarly, the flags IF and TF are used to enable/disable interrupts and the single-step mode of operation, respectively. The instruction set of the 8086 includes instructions for saving, loading, and manipulating these flags.

3.3 ASSEMBLY LANGUAGE AND MACHINE LANGUAGE

Now that we have introduced the software model of the 8086, let us continue with the concepts of *assembly language* and *machine language* instructions and programs. It is essential to become familiar with these ideas before attempting to learn the functions of the instructions in the instruction set and their use in writing programs.

Assembly Language Instructions

Assembly language instructions are provided to describe each of the basic operations that can be performed by a microprocessor. They are written using *alphanumeric symbols* instead of the 0s and 1s of the microprocessor's machine code. An example of a short assembly language program is shown in Fig. 3.2(a). The assembly language statements are located on the left. Frequently, comments describing the statements are included on the right. This type of documentation makes it easier for programmers to write, read, and debug code. By the term "code" we mean programs written in the language of the microprocessor. Programs written in assembly language are called *source code*.

Each instruction in the source program corresponds to one assembly language statement. The statement must specify which operation is to be performed and what data operands are to be processed. For this reason, an instruction can be divided into two separate parts: its *opcode* and its *operands*. The opcode is the part of the instruction that identifies the operation that is to be performed. For example, typical operations are add, subtract, and move.

In assembly language, we assign a unique one-, two-, or three-letter combination to each operation. This letter combination is referred to as a *mnemonic* for the instruction. For instance, the 8086 assembly language mnemonics for add, subtract, and move are ADD, SUB, and MOV, respectively.

Operands identify the data that are to be processed by the microprocessor as it carries out the operation specified by the opcode. For instance, in an instruction that adds the contents of the base register to the accumulator, BX and AX are the operands. An assembly language description of this instruction is

ADD AX,BX

In this example, the contents of BX and AX are added together and their sum is put in AX. Therefore, BX is considered to be the *source operand* and AX the *destination operand*.

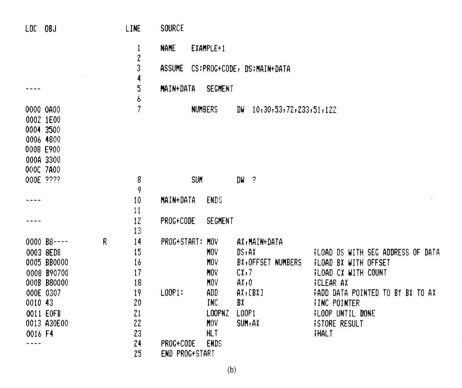

```
             NAME    EXAMPLE+1

             ASSUME  CS:PROG+CODE, DS:MAIN+DATA

             MAIN+DATA   SEGMENT

                     NUMBERS    DW   10,30,53,72,233,51,122
                     SUM        DW   ?

             MAIN+DATA   ENDS

             PROG+CODE   SEGMENT

             PROG+START: MOV    AX,MAIN+DATA
                         MOV    DS,AX              ;LOAD DS WITH SEG ADDRESS OF DATA
                         MOV    BX,OFFSET NUMBERS  ;LOAD BX WITH OFFSET
                         MOV    CX,7               ;LOAD CX WITH COUNT
                         MOV    AX,0               ;CLEAR AX
             LOOP1:      ADD    AX,[BX]            ;ADD DATA POINTED TO BY BX TO AX
                         INC    BX                 ;INC POINTER
                         LOOPNZ LOOP1              ;LOOP UNTIL DONE
                         MOV    SUM,AX             ;STORE RESULT
                         HLT                       ;HALT
             PROG+CODE   ENDS
             END PROG+START
```

(a)

```
LOC  OBJ            LINE    SOURCE

                    1    NAME    EXAMPLE+1
                    2
                    3    ASSUME  CS:PROG+CODE, DS:MAIN+DATA
                    4
----                5    MAIN+DATA   SEGMENT
                    6
0000 0A00           7            NUMBERS    DW   10,30,53,72,233,51,122
0002 1E00
0004 3500
0006 4800
0008 E900
000A 3300
000C 7A00
000E ????           8            SUM        DW   ?
                    9
----                10   MAIN+DATA   ENDS
                    11
----                12   PROG+CODE   SEGMENT
                    13
0000 B8----    R    14   PROG+START: MOV    AX,MAIN+DATA
0003 8ED8           15               MOV    DS,AX              ;LOAD DS WITH SEG ADDRESS OF DATA
0005 BB0000         16               MOV    BX,OFFSET NUMBERS  ;LOAD BX WITH OFFSET
0008 B90700         17               MOV    CX,7               ;LOAD CX WITH COUNT
000B B80000         18               MOV    AX,0               ;CLEAR AX
000E 0307           19   LOOP1:      ADD    AX,[BX]            ;ADD DATA POINTED TO BY BX TO AX
0010 43             20               INC    BX                 ;INC POINTER
0011 E0FB           21               LOOPNZ LOOP1              ;LOOP UNTIL DONE
0013 A30E00         22               MOV    SUM,AX             ;STORE RESULT
0016 F4             23               HLT                       ;HALT
----                24   PROG+CODE   ENDS
                    25   END PROG+START
```

(b)

Figure 3.2   (a) Typical 8086 assembly language program (Intel Corporation); (b) assembled machine code (Intel Corporation).

Here is another example of an assembly language statement:

LOOP: MOV AX,BX   ;COPY BX INTO AX

This instruction statement starts with the word LOOP. It is an address identifier for the instruction MOV AX,BX. This type of identifier is called a *label* or *tag*. The instruction is followed by "COPY BX INTO AX." This part of the statement is called a *comment*. Thus a general format for writing an assembly language statement is

LABEL: INSTRUCTION   ;COMMENT

Machine Language

Before a source program can be executed by the microprocessor, it must first be run through a process known as *assembling*. This is normally done on a minicomputer or microcomputer with a program called an *assembler*. The result produced by this step is an equivalent program expressed in the *machine code* that is executed by the microprocessor. That is, it is the equivalent of the source program but now written in 0s and 1s. This program is also referred to as *object code*.

Figure 3.2(b) is a listing that includes the machine language program for the assembly language program in Fig. 3.2(a). It was produced by an 8086 assembler. Reading from left to right, this listing contains addresses of memory locations, followed by the machine code instructions, the original assembly language statements, and comments. Notice that for simplicity the machine code instructions are expressed in hexadecimal notation and not as binary numbers.

3.4 THE 8086 ADDRESSING MODES

When the 8086 executes an instruction, it performs the specified function on data. These data are called its *operands* and may be part of the instruction, reside in one of the internal registers of the 8086, stored at an address in memory, or held at an I/O port. To access these different types of operands, the 8086 is provided with various *addressing modes*. Here are the modes available on the 8086: *register addressing, immediate addressing, direct addressing, register indirect addressing, based addressing, indexed addressing, based indexed addressing, string addressing,* and *port addressing.*

Of these nine modes, all but register addressing and immediate addressing make reference to an operand stored in memory. Therefore, they require the BIU to initiate a read or write bus cycle to the memory subsystem. Thus the addressing modes provide different ways of computing the address of the operand that is output on the address bus during the bus cycle. Let us now consider in detail each of these addressing modes.

Register Addressing Mode

With the register addressing mode, the operand to be accessed is specified as residing in an internal register of the 8086. An example of an instruction that uses this addressing mode is

MOV AX,BX

This stands for move the contents of BX, the *source operand*, to AX, the *destination operand*. Both the source and destination operands have been specified as the contents of internal registers of the 8086.

Let us now look at the effect of executing the register addressing mode MOV instruction. In Fig. 3.3(a) we see the state of the 8086 just prior to fetching the instruction. Notice that IP and CS point to the MOV AX,BX instruction at address 01000_{16}. Prior to execution of this instruction, the contents of BX are $ABCD_{16}$ and the contents of AX represent a don't-care state. As shown in Fig. 3.3(b), the result of executing the instruction is that $ABCD_{16}$ is copied into AX.

Immediate Addressing Mode

If a source operand is part of the instruction instead of the contents of a register or memory location, it represents what is called an *immediate operand* and is accessed using the immediate addressing mode. Typically, immediate operands represent constant data.

Immediate operands can be either a byte or word of data. In the instruction

MOV AL,015H

the source operand 15_{16} is an example of a byte-wide immediate source operand. The destination operand, which comprises the contents of AL, uses register addressing. Thus this instruction employs both the immediate and register addressing modes.

Figure 3.4(a) and (b) illustrate fetch and execution of this instruction. Here we find that the immediate operand 15_{16} is stored in program storage memory in the byte location immediately following the opcode of the instruction. This value is also fetched into the instruction queue in the BIU. When the EU performs the MOV operation, the source operand is fetched from the instruction queue; therefore, no external memory bus cycle is initiated. The result of executing this instruction is that the immediate operand is loaded into the lower byte part (AL) of the accumulator register.

Direct Addressing Mode

Direct addressing differs from immediate addressing in that the locations following the instruction opcode hold an *effective memory address* (EA) instead of data. This effective address is a 16-bit offset of the storage location of the operand from the current value in the data segment (DS) register. EA is combined with the contents of DS in the BIU to produce the *physical address* of the operand.

An example of an instruction that uses direct addressing for its source operand is

MOV CX,BETA

This stands for ''move the contents of the memory location which is offset by BETA from the current value in DS into internal register CX.''

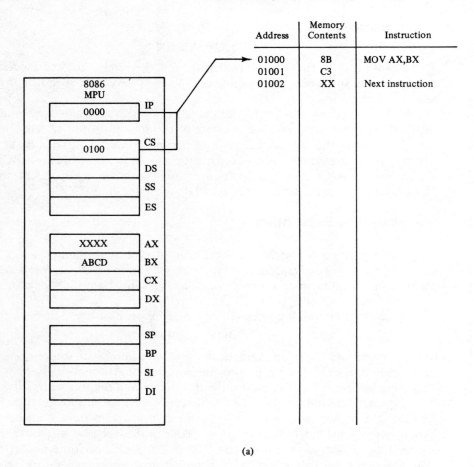

Address	Memory Contents	Instruction
01000	8B	MOV AX,BX
01001	C3	
01002	XX	Next instruction

(a)

Figure 3.3 (a) Register addressing mode instruction before execution; (b) after execution.

In Fig. 3.5(a) we find that the value of the offset is stored in the two byte locations that follow the instruction. It is also known as the *displacement*. Notice that the value assigned to BETA is 1234_{16}. As the instruction is executed, the BIU combines 1234_{16} with 0200_{16} to get the physical address of the source operand. This gives

$$PA = 02000_{16} + 1234_{16}$$
$$= 03234_{16}$$

Then it initiates an external memory bus cycle to read the word of data starting at this address. This value is $BEED_{16}$. The execution unit causes this value to be loaded in the CX register. This result is illustrated in Fig. 3.5(b).

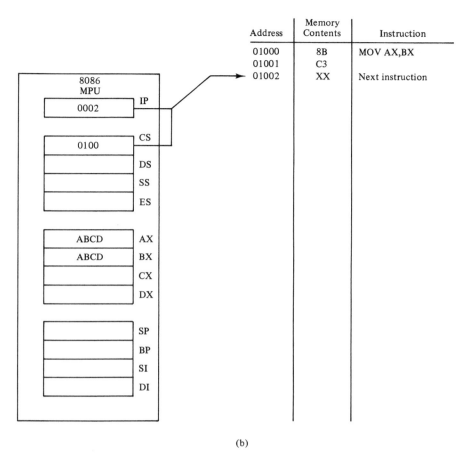

(b)

Figure 3.3 *(continued)*

Register Indirect Addressing Mode

Register indirect addressing is similar to direct addressing in that an effective address is combined with the contents of DS to obtain a physical address. However, it differs in the way the offset is specified. This time EA resides in either a pointer register or an index register within the 8086. The pointer register can be either base register BX or base pointer register BP, and the index register can be source index register SI, or destination index register DI.

An example of an instruction that uses register indirect addressing is

MOV AX,[SI]

This instruction moves the contents of the memory location offset by the value of EA in SI from the current value in DS to the AX register.

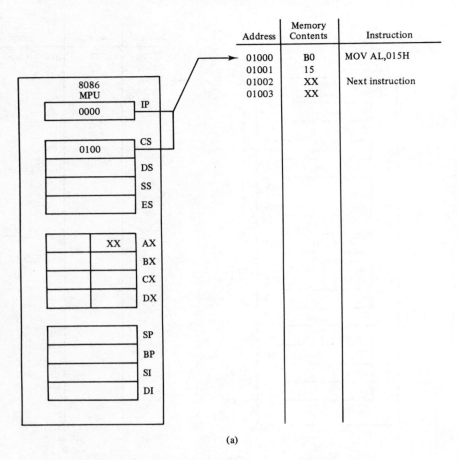

Address	Memory Contents	Instruction
01000	B0	MOV AL,015H
01001	15	
01002	XX	Next instruction
01003	XX	

(a)

Figure 3.4   (a) Immediate addressing mode instruction before execution; (b) after execution.

For instance, as shown in Fig. 3.6(a) and (b), if SI contains 1234_{16} and DS contains 0200_{16}, the result produced by executing the instruction is that the contents of memory location

$$PA = 02000_{16} + 1234_{16}$$
$$= 03234_{16}$$

are moved to the AX register. Notice in Fig. 3.6(b) that this value is $BEED_{16}$. In this example, the value 1234_{16} that was found in the SI register must be loaded with another instruction prior to the MOV instruction.

Notice that the result produced by executing this instruction and the example for the direct addressing mode are the same. However, they differ in the way in which the physical address was generated. The direct addressing method lends itself to ap-

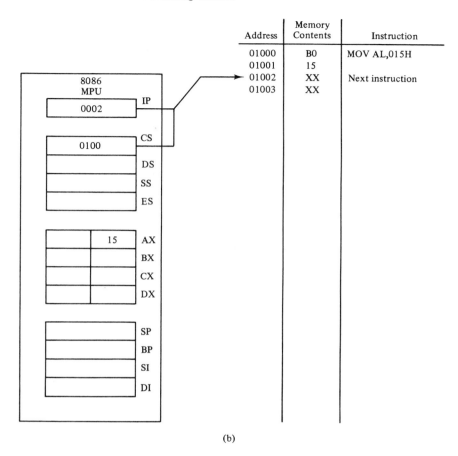

(b)

Figure 3.4 *(continued)*

plications where the value of EA is a constant. On the other hand, register indirect addressing can be used when the value of EA is calculated and stored, for example, in SI by a previous instruction. That is, EA is a variable.

Based Addressing Mode

In the based addressing mode, the physical address of the operand is obtained by adding a direct or indirect displacement to the contents of either base register BX or base pointer register BP and the current value in DS and SS, respectively. A MOV instruction that uses based addressing to specify the location of its destination operand is as follows:

MOV [BX].BETA,AL

This instruction uses base register BX and direct displacement BETA to derive the

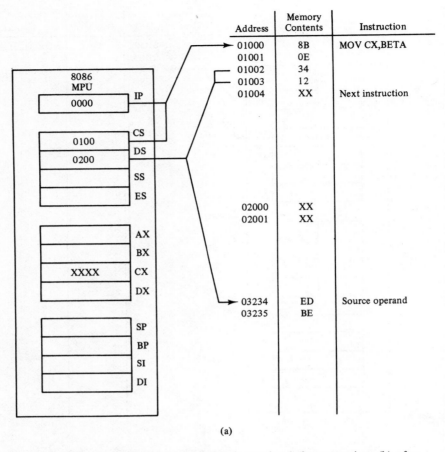

(a)

Figure 3.5 (a) Direct addressing mode instruction before execution; (b) after execution.

EA of the destination operand. The based addressing mode is implemented by specifying the base register in brackets followed by a period and the direct displacement. The source operand in this example is located in byte accumulator AL.

As shown in Fig. 3.7(a) and (b), the fetch and execution of this instruction causes the BIU to calculate the physical address of the destination operand from the contents of DS, BX, and the direct displacement. The result is

$$PA = 02000_{16} + 1000_{16} + 1234_{16}$$
$$= 04234_{16}$$

Then upon request of the EU it initiates a write bus cycle such that the source operand, AL, is written into the storage location at 04234_{16}. The result is that ED_{16} is copied into the destination memory location.

If BP is used instead of BX, the calculation of the physical address is performed

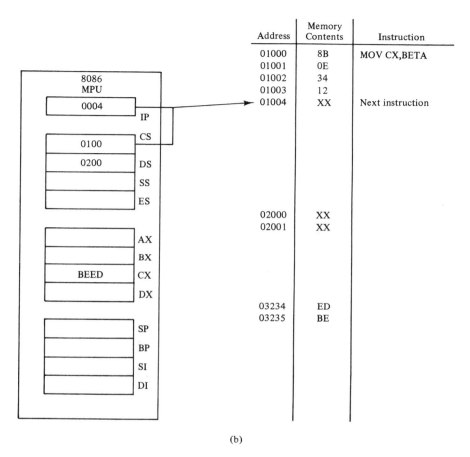

Address	Memory Contents	Instruction
01000	8B	MOV CX,BETA
01001	0E	
01002	34	
01003	12	
01004	XX	Next instruction
02000	XX	
02001	XX	
03234	ED	
03235	BE	

(b)

Figure 3.5 *(continued)*

using the contents of the stack segment (SS) register instead of DS. This permits access to data in the stack segment of memory.

Indexed Addressing Mode

Indexed addressing works identically to the based addressing we just described; however, it uses the contents of one of the index registers, instead of BX or BP, in the generation of the physical address. Here is an example:

MOV AL,ARRAY[SI]

The source operand has been specified using direct indexed addressing. Notice that the notation this time is such that ARRAY, which is a direct displacement, prefixes the selected index register, SI. Just like for the base register in based addressing, the index register is enclosed in brackets.

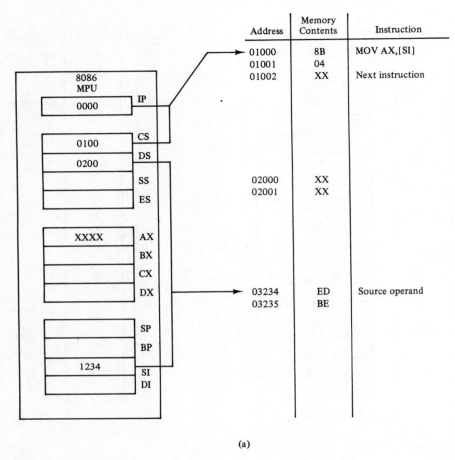

(a)

Figure 3.6   (a) Register indirect addressing mode instruction before execution; (b) after execution.

The effective address is calculated as

$$EA = (SI) + ARRAY$$

and the physical address is obtained by combining the contents of DS with EA.

The example in Fig. 3.8(a) and (b) shows the result of executing the MOV instruction. First the physical address of the source operand is calculated from DS, SI, and the direct displacement.

$$PA = 02000_{16} + 2000_{16} + 1234_{16}$$
$$= 05234_{16}$$

Then the byte of data stored at this location, which is BE_{16}, is read into lower byte AL of the accumulator register.

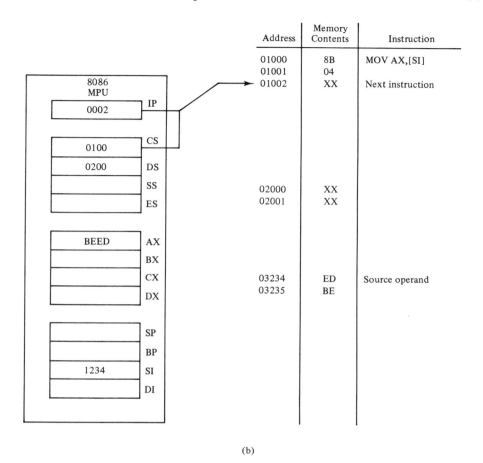

(b)

Figure 3.6   *(continued)*

Based Indexed Addressing Mode

Combining the based addressing mode and the indexed addressing mode together results in a new, more powerful mode known as based indexed addressing. Let us consider an example of a MOV instruction using this type of addressing.

$$MOV\ AH,[BX].BETA[SI]$$

Notice that the source operand is accessed using the based indexed addressing mode. Therefore, the effective address of the source operand is obtained as

$$EA = (BX) + BETA + (SI)$$

and the physical address of the operand from the current DS and the calculated EA.

An example of executing this instruction is illustrated in Fig. 3.9(a) and (b).

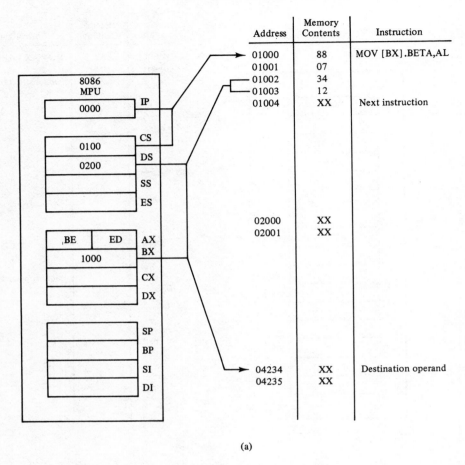

(a)

Figure 3.7   (a) Direct base pointer addressing mode instruction before execution; (b) after execution.

The address of the source operand is calculated as

$$PA = 02000_{16} + 1000_{16} + 1234_{16} + 2000_{16}$$
$$= 6234_{16}$$

Execution of the instruction causes the value stored at this location to be written into AH.

String Addressing Mode

The string instructions of the 8086's instruction set automatically use the source and destination index registers to specify the effective addresses of the source and destination operands, respectively. The move string instruction

MOVS

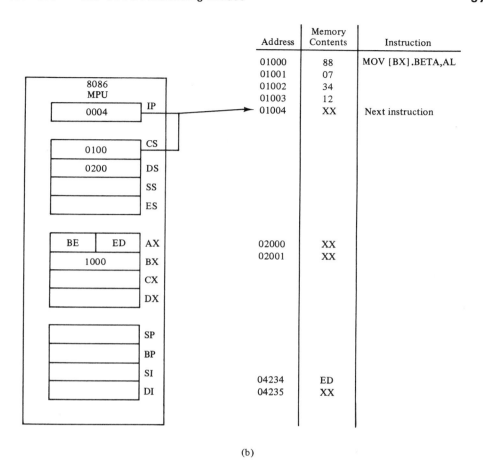

(b)

Figure 3.7 *(continued)*

is an example. Notice that neither SI nor DI appears in the string instruction, but both are used during its execution.

Port Addressing Mode

Port addressing is used in conjunction with the IN and OUT instructions to access input and output ports. Any of the memory addressing modes can be used for the port address for memory-mapped ports. For ports in the I/O address space, only the direct addressing mode and an indirect addressing mode using DX are available. For example, direct addressing of an input port is used in the instruction

IN AL,15H

This stands for "input the data from the byte-wide input port at address 15_{16} of the I/O address space to register AL."

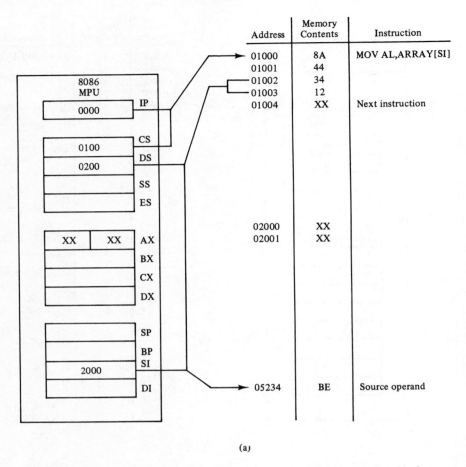

Address	Memory Contents	Instruction
01000	8A	MOV AL,ARRAY[SI]
01001	44	
01002	34	
01003	12	
01004	XX	Next instruction
02000	XX	
02001	XX	
05234	BE	Source operand

(a)

Figure 3.8   (a) Direct indexed addressing mode instruction before execution; (b) after execution.

Next, let us consider another example. Using indirect port addressing for the source operand in an IN instruction, we get

$$\text{IN AL,DX}$$

It means "input the data from the byte-wide input port whose address is specified by the contents of register DX." For instance, if (DX) equals 1234_{16}, the contents of the port at this I/O address are loaded into AL.

3.5 INSTRUCTION SET

Having introduced a software model and the various addressing modes of the 8086 microprocessor, we will now continue with its *instruction set*.

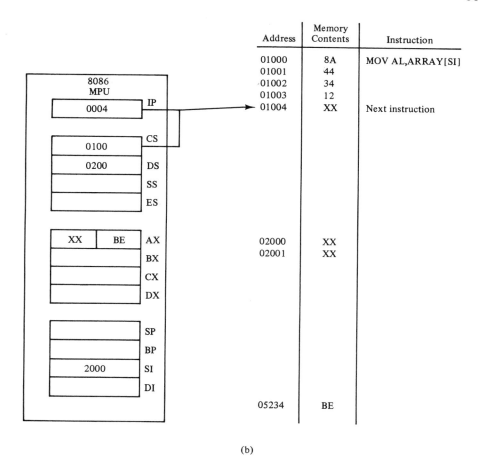

(b)

Figure 3.8 *(continued)*

The 8086 microprocessor provides a powerful instruction set containing 117 basic instructions. The wide range of operands and addressing modes permitted for use with these instructions further expands the instruction set into many more instructions executable at the machine code level. For instance, the basic MOV instruction expands into 28 different machine level instructions.

For the purpose of discussion, the instruction set will be divided into a number of groups of functionally related instructions. In this chapter we consider the data transfer instructions, arithmetic instructions, logic instructions, shift instructions, and rotate instructions. Advanced instructions such as those for program and processor control are described in Chapter 4.

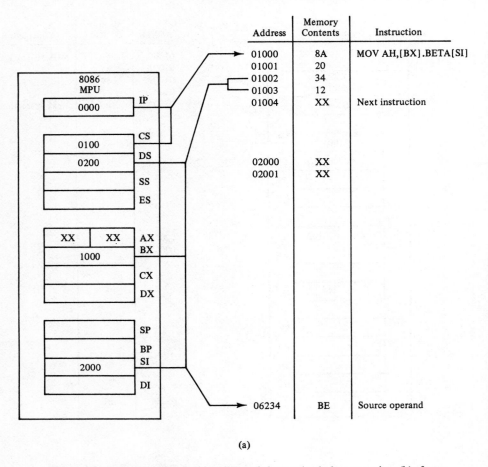

Address	Memory Contents	Instruction
01000	8A	MOV AH,[BX].BETA[SI]
01001	20	
01002	34	
01003	12	
01004	XX	Next instruction
02000	XX	
02001	XX	
06234	BE	Source operand

(a)

Figure 3.9   (a) Based indexed addressing mode instruction before execution; (b) after execution.

3.6 DATA TRANSFER INSTRUCTIONS

The 8086 microprocessor has a group of *data transfer instructions* that are provided to move data either between its internal registers or between an internal register and a storage location in memory. This group includes the *move byte or word* (MOV) instruction, *exchange byte or word* (XCHG) instruction, *translate byte* (XLAT) instruction, *load effective address* (LEA) instruction, *load data segment* (LDS) instruction, and *load extra segment* (LES) instruction. These instructions are discussed in this section.

The MOV Instruction

The MOV instruction of Fig. 3.10(a) is used to transfer a byte or a word of data from a source operand to a destination operand. These operands can be internal

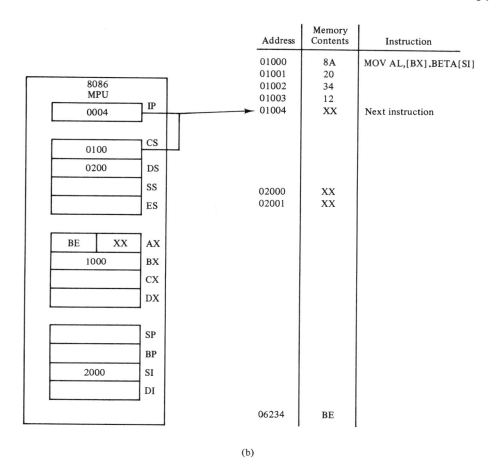

Address	Memory Contents	Instruction
01000	8A	MOV AL,[BX].BETA[SI]
01001	20	
01002	34	
01003	12	
01004	XX	Next instruction
02000	XX	
02001	XX	
06234	BE	

(b)

Figure 3.9 *(continued)*

registers of the 8086 and storage locations in memory. Figure 3.10(b) shows the valid source and destination operand variations. This large choice of operands results in many different MOV instructions. Looking at this list of operands, we see that data can be moved between general-purpose registers, between a general-purpose register and a segment register, between a general-purpose register or segment register and memory, or between a memory location and the accumulator.

Notice that the MOV instruction cannot transfer data directly between a source and a destination that both reside in external memory. Instead, the data must first be moved from memory into an internal register, such as to the accumulator (AX), with one move instruction and then moved to the new location in memory with a second move instruction.

All transfers between general-purpose registers and memory can involve either a byte or word of data. The fact that the instruction corresponds to byte or word data is designated by the way in which its operands are specified. For instance, AL

(a)

Mnemonic	Meaning	Format	Operation	Flags Affected
MOV	Move	MOV D,S	(S) → (D)	None

(b)

Destination	Source
Memory	Accumulator
Accumulator	Memory
Register	Register
Register	Memory
Memory	Register
Register	Immediate
Memory	Immediate
Seg-reg	Reg16
Seg-reg	Mem16
Reg16	Seg-reg
Mem16	Seg-reg

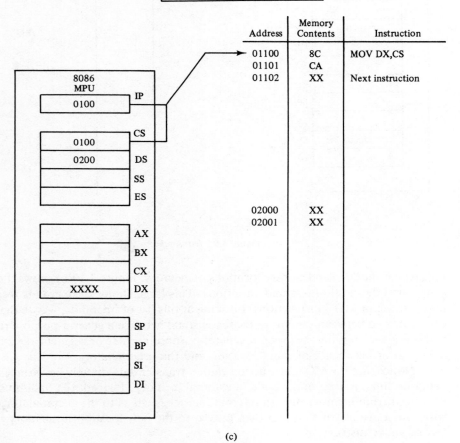

(c)

Figure 3.10 (a) MOV data transfer instruction; (b) allowed operands; (c) MOV DX,CS instruction before execution; (d) after execution.

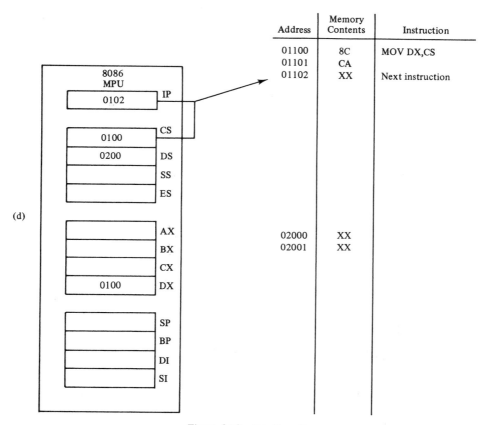

Address	Memory Contents	Instruction
01100	8C	MOV DX,CS
01101	CA	
01102	XX	Next instruction
02000	XX	
02001	XX	

(d)

Figure 3.10   *(continued)*

or AH would be used to specify a byte operand, and AX a word operand. On the other hand, data moved between one of the general-purpose registers and a segment register or between a segment register and a memory location must always be word-wide.

In Fig. 3.10(a) we also find additional important information. For instance, flag bits within the 8086 are not modified by execution of a MOV instruction.

An example of a segment register to general-purpose register MOV instruction shown in Fig. 3.10(c) is

$$MOV\ DX,CS$$

In this instruction, the code segment register is the source operand and the data register is the destination. It stands for "move the contents of CS into DX." That is,

$$(CS) \longrightarrow (DX)$$

For example, if the contents of CS are 0100_{16}, execution of the instruction MOV DX,CS as shown in Fig. 3.10(d) makes

$$(DX) = (CS) = 0100_{16}$$

In all memory reference MOV instructions, the machine code for the instruction includes an offset address relative to the contents of the data segment register. An example of this type of instruction is

MOV SUM,AX

In this instruction, the memory location identified by the variable SUM is specified using direct addressing. That is, the value of the offset is included in the two byte locations that follow its opcode in program memory.

Let us assume that the contents of DS equals 0200_{16} and that SUM corresponds to a displacement of 1212_{16}; then this instruction means "move the contents of accumulator AX to the memory location offset by 1212_{16} from the starting location of the current data segment." The physical address of this location is obtained as

$$PA = 02000_{16} + 1212_{16} = 03212_{16}$$

Thus the effect of the instruction is

$$(AL) \longrightarrow (\text{MEMORY LOCATION } 03212_{16})$$

$$(AH) \longrightarrow (\text{MEMORY LOCATION } 03213_{16})$$

Now let us consider another example:

MOV CX,[0ABCDH]

This instruction has the following effect

$$(\text{MEMORY LOCATION } (DS)0_{16} + ABCD_{16}) \longrightarrow (CL)$$

$$(\text{MEMORY LOCATION } (DS)0_{16} + ABCD_{16} + 1_{16}) \longrightarrow (CH)$$

In this example, source operand $ABCD_{16}$ has been considered to be the direct address of a memory location. The question is why $ABCD_{16}$ does not represent immediate data that are to be loaded into CX. The answer to this question is given by how the 8086's assembler codes instructions. An immediate mode transfer is specified by preceding $ABCD_{16}$ with a zero. Therefore, the instruction would have to have been written as

MOV CX,0ABCD

to represent an immediate data operand. The result produced by this instruction is

$$ABCD_{16} \longrightarrow (CX)$$

The XCHG Instruction

In our study of the move instruction, we found that it could be used to copy the contents of a register or memory location into a register or contents of a memory location to a register. In all cases, the original contents of the source location are preserved and the original contents of the destination are destroyed. In some applications, it is required to interchange the contents of two registers. For instance, we might want to exchange the data in the AX and BX registers.

This could be done using multiple move instructions and storage of the data in a temporary register such as DX. However, to perform the exchange function more efficiently, a special instruction has been provided in the instruction set of the 8086. This is the exchange (XCHG) instruction. The forms of the XCHG instruction and its allowed operands are shown in Fig. 3.11(a) and (b). Here we see that it can be used to swap data between two general-purpose registers or between a general-purpose register and a storage location in memory. In particular, it allows for the exchange of words of data between one of the general-purpose registers, including the pointers and index registers, and the accumulator (AX); exchange of a byte or word of data between one of the general-purpose registers and a location in memory; or between two of the general-purpose registers.

Let us consider an example of an exchange between two internal registers. Here is a typical instruction:

$$\text{XCHG AX,DX}$$

Its execution by the 8086 swaps the contents of AX with that of DX. That is,

$$(\text{AX original}) \longrightarrow (\text{DX})$$
$$(\text{DX original}) \longrightarrow (\text{AX})$$

or

$$(\text{AX}) \longleftrightarrow (\text{DX})$$

Example 3.1

For the data shown in Fig. 3.11(c), what is the result of executing the instruction

$$\text{XCHG SUM,BX ?}$$

Solution.   Execution of this instruction performs the function

$$((\text{DS})0 + \text{SUM}) \longleftrightarrow (\text{BX})$$

In Fig. 3.11(c) we see that $(\text{DS}) = 0200_{16}$ and the direct address $\text{SUM} = 1234_{16}$. Therefore, the physical address is

$$\text{PA} = 02000_{16} + 1234_{16} = 03234_{16}$$

Notice that this location contains FF_{16} and the address that follows contains 00_{16}. Moreover, note that BL contains AA_{16} and BH contains 11_{16}.

Execution of the instruction performs the following 16-bit swap.

$$(03234_{16}) \longleftrightarrow (\text{BL})$$
$$(03235_{16}) \longleftrightarrow (\text{BH})$$

As shown in Fig. 3.11(d), we get

$$(\text{BX}) = 00\text{FF}_{16}$$
$$(\text{SUM}) = 11\text{AA}_{16}$$

Mnemonic	Meaning	Format	Operation	Flags Affected
XCHG	Exchange	XCHG D,S	(D) ↔ (S)	None

(a)

Destination	Source
Accumulator	Reg16
Memory	Register
Register	Register

(b)

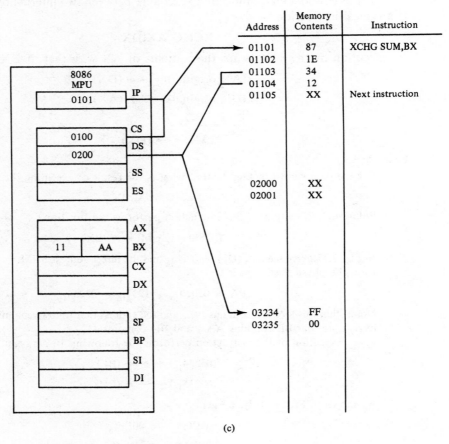

(c)

Figure 3.11 (a) XCHG data transfer instruction; (b) allowed operands; (c) XCHG SUM,BX instruction before execution; (d) after execution.

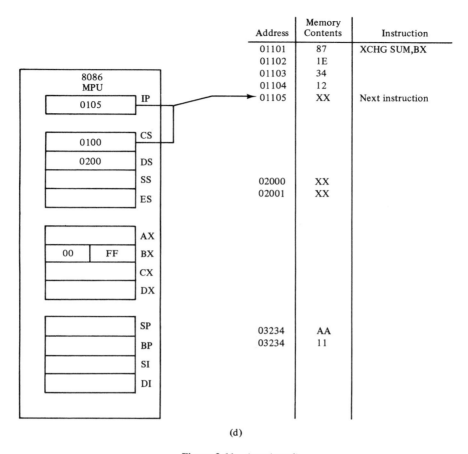

(d)

Figure 3.11 *(continued)*

The XLAT Instruction

The translate (XLAT) instruction has been provided in the instruction set of the 8086 to simplify implementation of the lookup-table operation. This instruction is described in Fig. 3.12. When using XLAT, the contents of register BX represent the offset of the starting address of the *lookup table* from the beginning of the current data segment. Also, the contents of AL represent the offset of the element to be accessed from the beginning of the lookup table. This 8-bit element address permits a table with up to 256 elements. The values in both of these registers must be initialized prior to execution of the XLAT instruction.

Execution of XLAT replaces the contents of AL by the contents of the accessed lookup-table location. The physical address of this element in the table is derived as

$$PA = (DS)0 + (BX) + (AL)$$

An example of the use of this instruction would be for software *code conver-*

Mnemonic	Meaning	Format	Operation	Flags Affected
XLAT	Translate	XLAT Source-table	$((AL) + (BX) + (DS)0) \rightarrow (AL)$	None

Figure 3.12 XLAT data transfer instruction.

sions: for instance, an ASCII-to-EBCDIC conversion. This requires an EBCDIC table in memory. The individual EBCDIC codes are located in the table at element displacements (AL) equal to their equivalent ASCII character value. That is, the EBCDIC code $B1_{16}$ for letter A would be positioned at displacement 41_{16}, which equals ASCII A, from the start of the table. The start of this ASCII-to-EBCDIC table in the current data segment is identified by the contents of BX.

As an illustration of XLAT, let us assume that the $(DS) = 0300_{16}$, $(BX) = 0100_{16}$, and $(AL) = 0D_{16}$. $0D_{16}$ represents the ASCII character CR (carriage return). Execution of XLAT replaces the contents of AL by the contents of the memory location given by

$$PA = (DS)0 + (BX) + (AL)$$
$$= 03000_{16} + 00100_{16} + 0000D_{16}$$
$$= 0310D_{16}$$

Thus the execution can be described by

$$(0310D_{16}) \longrightarrow (AL)$$

Assuming that this memory location contains 52_{16}, this value is placed in AL.

$$(AL) = 52_{16}$$

The LEA, LDS, and LES Instructions

Another type of data transfer operation that is important is to load a segment or general-purpose register with an address directly from memory. Special instructions are provided in the instruction set of the 8086 to give a programmer this capability. These instructions are described in Fig. 3.13(a). They are load register with effective address (LEA), load register and data segment register (LDS), and load register and extra segment register (LES).

Looking at Fig. 3.13(a), we see that these instructions provide the ability to manipulate memory addresses by loading a specific register with a 16-bit offset address or a 16-bit offset address together with a 16-bit segment address into either DS or ES.

The LEA instruction is used to load a specified register with a 16-bit offset address. An example of this instruction is

LEA SI,INPUT

When executed, it loads the SI register with an offset address value. The value of this offset is represented by the value of INPUT. INPUT is stored following the in-

Mnemonic	Meaning	Format	Operation	Flags Affected
LEA	Load effective address	LEA Reg16,Mem16	Mem16 → (Reg16)	None
LDS	Load register and DS	LDS Reg16,Mem32	(Mem32) → (Reg16) (Mem32+2) → (DS)	None
LES	Load register and ES	LES Reg16,Mem32	(Mem32) → (Reg16) (Mem32+2) → (ES)	None

(a)

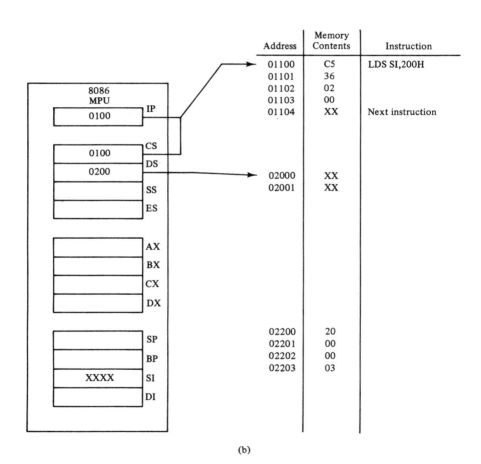

(b)

Figure 3.13   (a) LEA, LDS, and LES data transfer instructions; (b) LDS SI, 200H instruction before execution; (c) after execution.

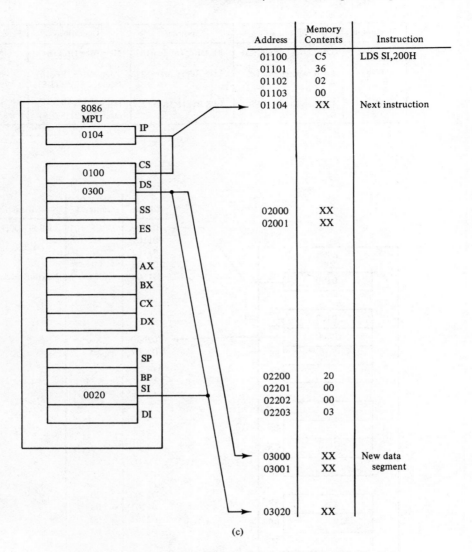

Address	Memory Contents	Instruction
01100	C5	LDS SI,200H
01101	36	
01102	02	
01103	00	
01104	XX	Next instruction
02000	XX	
02001	XX	
02200	20	
02201	00	
02202	00	
02203	03	
03000	XX	New data
03001	XX	segment
03020	XX	

(c)

Figure 3.13   *(continued)*

struction opcode in program memory. This value is prefetched by the BIU; therefore, the instruction does not require any external bus cycles during its execution.

The other two instructions, LDS and LES, are similar to LEA except that they load the specified register as well as the DS or ES segment register. For instance, the instruction

LDS SI,200H

loads the SI register from the word location in memory whose offset address with respect to the current data segment is 200_{16}. Figure 3.13(b) shows that the contents of DS are 0200_{16}. This gives a physical address of

$$PA = 02000_{16} + 0200_{16} = 02200_{16}$$

It is the contents of this location and the one that follows that are loaded into SI. Therefore, in Fig. 3.13(c), we find that SI contains 0020_{16}. The next two bytes, that is, the contents of addresses 2202_{16} and 2203_{16}, are loaded into the DS register. As shown, this defines a new data segment address of 03000_{16}.

3.7 ARITHMETIC INSTRUCTIONS

The instruction set of the 8086 microprocessor contains an extensive complement of *arithmetic instructions*. They include instructions for the *addition, subtraction, multiplication*, and *division* operations. Moreover, these operations can be performed on numbers expressed in a variety of numeric data formats. They include: *unsigned or signed binary bytes or words, unpacked or packed decimal bytes*, or *ASCII numbers*. By "packed decimal," we mean that two BCD digits are packed into a byte register or memory location. Unpacked decimal numbers are stored one BCD digit per byte. These decimal numbers are always unsigned. Moreover, ASCII numbers are expressed in ASCII code and stored one number per byte.

The status that results from the execution of an arithmetic instruction is recorded in the flags of the 8086. The flags that are affected by the arithmetic instructions are: carry flag (CF), auxiliary flag (AF), sign flag (SF), zero flag (ZF), parity flag (PF), and overflow flag (OF). Each of these flags was discussed in Chapter 2.

For the purpose of discussion, we will divide the arithmetic instructions into the subgroups shown in Fig. 3.14.

Addition Instructions—ADD, ADC, INC, AAA, and DAA

The form of each of the instructions in the *addition group* is shown in Fig. 3.15(a) and their allowed operand variations, for all but the INC instruction, are shown in Fig. 3.15(b). Let us begin by looking more closely at the *add* (ADD) instruction. Notice in Fig. 3.15(b) that it can be used to add to the contents of the accumulator an immediate operand, the contents of another register, or the contents of a storage location in memory. It also allows us to add the contents of two registers or the contents of a register and a memory location.

In general, the result of executing the instruction is expressed as

$$(S) + (D) \longrightarrow (D)$$

That is, the contents of the source operand are added to those of the destination operand and the sum that results is put into the location of the destination operand.

Example 3.2

Assume that the AX and BX registers contain 1100_{16} and $0ABC_{16}$, respectively. What are the results of executing the instruction ADD AX,BX?

Addition	
ADD	Add byte or word
ADC	Add byte or word with carry
INC	Increment byte or word by 1
AAA	ASCII adjust for addition
DAA	Decimal adjust for addition
Subtraction	
SUB	Subtract byte or word
SBB	Subtract byte or word with borrow
DEC	Decrement byte or word by 1
NEG	Negate byte or word
AAS	ASCII adjust for subtraction
DAS	Decimal adjust for subtraction
Multiplication	
MUL	Multiply byte or word unsigned
IMUL	Integer multiply byte or word
AAM	ASCII adjust for multiply
Division	
DIV	Divide byte or word unsigned
IDIV	Integer divide byte or word
AAD	ASCII adjust for division
CBW	Convert byte to word
CWD	Convert word to doubleword

Figure 3.14 Arithmetic instructions (Intel Corporation).

Solution. Execution of the ADD instruction causes the contents of source operand BX to be added to the contents of destination register AX. This gives

$$(BX) + (AX) = 0ABC_{16} + 1100_{16} = 1BBC_{16}$$

This sum ends up in destination register AX.

$$(AX) = 1BBC_{16}$$

Execution of this instruction is illustrated in Fig. 3.16(a) and (b).

The instruction *add with carry* (ADC) works similarly to ADD. But in this case, the content of the carry flag is also added; that is,

$$(S) + (D) + (CF) \rightarrow (D)$$

The valid operand combinations are the same as those for the ADD instruction.

Another instruction that can be considered as part of the addition subgroup of arithmetic instructions is the *increment* (INC) instruction. As shown in Fig. 3.15(c), its operands can be the contents of a 16-bit internal register, an 8-bit internal register, or a storage location in memory. Execution of the INC instruction adds 1 to the specified operand. An example of an instruction that increments the high byte of AX is INC AH.

Looking at Fig. 3.15(a), we see that execution of any one of these three instructions affects all six of the flags mentioned earlier.

Mnemonic	Meaning	Format	Operation	Flags Affected
ADD	Addition	ADD D, S	$(S) + (D) \rightarrow (D)$ Carry $\rightarrow$ (CF)	OF, SF, ZF, AF, PF, CF
ADC	Add with carry	ADC D, S	$(S) + (D) + (CF) \rightarrow (D)$ Carry $\rightarrow$ (CF)	OF, SF, ZF, AF, PF, CF
INC	Increment by 1	INC D	$(D) + 1 \rightarrow (D)$	OF, SF, ZF, AF, PF, CF
AAA	ASCII adjust for addition	AAA		OF, SF, ZF, AF, PF, CF
DAA	Decimal adjust for addition	DAA		OF, SF, ZF, AF, PF, CF

(a)

Destination	Source
Register	Register
Register	Memory
Memory	Register
Register	Immediate
Memory	Immediate
Accumulator	Immediate

(b)

Destination
Reg16
Reg8
Memory

(c)

Figure 3.15 (a) Addition arithmetic instructions; (b) allowed operands for ADD and ADC instructions; (c) allowed operands for INC instruction.

Example 3.3

The original contents of AX, BL, memory location SUM, and carry flag (CF) are 1234_{16}, AB_{16}, $00CD_{16}$, and 0_{16}, respectively. Describe the results of executing the following sequence of instructions:

$$ADD \quad AX,SUM$$

$$ADC \quad BL,05H$$

$$INC \quad SUM$$

Solution. By executing the first instruction, we add the word in the accumulator to the contents of the memory location identified as SUM. The result is placed in the accumulator. That is,

$$(AX) \longleftarrow (AX) + (SUM)$$
$$= 1234_{16} + 00CD_{16} = 1301_{16}$$

The carry flag remains reset.

The second instruction adds the lower byte of the base register (BL), immediate operand 5_{16}, and the carry flag, which is 0_{16}. This gives

$$(BL) \longleftarrow (BL) + IOP + (CF)$$
$$= AB_{16} + 5_{16} + 0_{16} = B0_{16}$$

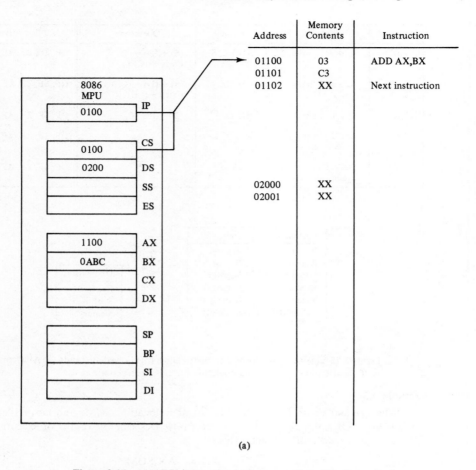

(a)

Figure 3.16   (a) ADD instruction before execution; (b) after execution.

Again CF stays reset.

The last instruction increments the contents of memory location SUM by 1. That is

$$(SUM) \longleftarrow (SUM) + 1_{16}$$
$$= 00CD_{16} + 1_{16} = 00CE_{16}$$

These results are summarized in Fig. 3.17.

The addition instructions we just covered can also be used directly to add numbers expressed in ASCII code. This eliminates the need for doing a code conversion on ASCII form data prior to processing it with addition operations. Whenever the 8086 does an addition on ASCII format data, an adjustment must be performed on the result to convert it to a decimal number. It is specifically for this purpose that the *ASCII adjust for addition* (AAA) instruction is provided in the instruction

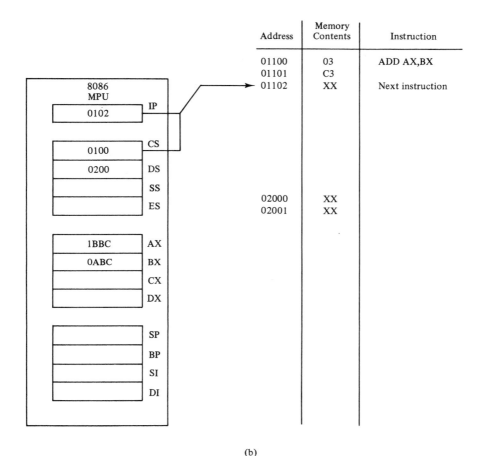

(b)

Figure 3.16 *(continued)*

Instruction	(AX)	(BL)	(SUM)	(CF)
Initial state	1234	AB	00CD	0
ADD AX,SUM	1301	AB	00CD	0
ADC BL,05H	1301	B0	00CD	0
INC SUM	1301	B0	00CE	0

Figure 3.17   Results due to execution
of arithmetic instructions.

set of the 8086. The AAA instruction should be executed immediately after the instruction that adds ASCII data.

Assuming that AL contains the result produced by adding two ASCII-coded numbers, execution of the AAA instruction causes the contents of AL to be replaced by its equivalent decimal value. If the sum is greater than 9, AL contains the LSDs, and AH is incremented by 1. Otherwise, AL contains the sum and AH is cleared. Both the AF and CF flags can get affected. Since AAA can only adjust data that are in AL, the destination register for ADD instructions that process ASCII numbers should be AL.

Example 3.4

What is the result of executing the following instruction sequence?

$$\text{ADD AL,BL}$$

$$\text{AAA}$$

Assume that AL contains 32_{16}, which is the ASCII code for number 2, BL contains 34_{16}, which is the ASCII code for number 4, and AH has been cleared.

Solution.   Executing the ADD instruction gives

$$(\text{AL}) \longleftarrow (\text{AL}) + (\text{BL})$$

$$= 32_{16} + 34_{16} = 66_{16}$$

Next the result is adjusted to give its equivalent decimal number. This is done by execution of the AAA instruction. The equivalent of adding 2 and 4 is decimal 6 with no carry. Therefore, the result after the AAA instruction is

$$(\text{AL}) = 06_{16}$$

$$(\text{AH}) = 00_{16}$$

and both AF and CF remain cleared.

The instruction set of the 8086 includes another instruction, called *decimal adjust for addition* (DAA). This instruction is used to perform an adjust operation similar to that performed by AAA but for the addition of packed BCD numbers instead of ASCII numbers. Information about this instruction is also provided in Fig. 3.15. Similar to AAA, DAA performs an adjustment on the value in AL. A typical instruction sequence is

$$\text{ADD AL,BL}$$

$$\text{DAA}$$

Remember that the contents of AL and BL must be packed BCD numbers. That is, two BCD digits packed into a byte. The adjusted result in AL is again a packed BCD byte.

Subtraction Instructions—SUB, SBB, DEC, AAS, DAS, and NEG

The instruction set of the 8086 includes an extensive set of instructions provided for implementing subtraction. As shown in Fig. 3.18, the subtraction subgroup is similar to the addition subgroup. It includes instructions for subtracting a source and destina-

Mnemonic	Meaning	Format	Operation	Flags affected
SUB	Subtract	SUB D,S	$(D) - (S) \rightarrow (D)$ Borrow $\rightarrow$ (CF)	OF, SF, ZF, AF, PF, CF
SBB	Subtract with borrow	SBB D,S	$(D) - (S) - (CF) \rightarrow (D)$	OF, SF, ZF, AF, PF, CF
DEC	Decrement by 1	DEC D	$(D) - 1 \rightarrow (D)$	OF, SF, ZF, AF, PF, CF
NEG	Negate	NEG D	$0 - (D) \rightarrow (D)$ $1 \rightarrow (CF)$	OF, SF, ZF, AF, PF, CF
DAS	Decimal adjust for subtraction	DAS		OF, SF, ZF, AF, PF, CF
AAS	ASCII adjust for subtraction	AAS		OF, SF, ZF, AF, PF, CF

(a)

Destination	Source
Register	Register
Register	Memory
Memory	Register
Accumulator	Immediate
Register	Immediate
Memory	Immediate

(b)

Destination
Reg16
Reg8
Memory

(c)

Destination
Register
Memory

(d)

Figure 3.18 (a) Subtraction arithmetic instructions; (b) allowed operands for SUB and SBB instructions; (c) allowed operands for DEC instruction; (d) allowed operands for NEG instruction.

tion operand, decrementing an operand, and for adjusting subtractions of ASCII and BCD data. An additional instruction in this subgroup is negate.

The *subtract* (SUB) instruction is used to subtract the value of a source operand from a destination operand. The result of this operation in general is given as

$$(D) \longleftarrow (D) - (S)$$

As shown in Fig. 3.18(b), it can employ the identical operand combinations as the ADD instruction.

The *subtract with borrow* (SBB) instruction is similar to SUB; however, it also subtracts the content of the carry flag from the destination. That is,

$$(D) \longleftarrow (D) - (S) - (CF)$$

Just as the INC instruction could be used to add 1 to an operand, the *decrement* (DEC) instruction can be used to subtract 1 from its operand. The allowed operands are shown in Fig. 3.18(c).

In Fig. 3.18(d) we see that the *negate* (NEG) instruction can operate on operands in a general-purpose register or a storage location in memory. Execution of this instruction causes the value of its operand to be replaced by its negative. The way this is actually done is through subtraction. That is, the contents of the specified operand are subtracted from zero using 2's-complement arithmetic and the result is returned to the operand location.

Example 3.5

Assuming that register BX contains $3A_{16}$, what is the result of executing the instruction

$$\text{NEG BX ?}$$

Solution. Executing the NEG instruction causes the 2's-complement subtraction that follows:

$$0000_{16} - (BX) = 0000_{16} + \text{2's complement of } 3A_{16}$$
$$= 0000_{16} + \text{FFC6}_{16}$$
$$= \text{FFC6}_{16}$$

This value is returned to BX.

$$(BX) = \text{FFC6}_{16}$$

In our study of the addition instruction subgroup, we found that the 8086 was capable of directly adding ASCII and BCD numbers. The SUB and SBB instructions can also subtract numbers represented in these formats. Just as for addition, the results that are obtained must be adjusted to produce their corresponding decimal numbers. In the case of ASCII subtraction, we use the *ASCII adjust for subtraction* (AAS) instruction, and for packed BCD subtraction we use the *decimal adjust for subtract* (DAS) instruction.

An example of an instruction sequence for direct ASCII subtraction is

$$\text{SUB AL,BL}$$

$$\text{AAS}$$

ASCII numbers must be loaded into AL and BL before the execution of the subtract instruction. Notice that the destination of the subtraction should be AL. After execution of AAS, AL contains the difference of the two numbers and AH is cleared if no borrow takes place or is decremented by 1 if a borrow occurs.

Multiplication and Division Instructions—MUL, DIV, IMUL, IDIV, AAM, AAD, CBW, and CWD

The 8086 has instructions to support multiplication and division of binary and BCD numbers. Two basic types of multiplication and division instructions, those for the processing of unsigned numbers and signed numbers, are available. To do these operations on unsigned numbers, the instructions are MUL and DIV. On the other hand, to multiply or divide signed numbers, the instructions are IMUL and IDIV.

Figure 3.19(a) describes these instructions. Notice in Fig. 3.19(b) that only a byte-wide or word-wide operand is specified in a multiplication instruction. It is the

Mnemonic	Meaning	Format	Operation	Flags Affected
MUL	Multiply (unsigned)	MUL S	$(AL) \cdot (S8) \rightarrow (AX)$ $(AX) \cdot (S16) \rightarrow (DX),(AX)$	OF, SF, ZF, AF, PF, CF
DIV	Division (unsigned)	DIV S	(1) $Q((AX)/(S8)) \rightarrow (AL)$ $R((AX)/(S8)) \rightarrow (AH)$ (2) $Q((DX,AX)/(S16)) \rightarrow (AX)$ $R((DX,AX)/(S16)) \rightarrow (DX)$ If Q is FF_{16} in case (1) or $FFFF_{16}$ in case (2), then type 0 interrupt occurs	OF, SF, ZF, AF, PF, CF
IMUL	Integer multiply (signed)	IMUL S	$(AL) \cdot (S8) \rightarrow (AX)$ $(AX) \cdot (S16) \rightarrow (DX),(AX)$	OF, SF, ZF, AF, PF, CF
IDIV	Integer divide (signed)	IDIV S	(1) $Q((AX)/(S8)) \rightarrow (AX)$ $R((AX)/(S8)) \rightarrow (AH)$ (2) $Q((DX,AX)/(S16)) \rightarrow (AX)$ $R((DX,AX)/(S16)) \rightarrow (DX)$ If Q is $7F_{16}$ in case (1) or $7FFF_{16}$ in case (2), then type 0 interrupt occurs	OF, SF, ZF, AF, PF, CF
AAM	Adjust AL for multiplication	AAM	$Q((AL)/10) \rightarrow AH$ $R((AL)/10) \rightarrow AL$	OF, SF, ZF, AF, PF, CF
AAD	Adjust AX for division	AAD	$(AH) \cdot 10 + AL \rightarrow AL$ $00 \rightarrow AH$	OF, SF, ZF, AF, PF, CF
CBW	Convert byte to word	CBW	(MSB of AL) $\rightarrow$ (All bits of AH)	None
CWD	Convert word to double word	CWD	(MSB of AX) $\rightarrow$ (All bits of DX)	None

(a)

Source
Reg8
Reg16
Mem8
Mem16

(b)

Figure 3.19 (a) Multiplication and division arithmetic instructions; (b) allowed operands.

source operand. As shown in Fig. 3.19(a), the other operand, which is the destination, is assumed already to be in AL for 8-bit multiplications or in AX for 16-bit multiplications.

The result of executing a MUL or IMUL instruction on byte data can be represented as

$$(AX) \longleftarrow (AL) \times (\text{8-BIT OPERAND})$$

That is, the resulting 16-bit product is produced in the AX register. On the other hand, for multiplications of data words, the 32-bit result is given by

$$(DX,AX) \longleftarrow (AX) \times (16\text{-BIT OPERAND})$$

where AX contains the 16 LSBs and DX the 16 MSBs.

For the division operation, again just the source operand is specified. The other operand is either the contents of AX for 16-bit dividends or the contents of both DX and AX for 32-bit dividends. The result of a DIV or IDIV instruction for an 8-bit divisor is represented by

$$(AH),(AL) \longleftarrow (AX)/(8\text{-BIT OPERAND})$$

where (AH) is the remainder and (AL) the quotient. For 16-bit divisions, we get

$$(DX),(AX) \longleftarrow (DX,AX)/(16\text{-BIT OPERAND})$$

Here AX contains the quotient and DX contains the remainder.

As shown in Fig. 3.19(a), adjust instructions for BCD multiplication and division are also provided. They are *adjust AL for multiply* (AAM) and *adjust AX for divide* (AAD). The multiplication performed just before execution of AAM instruction is assumed to have been performed on two unpacked BCD numbers with the product in AL. The AAD instruction assumes that AH and AL contain unpacked BCD numbers.

The division instructions can also be used to divide an 8-bit dividend in AL by an 8-bit divisor. However, to do this, the sign of the dividend must first be extended to fill the AX register. That is, AH is filled with zeros if the number in AL is positive or with ones if it is negative. This conversion is automatically done by executing the *convert byte to word* (CBW) instruction.

In a similar way, the 32-bit by 16-bit division instructions can be used to divide a 16-bit dividend in AX by a 16-bit divisor. In this case, the sign bit of AX must be extended by 16 bits into the DX register. This can be done by another instruction, which is known as *convert word to double word* (CWD). These two sign-extension instructions are also shown in Fig. 3.19(a).

Notice that the CBW and CWD instructions are provided to handle operations where the result or intermediate results of an operation cannot be held in the correct word length for use in other arithmetic operations. Using these instructions, we can extend a byte or word of data to its equivalent word or double word.

Example 3.6

What is the result of executing the following sequence of instructions?

MOV   AL,0A1H

CBW

CWD

Solution.   The first instruction loads AL with $A1_{16}$. This gives

$$(AL) = A1_{16} = 10100001_2$$

Executing the second instruction extends the most significant bit of AL, which is 1, into all bits of AH. The result is

$$(AH) = 11111111_2 = FF_{16}$$
$$(AX) = 1111111110100001_2 = FFA1_{16}$$

This completes conversion of the byte in AL to a word in AX.

The last instruction loads each bit of DX with the most significant bit of AX. This bit is also 1. Therefore, we get

$$(DX) = 1111111111111111_2 = FFFF_{16}$$

Now the word in AX has been extended to the double word

$$(AX) = FFA1_{16}$$
$$(DX) = FFFF_{16}$$

3.8 LOGIC INSTRUCTIONS

The 8086 has instructions for performing the logic operations *AND, OR, exclusive-OR*, and *NOT*. As shown in Fig. 3.20(a), the AND, OR, and XOR instructions perform their respective logic operations bit by bit on the specified source and destination operands, the result being represented by the final contents of the destination operand. Figure 3.20(b) shows the allowed operand combinations for the AND, OR, and XOR instructions.

For example, the instruction

AND AX,BX

causes the contents of BX to be ANDed with the contents of AX. The result is reflected by the new contents of AX. If AX contains 1234_{16} and BX contains $000F_{16}$, the result produced by the instruction is

$$1234_{16} \cdot 000F_{16} = 0001001000110100_2 \cdot 0000000000001111_2$$
$$= 0000000000000100_{16}$$
$$= 0004_{16}$$

This result is stored in the destination operand.

$$(AX) = 0004_{16}$$

In this way we see that the AND instruction was used to mask off the 12 most significant bits of the destination operand.

The NOT logic instruction differs from those for AND, OR, and exclusive-OR in that it operates on a single operand. Looking at Fig. 3.20(c), which shows the allowed operands of the NOT instruction, we see that this operand can be the contents of an internal register or a location in memory.

Mnemonic	Meaning	Format	Operation	Flags Affected
AND	Logical AND	AND D,S	$(S) \cdot (D) \to (D)$	OF, SF, ZF, AF, PF, CF
OR	Logical Inclusive-OR	OR D,S	$(S) + (D) \to (D)$	OF, SF, ZF, AF, PF, CF
XOR	Logical Exclusive-OR	XOR D,S	$(S) \oplus (D) \to (D)$	OF, SF, ZF, AF, PF, CF
NOT	Logical NOT	NOT D	$(\overline{D}) \to (D)$	None

(a)

Destination	Source
Register	Register
Register	Memory
Memory	Register
Register	Immediate
Memory	Immediate
Accumulator	Immediate

(b)

Destination
Register
Memory

(c)

Figure 3.20 (a) Logic instructions; (b) allowed operands for AND, OR, and XOR instructions; (c) allowed operands for NOT instruction.

Example 3.7

Describe the result of executing the following sequence of instructions.

$$\text{MOV} \quad \text{AL,01010101B}$$

$$\text{AND} \quad \text{AL,00011111B}$$

$$\text{OR} \quad \text{AL,11000000B}$$

$$\text{XOR} \quad \text{AL,00001111B}$$

$$\text{NOT} \quad \text{AL}$$

Solution. The first instruction moves the immediate operand 01010101_2 into the AL register. This loads the data that are to be manipulated with the logic instructions. The next instruction performs a bit-by-bit AND operation of the contents of AL with immediate operand 00011111_2. This gives

$$01010101_2 \cdot 00011111_2 = 00010101_2$$

This result is produced in destination register AL. Note that this operation has masked off the 3 most significant bits of AL.

The next instruction performs a bit-by-bit logical OR of the present contents of AL with immediate operand $C0_{16}$. This gives

$$00010101_2 + 11000000_2 = 11010101_2$$

$$(AL) = 11010101$$

This operation is equivalent to setting the two most significant bits of AL.

Instruction	(AL)
MOV AL,01010101B	01010101
AND AL,00011111B	00010101
OR AL,11000000B	11010101
XOR AL,00001111B	11011010
NOT AL	00100101

Figure 3.21 Results of example program using logic instructions.

The fourth instruction is an exclusive-OR operation of the contents of AL with immediate operand 00001111_2. We get

$$11010101_2 \oplus 00001111_2 = 11011010_2$$

$$(AL) = 11011010$$

Note that this operation complements the logic state of those bits in AL that are ones in the immediate operand.

The last instruction, NOT AL, inverts each bit of AL. Therefore, the final contents of AL become

$$(AL) = \overline{11011010_2} = 00100101_2$$

These results are summarized in Fig. 3.21.

3.9 SHIFT INSTRUCTIONS

The four *shift instructions* of the 8086 can perform two basic types of shift operations. They are the *logical shift* and the *arithmetic shift*. Moreover, each of these operations can be performed to the right or to the left. The shift instructions are *shift logical left* (SHL), *shift arithmetic left* (SAL), *shift logical right* (SHR), and *shift arithmetic right* (SAR).

The logical shift instructions, SHL and SHR, are described in Fig. 3.22(a). Notice in Fig. 3.22(b) that the destination operand, the data whose bits are to be shifted, can be either the contents of an internal register or a storage location in memory. Moreover, the source operand can be specified in two ways. If it is assigned the value 1, a 1-bit shift will take place. For instance, as illustrated in Fig. 3.23(a), executing

SHL AX,1

causes the 16-bit content of the AX register to be shifted one bit position to the left. Here we see that the vacated LSB location is filled with 0 and the bit shifted out of the MSB is saved in CF.

On the other hand, if the source operand is specified as CL instead of 1, the count in this register represents the number of bit positions the operand is to be shifted. This permits the count to be defined under software control and allows a range of shifts from 1 to 256 bits.

An example of an instruction specified in this way is

SHR   AX,CL

Mnemonic	Meaning	Format	Operation	Flags Affected
SAL/SHL	Shift arithmetic left/shift logical left	SAL/SHL D,Count	Shift the (D) left by the number of bit positions equal to Count and fill the vacated bits positions on the right with zeros	OF, CF
SHR	Shift logical right	SHR D,Count	Shift the (D) right by the number of bit positions equal to Count and fill the vacated bit positions on the left with zeros	OF, CF
SAR	Shift arithmetic right	SAR D,Count	Shift the (D) right by the number of bit positions equal to Count and fill the vacated bit positions on the left with the original most significant bit	OF, SF, ZF, AF, PF, CF

(a)

Destination	Count
Register	1
Register	CL
Memory	1
Memory	CL

(b)

Figure 3.22 (a) Shift instructions; (b) allowed operands.

Assuming that CL contains the value 02_{16}, the logical shift right that occurs is shown in Fig. 3.23(b). Notice that the two MSBs have been filled with 0s and the last bit shifted out at the LSB, which is 0, is maintained in the carry flag.

In an arithmetic shift to the left, SAL operation, the vacated bits at the right of the operand are filled with zeros, whereas in an arithmetic shift to the right, SAR operation, the vacated bits at the left are filled with the value of the original MSB of the operand. Thus in an arithmetic shift to the right, the original sign of the number is extended. This operation is equivalent to division by 2 as long as the bit shifted out of the LSB is a zero.

Figure 3.23(c) shows the effect of executing the instruction

$$\text{SAR} \quad \text{AX,CL}$$

Assuming that CL contains 02_{16}, a shift right by two bit locations takes place and the original sign bit, which is logic 0, is extended to the two vacated bit positions. Moreover, the last bit shifted from the LSB location is maintained in CF. Therefore, CF is 1.

Example 3.8

Write a program to implement the following expression using shift instructions to perform the arithmetic.

$$3(AX) + 7(BX) \longrightarrow (DX)$$

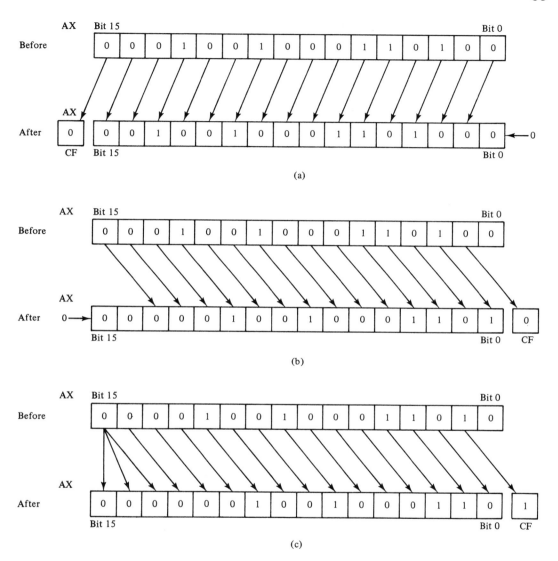

Figure 3.23 (a) Result of executing SHL AX,1; (b) result of executing SHR AX,CL; (c) result of executing SAR AX,CL.

Solution. Shifting left by 1 bit gives a multiplication by 2. However, to perform multiplication by an odd number, we can use a shift instruction to multiply to the nearest multiple of 2 and then add or subtract the appropriate value to get the desired result.

The algorithm for performing the expression starts by shifting (AX) left by 1 bit. This gives 2 times (AX). Adding the original (AX) gives multiplication by 3. Next, the contents of BX are shifted left by 3 bits to give 8 times its value. Subtracting the original

(BX) once gives multiplication by 7. Expressing this with instructions, we get

```
MOV   SI,AX    ; COPY (AX) INTO SI
SAL   SI,1     ; 2(AX)
ADD   SI,AX    ; 3(AX)
MOV   DX,BX    ; COPY (BX) INTO DX
MOV   CL,03H   ; LOAD SHIFT COUNT
SAL   DX,CL    ; 8(BX)
SUB   DX,BX    ;7(BX)
ADD   DX,SI    ; RESULT
```

It is important to note that we have assumed that to obtain any intermediate result or the final result, overflow does not occur. For instance, if 8(BX) cannot be accommodated in the 16 bits of BX, the result produced may be incorrect.

3.10 ROTATE INSTRUCTIONS

Another group of instructions, known as the *rotate instructions*, are similar to the shift instructions we just introduced. This group, as shown in Fig. 3.24(a), includes the *rotate left* (ROL), *rotate right* (ROR), *rotate left through carry* (RCL), and *rotate right through carry* (RCR) instructions.

Mnemonic	Meaning	Format	Operation	Flags Affected
ROL	Rotate left	ROL D,Count	Rotate the (D) left by the number of bit positions equal to Count. Each bit shifted out from the leftmost bit goes back into the rightmost bit position.	OF, CF
ROR	Rotate right	ROR D,Count	Rotate the (D) right by the number of bit positions equal to Count. Each bit shifted out from the rightmost bit goes into the leftmost bit position.	OF, CF
RCL	Rotate left through carry	RCL D,Count	Same as ROL except carry is attached to (D) for rotation.	OF, CF
RCR	Rotate right through carry	RCR D,Count	Same as ROR except carry is attached to (D) for rotation.	OF, CF

(a)

Destination	Count
Register	1
Register	CL
Memory	1
Memory	CL

(b)

Figure 3.24   (a) Rotate instructions; (b) allowed operands.

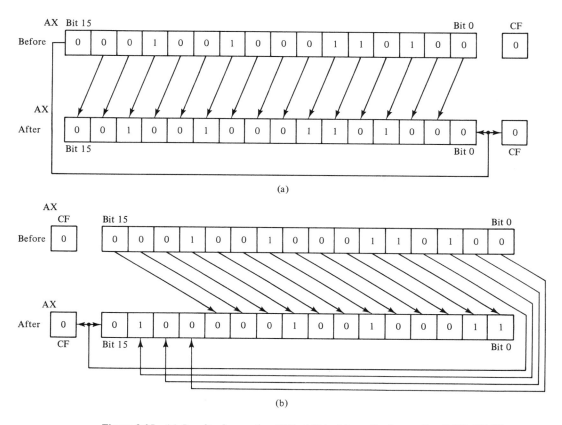

Figure 3.25   (a) Result of executing ROL AX,1; (b) result of executing ROR AX,CL.

As shown in Fig. 3.24(b), the rotate instructions are similar to the shift instructions in several ways. They have the ability to shift the contents of either an internal register or storage location in memory. Also, the shift that takes place can be from 1 to 256 bit positions to the left or to the right. Moreover, in the case of a multibit shift, the number of bit positions to be shifted is again specified by the contents of CL. Their difference from the shift instructions lies in the fact that the bits moved out at either the MSB or LSB end are not lost; instead, they are reloaded at the other end.

As an example, let us look at the operation of the ROL instruction. Execution of ROL causes the contents of the selected operand to be rotated left the specified number of bit positions. Each bit shifted out at the MSB end is reloaded at the LSB end. Moreover, the contents of CF reflects the state of the last bit that was shifted out. For instance, the instruction

ROL AX,1

causes a 1-bit rotate to the left. Figure 3.25(a) shows the result produced by execut-

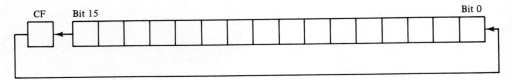

Figure 3.26   Rotation caused by execution of the RCL instruction.

ing this instruction. Notice that the original value of bit 15 is 0. This value has been rotated into CF and bit 0 of AX. All other bits have been rotated one bit position to the left.

The ROR instruction operates the same way as ROL except that it causes data to be rotated to the right instead of to the left. For example, execution of

$$\text{ROR AX,CL}$$

causes the contents of AX to be rotated right by the number of bit positions specified in CL. The result for CL equal to 4 is illustrated in Fig. 3.25(b).

The other two rotate instructions, RCL and RCR, differ from ROL and ROR in that the bits are rotated through the carry flag. Figure 3.26 illustrates the rotation that takes place due to execution of the RCL instruction. Notice that the bit returned to bit 0 is the prior contents of CF and not bit 15. The bit shifted out of bit 15 goes into the carry flag. Thus the bits rotate through carry.

Example 3.9

What is the result in BX and CF after execution of the following instruction?

$$\text{RCR BX,CL}$$

Assume that prior to execution of the instruction $(CL) = 04_{16}$, $(BX) = 1234_{16}$, and $(CF) = 0$.

Solution.   The original contents of BX are

$$(BX) = 0001001000110100_2 = 1234_{16}$$

Execution of the ROR instruction causes a 4-bit rotate right through carry to take place on the data in BX. Therefore, the original content of bit 3, which is 0, resides in carry; $CF = 0$ and 1000 has been reloaded from bit 15. The resulting contents of BX are

$$(BX) = 1000000100100011_2 = 8123_{16}$$

ASSIGNMENT

Section 3.2

1. Can the 8086 directly store a word of data starting at an odd address?
2. What type of information is contained in the software model of the 8086?
3. Which registers of the 8086 are used in memory segmentation?
4. Categorize each flag bit of the 8086 as either a control flag or a flag to monitor the effect of instruction execution.

Section 3.3

5. Identify the three parts of an assembly language instruction in each of the following state-ments:

> AGAIN: ADD   AX,CX   ;ADD THE REGISTERS
>
> MOV   BX,AX   ;SAVE RESULT

6. Identify the source and destination operands for each of the statements in problem 5.

Section 3.4

7. Make a list of the addressing modes available on the 8086.

8. Identify the addressing modes for both the source and destination operands in the in-structions that follow.

    (a) MOV AL,BL
    (b) MOV AX,0FFH
    (c) MOV [SI],AX
    (d) MOV SI,[DI]
    (e) MOV [BX].XYZ,CX
    (f) MOV XYZ[SI],AH
    (g) MOV [BX].XYZ[DI],AL

9. Compute the memory address, the specified register, or the immediate value for the source operand and destination operand in each of the instructions in problem 8.

10. Write an instruction that loads AL from memory address $A000_{16}$ using three different addressing modes. Specify all assumptions made.

Section 3.6

11. Write an instruction sequence equivalent to

> XCHG AX,BX

12. Two code conversion tables starting with offsets TABL1 and TABL2 in the data segment starting at $A000_{16}$ are to be accessed. Write a routine that initializes the needed registers and then replaces the contents of memory locations MEM1 and MEM2 (offsets in the data segment) by the equivalent converted codes from the code conversion tables.

Section 3.7

13. Two word-wide unsigned integers are stored at the memory addresses $A000_{16}$ and $B000_{16}$, respectively. Write an instruction sequence that computes and stores their sum, differ-ence, product, and quotient. Store these results at consecutive memory locations starting at address $C000_{16}$ in memory. To obtain the difference, subtract the integer at $B000_{16}$ from the integer at $A000_{16}$. For the division, divide the integer at $A000_{16}$ by the integer at $B000_{16}$. Use register indirect relative addressing mode to store the various results.

14. Two word-long BCD integers are stored at the symbolic addresses NUM1 and NUM2, respectively. Write an instruction sequence to generate their difference and store it at NUM3. The difference is to be formed by subtracting the value at NUM1 from that at NUM2.

Section 3.8

15. Write an instruction sequence that generates a byte-size integer in the memory location identified by label RESULT. The value of the byte integer is to be calculated as follows:

$$RESULT = AL \cdot NUM1 + (\overline{NUM2 \cdot AL + BL})$$

Assume that all parameters are byte size.

Section 3.9

16. Implement the following operation using shift and arithmetic instructions.

$$7(AX) - 5(BX) - \tfrac{1}{8}(BX) \longrightarrow (AX)$$

Assume that all parameters are word size.

Section 3.10

17. Write a program that saves the content of bit 5 in AL in BX as a word.

4

8086 Microprocessor Programming 2

4.1 INTRODUCTION

In Chapter 3 we discussed many of the instructions that can be executed by the 8086 microprocessor. Furthermore, we used these instructions to write simple programs. In this chapter we introduce the rest of the instruction set and at the same time cover some more complicated programming techniques. The following topics are discussed in this chapter:

1. Flag control instructions
2. Compare instruction
3. Jump instructions
4. Program examples employing loops
5. Subroutines and subroutine handling instructions
6. Example program employing subroutines
7. Loop instructions
8. String instructions

4.2 FLAG CONTROL INSTRUCTIONS

The 8086 microprocessor has a set of flags which either monitor the status of executing instructions or control options available in its operation. These flags were described in detail in Chapter 2. The instruction set includes a group of instructions which when executed directly affect the setting of the flags. These instructions, shown

Mnemonic	Meaning	Operation	Flags Affected
LAHF	Load AH from flags	$(AH) \leftarrow (Flags)$	None
SAHF	Store AH into flags	$(Flags) \leftarrow (AH)$	SF, ZF, AF, PF, CF
CLC	Clear carry flag	$(CF) \leftarrow 0$	CF
STC	Set carry flag	$(CF) \leftarrow 1$	CF
CMC	Complement carry flag	$(CF) \leftarrow (\overline{CF})$	CF
CLI	Clear interrupt flag	$(IF) \leftarrow 0$	IF
STI	Set interrupt flag	$(IF) \leftarrow 1$	IF

Figure 4.1 Flag control instructions.

in Fig. 4.1, are: *load AH from flags* (LAHF), *store AH into flags* (SAHF), *clear carry* (CLC), *set carry* (STC), *complement carry* (CMC), *clear interrupt* (CLI), and *set interrupt* (STI). A few more instructions exist that can directly affect the flags; however, we will not cover them until later in the chapter when we introduce the subroutine and string instructions.

Looking at Fig. 4.1, we see that the first two instructions, LAHF and SAHF, can be used either to read the flags or to change them, respectively. Notice that the data transfer that takes place is always between the AH register and the flag register. For instance, we may want to start an operation with certain flags set or reset. Assume that we want to preset all flags to logic 1. To do this, we can first load AH with FF_{16} and then execute the SAHF instruction.

The next three instructions, CLC, STC, and CMC, are used to manipulate the carry flag. They permit CF to be cleared, set, or complemented to its inverse logic level, respectively. For example, if CF is 1 and the CMC instruction is executed, it becomes 0.

The last two instructions are used to manipulate the interrupt flag. Executing the clear interrupt (CLI) instruction sets IF to logic 0 and disables the interrupt interface. On the other hand, executing the STI instruction sets IF to 1 and the microprocessor starts accepting interrupts from that point on.

4.3 COMPARE INSTRUCTION

There is an instruction included in the instruction set of the 8086 which can be used to compare two 8-bit or 16-bit numbers. It is the *compare* (CMP) instruction of Fig. 4.2(a). Figure 4.2(b) shows that the operands can reside in a storage location in memory, a register within the MPU, or as part of the instruction. For instance, a byte-wide number in a register such as BL can be compared to a second byte-wide number that is supplied as immediate data.

The result of the comparison is reflected by changes in six of the status flags of the 8086. Notice in Fig. 4.2(a) that it affects the overflow flag, sign flag, zero

Mnemonic	Meaning	Format	Operation	Flags Affected
CMP	Compare	CMP D,S	(D) − (S) is used in setting or resetting the flags	CF, AF, OF, PF, SF, ZF

(a)

Destination	Source
Register	Register
Register	Memory
Memory	Register
Register	Immediate
Memory	Immediate
Accumulator	Immediate

(b)

Figure 4.2   (a) Compare instruction; (b) allowed operands.

flag, auxiliary carry flag, parity flag, and carry flag. The logic state of these flags can be referenced by instructions in order to make a decision whether or not to alter the sequence in which the program executes.

The process of comparison performed by the CMP instruction is basically a subtraction operation. The source operand is subtracted from the destination operand. However, the result of this subtraction is not saved. Instead, based on the result the appropriate flags are set or reset.

The subtraction is done using 2's-complement arithmetic. For example, let us assume that the destination operand equals $10011001_2 = -103_{10}$ and that the source operand equals $00011011_2 = +27_{10}$. Subtracting the source from the destination, we get

$$10011001_2 = -103_{10}$$
$$- \ 00011011_2 = -(+27_{10})$$

Replacing the destination operand with its 2's complement and adding yields

$$10011001_2 = -103_{10}$$
$$+ \ 11100101_2 = - \ 27_{10}$$
$$\overline{01111110_2 = +126_{10}}$$

In the process of obtaining this result, we set the status that follows:

1. No carry is generated from bit 3 to bit 4; therefore, the auxiliary carry flag AF is at logic 0.
2. There is a carry out from bit 7. Thus carry flag CF is set.
3. Even though a carry out of bit 7 is generated, there is no carry from bit 6 to bit 7. This is an overflow condition and the OF flag is set.

4. There are an even number of 1s; therefore, this makes parity flag PF equal to 1.

5. Bit 7 is zero and therefore sign flag SF is at logic 0.

6. The result that is produced is nonzero, which makes zero flag ZF logic 0.

Notice that the result produced by the subtraction of the two 8-bit numbers is not correct. This condition was indicated by setting the overflow flag.

Example 4.1

Describe what happens to the status flags as the sequence of instructions that follow is executed.

$$\text{MOV} \quad \text{AX,01234H}$$

$$\text{MOV} \quad \text{BX,0ABCDH}$$

$$\text{CMP} \quad \text{AX,BX}$$

Assume that flags ZF, SF, CF, AF, OF, and PF are all initially reset.

Solution. The first instruction loads AX with 1234_{16}. No status flags are affected by the execution of a MOV instruction. The second instruction puts $ABCD_{16}$ into the BX register. Again status is not affected. Thus, after execution of these two move instructions, the contents of AX and BX are

$$(AX) = 1234_{16} = 0001001000110100_2$$

and

$$(BX) = ABCD_{16} = 1010101111001101_2$$

The third instruction is a 16-bit comparison with AX representing the destination and BX the source. Therefore, the contents of BX are subtracted from that of AX.

$$(AX) - (BX) = 0001001000110100_2 - 1010101111001101_2$$

Replacing (BX) with its 2's complement and adding, we get

$$(AX) + 2\text{'s complement } (BX) = 0001001000110100_2 + 0101010000110010_2 + 1_2$$

$$= 0110011001100111_2$$

The flags are either set or reset based on the result of this subtraction. Notice that the result is nonzero and positive. This makes ZF and SF equal to zero. Moreover, the carry, auxiliary carry, and no overflow conditions have occurred. Therefore, CF and AF are at logic 1 while OF is at logic 0.

Finally, the result has odd parity; therefore, PF is set to 0. These results are summarized in Fig. 4.3.

Instruction	ZF	SF	CF	AF	OF	PF
Initial state	0	0	0	0	0	0
MOV AX,01234H	0	0	0	0	0	0
MOV BX,0ABCDH	0	0	0	0	0	0
CMP AX,BX	0	0	1	1	0	0

Figure 4.3 Effect on flags of executing instructions.

4.4 JUMP INSTRUCTIONS

The purpose of a *jump* instruction is to alter the execution path of instructions in the program. In the 8086 microprocessor, the code segment register and instruction pointer keep track of the next instruction to be executed. Thus a jump instruction involves altering the contents of these registers. In this way, execution continues at an address other than that of the next sequential instruction. That is, a jump occurs to another part of the program. Typically, program execution is not intended to return to the next sequential instruction after the jump instruction. Therefore, no return linkage is saved when the jump takes place.

The 8086 microprocessor allows two different types of jump instructions. They are the *unconditional jump* and the *conditional jump*. In an unconditional jump, no status requirements are imposed for the jump to occur. That is, as the instruction is executed, the jump always takes place to change the execution sequence.

On the other hand, for a conditional jump instruction, status conditions that exist at the moment the jump instruction is executed decide whether or not the jump will occur. If this condition or conditions are met, the jump takes place; otherwise, execution continues with the next sequential instruction of the program. The conditions that can be referenced by a conditional jump instruction are status flags such as carry (CF), parity (PF), and overflow (OF).

Unconditional Jump Instruction

The unconditional jump instruction of the 8086 is shown in Fig. 4.4(a) together with its valid operand combinations in Fig. 4.4(b). There are two basic kinds of unconditional jumps. The first, called an *intrasegment jump*, is limited to addresses within the current code segment. This type of jump is achieved by just modifying the value

Mnemonic	Meaning	Format	Operation	Flags Affected
JMP	Unconditional jump	JMP Operand	Jump is initiated to the address specified by Operand	None

(a)

Operand
Short-label
Near-label
Far-label
Memptr16
Regptr16
Memptr32

(b)

Figure 4.4   (a) Unconditional jump instruction; (b) allowed operands.

in IP. The other kind of jump, the *intersegment jump*, permits jumps from one code segment to another. Implementation of this type of jump requires modification of the contents of both CS and IP.

Jump instructions specified with a *Short-label, Near-label, Memptr16,* or *Regptr16 operand* represent intrasegment jumps. The Short-label and Near-label operands specify the jump relative to the address of the jump instruction itself. For example, in a Short-label jump instruction an 8-bit number is coded as an immediate operand to specify the *signed displacement* of the next instruction to be executed from the location of the jump instruction. When the jump instruction is executed, IP is reloaded with a new value equal to the updated value in IP, which is (IP) + 2, plus the signed displacement. The new value of IP and current value in CS give the address of the next instruction to be fetched and executed. With an 8-bit displacement, the Short-label operand can only be used to initiate a jump in the range − 126 to + 129 bytes from the location of the jump instruction.

On the other hand, Near-label operands specify the displacement with a 16-bit immediate operand. This corresponds to a range equal to 32K bytes forward or backward from the jump instruction. The displacement is automatically calculated by the 8086's assembler during program assembly. Thus a programmer can use symbolic labels as operands.

An example is the instruction

JMP LABEL

This means to jump to the point in the program corresponding to the tag LABEL. The programmer does not have to worry about counting the number of bytes from the jump instruction to the location to which control is to be passed. Moreover, the fact that it is coded as a Short- or Near-label displacement is also determined by the assembler.

The jump to address can also be specified indirectly by the contents of a memory location or the contents of a register. These two types correspond to the Memptr16 and Regptr16 operands, respectively. Just as for the Near-label operand, they both permit a jump of + or − 32K bytes from the address of the jump instruction.

For example,

JMP BX

uses the contents of register BX for the displacement. That is, the value in BX is copied into IP. Then the physical address of the next instruction is obtained by using the current contents of CS and this new value in IP.

To specify an operand to be used as a pointer, the various addressing modes available with the 8086 can be used. For instance,

JMP [BX]

uses the contents of BX as the address of the memory location that contains the offset address. This offset is loaded into IP, where it is used together with the current contents of CS to compute the "jump to" address.

The intersegment unconditional jump instructions correspond to the *Far-label* and *Memptr32 operands* that are shown in Fig. 4.4(b). Far-label uses a 32-bit immediate operand to specify the jump to address. The first 16 bits of this 32-bit pointer are loaded into IP and are an offset address relative to the contents of the code segment register. The next 16 bits are loaded into the CS register and define the new 64K-byte code segment.

An indirect way to specify the offset and code segment address for an intersegment jump is by using the Memptr32 operand. This time four consecutive memory bytes starting at the specified address contain the offset address and the new code segment address, respectively. Just like the Memptr16 operand, the Memptr32 operand may be specified using any one of the various addressing modes of the 8086.

An example is the instruction

JMP FARSEG[DI]

It uses the contents of DS and DI to calculate the address of the memory location that contains the first word of the pointer that identifies the location to which the jump will take place. The two-word pointer starting at this address is read into IP and CS to pass control to the new point in the program.

Conditional Jump Instruction

The second type of jump instructions are those which perform conditional jump operations. Figure 4.5(a) shows a general form of this instruction and Fig. 4.5(b) is a list of each of the conditional jump instructions in the 8086's instruction set. Notice that each of these instructions tests for the presence or absence of certain conditions.

For instance, the *jump on carry* (JC) instruction makes a test to determine if carry flag (CF) is set. Depending on the result of the test, the jump to the location specified by its operand either takes place or does not. If CF equals 0, the test fails and execution continues with the instruction at the address following the JC instruction. On the other hand, if CF is set to 1, the test condition is satisfied and the jump is performed.

Notice that for some of the instructions in Fig. 4.5(b) two different mnemonics can be used. This feature can be used to improve program readability. That is, for each occurrence of the instruction in the program, it can be identified with the mnemonic that best describes its function.

For instance, the instruction *jump on parity* (JP)/*jump on parity even* (JPE) can be used to test parity flag PF for logic 1. Since PF is set to 1 if the result from a computation has even parity, this instruction can initiate a jump based on the occurrence of even parity. The reverse instruction JNP/JNPE is also provided. It can be used to initiate a jump based on the occurrence of a result with odd parity instead of even parity.

In a similar manner, the instructions *jump if equal* (JE) and *jump if zero* (JZ) have the same function. Either notation can be used in a program to determine if the result of a computation was zero.

All other conditional jump instructions work in a similar way except that they test different conditions to decide whether or not the jump is to take place. Examples

Mnemonic	Meaning	Format	Operation	Flags Affected
Jcc	Conditional jump	Jcc Operand	If the specific condition cc is true, the jump to the address specified by the Operand is initiated; otherwise, the next instruction is executed	None

(a)

Mnemonic	Meaning
JA/JNBE	Jump if above/jump if not below or equal
JAE/JNB	Jump if above or equal/jump if not below
JB/JNAE	Jump if below/jump if not above or equal
JBE/JNA	Jump if below or equal/jump if not above
JC	Jump if carry
JCXZ	Jump if CX is zero
JE/JZ	Jump if equal/jump if zero
JG/JNLE	Jump if greater/jump if not less or equal
JGE/JNL	Jump if greater or equal/jump if not less
JLE/JNG	Jump if less or equal/jump if not greater
JNC	Jump if not carry
JNE/JNZ	Jump if not equal/jump if not zero
JNO	Jump if not overflow
JNP/JPO	Jump if not parity/jump if parity odd
JNS	Jump if not sign
JO	Jump if overflow
JP/JPE	Jump if parity/jump if parity even
JS	Jump if sign

(b)

Figure 4.5 (a) Conditional jump instruction; (b) types of conditional jump instructions.

of these conditions are that the contents of CX are zero, an overflow has occurred, or the result is negative.

To distinguish between comparisons of signed and unsigned numbers by jump instructions, two different names, which seem to be the same, have been devised. They are above and below for comparison of unsigned numbers and less and greater for comparison of signed numbers. For instance, the number $ABCD_{16}$ is above the number 1234_{16} if considered as an unsigned number. On the other hand, if they are considered as signed numbers, $ABCD_{16}$ is negative and 1234_{16} is positive. Therefore, $ABCD_{16}$ is less than 1234_{16}.

Example 4.2

Write a program to move a block of N bytes of data starting at offset address BLK1ADDR to another block starting at offset address BLK2ADDR. Assume that both blocks are in the same data segment, whose starting point is defined by the data segment address DATASEGADDR.

Solution. The steps to be implemented to solve this problem are outlined in the flow-chart in Fig. 4.6(a). It has four basic operations. The first operation is initialization. Initialization involves establishing the initial address of the data segment. This is done by loading the DS register with the value DATASEGADDR. Furthermore, source index register SI and destination index register DI are initialized with addresses BLK1ADDR and BLK2ADDR, respectively. In this way, they point to the beginning of the source block and the beginning of the destination block, respectively. To keep track of the count, register CX is initialized with N, the number of points to be moved. This leads us to the following assembly language statements.

MOV	AX,DATASEGADDR
MOV	DS,AX
MOV	SI,BLK1ADDR
MOV	DI,BLK2ADDR
MOV	CX,N

Notice that DS cannot be directly loaded by immediate data with a MOV instruction. Therefore, the address was first loaded into AX and then moved to DS. SI, DI, and CX can be loaded directly with immediate data.

The next operation that must be performed is the actual movement of data from the source block of memory to the destination block. The offset addresses are already loaded into SI and DI; therefore, move instructions that employ indirect addressing can be used to accomplish the data transfer operation. Remember that the 8086 does not allow direct memory-to-memory moves. For this reason, AX will be used as an inter-mediate storage location for data. The source byte is moved into AX with one instruction and then another instruction is needed to move it from AX to the destination location. Thus the data move is accomplished by the following instructions:

NXTPT:	MOV	AH,[SI]
	MOV	[DI],AH

Notice that for a byte move only the higher 8 bits of AX are used. Therefore, the operand is specified as AH instead of AX.

The next operation is to update the pointers in SI and DI so that they are ready for the next byte move. Also, the counter must be decremented so that it corresponds to the number of bytes that remain to be moved. These updates can be done by the following sequence of instructions:

INC	SI
INC	DI
DEC	CX

The test operation involves determining whether or not all the data points have been moved. The contents of CX represents this condition. When its value is nonzero, there still are points to be moved; whereas a value of zero indicates that the block move is complete. This zero condition is reflected by 1 in ZF. The instruction needed to perform this test is

JNZ NXTPT

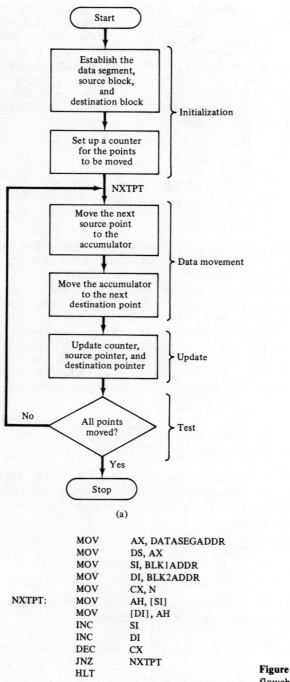

(a)

```
          MOV     AX, DATASEGADDR
          MOV     DS, AX
          MOV     SI, BLK1ADDR
          MOV     DI, BLK2ADDR
          MOV     CX, N
NXTPT:    MOV     AH, [SI]
          MOV     [DI], AH
          INC     SI
          INC     DI
          DEC     CX
          JNZ     NXTPT
          HLT
```

(b)

Figure 4.6 (a) Block transfer flowchart; (b) program.

Here NXTPT is a label that corresponds to the first instruction in the data move operation. The last instruction in the program can be a *halt* (HLT) instruction to indicate the end of the block move operation. The entire program is shown in Fig. 4.6(b).

Example 4.3

It is required to determine the average of a set of data points stored in a buffer. The number of points in the buffer, the offset address of the beginning of the buffer, and the data segment address are stored in a table called a parameter table. Figure 4.7(a) shows the parameters needed for the average program. Notice that the beginning address of this table is $ABCD0_{16}$. This first address holds the number that indicates how many data points are in the buffer. Since a byte is used to specify the number of data points, the size of the buffer is limited to 256 bytes. The offset address of the beginning of the buffer is stored at table locations $ABCD1_{16}$ and $ABCD2_{16}$. This buffer table offset address is with respect to the data segment defined by the address in locations $ABCD3_{16}$ and $ABCD4_{16}$. Assuming that the data points are signed 8-bit binary numbers, write a program to find their average.

Solution.   The average can be found by adding all the signed numbers and then dividing their sum by the number of points that were added. Even though 8-bit data points are being added, the sum that results can be more than 8 bits. Therefore, we will consider a 16-bit result for the sum and it will be held in register DX. The average that is obtained turns out to be just 8 bits long. It will be available in AL at the completion of the program.

Our plan for the program that will solve this problem is shown in Fig. 4.7(b). This flowchart can be divided into six basic operations, which are: initialization, preparing the next point for addition, performing the addition, updating the counter and pointer, testing for the end of the summation, and computing the average.

Initialization involves establishing the data segment and data buffer addresses and loading the data point counter. This is achieved by loading the appropriate registers within the 8086 with parameters from the parameter table. The instructions that perform this initialization are:

            MOV   AX,0A000H

            MOV   DS,AX

            MOV   DI,0BCD0H

            MOV   CL,[DI]

            MOV   BL,CL

            LDS   SI,[DI + 1]

The first two instructions define the data segment in which the parameter table resides. This is achieved by first loading AX with the immediate operand $A000_{16}$ of a MOV instruction and then copying it into DS. Then another MOV instruction establishes a pointer to the parameter table in register DI. This is done by loading DI with immediate operand $BCD0_{16}$. The instruction that follows this uses DI as a pointer to load CL from the first address in the parameter table. This address is $ABCD0_{16}$ and contains the number of points to be used in forming the average. Looking at Fig. 4.7(a), we see that this value is FF_{16}. The next instruction copies the number in CL into BL for later use. The LDS

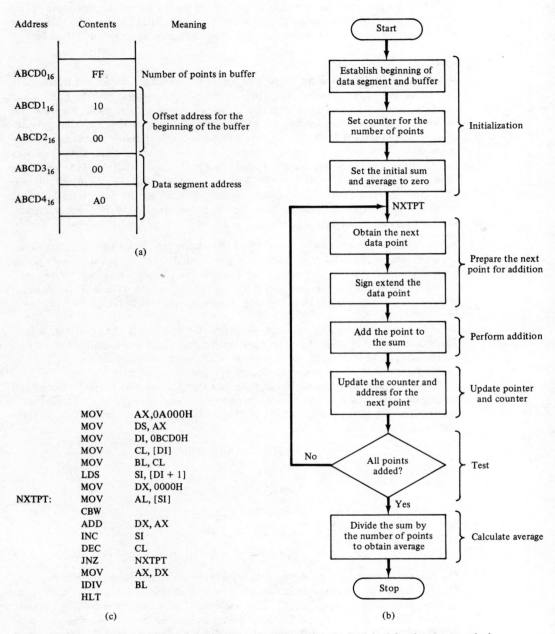

Address	Contents	Meaning
$ABCD0_{16}$	FF	Number of points in buffer
$ABCD1_{16}$	10	Offset address for the beginning of the buffer
$ABCD2_{16}$	00	
$ABCD3_{16}$	00	Data segment address
$ABCD4_{16}$	A0	

(a)

```
                MOV     AX,0A000H
                MOV     DS, AX
                MOV     DI, 0BCD0H
                MOV     CL, [DI]
                MOV     BL, CL
                LDS     SI, [DI + 1]
                MOV     DX, 0000H
NXTPT:          MOV     AL, [SI]
                CBW
                ADD     DX, AX
                INC     SI
                DEC     CL
                JNZ     NXTPT
                MOV     AX, DX
                IDIV    BL
                HLT
```

(c)

Flowchart (b):

Start

Establish beginning of data segment and buffer ⎫
Set counter for the number of points ⎬ Initialization
Set the initial sum and average to zero ⎭

NXTPT
Obtain the next data point ⎫ Prepare the next
Sign extend the data point ⎭ point for addition

Add the point to the sum ⎬ Perform addition

Update the counter and address for the next point ⎬ Update pointer and counter

All points added? — No ⎬ Test

Yes
Divide the sum by the number of points to obtain average ⎬ Calculate average

Stop

(b)

Figure 4.7 (a) Parameter table for average calculations; (b) flowchart for the average calculation program; (c) program.

instruction is used to define the buffer together with the data segment in which it resides. This instruction first loads SI with the offset address of the beginning of the buffer from table locations $ABCD1_{16}$ and $ABCD2_{16}$ and then DS with the address of the data segment in which the data table lies from table locations $ABCD3_{16}$ and $ABCD4_{16}$. The sum must start with zero; therefore, register DX, which is to hold the sum, is loaded with zeros by the instruction.

$$\text{MOV DX,0000H}$$

The next operation involves obtaining a byte of data from the buffer, making it into a 16-bit number by sign extension, and adding it to the contents of the DX register. This is accomplished by the following sequence of instructions:

```
NXTPT:  MOV   AL,[SI]
        CBW
        ADD   DX,AX
```

The first instruction loads AL with the element in the buffer that is pointed to by the address in SI. The CBW instruction converts the signed byte in AL to a signed word in AX by extending its sign. Next the 16-bit signed number in AX is added to the sum in DX. Notice that the label NXTPT (next point) has been used on the first instruction.

To prepare for the next addition, we must increment the value in SI such that it points to the next element in the buffer and decrement the count in CL. To do this, we use the following instructions:

```
INC   SI
DEC   CL
```

If the contents of CL at this point are nonzero, we should go back to obtain and add the next element from the buffer; otherwise, we just proceed with the next instruction in the program. To do this, we execute the following instruction:

```
JNZ NXTPT
```

Execution of this instruction tests the value in ZF that results from the DEC CL instruction. If this flag is not set to 1, a jump is initiated to the instruction corresponding to the label NXTPT. Remember that NXTPT is placed at the instruction used to move a byte into AL for addition to the sum. In this way, we see that this part of the program will be repeated until all data points have been added. After this is complete, the sum resides in DX.

The average is obtained by dividing the accumulated sum in DX by the number of data points. The count of data points was saved earlier in BL. However, the contents of DX cannot be divided directly. It must first be moved into AX. Once there, the signed divide instruction can be used to do the division. This gives the following instructions:

```
MOV   AX,DX
IDIV  BL
```

The result of the division, which is the average, is now in AL. The entire average calculation program is shown in Fig. 4.7(c).

Example 4.4

It is required to sort an array of 16-bit signed binary numbers such that they are arranged in ascending order. For instance, if the original array is

$$5, 1, 29, 15, 38, 3, -8, -32$$

after sorting, the array that results would be

$$-32, -8, 1, 3, 5, 15, 29, 38$$

Assume that the array of numbers is stored at consecutive memory locations from addresses $A0400_{16}$ through $A04FE_{16}$ in memory. Write a sort program.

Solution.   First we will develop an algorithm that can be used to sort an array of elements A(0), A(1), A(2), through A(N) into ascending order. One way of doing this is to take the first number in the array, which is A(0), and compare it to the second number A(1). If A(0) is greater than A(1), the two numbers are swapped; otherwise, they are left alone. Next A(0) is compared to A(2) and based on the result of this comparison they are either swapped or left alone. This sequence is repeated until A(0) has been compared with all numbers up through A(N). When this is complete, the smallest number will be in the A(0) position.

Now A(1) must be compared to A(2) through A(N) in the same way. After this is done, the second smallest number is in the A(1) position. Up to this point, just two of the N numbers have been put in ascending order. Therefore, the procedure must be continued for A(2) through A(N − 1) to complete the sort.

Figure 4.8(a) illustrates the use of this algorithm for an array with just four numbers. The numbers are A(0) = 5, A(1) = 1, A(2) = 29, and A(3) = − 8. During the sort sequence, A(0) = 5 is first compared to A(1) = 1. Since 5 is greater than 1, A(0) and A(1) are swapped. Now A(0) = 1 is compared to A(2) = 29. This time 1 is less than 29; therefore, the numbers are not swapped and A(0) remains equal to 1. Next, A(0) = 1 is compared with A(3) = − 8. A(0) is greater than A(3). Thus A(0) and A(3) are swapped and A(0) becomes equal to − 8. Notice in Fig. 4.8(a) that the lowest of the four numbers now resides in A(0).

The sort sequence in Fig. 4.8(a) continues with A(1) = 5 being compared first to A(2) = 29 and then to A(3) = 1. In the first comparison, A(1) is less than A(2). For this reason, their values are not swapped. But in the second comparison, A(1) is greater than A(3); therefore, the two values are swapped. In this way, the second lowest number, which is 1, is sorted into A(1).

It just remains to sort A(2) and A(3). Comparing these two values, we see that 29 is greater than 5. This causes the two values to be swapped such that A(2) = 5 and A(3) = 29. As shown in Fig. 4.8(a), the sorting of the array is now complete.

Now we will implement the algorithm on the 8086 microprocessor. The flowchart for its implementation is shown in Fig. 4.8(b). The first block in the flowchart represents the initialization of data segment register DS and pointers $PNTR_1$ and $PNTR_3$. The DS register is initialized with $A000_{16}$ to define a data segment starting from memory address $A0000_{16}$. $PNTR_1$ points to the first element in the array. It will be register SI and will be initialized to 0400_{16}. Therefore, the first element of the array is at address $A0400_{16}$. For pointer $PNTR_3$, we will use register BX and will initialize it to $04FE_{16}$. It points to the last element in the array, which is at address $A04FE_{16}$. Next, $PNTR_2$, the moving pointer, is initialized so that it points to the second element in the array.

Register DI will be used for this pointer. This leads to the following instruction sequence for initialization:

$$\text{MOV}\quad \text{AX,0A000H}$$

$$\text{MOV}\quad \text{DS,AX}$$

$$\text{MOV}\quad \text{SI,0400H}$$

$$\text{MOV}\quad \text{BX,04FEH}$$

AA: MOV   DI,SI

$$\text{ADD}\quad \text{DI,02H}$$

Notice that DS was loaded via AX with the immediate data $A000_{16}$ to define a data segment starting at $A0000_{16}$. SI and BX, which are $PNTR_1$ and $PNTR_3$, respectively, are loaded with immediate operands 0400_{16} and $04FE_{16}$. In this way, they point to the first and last elements of the array, respectively. Finally, register DI, which is $PNTR_2$, is loaded with 0400_{16} from SI and then incremented by 2 with an ADD instruction such that it points to the second element in the array. This completes the initialization process.

Next, the array element pointed to by $PNTR_1$ is to be compared to the element pointed to by $PNTR_2$. If the element corresponding to $PNTR_1$ is arithmetically less than the element corresponding to pointer $PNTR_2$, the two elements are already in ascending order. But if this is not the case, the two elements must be interchanged. Both of these elements are in memory. However, the 8086 cannot directly compare two values in memory. For this reason, one of the two elements must be moved to a register within the 8086. We will use AX for this purpose. The resulting code is as follows:

BB: MOV   AX,[SI]

$$\text{CMP}\quad \text{AX,[DI]}$$

$$\text{JLE}\quad \text{CC}$$

I	0	1	2	3	Status
A(I)	5	1	29	−8	Original array
A(I)	1	5	29	−8	Array after comparing A(0) and A(1)
A(I)	1	5	29	−8	Array after comparing A(0) and A(2)
A(I)	−8	5	29	1	Array after comparing A(0) and A(3)
A(I)	−8	5	29	1	Array after comparing A(1) and A(2)
A(I)	−8	1	29	5	Array after comparing A(1) and A(3)
A(I)	−8	1	5	29	Array after comparing A(2) and A(3)

(a)

Figure 4.8   (a) Sort operation example; (b) flowchart for the sort program; (c) sort program.

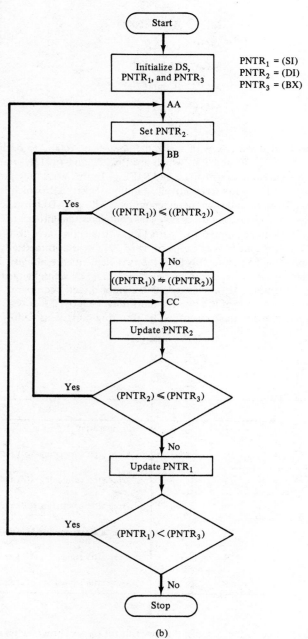

(b)   **Figure 4.8** *(continued)*

		MOV	AX, 0A000H
		MOV	DS, AX
		MOV	SI, 0400H
		MOV	BX, 04FEH
	AA:	MOV	DI, SI
		ADD	DI, 02H
	BB:	MOV	AX, [SI]
		CMP	AX, [DI]
		JLE	CC
(c)		MOV	[SI], [DI]
		MOV	[DI], AX
	CC:	INC	DI
		INC	DI
		CMP	DI, BX
		JBE	BB
		INC	SI
		INC	SI
		CMP	SI, BX
		JB	AA
		HLT	

Figure 4.8 *(continued)*

```
        MOV    DX,[DI]
        MOV    [SI],DX
        MOV    [DI],AX
CC:
```

The first instruction moves the element pointed to by $PNTR_1$ into AX. The second instruction compares the value in AX with the element pointed to by $PNTR_2$. The result of this comparison is reflected in the status flags. The jump on less than or equal to instruction that follows checks if the first element is arithmetically less than or equal to the second element. If the result of this check is yes, control is transferred to CC. CC is a label to be used in the segment of program that will follow. If the check fails, the two elements must be interchanged. In this case, the instructions executed next move the element pointed to by $PNTR_2$ into the location pointed to by $PNTR_1$. Then the copy of the original value pointed to by $PNTR_1$, which is saved in AX, is moved to the location pointed to by $PNTR_2$.

To continue sorting through the rest of the elements in the array, we update $PNTR_2$ such that it points to the next element in the array. This comparison should be repeated until the first element has been compared to each of the other elements in the array. This condition is satisfied when $PNTR_2$ points to the last element in the array. That is, $PNTR_2$ equals $PNTR_3$. This part of the program can be done with a code:

```
CC:     INC    DI
        INC    DI
        CMP    DI,BX
        JBE    BB
```

The first two instructions update $PNTR_2$ such that it points to the next element. The third instruction compares $PNTR_2$ to $PNTR_3$ to determine whether or not they are equal. If they are equal to each other, the first element has been compared to the last element and we are ready to continue with the second element. Otherwise, we must repeat from the label BB. This test is done with the jump on below or equal instruction. Notice that label BB corresponds to the beginning of the part of the program that compares the elements of the array. Once we fall through the JBE instruction, we have placed the smallest number in the array into the position pointed to by $PNTR_1$. To process the rest of the elements in the array in a similar way, $PNTR_1$ must be moved over the entire range of elements and the foregoing procedure repeated. This can be done by implementing the code that follows:

```
INC   SI
INC   SI
CMP   SI,BX
JB    AA
HLT
```

The first two instructions increment pointer $PNTR_1$ such that it points to the next element in the array. The third instruction checks if all the elements have been sorted. The fourth instruction passes control back to the sorting sequence of instructions if $PNTR_1$ does not point to the last element. However, if all elements of the array have been sorted, we come to a halt at the end of the program. The entire program appears in Fig. 4.8(c).

4.5 SUBROUTINES AND SUBROUTINE-HANDLING INSTRUCTIONS

Subroutines are procedures written separate from the main program. Whenever the main program must perform a function that is defined by a subroutine, it calls the subroutine into operation. In order to do this, control must be passed from the main program to the starting point of the subroutine. Execution continues with the subroutine and upon completion control is returned back to the main program at the instruction that follows the one that called the subroutine. Notice that the difference between the operation of a subroutine call and a jump is that a call to a subroutine not only produces a jump to an appropriate address in program storage memory, but it also has a mechanism for saving information such as IP and CS, which is needed to return back to the main program.

CALL and RET Instructions

There are two basic instructions in the instruction set of the 8086 for subroutine handling. They are the *call* (CALL) and *return* (RET) instructions. Together they provide the mechanism for calling a subroutine into operation and returning control back to the main program at its completion. We will first discuss these two instructions and later introduce other instructions which can be used in conjunction with subroutines.

　　Just like the JMP instruction, CALL allows implementation of two types of operations, the *intrasegment call* and the *intersegment call*. The CALL instruction

Mnemonic	Meaning	Format	Operation	Flags Affected
CALL	Subroutine call	CALL operand	Execution continues from the address of the subroutine specified by the operand. Information required to return back to the main program such as IP and CS are saved on the stack.	None

(a)

Operand
Near-proc
Far-proc
Memptr16
Regptr16
Memptr32

(b)

Figure 4.9   (a) Subroutine call instruction; (b) allowed operands.

is shown in Fig. 4.9(a) and its allowed operand variations are shown in Fig. 4.9(b).

It is the operand that initiates either an intersegment or an intrasegment call. The operands Near-proc, Memptr16, and Regptr16 all specify intrasegment calls to a subroutine. In all three cases, execution of the instruction causes the contents of IP to be saved on the stack. Then the stack pointer (SP) is decremented by 2. The saved values of IP is the address of the instruction that follows the CALL instruction. After saving the return address, a new 16-bit value, which corresponds to the storage location of the first instruction in the subroutine, is loaded into IP.

The three types of intrasegment operands represent different ways of specifying this new value of IP. In a Near-proc operand, the displacement of the first instruction of the subroutine from the current value of IP is supplied directly by the instruction. An example is

CALL NEAR PROC

Here the label NEAR determines the 16-bit displacement and is coded as an immediate operand following the opcode for the call instruction. Call is actually a relative addressing mode instruction; that is, the offset address is calculated relative to the address of the call instruction itself. With 16 bits, the displacement is limited to + or − 32K bytes.

The Memptr16 and Regptr16 operands provide indirect subroutine addressing by specifying a memory location or an internal register, respectively, as the source of a new value for IP. The value specified in this way is not a displacement. It is the actual offset that is to be loaded into IP. An example of the Regptr16 operand is

CALL BX

When this instruction is executed, the contents of BX are loaded into IP and execution continues with the subroutine starting at a physical address derived from CS and IP.

By using one of the various addressing modes of the 8086, an internal register can be used as a pointer to an operand that resides in memory. This represents a Memptr16 type of operand. In this case, the value of the physical address of the offset is obtained from the current contents of the data segment register DS and the address or addresses held in the specified registers. For instance, the instruction

CALL [BX]

has its subroutine offset address at the memory location whose physical address is derived from the contents of DS and BX. The value stored at this memory location is loaded into IP. Again the current contents of CS and the new value in IP point to the first instruction of the subroutine.

Notice that in both intrasegment call examples the subroutine was located within the same code segment as the call instruction. The other type of CALL instruction, the intersegment call, permits the subroutine to reside in another code segment. It corresponds to the Far-proc and Memptr32 operands. These operands specify both a new offset address for IP and a new segment address for CS. In both cases, execution of the call instruction causes the contents of the CS and IP registers to be saved on the stack and then new values are loaded into IP and CS. The saved values of CS and IP permit return to the main program from a different code segment.

Far-proc represents a 32-bit immediate operand that is stored in the four bytes that follow the opcode of the call instruction in program memory. These two words are loaded directly from code segment memory into IP and CS with execution of the CALL instruction. An example is the instruction

CALL FAR PROC

On the other hand, when the operand is Memptr32, the pointer for the subroutine is stored as four bytes in data memory. The location of the first byte of the pointer can be specified indirectly by one of the 8086's registers. An example is

CALL FAR [DI]

Here the physical address of the first byte of the four-byte pointer in memory is derived from the contents of DS and DI.

Every subroutine must end by executing an instruction that returns control to the main program. This is the return (RET) instruction. It is described in Fig. 4.10(a) and (b). Notice that its execution causes the value of IP or both the values of IP and CS that were saved on the stack to be returned back to their corresponding registers. In general, an intrasegment return results from an intrasegment call and an intersegment return results from an intersegment call.

There is an additional option with the return instruction. It is that a two-byte code following the return instruction can be included. This code gets added to the stack pointer after restoring the return address into IP or IP and CS for Far-proc calls. The purpose of this stack pointer displacement is to provide a simple means

Mnemonic	Meaning	Format	Operation	Flags Affected
RET	Return	RET or RET Operand	Return to the main program by restoring IP (and CS for fat-proc). If Operand is present, it is added to the contents of SP.	None

(a)

(b)

Figure 4.10   (a) Return instruction; (b) allowed operands.

by which the *parameters* that were saved on the stack before the call to the subroutine was initiated, can be discarded.

PUSH and POP Instructions

After the context switch to a subroutine, we find that it is usually necessary to save the contents of certain registers or some other main program parameters. These values are saved by pushing them onto the stack. Typically, these data correspond to registers and memory locations that are used by the subroutine. In this way, their original contents are kept intact in the stack segment of memory during the execution of the subroutine. Before a return to the main program takes place, the saved registers and main program parameters are restored. This is done by popping the saved values from the stack back into their original locations. Thus a typical structure of a subroutine is that shown in Fig. 4.11.

The instruction that is used to save parameters on the stack is the *push* (PUSH) instruction and that used to retrieve them back is the *pop* (POP) instruction. Notice in Fig. 4.12(a) that the standard PUSH and POP instructions can be written with a general-purpose register, a segment register (excluding CS), or a storage location in memory as their operand.

Execution of a PUSH instruction causes the data corresponding to the operand to be pushed onto the top of the stack. For instance, if the instruction is

PUSH AX

the result is as follows:

$$((SP) - 1) \leftarrow (AH)$$
$$((SP) - 2) \leftarrow (AL)$$
$$(SP) \leftarrow (SP) - 2$$

This shows that the two bytes of AX are saved in the stack part of memory and the

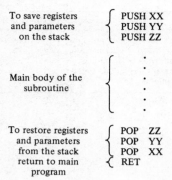

To save registers
and parameters
on the stack

PUSH XX
PUSH YY
PUSH ZZ

Main body of the
subroutine

To restore registers
and parameters
from the stack
return to main
program

POP　ZZ
POP　YY
POP　XX
RET

Figure 4.11　Structure of a subroutine.

Mnemonic	Meaning	Format	Operation	Flags Affected
PUSH	Push word onto stack	PUSH S	$((SP)) \leftarrow (S)$	None
POP	Pop word off stack	POP D	$(D) \leftarrow ((SP))$	None

(a)

Operand (S or D)
Register
Seg-reg (CS illegal)
Memory

(b)

Figure 4.12　(a) PUSH and POP instructions; (b) allowed operands.

stack pointer is decremented by 2 such that it points to the new top of the stack. On the other hand, if the instruction is

$$POP\ AX$$

its execution results in

$$(AL) \longleftarrow ((SP))$$
$$(AH) \longleftarrow ((SP) + 1)$$
$$(SP) \longleftarrow (SP) + 2$$

In this manner, the saved contents of AX are restored back into the register.

At times, we also want to save the contents of the flag register and if saved we will later have to restore them. These operations can be accomplished with the *push flags* (PUSHF) and *pop flags* (POPF) instructions, respectively. These instructions are shown in Fig. 4.13. Notice that PUSHF saves the contents of the flag register on the top of the stack. On the other hand, POPF returns the flags from the top of the stack to the flag register.

Mnemonic	Meaning	Operation	Flags Affected
PUSHF	Push flags onto stack	((SP)) ← (Flags)	None
POPF	Pop flags from stack	(Flags) ← ((SP))	OF, DF, IF, TF, SF, ZF, AF, PF, CF

Figure 4.13 PUSHF and POPF instructions.

Example 4.5

Write a program to generate the first 20 elements of a Fibonacci series. In this series, the first and second elements are 0 and 1, respectively. Each element that follows is obtained by adding the previous two elements. Use a subroutine to generate the next element from the previous two elements. Store the elements of the series starting at address FIBSER.

Solution.   Our plan for the solution of this problem is shown in Fig. 4.14(a). This flowchart shows the use of a subroutine to generate an element of the series, store it in memory, and prepare for generation of the next element.

The first step in the solution is initialization. It involves setting up a data segment, generating the first two numbers of the series, and storing them at memory locations with offset addresses FIBSER and FIBSER + 1. Then a pointer must be established to address the locations for other terms of the series. This address will be held in the DI register. Finally, a counter with initial value equal to 18 can be set up in CX to keep track of how many numbers remain to be generated. The instructions needed for initialization are:

$$\text{MOV} \quad \text{AX,DATASEGSTART}$$

$$\text{MOV} \quad \text{DS,AX}$$

$$\text{MOV} \quad \text{NUM1,0H}$$

$$\text{MOV} \quad \text{NUM2,01H}$$

$$\text{MOV} \quad \text{FIBSER,0H}$$

$$\text{MOV} \quad \text{FIBSER + 1,01H}$$

$$\text{LEA} \quad \text{DI,FIBSER + 2}$$

$$\text{MOV} \quad \text{CX,012H}$$

Notice that the data segment address which is defined by variable DATASEGSTART is first moved into AX and then DS is loaded from AX with another MOV operation. Next the memory locations assigned to NUM_1 and NUM_2 are loaded with immediate data 0000_{16} and 0001_{16}, respectively. These same values are then copied into the storage locations for the first two series elements, FIBSER and FIBSER + 1. Now DI is loaded with the address of FIBSER + 2, which is a pointer to the storage location of the third element of the series. Finally, CX is loaded with 12_{16}, which is the hexadecimal equivalent of 18_{10}.

To generate the next term in the series we call a subroutine. This subroutine generates and stores the elements. Before returning to the main program, it also updates memory locations NUM_1 and NUM_2 with the values of the immediate past two elements. After this, the counter in CX is decremented to record that a series element

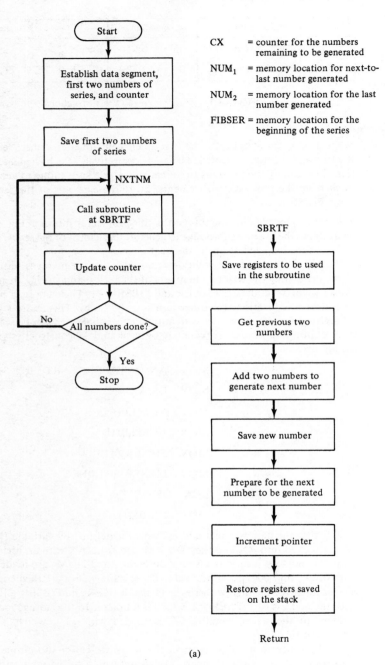

(a)

Figure 4.14   (a) Flowchart for generation of a Fibonacci series; (b) program.

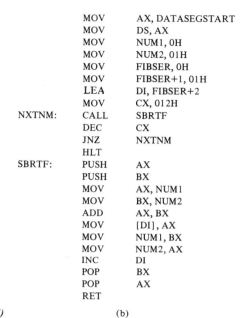

	MOV	AX, DATASEGSTART
	MOV	DS, AX
	MOV	NUM1, 0H
	MOV	NUM2, 01H
	MOV	FIBSER, 0H
	MOV	FIBSER+1, 01H
	LEA	DI, FIBSER+2
	MOV	CX, 012H
NXTNM:	CALL	SBRTF
	DEC	CX
	JNZ	NXTNM
	HLT	
SBRTF:	PUSH	AX
	PUSH	BX
	MOV	AX, NUM1
	MOV	BX, NUM2
	ADD	AX, BX
	MOV	[DI], AX
	MOV	NUM1, BX
	MOV	NUM2, AX
	INC	DI
	POP	BX
	POP	AX
	RET	

Figure 4.14   *(continued)*   (b)

has been generated and stored. This process must be repeated until the counter becomes equal to zero. This leads to the following assembly language code:

```
NXTNM:   CALL   SBRTF

         DEC    CX

         JNZ    NXTNM

         HLT
```

The call is to the subroutine labeled SBRTF. After the subroutine runs to completion, program control returns to the DEC CX statement. This statement causes the count in CX to be decremented by 1. Next, a conditional jump instruction tests the zero flag to determine if the result after decrementing CX is zero. If CX is not zero, control is returned to the CALL instruction at NXTNM. If it is zero, the program is complete and execution halts.

The subroutine itself is given next.

```
SBRTF:   PUSH   AX

         PUSH   BX

         MOV    AX,NUM1

         MOV    BX,NUM2

         ADD    AX,BX

         MOV    [DI],AX

         MOV    NUM1,BX
```

MOV   NUM2,AX

INC   DI

POP   BX

POP   AX

RET

First we save the contents of AX and BX on the stack. Then NUM_1 and NUM_2 are copied into AX and BX, respectively. They are then added together to form the next element. The resulting sum is produced in AX. Now the new element is stored in memory indirectly through DI. Remember that DI holds a pointer to the storage location of the next element of the series in memory. Then the second element, which is held in BX, becomes the new first element by copying it into NUM_1. The sum, which is in AX, becomes the new second term by copying it into NUM_2. Finally, DI is incremented by 1 such that it points to the next element of the series. The registers saved on the stack are restored and we then return back to the main program.

Notice that both the subroutine call and its return have Near-proc operands. The entire program is presented in Fig. 4.14(b).

4.6 LOOP INSTRUCTIONS

The 8086 microprocessor has three instructions specifically designed for implementing *loop operations*. These instructions can be used in place of certain conditional jump instructions and give the programmer a simpler way of writing loop sequences. The loop instructions are listed in Fig. 4.15.

The first instruction, *loop* (LOOP), works with respect to the contents of the CX register. CX must be preloaded with a count representing the number of times the loop is to be repeated. Whenever LOOP is executed, the contents of CX are first

Mnemonic	Meaning	Format	Operation
LOOP	Loop	LOOP Short-label	$(CX) \leftarrow (CX) - 1$ Jump is initiated to location defined by short-label if $(CX) \neq 0$; otherwise, execute next sequential instruction
LOOPE/LOOPZ	Loop while equal/ loop while zero	LOOPE/LOOPZ Short-label	$(CX) \leftarrow (CX) - 1$ Jump to location defined by short-label if $(CX) \neq 0$ and $(ZF) \neq 0$; otherwise, execute next sequential instruction
LOOPNE/ LOOPNZ	Loop while not equal/ loop while not zero	LOOPNE/LOOPNZ Short-label	$(CX) \leftarrow (CX) - 1$ Jump to location defined by short-label if $(CX) \neq 0$ and $(ZF) = 0$; otherwise, execute next sequential instruction

Figure 4.15 Loop instructions.

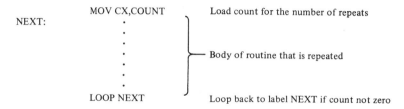

Figure 4.16   Typical loop routine structure.

decremented by 1 and then checked to determine if they are equal to zero. If equal to zero, the loop is complete and the instruction following LOOP is executed; otherwise, control is returned to the instruction at the label specified in the loop instruction. In this way, we see that LOOP is a single instruction that functions the same as a decrement CX instruction followed by a JNZ instruction.

For example, the LOOP instruction sequence shown in Fig. 4.16 will cause the part of the program from the label NEXT through the instruction LOOP to be repeated a number of times equal to the value of count stored in CX. For example, if CX contains $000A_{16}$, the sequence of instructions included in the loop is executed 10 times.

The other two instructions in Fig. 4.15 operate in a similar way except that they check for two conditions. For instance, the instruction *loop while equal* (LOOPE)/*loop while zero* (LOOPZ) checks the contents of both CX and the ZF flag. Each time the loop instruction is executed, CX decrements by 1 without affecting the flags, its contents are checked for zero, and the state of ZF that results from execution of the previous instruction is tested for 1. If CX equals 0 and ZF equals 1, a jump is initiated to the location specified with the Short-label operand and the loop continues. If either CX is not 0 or ZF is not 1, the loop is complete and the instruction following the loop instruction is executed.

Instruction *loop while not equal* (LOOPNE)/*loop while not zero* (LOOPNZ) works in a similar way to the LOOPE/LOOPZ instruction. The difference is that it checks ZF and CX looking for ZF equal to 0 together with CX not equal to 0. If these conditions are met, the jump back to the location specified with the Short-label operand is performed and the loop continues.

4.7 STRING INSTRUCTIONS

The 8086 microprocessor is equipped with special instructions to handle *string operations*. By "string" we mean a series of data words or bytes that reside in consecutive memory locations. The string instructions of the 8086 permit a programmer to implement operations such as to move data from one block of memory to a block elsewhere in memory. A second type of operation that is easily performed is to scan a string of data elements stored in memory looking for a specific value. Other examples are to compare the elements of two strings together in order to determine whether they are the same or different, and to initialize a set of consecutive memory loca-

Mnemonic	Meaning	Format	Operation	Flags Affected
MOVS	Move string	MOVS Operand	$((ES)0 + (DI)) \leftarrow ((DS)0 + (SI))$ $(SI) \leftarrow (SI) \pm 1$ or 2 $(DI) \leftarrow (DI) \pm 1$ or 2	None
MOVSB	Move string byte	MOVSB	$((ES)0 + (DI)) \leftarrow ((DS)0 + (SI))$ $(SI) \leftarrow (SI) \pm 1$ $(DI) \leftarrow (DI) \pm 1$	None
MOVSW	Move string word	MOVSW	$((ES)0 + (DI)) \leftarrow ((DS)0 + (SI))$ $((ES)0 + (DI) + 1) \leftarrow ((DS)0 + (SI) + 1)$ $(SI) \leftarrow (SI) \pm 2$ $(DI) \leftarrow (DI) \pm 2$	None
CMPS	Compare string	CMPS Operand	Set flags as per $((DS)0 + (SI)) - ((ES)0 + (DI))$ $(SI) \leftarrow (SI) \pm 1$ or 2 $(DI) \leftarrow (DI) \pm 1$ or 2	CF, PF, AF, ZF, SF, OF
SCAS	Scan string	SCAS Operand	Set flags as per $(AL$ or $AX) - ((ES)0 + (DI))$ $(DI) \leftarrow (DI) \pm 1$ or 2	CF, PF, AF, ZF, SF, OF
LODS	Load string	LODS Operand	$(AL$ or $AX) \leftarrow ((DS)0 + (SI))$ $(SI) \leftarrow (SI) \pm 1$ or 2	None
STOS	Store string	STOS Operand	$((ES)0 + (DI)) \leftarrow (AL$ or $AX) \pm 1$ or 2 $(DI) \leftarrow (DI) \pm 1$ or 2	None

Figure 4.17 Basic string instructions.

tions. Complex operations such as these typically require several nonstring instructions to be implemented.

There are five basic string instructions in the instruction set of the 8086. These instructions, as listed in Fig. 4.17, are *move byte* or *word string* (MOVS, MOVSB/MOVSW), *compare strings* (CMPS), *scan string* (SCAS), *load string* (LODS), and *store string* (STOS). They are called the *basic string instructions* because each defines an operation for one element of a string. Thus these operations must be repeated to handle a string of more than one element. Let us first look at the basic operations performed by these instructions.

Move String—MOVS, MOVSB/MOVSW

The instructions MOVS, MOVSB, and MOVSW all perform the same basic operation. An element of the string specified by the source index (SI) register with respect to the current data segment (DS) register is moved to the location specified by the destination index (DI) register with respect to the current extra segment (ES) register. The move can be performed on a byte or a word of data. After the move is complete, the contents of both SI and DI are automatically incremented or decremented by 1 for a byte move and by 2 for a word move. Remember the fact that the address pointers in SI and DI increment or decrement depends on how the direction flag DF is set. The instruction MOVS requires that an operand be specified, whereas MOVSB and MOVSW have no operands. This operand is simply either WORD or BYTE. For example, one way of writing a MOVS instruction is

MOVS BYTE

This instruction could also be written simply as

MOVSB

Compare Strings and Scan Strings—CMPS and SCAS

The CMPS instruction can be used to compare two elements in the same or different strings. It subtracts the destination operand from the source operand and adjusts flags CF, PF, AF, ZF, SF, and OF accordingly. The result of subtraction is not saved; therefore, the operation does not affect the operands in any way.

An example of a compare strings instruction for bytes of data is

CMPS BYTE

Again, the source element is pointed to by the address in SI with respect to the current value in DS and the destination element is specified by the contents of DI relative to the contents of ES. Moreover, both SI and DI are updated such that they point to the next elements in their respective strings.

The scan string (SCAS) instruction is similar to CMPS; however, it compares the byte or word element of the destination string at the physical address derived from DI and ES to the contents of AL or AX, respectively. The flags are adjusted based on this result and DI incremented or decremented.

Load and Store Strings—LODS and STOS

The last two instructions in Fig. 4.17, load string (LODS) and store string (STOS), are specifically provided to move string elements between the accumulator and memory. LODS loads either a byte or a word from a string in memory into AL or AX, respectively. The address in SI is used relative to DS to determine the address of the memory location of the string element. For instance, the instruction

LODS WORD

indicates that the word string element at the physical address derived from DS and SI is to be loaded into AX. Then the index in SI is automatically incremented by 2.

On the other hand, STOS stores a byte from AL or a word from AX into a string location in memory. This time the contents of ES and DI are used to form the address of the storage location in memory.

Repeat String—REP

In most applications, the basic string operations must be repeated in order to process arrays of data. This is done by inserting a repeat prefix before the instruction that is to be repeated. The *repeat prefixes* of the 8086 are shown in Fig. 4.18.

Prefix	Used with:	Meaning
REP	MOVS STOS	Repeat while not end of string CX ≠ 0
REPE/REPZ	CMPS SCAS	Repeat while not end of string and strings are equal CX ≠ 0 and ZF = 1
REPNE/REPNZ	CMPS SCAS	Repeat while not end of string and strings are not equal CX ≠ 0 and ZF = 0

Figure 4.18 Prefixes for use with the basic string instructions.

The first prefix, REP, causes the basic string operation to be repeated until the contents of register CX become equal to zero. Each time the instruction is executed, it causes CX to be tested for zero. If CX is found to be nonzero, it is decremented by 1 and the basic string operation is repeated. On the other hand, if it is 0, the repeat string operation is done and the next instruction in the program is executed. The repeat count must be loaded into CX prior to executing the repeat string instruction.

For instance, let us consider the following sequence of instructions:

MOV	AX,DATA_SEGMENT
MOV	DS,AX
MOV	AX,EXTRA_SEGMENT
MOV	ES,AX
MOV	CX,020H
MOV	SI,MASTER
MOV	DI,COPY
REPMOVSB	

The first two instructions initialize DS with the value DATA_SEGMENT. It is followed by two instructions that load ES with the value EXTRA_SEGMENT. Then the number of repeats, 020_{16}, is loaded into CX. The next two instructions load SI and DI with beginning offset addresses MASTER and COPY for the source and destination strings. Now we are ready to perform the string operation. Execution of REPMOVSB moves a block of 32 consecutive bytes from the block of memory locations starting at offset address MASTER with respect to the current data segment (DS) to a block of locations starting at offset address COPY with respect to the current extra segment (ES).

The prefixes REPE and REPZ stand for the same function. They are meant for use with the CMPS and SCAS instructions. With REPE/REPZ, the basic compare or scan operation can be repeated as long as both the contents of CX are not equal to zero and the zero flag is 1. The first condition CX not equal to zero indicates that the end of the string has not yet been reached and the second condition ZF = 1 indicates that the elements that were compared are equal.

The last prefix, REPNE/REPNZ, works similarly to REPE/REPZ except that now the operation is repeated as long as CX is not equal to zero and ZF is zero. That is, the comparison or scanning is to be performed as long as the string elements are unequal and the end of the string is not yet found.

Autoindexing for String Instructions

Earlier we pointed out that during the execution of a string instruction the address indices in SI and DI are either automatically incremented or decremented. Moreover, we indicated that the decision to increment or decrement is made based on the setting of the direction flag DF. The 8086 provides two instructions, clear direction flag (CLD) and set direction flag (STD), to permit selection between *autoincrement* and *autodecrement mode* of operation. These instructions are shown in Fig. 4.19. When CLD is executed, DF is set to 0. This selects autoincrement mode and each time a string operation is performed SI and/or DI are incremented by 1 if byte data are processed and by 2 if word data are processed.

Mnemonic	Meaning	Format	Operation	Flags Affected
CLD	Clear DF	CLD	(DF) ← 0	DF
STD	Set DF	STD	(DF) ← 1	DF

Figure 4.19 Instructions for autoincrementing and autodecrementing in string instructions.

Example 4.6

Given a string of 100 EBCDIC characters stored starting at offset address EBCDIC__CHAR, convert them to their equivalent string of ASCII characters and store them at offset address ASCII__CHAR. The translation may be done using an EBCDIC-to-ASCII conversion table that starts at offset memory address EBCDIC _ TO _ ASCII.

Solution.   The problem to be programmed is illustrated in Fig. 4.20(a). Here we have assumed that the various data elements—the 100 given EBCDIC characters, the conversion table for EBCDIC to ASCII, and the generated ASCII characters—all reside in the same data segment. This data segment starts at the address DATA _ SEGMENT. With respect to this data segment, the offset addresses EBCDIC _ CHAR, ASCII _ CHAR, and EBCDIC _TO _ ASCII are as shown in the diagram. Moreover, we are assuming that the string of 100 EBCDIC characters and the EBCDIC _ TO _ ASCII table already exist at the correct locations in memory.

Our solution to the problem is flowcharted in Fig. 4.20(b). We will use the string, translate, and loop instructions to implement the solution. Moreover, we will also use autoincrement mode for the string operations.

The initialization involves setting up the data segment (DS) register to address the area in memory that stores the 100 given EBCDIC characters and conversion table. The same memory area will be used to store the converted ASCII characters; therefore, we will make the extra segment, which is needed by the string instructions, overlap the data segment by loading both DS and ES with the same address. This is the value assigned to variable DATA _SEGMENT. Then SI and DI must be loaded with addresses that point to the first characters in the EBCDIC string and the ASCII string, respectively.

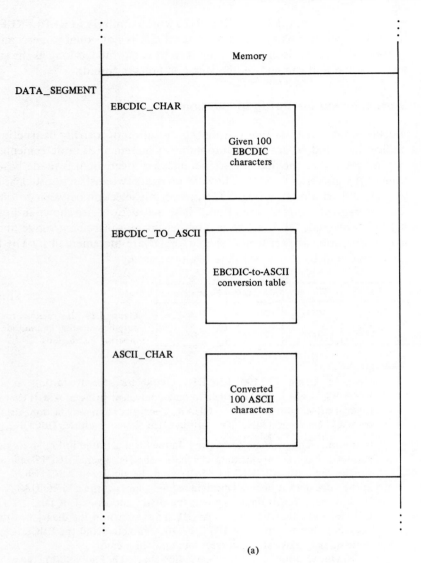

(a)

Figure 4.20   (a) EBCDIC-to-ASCII conversion; (b) flowchart; (c) program.

These addresses are equal to EBCDIC _ CHAR and ASCII _CHAR, respectively. The code translation is made using a conversion table and the XLAT instruction. XLAT requires that BX hold a pointer to the beginning of the conversion table. Therefore, BX must be loaded with the address corresponding to EBCDIC_ TO _ ASCII. To keep track of the number of characters that are converted, CX will be loaded with 100_{10} equal to 64_{16}. Finally, the autoincrement feature is invoked by resetting the direction flag DF.

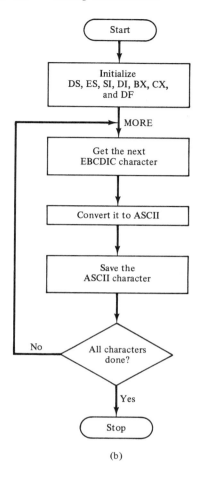

(b)

```
            MOV        AX, DATA_SEGMENT
            MOV        DS, AX
            MOV        ES, AX
            MOV        SI, EBCDIC_CHAR
            MOV        DI, ASCII_CHAR
            MOV        BX, EBCDIC_TO_ASCII
            MOV        CX, 064H
            CLD
MORE:       LODS       BYTE
            XLAT
            STOS       BYTE
            LOOP       MORE
            HLT
```

(c)   **Figure 4.20**   *(continued)*

This leads to the following initialization code:

MOV	AX,DATA _ SEGMENT
MOV	DS,AX
MOV	ES,AX
MOV	SI,EBCDIC_ CHAR
MOV	DI,ASCII_ CHAR
MOV	BX,EBCDIC_ TO_ ASCII
MOV	CX,064H
CLD	

Next, an EBCDIC character can be loaded, translated to its corresponding ASCII character, and stored in the memory area reserved for storage of ASCII characters. This gives us the instructions

MORE:	LODS	BYTE
	XLAT	
	STOS	BYTE

Execution of the LODS instruction loads the first element of the EBCDIC string into AL. Notice that use of autoincrementing prepares SI to handle the next conversion. Next, the XLAT instruction uses the EBCDIC character code in AL as an offset to address the equivalent ASCII character in the table at EBCDIC _ TO _ ASCII. This ASCII character is transferred to AL. The translation is now complete; however, the resulting character must be stored in the table defined by the address ASCII _ CHAR. This is done with the STOS instruction. During the execution of this instruction, DI is automatically incremented so that it points to the next storage location in the ASCII string.

To repeat the process starting from label MORE, we can use a loop instruction that will decrement CX and jump to MORE as long as the contents of CX are not zero. This assures that translation is repeated for each of the 100 characters in the EBCDIC string. To do this, the instruction is

LOOP	MORE

To end the program, the halt (HLT) instruction can be executed. The entire program is repeated in Fig. 4.20(c).

ASSIGNMENT

Section 4.2

1. Write an instruction sequence to configure the 8086 as follows: interrupts not accepted; save the original contents of flags SF, ZF, AF, PF, and CF at the address $A000_{16}$; and then clear CF.

Section 4.3

2. Describe the difference in operation and effect on status flags due to execution of the subtract words and compare words instructions.

3. What happens to the ZF and CF status flags as the following sequence of instructions is executed? Assume that they are both initially cleared.

$$\begin{array}{ll} \text{MOV} & \text{BX,01111H} \\ \text{MOV} & \text{AX,0BBBBH} \\ \text{CMP} & \text{AX,BX} \end{array}$$

Section 4.4

4. The program that follows implements what is known as a *delay loop*.

$$\begin{array}{lll} & \text{MOV} & \text{CX,01000H} \\ \text{DLY:} & \text{DEC} & \text{CX} \\ & \text{JNZ} & \text{DLY} \\ \text{NXT:} & \text{---} & \text{---} \end{array}$$

   (a) How many times does the JNZ DLY instruction get executed?
   (b) Change the program so that JNZ DLY is executed just 17 times.
   (c) Change the program so that JNZ DLY is executed 2^{32} times.

5. Given a number N in the range $0 < N \le 5$, write a program that computes its factorial and saves the result in memory location FACT.

6. Write a program that compares the elements of two arrays, A(I) and B(I). Each array contains 100 16-bit signed numbers. The comparison is to be done by comparing the corresponding elements of the two arrays until either two elements are found to be unequal or all elements of the arrays have been compared and found to be equal. Assume that the arrays start at addresses $A000_{16}$ and $B000_{16}$, respectively. If the two arrays are found to be unequal, save the address of the first unequal element of A(I) in memory location FOUND; otherwise, write all 0s into this location.

7. Given an array A(I) of 100 16-bit signed numbers that are stored in memory starting at address $A000_{16}$, write a program to generate two arrays from the given array such that one P(J) consists of all the positive numbers and the other N(K) contains all of the negative numbers. Store the array of positive numbers in memory starting at address $B000_{16}$ and the array of negative numbers starting at address $C000_{16}$.

8. Given a 16-bit binary number in DX, write a program that converts it to its equivalent BCD number in DX. If the result is bigger than 16 bits, place all 1s in DX.

9. Given an array A(I) with 100 16-bit signed integer numbers, write a program to generate a new array B(I) as follows:

$$B(I) = A(I) \quad \text{for I} = 1, 2, 99, \text{ and } 100$$

and

$$B(I) = \text{median value of A}(I-2), \text{ A}(I-1), \text{ A}(I),$$
$$\text{A}(I+1), \text{ and A}(I+2) \quad \text{for all other Is}$$

Section 4.5

10. Write a subroutine that converts a given 16-bit BCD number to its equivalent binary number. The BCD number is to be passed to a subroutine through register DX and the routine returns the equivalent binary number in DX.

11. Given an array A(I) of 100 16-bit signed integer numbers, write a subroutine to generate a new array B(I) such that

$$B(I) = A(I) \qquad \text{for } I = 1 \text{ and } 100$$

and

$$B(I) = \frac{1}{4}(A(I - 1) - 5A(I) + 9A(I + 1)) \qquad \text{for all other Is}$$

The values of A(I − 1), A(I), and A(I + 1) are to be passed to the subroutine in registers AX, BX, and CX and the subroutine returns the result B(I) in register AX.

12. Write a segment of main program and show its subroutine structure to perform the following operations. The program is to check continuously the three most significant bits in register DX and depending on their setting executes one of three subroutines: SUBA, SUBB, or SUBC. The subroutines are selected as follows:
    (a) If bit 15 of DX is set, initiate SUBA.
    (b) If bit 14 of DX is set and bit 15 is not set, initiate SUBB.
    (c) If bit 13 of DX is set and bits 14 and 15 are not set, initiate SUBC.
    If the subroutine is executed, the corresponding bits of DX are to be cleared and then control returned to the main program. After returning from the subroutine, the main program is repeated.

Section 4.6

13. Using loop instructions, implement the program in problem 5.
14. Using loop instructions, implement the program in problem 6.

Section 4.7

15. Use string instructions to implement the program in problem 6.
16. Write a program to convert a table of 100 ASCII characters stored starting at offset address ASCII _CHAR into their equivalent table of EBCDIC characters and store them at offset address EBCDIC_ CHAR. The translation is to be done using an ASCII-to-EBCDIC conversion table starting at offset address ASCII_ TO_ EBCDIC. Assume that all three tables are located in different segments of memory.

5

Memory Interface of the 8086 Microprocessor

5.1 INTRODUCTION

Up to this point in the book, we have introduced the 8086 microprocessor, its signal leads, and internal architecture. Moreover, from a software point of view, we have covered its instruction set and how to write programs in assembly language. Now we will begin to examine the hardware interfaces of the 8086. This chapter is devoted to its memory interface and external memory subsystems. For this purpose, we have included the following topics in the chapter:

1. Memory interface block diagram
2. Address space and data organization
3. Dedicated and general use of memory
4. Generating a physical memory address
5. Hardware organization of the memory address space
6. Memory bus status codes and memory control signals
7. Read and write bus cycles
8. The stack and stack pointer
9. Demultiplexing the address/data bus
10. 4K-word program storage memory
11. 1K-word static RAM data storage memory
12. 128K-byte dynamic RAM subsystem

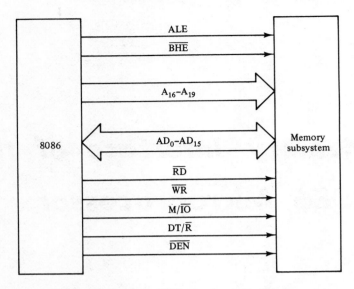

Figure 5.1 Minimum 8086 system memory interface.

5.2 MEMORY INTERFACE BLOCK DIAGRAM

In either the minimum- or maximum-mode-system configuration, the 8086 micro-processor can address up to 1M bytes of memory. However, the interface to the memory subsystem is different for each of these two modes of operation. The circuit diagram in Fig. 5.1 is that of the minimum-system memory interface. Here we find that it consists of the *multiplexed address/data bus lines* AD_0 through AD_{15} together with *additional address lines* A_{16} through A_{19} and *bank high enable* ($\overline{BHE}$). Notice that *memory control signals* ALE, $\overline{RD}$, $\overline{WE}$, $M/\overline{IO}$, $DT/\overline{R}$, and $\overline{DEN}$ are produced by the 8086.

The maximum-mode memory interface is shown in Fig. 5.2. This circuit configuration includes an 8288 bus controller device. Notice that bus *status signals* $\overline{S}_0$ through $\overline{S}_2$ are input to this device. It decodes this 3-bit code to identify the type of bus cycle that is to be initiated. In turn, it generates *read/write signals* $\overline{MRDC}$, $\overline{MWTC}$, and $\overline{AMWC}$ as well as *control signals* ALE, $DT/\overline{R}$, and $\overline{DEN}$. In this way we see that in the maximum-mode system the bus controller instead of the 8086 generates most of the timing and control signals for the memory interface.

Address Space and Data Organization

Looking at Figs. 5.1 and 5.2, we find that the 8086 has a 20-bit address bus. This bus consists of address lines AD_0 through AD_{15} and A_{16} through A_{19}. Of these, AD_0 is the LSB of the address and A_{19} the MSB. With this 20-bit *physical address*, it can directly address up to 1,048,576 bytes (1M byte) of memory. As shown in the memory

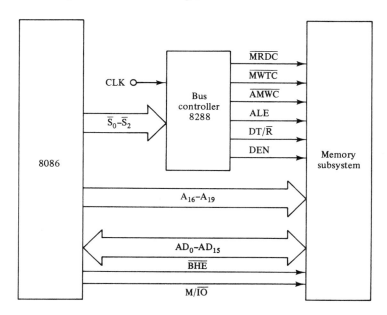

Figure 5.2 Maximum 8086 system memory interface.

map of Fig. 5.3, these byte storage locations are assigned to consecutive addresses over the range from 00000_{16} to $FFFFF_{16}$.

In this way we see that the memory subsystem in an 8086 microcomputer system is actually organized as 8-bit bytes, not as 16-bit words. However, any two consecutive bytes can be accessed as a word. The lower-addressed byte is the least significant byte of the word and the higher-addressed byte is its most significant byte.

Figure 5.4(a) demonstrates the storage of a word. Notice that the storage location at the lower address, 00724_{16}, contains the value $00000010_2 = 02_{16}$. Moreover, the contents of the next-higher-addressed storage location 00725_{16} are $01010101_2 = 55_{16}$. These two bytes represent the word $0101010100000010_2 = 5502_{16}$.

To permit efficient use of memory, words of data can be stored at even- or odd-address boundaries. The LSB A_0 of the address determines the type of *word*

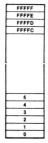

Figure 5.3 Address space of the 8086.

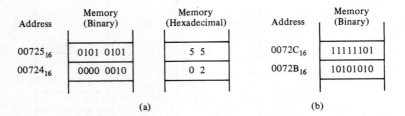

Figure 5.4 (a) Storage of a word at an even-address boundary (Intel Corporation); (b) word storage example (Intel Corporation).

boundary. If this bit is 0, the word is said to be held at an *even-address boundary.* That is, a word at an even-address boundary corresponds to two consecutive bytes with the least significant byte located at an even address.

For example, the word in Fig. 5.4(a) has its least significant byte at address 00724_{16}. Therefore, it is stored at an even-address boundary.

Example 5.1

What is the data word shown in Fig. 5.4(b)? Express the result in hexadecimal form. Is it stored at an even- or an odd-address boundary?

Solution: The most significant byte of the word is stored at address $0072C_{16}$ and equals

$$11111101_2 = FD_{16}$$

Its least significant byte is stored at address $0072B_{16}$ and is

$$10101010_2 = AA_{16}$$

Together these two bytes give the word

$$1111110110101010_2 = FDAA_{16}$$

Expressing the address of the least significant byte in binary form gives

$$0072B_{16} = 00000000011100101011_2$$

Since bit A_0 is logic 1, the word is stored at an odd-address boundary in memory.

All data bytes and words at even-address boundaries can be accessed by the 8086 in one bus cycle. With the 5-MHz 8086, this takes 800 ns. On the other hand, accesses of words at odd-address boundaries require two bus cycles instead of one. This takes 1.6 μs when the 8086 is operating at a 5-MHz clock rate.

Data can be accessed either as bytes or words and can be stored at even- or odd-address boundaries. However, instructions are always accessed as words. For this reason they should always be stored at even-address boundaries. This minimizes the number of bus cycles needed to fetch them for execution, thereby maximizing performance.

The *double word* is another data form that can be processed in an 8086 system. A double word corresponds to two consecutive words of data stored in memory. An example of double-word data is a pointer that is used to address data or code outside the current segment. The word of the pointer that is stored at the higher address is

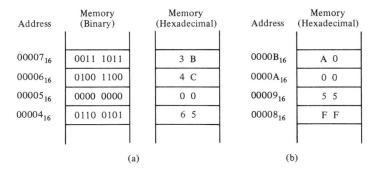

Figure 5.5 (a) Storage of a double-word pointer (Intel Corporation); (b) another double-word pointer (Intel Corporation).

the segment base address and the word at the lower address is the offset value.

An example showing storage of a pointer in memory is given in Fig. 5.5(a). Here we find that the higher-addressed word, which represents the segment address, is stored starting at even-address boundary 00006_{16}. The most significant byte of this word is at address 00007_{16} and equals $00111011_2 = 3B_{16}$. Its least significant byte is at address 00006_{16} and equals $01001100_2 = 4C_{16}$. Combining these two values, we get the segment base address, which equals $0011101101001100_2 = 3B4C_{16}$.

The offset part of the pointer is the lower-addressed word. Its least significant byte is stored at address 00004_{16}. This location contains $01100101_2 = 65_{16}$. The most significant byte is at address 00005_{16}, which contains $00000000_2 = 00_{16}$. The resulting offset is $0000000001100101_2 = 0065_{16}$.

Example 5.2

How should the pointer with segment base address equal to $A000_{16}$ and offset address $55FF_{16}$ be stored at an even-address boundary starting at 00008_{16}?

Solution. Storage of the two-word pointer requires four consecutive byte locations in memory starting at address 00008_{16}. The least significant byte of the offset is stored at address 00008_{16}. This value is shown as $11111111_2 = FF_{16}$ in Fig. 5.5(b). The most significant byte of the offset, which is 55_{16}, is stored at address 00009_{16}. These two bytes are followed by the least significant byte of the segment base address, 00_{16}, at address $0000A_{16}$ and its most significant byte, $A0_{16}$, at address $0000B_{16}$.

The 1M-byte address space of the 8086 is actually organized into *64K-byte segments*. These segments represent independently addressable units of memory consisting of 64K consecutive byte storage locations. Each segment is assigned a base address that identifies its lowest-addressed byte storage location.

Only four of these 64K-byte segments are active at a time. The segments that are active, as shown in Fig. 5.6(a), are identified by the values held in the four internal address segment registers: CS (code segment), SS (stack segment), DS (data segment), and ES (extra segment). This gives a logical address space of 256K bytes of active memory. Of this, 64K bytes are allocated for code (program) storage, 64K bytes for a stack, and 128K bytes for data storage.

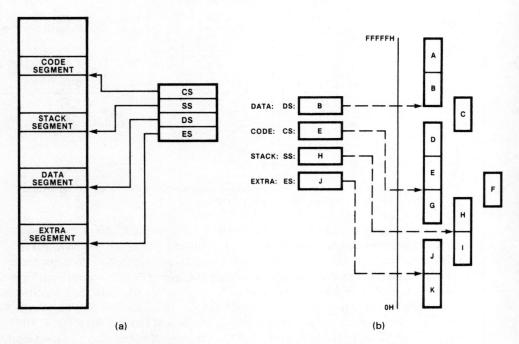

Figure 5.6   (a) Active nonoverlapping memory segments (Intel Corporation); (b) active overlapping memory segments (Intel Corporation).

Figure 5.6(b) illustrates the segmentation of system memory. In this diagram we have identified 64K-byte segments with letters such as A, B, and C. The data segment (DS) register presently contains the value B. Therefore, the 64K-byte segment of memory labeled B acts as the data storage segment. Segment E is selected for the current code segment. It is this part of memory from which the 8086 fetches instructions of the program. The stack segment (SS) register contains H, thereby selecting the 64K-byte segment labeled as H for use as a stack. Finally, the extra segment register ES is loaded with J such that segment J of memory can function as a second data storage segment.

The values in the internal segment registers can be modified through software. Therefore, for a program to gain access to another part of memory it just has to change the value of the appropriate register or registers. For instance, a new 128K-byte data space can be brought in by simply changing the values in DS and ES. This can be done with the load data segment (LDS) instruction and load extra segment (LES) instruction, respectively.

There is one restriction on the value that can be assigned to a segment as a base address: this is that it must reside on a 16-byte address boundary. Valid examples are 00000_{16}, 00010_{16}, and 00020_{16}. Other than this restriction, segments can be *contiguous, adjacent, disjointed*, or even *overlapping*. For example, in Fig. 5.6(b), segments A and B are contiguous, whereas segments B and C are overlapping.

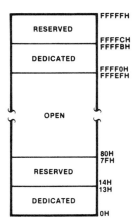

Figure 5.7 Dedicated and general use memory (Intel Corporation).

Dedicated Memory Locations

Any part of the 1M-byte address space of the 8086 can be implemented with either ROM or RAM. However, some address locations have dedicated functions. These locations should not be used as general memory space for data or program storage.

Figure 5.7 shows the *reserved* and *general use (open) parts* of the 8086's *address space*. Notice that storage locations from address 00000_{16} to $0007F_{16}$ are dedicated. These 128 bytes of memory are reserved for storage of pointers to interrupt service routines. As indicated earlier, each pointer requires four bytes of memory. Two bytes hold the 16-bit segment address and the other two hold the 16-bit offset.

At the high end of the memory address space is another pointer area. It is located from address $FFFFC_{16}$ through $FFFFF_{16}$. These four memory locations are reserved for storage of the pointer to the hardware reset function. Moreover, Intel Corporation has identified the 12 storage locations from address $FFFF0_{16}$ through $FFFFB_{16}$ as dedicated for use with future products.

Generating a Memory Address

The *logical addresses* that occur in the program of the 8086 are always 16 bits in length. This is because all registers and memory locations are 16 bits in length. However, the physical address that is placed on the address bus during a memory cycle is 20 bits. The generation of the physical address involves combining a 16-bit offset value that is located in either an index register or pointer register and a 16-bit base value that is located in a segment register. Together the base value and offset represent the logical address.

The source of the offset address depends on which type of memory reference is taking place. It can be the base pointer (BP) register, base (BX) register, source index (SI) register, destination index (DI) register, or instruction pointer (IP). On the other hand, the base value always resides in one of the segment registers: CS, DS, SS, or ES.

For instance, when an instruction acquisition takes place, the source of the base address is always the code segment (CS) register and the source of the offset is always the instruction pointer (IP).

Moreover, if the value of a variable is being written to memory during the execution of an instruction, typically, the base segment address will be in the data segment (DS) register and the offset will be in the destination index (DI) register. Segment override prefixes can be used to change the segment from which the variable is accessed.

Another example is the stack address that is needed when pushing words onto the stack. This address is formed from the contents of the stack segment (SS) register and stack pointer (SP).

Remember that the base segment address represents the starting location of the 64K-byte segment in memory: that is, the lowest-addressed byte in the segment. The offset identifies the distance in bytes that the storage location of interest resides from this starting address. Therefore, the lowest-addressed byte in a segment has an offset of 0000_{16} and the highest-addressed byte has an offset of $FFFF_{16}$.

Figure 5.8 shows how a segment address and offset value are combined to give a physical address. What happens is that the value in the segment register is shifted left by 4 bits with its LSBs being filled with 0s. Then the offset value is added to the 16 LSBs of the shifted segment address. The result of this addition is the 20-bit physical address.

The example in Fig. 5.8 represents a base segment address of 1234_{16} and an offset address of 0022_{16}. First let us express the base address in binary form. This gives

$$1234_{16} = 0001001000110100_2$$

Shifting left four times and filling with zeros results in

$$00010010001101000000_2 = 12340_{16}$$

The offset in binary form is

$$0022_{16} = 0000000000100010_2$$

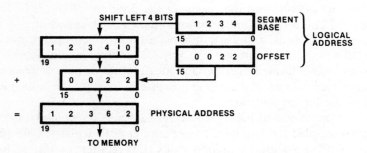

Figure 5.8 Generating a physical address (Intel Corporation).

Adding the shifted address and offset, we get

$$0001001000110100000_2 + 0000000000100010_2 = 0001001000110110000_2$$
$$= 12362_{16}$$

The bus interface unit does this address calculation each time a memory access is initiated.

Example 5.3

What would be the offset required to map to address location $002C3_{16}$ if the segment base address is $002A_{16}$?

Solution.   The offset value can be obtained by shifting the segment base address left 4 bits and then subtracting it from the physical address. Shifting left gives

$$002A0_{16}$$

Now subtracting, we get the value of the offset:

$$002C3_{16} - 002A0_{16} = 0023_{16}$$

Actually, many different logical addresses can be mapped to the same physical address location in memory. This is done by simply changing the values of the base address in the segment register and its corresponding offset. The diagram in Fig. 5.9

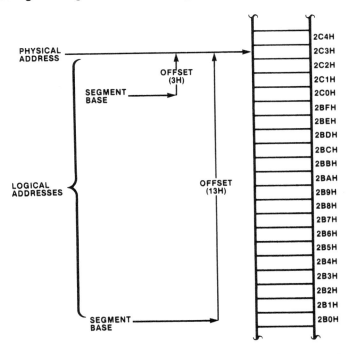

Figure 5.9   Relationship between logical segment address and offset, and physical memory address (Intel Corporation).

demonstrates this idea. Notice that base $002B_{16}$ with offset 0013_{16} maps to physical address $002C3_{16}$ in memory. However, if the segment base address is changed to $002C_{16}$ with a new offset of 0003_{16}, the physical address is still $002C3_{16}$.

5.3 HARDWARE ORGANIZATION OF THE MEMORY ADDRESS SPACE

From a hardware point of view, the memory address space of the 8086 is implemented as two independent 512K-byte banks. They are called the *low (even) bank* and the *high (odd) bank.* Data bytes associated with an even address (00000_{16}, 00002_{16}, etc.) reside in the low bank and those with odd addresses (00001_{16}, 00003_{16}, etc.) reside in the high bank.

Looking at the circuit diagram in Fig. 5.10, we see that address bits A_1 through A_{19} select the storage location that is to be accessed. Therefore, they are applied to both banks in parallel. A_0 and bank high enable ($\overline{BHE}$) are used as bank select signals. Logic 0 at A_0 identifies an even-addressed byte of data and causes the low bank of memory to be enabled. On the other hand, $\overline{BHE}$ equal to 0 enables the high bank for access of an odd-addressed byte of data. Each of the memory banks provides half of the 8086's 16-bit data bus. Notice that the lower bank transfers bytes of data over data lines D_0 through D_7, while data transfers for the high bank use D_8 through D_{15}.

Figure 5.11(a) shows that when a byte memory operation is performed to address X, which is an even address, a storage location in the low bank is accessed. Therefore, A_0 is set to logic 0 to enable the low bank of memory and $\overline{BHE}$ to logic 1 to disable the high bank. As shown in the circuit diagram, data are transferred to or from the low bank over data bus lines D_0 through D_7. D_7 carries the MSB of the byte and D_0 the LSB.

On the other hand, to access a byte of data at an odd address such as X + 1 in Fig. 5.11(b), A_0 is set to logic 1 and $\overline{BHE}$ to logic 0. This enables the high bank of memory and disables the low bank. Data are transferred between the 8086 and the high bank over bus lines D_8 through D_{15}. Here D_{15} represents the MSB and D_8 the LSB.

Whenever an even-addressed word of data is accessed, both the high and low banks are accessed at the same time. Figure 5.11(c) illustrates how a word at even

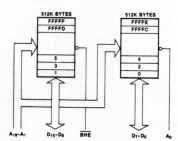

Figure 5.10 High and low memory banks (Intel Corporation).

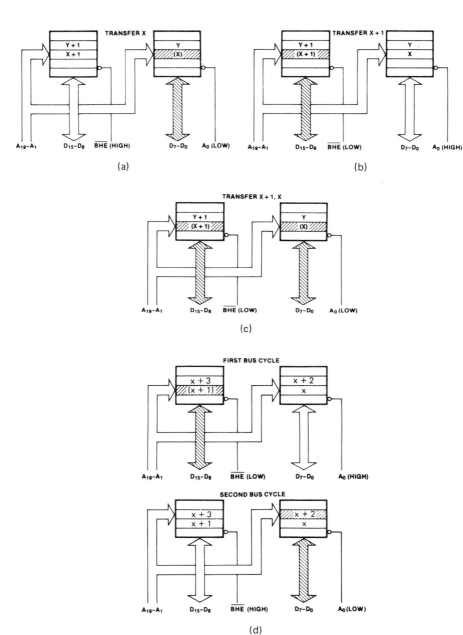

Figure 5.11   (a) Even-addressed byte transfer (Intel Corporation); (b) odd-addressed byte transfer (Intel Corporation); (c) even-addressed word transfer (Intel Corporation); (d) odd-addressed word transfer (Intel Corporation).

address X is accessed. Notice that both A_0 and $\overline{BHE}$ equal 0; therefore, both banks are enabled. In this case, a byte of data is transferred from or to both the low and high banks at the same time. This 16-bit word is transferred over the complete data bus D_0 through D_{15}. The bytes of an even-addressed word are said to be aligned and can be transferred with a memory operation that takes just one bus cycle.

A word at an odd-addressed boundary is different. It is said to be unaligned. That is, the least significant byte is at the lower address location in the high memory bank. This is demonstrated in Fig. 5.11(d). Here we see that the odd byte of the word is located at address $X + 1$ and the even byte at address $X + 2$.

Two bus cycles are required to access this word. During the first bus cycle, the odd byte of the word, which is located at address $X + 1$ in the high bank, is accessed. This is accompanied by select signals $A_0 = 1$ and $\overline{BHE} = 0$ and a data transfer over D_8 through D_{15}.

Next the 8086 automatically increments the address such that $A_0 = 0$. This represents the next address in memory which is even. Then a second memory bus cycle is initiated. During this second cycle, the even byte located at $X + 2$ in the low bank is accessed. The data transfer takes place over bus lines D_0 through D_7. This transfer is accompanied by $A_0 = 0$ and $\overline{BHE} = 1$.

5.4 MEMORY BUS STATUS CODES

Whenever a memory bus cycle is in progress, an address bus status code $S_3 S_4$ is output on the multiplexed address lines A_{16} and A_{17}. This two-bit code is output at the same time the data are carried over the other bus lines.

Bits S_3 and S_4 together form a 2-bit binary code that identifies which one of the four segment registers was used to generate the physical address that was output during the address period in the bus cycle. The four *address bus status codes* are listed in Fig. 5.12. Here we find that code $S_3 S_4 = 00$ identifies the extra segment register, 10 identifies the stack segment register, 01 identifies the code segment register, and 11 identifies the data segment register.

These status codes are output in both the minimum and the maximum system modes. They can be decoded with external circuitry to enable separate 1M-byte address spaces for ES, SS, CS, and DS. In this way, the memory address reach of the 8086 can be expanded to 4M bytes.

S_3	S_4	Address Status
0	0	Alternate (relative to the ES segment)
1	0	Stack (relative to the SS segment)
0	1	Code/None (relative to the CS segment or a default of zero)
1	1	Data (relative to the DS segment)

Figure 5.12 Address bus status codes (Intel Corporation).

5.5 MEMORY CONTROL SIGNALS

Earlier in the chapter we saw that similar control signals are produced in the maxi-mum- and minimum-mode systems. Moreover, we found that in the minimum system mode, the 8086 produces all of the control signals. But in the maximum system mode, they are produced by the 8288 bus controller. Here we will look more closely at each of these signals and their function.

Minimum-System Memory Control Signals

In the 8086 microcomputer system of Fig. 5.1, which is configured for the minimum system mode of operation, we found that the control signals provided to support the interface to the memory subsystem are: ALE, $\overline{BHE}$, M/$\overline{IO}$, DT/$\overline{R}$, $\overline{RD}$, $\overline{WR}$, and $\overline{DEN}$. These control signals are required to tell the memory subsystem when the bus is carrying a valid address, in which direction data are to be transferred over the bus, when valid write data are on the bus, and when to put read data on the bus.

For example, *address latch enable* (ALE) signals external circuitry that a valid address is on the bus. It is a pulse to the 1 logic level and is used to latch the address in external circuitry. Another important control signal involved in the memory inter-face is bank high enable ($\overline{BHE}$). Logic 0 is output on this line during the address part of the bus cycle whenever the high-bank part of the memory subsystem must be enabled.

The *memory/input-output* (M/$\overline{IO}$) and *data transmit/receive* (DT/$\overline{R}$) lines sig-nal external circuitry whether a memory or I/O bus cycle is in progress and whether the 8086 will transmit or receive data over the bus. During all memory bus cycles, M/$\overline{IO}$ is held at the 1 logic level. Moreover, when the 8086 switches DT/$\overline{R}$ to logic 1 during the data transfer part of the bus cycle, the bus is in the transmit mode and data are written into memory. On the other hand, it sets DT/$\overline{R}$ to logic 0 to signal that the bus is in the receive mode. This corresponds to reading of memory.

The signals *read* ($\overline{RD}$) and *write* ($\overline{WR}$), respectively, identify that a read or write bus cycle is in progress. The 8086 switches $\overline{WR}$ to logic 0 to signal memory that a write cycle is taking place over the bus. On the other hand, $\overline{RD}$ is switched to logic 0 whenever a read cycle is in progress. During all memory operations, the 8086 pro-duces one other control signal. It is *data enable* ($\overline{DEN}$). Logic 0 at this output is used to enable the data bus.

Maximum-System Memory Control Signals

When the 8086 is configured to work in the maximum mode, it does not directly pro-vide all the control signals to support the memory interface. Instead, an external *bus controller*, the 8288, provides memory commands and control signals that are com-patible with the *Multibus*. Figure 5.2 shows an 8086 connected in this way.

Specifically, the $\overline{WR}$, M/$\overline{IO}$, DT/$\overline{R}$, $\overline{DEN}$, ALE, and $\overline{INTA}$ signal lines on the 8086 are changed. They are replaced with *multiprocessor lock* signal ($\overline{LOCK}$), a *bus*

Status Inputs			CPU Cycle	8288 Command
$\overline{S}_2$	$\overline{S}_1$	$\overline{S}_0$		
0	0	0	Interrupt acknowledge	$\overline{INTA}$
0	0	1	Read I/O port	$\overline{IORC}$
0	1	0	Write I/O port	$\overline{IOWC}$, $\overline{AIOWC}$
0	1	1	Halt	None
1	0	0	Instruction fetch	$\overline{MRDC}$
1	0	1	Read memory	$\overline{MRDC}$
1	1	0	Write memory	$\overline{MWTC}$, $\overline{AMWC}$
1	1	1	Passive	None

Figure 5.13 Memory bus cycle status codes (Intel Corporation).

status code ($\overline{S}_2$ through $\overline{S}_0$), and a *queue status code* ($QS_1 QS_0$). The 8086 still does produce signals $\overline{BHE}$ and $\overline{RD}$. Moreover, these two signals provide the same functions as they did in minimum system mode.

The 3-bit bus status code $\overline{S}_2\text{-}\overline{S}_1\overline{S}_0$ is output prior to the initiation of each bus cycle. It identifies which type of bus cycle is to follow. This code is input to the 8288 bus controller. Here it is decoded to identify which type of bus cycle command signals must be generated.

Figure 5.13 shows the relationship between the bus status codes and the types of 8086 bus cycle produced. Also shown in this chart are the names of the corresponding command signals that are generated at the outputs of the 8288. For instance, the input code $\overline{S}_2\overline{S}_1\overline{S}_0$ equal 100 indicates that an instruction fetch cycle is to take place. This memory read makes the $\overline{MRDC}$ command output switch to logic 0.

Another bus command that is provided for the memory subsystem is $\overline{S}_2\overline{S}_1\overline{S}_0$ equal to 110. This represents a memory write cycle and it causes both the *memory write command* ($\overline{MWTC}$) and *advanced memory write command* ($\overline{AMWC}$) outputs to switch to the 0 logic level.

The control outputs produced by the 8288 are DEN, DT/$\overline{R}$, and ALE. These signals provide the same functions as those produced by the corresponding pins on the 8086 in the minimum system mode.

The other two status signals, QS_0 and QS_1, form an instruction queue code. This code tells external circuitry what type of information was removed from the queue during the previous clock cycle. Figure 5.14 shows the four different queue statuses. Notice that $QS_1 QS_0$ = 01 indicates that the first byte of an instruction was taken from the queue. The next byte of the instruction that is fetched is identified by queue status code 11. Whenever the queue is reset, for instance due to a transfer of control, the reinitialization code 10 is output. Moreover, if no queue operation occurred, status code 00 is output.

The last signal is bus priority lock ($\overline{LOCK}$). This signal is to be used as an input to the 8289 bus arbiter together with bus status code $\overline{S}_0$ through $\overline{S}_2$, and CLK. They are used to lock other processors off the system bus during execution of an instruc-

QS$_1$	QS$_0$	Queue Status
0	0	No Operation. During the last clock cycle, nothing was taken from the queue.
0	1	First Byte. The byte taken from the queue was the first byte of the instruction.
1	0	Queue Empty. The queue has been reinitialized as a result of the execution of a transfer instruction.
1	1	Subsequent Byte. The byte taken from the queue was a subsequent byte of the instruction.

Figure 5.14 Queue status codes (Intel Corporation).

tion. In this way the processor can be assured of uninterrupted access to common system resources such as *global memory*.

The *bus arbitration* signals produced by the 8289 are: *bus clock* ($\overline{BCLK}$), *bus request* ($\overline{BREQ}$), *bus priority in* ($\overline{BPRN}$), *bus priority out* ($\overline{BPRO}$), and *I/O busy* ($\overline{BUSY}$). These are the bus exchange signals of the Multibus. It is this bus arbiter that permits multiple processors to reside on the system bus by implementing the Multibus arbitration protocol in the 8086 microcomputer system.

5.6 READ AND WRITE BUS CYCLES

In the preceding section we introduced the status and control signals associated with the memory interface. Here we continue by studying the sequence in which they occur during the read and write bus cycles of memory.

Read Cycle

The memory interface signals of a minimum-mode 8086 system are shown in Fig. 5.15. Here their occurrence is illustrated relative to the four *time states* T_1, T_2, T_3, and T_4 of the 8086's bus cycle. Let us trace through the events that occur as data or instructions are read from memory.

The *read bus cycle* begins with state T_1. During this period, the 8086 outputs the 20-bit address of the memory location to be accessed on its multiplexed address/data bus AD$_0$ through AD$_{15}$ and A$_{16}$ through A$_{19}$. $\overline{BHE}$ is also output during this time. Notice that a pulse is also produced at ALE. The trailing edge of this pulse should be used to latch the address and $\overline{BHE}$ in external circuitry.

Also, we see that at the start of T_1, signals M/$\overline{IO}$ and DT/$\overline{R}$ are set to the 1 and 0 logic levels, respectively. This indicates to circuitry in the memory subsystem that a memory cycle is in progress and that the 8086 is going to receive data from

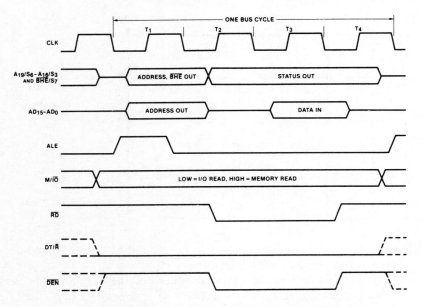

Figure 5.15 Memory read bus cycle (Intel Corporation).

the bus. Notice that both of these signals are maintained at these logic levels throughout all four periods of the bus cycle.

Beginning with state T_2, status bits S_3 through S_6 are output on the upper four bus lines A_{16} through A_{19}. Remember that bits S_3 and S_4 identify to external circuitry which segment register was used to generate the address just output. This status information is maintained through periods T_3 and T_4. The rest of the address/data bus lines, AD_0 through AD_{15}, are put in the high-Z state during T_2.

Late in period T_2, $\overline{RD}$ is switched to logic 0. This indicates to the memory subsystem that a read cycle is in progress. Then $\overline{DEN}$ is switched to logic 0 to tell external circuitry to put the data that are to be read from memory onto the bus.

As shown in the waveforms, input data are read by the 8086 during T_3, after which, as shown in T_4, the 8086 returns $\overline{RD}$ and $\overline{DEN}$ to the 1 logic level. The read cycle is now complete.

Write Cycle

The *write bus cycle* timing, shown in Fig. 5.16, is similar to that given for a read cycle in Fig. 5.15. Looking at the write cycle waveforms, we find that during T_1 the address and $\overline{BHE}$ are output and latched with the ALE pulse. This is identical to the read cycle. Moreover, $M/\overline{IO}$ is set to logic 1 to indicate that a memory cycle is in progress. However, this time $DT/\overline{R}$ is also switched to logic 1. This signals external circuits that the 8086 is going to transfer data over the bus.

As T_2 starts, the 8086 switches $\overline{WR}$ to logic 0. This tells the memory subsystem that a write operation is to follow over the bus. The 8086 puts the data on the bus

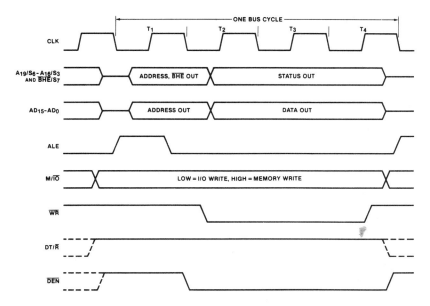

Figure 5.16   Memory write bus cycle (Intel Corporation).

late in T_2 and maintains the data valid through T_4. The write of data into memory should be initiated as $\overline{WR}$ returns from 0 to 1 early in T_4. This completes the write cycle.

Wait States in the Memory Bus Cycle

Wait states can be inserted to lengthen the memory bus cycles of the 8086. This is done with the *ready input* signal. Upon request from an event in hardware, for instance slow memory, the READY input is switched to logic 0. This signals the 8086 that the current bus cycle should not be completed. Instead, it is extended by inserting wait states with duration t_w equal 125 ns (for 8-MHz clock operation) between periods T_3 and T_4. The data that were on the bus during T_3 are maintained throughout the wait-state period. In this way, the bus cycle is not completed until READY is returned back to logic 1.

In the 8086 microcomputer system, the READY input of the 8086 is supplied by the READY output of the 8284 clock generator circuit.

5.7 THE STACK, STACK SEGMENT REGISTER, AND STACK POINTER

During interrupt and subroutine call types of operations, the contents of specific internal registers of the 8086 are pushed to a section of memory known as the *stack*. Here they are maintained temporarily. At the completion of the service routine or subroutine, these values are popped off the stack and put back into the same internal register where they originally resided.

For instance, when an interrupt occurs, the 8086 automatically pushes the current flags, the value in CS, and the value in IP to the stack. As part of the service routine for the interrupt, the contents of other registers can be pushed onto the stack by executing PUSH instructions. An example is the instruction PUSH SI. It causes the contents of the source index register to be pushed onto the stack.

At the end of the service routine, POP instructions can be included to pop values from the stack back into their corresponding internal registers. For example, POP SI causes the value at the top of the stack to be popped back into the source index register.

As indicated earlier, stack is implemented in the memory of the 8086 microcomputer system. It is 64K bytes long and is organized as 32K words. The lowest addressed byte in the current stack is pointed to by the address in the stack segment (SS) register.

Any number of stacks may exist in an 8086 microcomputer system. A new stack can be brought in by simply changing the value in the SS register through software. For instance, executing the instruction MOV SS,DX loads a new value from DX into SS. Even though many stacks can exist, only one can be active at a time.

Another register, the stack pointer (SP) contains an offset from the value in SS. The address obtained from the contents of SS and SP is the physical address of the last storage location in the stack to which data were pushed. This is known as the *top of the stack*. The value in the stack pointer starts at $FFFF_{16}$ upon initialization of the 8086. Combining this value with the current value in SS gives the highest-addressed location in the stack: that is, the *bottom of the stack*.

Since the data transfers to and from stack are always 16-bit words, it is important to configure the system such that all stack locations are at even word boundaries. This minimizes the number of memory cycles required to push or pop data for the stack and minimizes the amount of time required to perform a switch in program context.

The 8086 pushes data and addresses to the stack one word at a time. Each time a register value is to be pushed onto the top of the stack, the value in the stack pointer is first decremented by 2 and then the contents of the register are written into memory. In this way, we see that the stack grows down in memory from the bottom of the stack, which corresponds to the physical address derived from SS and $FFFF_{16}$, toward the end of the stack, which corresponds to the physical address obtained from SS and offset 0000_{16}.

When a value is popped from the top of the stack, the reverse of this sequence occurs. The physical address defined by SS and SP always points to the location of the last value pushed onto the stack. Its contents are first popped off the stack and put into the specified register within the 8086; then SP is incremented by 2. The top of the stack now corresponds to the previous value pushed onto the stack.

An example that shows how the contents of a register are pushed onto the stack is shown in Fig. 5.17(a). Here we find the state of the stack prior to execution of

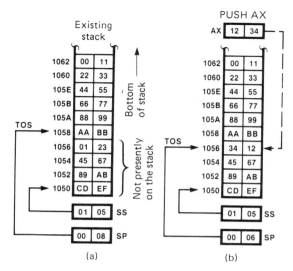

Figure 5.17 Pushing the contents of a register to the stack (Intel Corporation).

the PUSH instruction. Notice that the stack segment register contains 105_{16}. As indicated, the bottom of the stack resides at the physical address derived from SS with offset $FFFF_{16}$. This gives the bottom of stack address A_{BOS}

$$A_{BOS} = 1050_{16} + FFFF_{16}$$
$$= 1104F_{16}$$

Furthermore, the stack pointer, which represents the offset from the bottom of the stack to the top of the stack, equals 0008_{16}. Therefore, the current top of the stack is at physical address A_{TOS} equals

$$A_{TOS} = 1050_{16} + 0008_{16}$$
$$= 1058_{16}$$

Addresses with higher values than that of the top of stack, 1058_{16}, contain valid stack data. Those with lower addresses do not yet contain valid stack data. Notice that the last value pushed to the stack in Fig. 5.17(a) was $BBAA_{16}$.

Figure 5.17(b) demonstrates what happens when the PUSH AX instruction is executed. Here we see that AX contains the value 1234_{16}. Notice that execution of the PUSH instruction causes the stack pointer to be decremented by 2 but does not affect the contents of the stack segment register. Therefore, the next location to be accessed in the stack corresponds to address 1056_{16}. It is to this location that the value in AX is pushed. Notice that the most significant byte of AX, which equals 12_{16}, now resides in the least significant byte of the word in stack and the least significant byte 34_{16} is held in the most significant byte.

Now let us look at an example in which stack data are popped back into the register from which they were pushed. Figure 5.18 illustrates this operation. In Fig. 5.18(a), the stack is shown to be in the state that resulted due to our prior PUSH

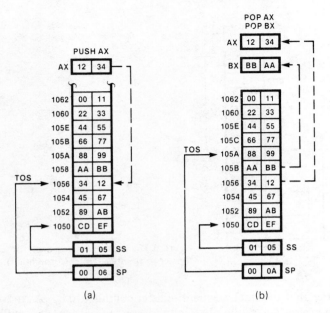

Figure 5.18 Popping the contents of a register from the stack (Intel Corporation).

AX example. That is, SP equals 0006_{16}, SS equals 105_{16}, the address of the top of the stack equals 1056_{16}, and the word at the top of the stack equals 1234_{16}.

Looking at Fig. 5.18(b), we see what happens when the instructions POP AX and POP BX are executed in that order. Here we see that execution of the first instruction causes the 8086 to read the value 1234_{16} from the top of the stack and put it into the AX register as 1234_{16}. Next, SP is incremented to give 0008_{16} and another read cycle is initiated from the stack. This second read corresponds to the POP BX instruction and it causes the value $BBAA_{16}$ to be loaded into the BX register. SP is incremented once more and now equals $000A_{16}$. Therefore, the new top of stack is at address $105A_{16}$.

From Fig. 5.18(b) we see that the values read out of 1056_{16} and 1058_{16} still remain at these addresses. But now they reside at locations that are considered to be above the top of the stack. Therefore, they no longer represent valid stack data.

5.8 DEMULTIPLEXING THE ADDRESS/DATA BUS

In an 8086 microcomputer system, memory, I/O devices, and the interrupt interface share use of the multiplexed address/data bus lines. In all three cases, a stable address is required and it must be available at the same time that data are to be transferred over the bus. For this reason, the address and data signals must be separated using external demultiplexing circuits to give a system bus. This *demultiplexed system bus* consists of the 20 address lines A_0 through A_{19}, 16 data bus lines D_0 through D_{15}, and memory control signals $\overline{BHE}$, $M/\overline{IO}$, $DT/\overline{R}$, $\overline{DEN}$, $\overline{WR}$, and $\overline{RD}$.

Several different techniques can be used to demultiplex the system bus. One approach is shown in Fig. 5.19. Here the microprocessor's bus is demultiplexed into a system bus just once at the MPU and then distributed to all other system elements. This is known as *local demultiplexing* and has the advantage of requiring minimal circuitry.

During bus cycles, a 20-bit address is output by the 8086 on AD_0 through A_{19} during period T_1 of the bus cycle. This address is accompanied by a pulse on the ALE (address latch enable) line. In this circuit, ALE tells external circuitry that a stable address is available and it should be latched.

In the circuit of Fig. 5.19 we have used three 8282 noninverting latches to demultiplex the address. These devices are octal latches. The ALE output of the 8086 is applied to the strobe (STB) input of all three latches. When pulsed at STB, the address applied to the DI_0 through DI_7 inputs of the 8282s is latched into their internal flip-flops. This happens on the 1-to-0 edge of ALE. Even though the address is latched, it is not yet available at address outputs A_0 through A_{19}. This is because the outputs of the octal latches are not yet enabled. To do this, we must switch the output enable (OE) input on the 8282s to the 0 logic level. In many applications, OE can be fixed at the 0 logic level. This permanently enables the outputs of the 8282s and the address is made available at A_0 through A_{19} as soon as it is latched. Notice that signal $\overline{BHE}$ is latched together with the address. In this way, the address is latched and maintained stable throughout the bus cycle.

This circuit configuration also increases the drive capability at the system bus. The outputs of the 8282 are rated to drive up to 32 mA. However, a propagation delay of 30 ns is introduced as signals pass through it.

The data bus D_0 through D_{15} can be directly formed from the AD_0 through

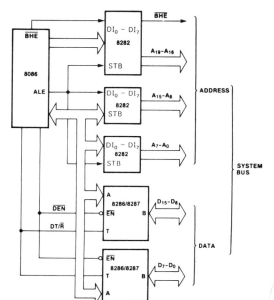

Figure 5.19 Local demultiplexing of the system bus (Intel Corporation).

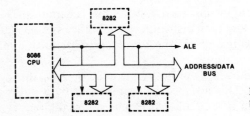

Figure 5.20 Remote demultiplexing of the system bus (Intel Corporation).

AD_{15} lines or buffered with bidirectional bus transceivers to increase drive capability. It is usually necessary to do this buffering because a large number of memory and peripheral devices are attached to the bus.

Two 8286 8-bit bidirectional transceiver devices can be used for this purpose. They are connected as shown in Fig. 5.19. Data can be passed in either direction between its A and B terminals. The direction of data transfer is determined by the logic level applied at the transfer (T) input. When T is logic 1, data are passed from A to B. This corresponds to the direction required for data transfers during write bus cycles. Changing the logic level of T to 0 causes data to be passed from B to A such as needed for read cycles. Moreover, logic 0 is needed at the $\overline{EN}$ input of the 8286 to enable the input and output drive circuitry selected by T. The bus side of the 8286 is able to drive up to 32 mA with propagation delays through the device equal to 30 ns.

From the circuit in Fig. 5.19, we see that the 8086 controls the direction and timing of data transfers through the 8286s with signals $DT/\overline{R}$ at the T input and $\overline{DEN}$ at its $\overline{EN}$ input. When $DT/\overline{R}$ is set to logic 1, the 8286s are set to pass data from MPU to memory. This sets the bus for a write operation. Switching $DT/\overline{R}$ to logic 0 changes the direction of data transfer through the 8286s such that the MPU can read data out of memory. $\overline{DEN}$ is switched to logic 0 whenever a data transfer is to take place over the bus and enables the output buffers of the 8286.

A second approach is shown in Fig. 5.20. This configuration is known as *remote demultiplexing*. In this case, the microprocessor's local bus signals are distributed to each part of the system and then demultiplexed by circuits provided in the memory or I/O sections.

5.9 4K-WORD PROGRAM STORAGE MEMORY

ROM, PROM, or EPROM devices are connected to the 8086 to implement a *program storage memory*. EPROM devices such as the 2716, 2732, and 2764 are organized with a byte-wide output. For this reason, two such devices are required to store the 16-bit instruction words of the 8086.

Figure 5.21 shows how two 2732 EPROMs are connected to the demultiplexed system bus of the 8086 to provide a 4K-word program storage memory. The upper of the two devices represents the high memory bank and the lower device the low memory bank. To select one of the 4K of storage locations, we need a 12-bit address. In the circuit diagram, this corresponds to A_1 through A_{12}. Notice that both EPROM devices are addressed in parallel over the bus.

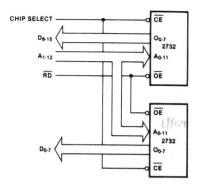

Figure 5.21 4K-word program storage memory (Intel Corporation).

The additional high-order bits of the 8086's address, which are not shown, must be decoded to produce the CHIP SELECT signal. The $\overline{CE}$ inputs of the two 2732s are connected in parallel and supplied by CHIP SELECT. Whenever the address on the system bus corresponds to program storage memory, the output of an address decoder circuit must switch this line to logic 0 to enable the EPROMs for operation.

Instructions are read as 16-bit words from the program storage memory over data bus lines D_0 through D_{15}. The upper 2732 devices provide the most significant byte of the instruction word. Looking at the circuit diagram in Fig. 5.21, we see that this byte is output on data bus lines D_8 through D_{15}. The lower 2732 outputs the least significant byte of the instruction word. This byte is carried over data bus lines D_0 through D_7. The data outputs of both devices are enabled by switching the signal $\overline{RD}$ to logic 0.

During an instruction acquisition cycle, the instruction fetch sequence of the 8086 causes a read bus cycle to be initiated. The values in CS and IP are combined in the bus interface unit to generate the address of a storage location in the address range of the program storage memory. This address is output on A_0 through A_{19} and latched in external circuitry. Bits A_1 through A_{12} are applied to both EPROMs in parallel to select the instruction word to be output. At the same time, the high-order bits of the address are decoded and switch CHIP SELECT to logic 0. Now the 2732s are enabled for operation.

When the 8086 switches read ($\overline{RD}$) to logic 0, the outputs of the two 2732s are enabled. This causes the two bytes of the instruction word to be put on data bus lines D_0 through D_{15}. The 8086 reads these two bytes simultaneously as a 16-bit word.

5.10 1K-WORD STATIC RAM DATA STORAGE MEMORY

Data are normally stored in random access read/write memory instead of read-only memory. If the amount of memory required in the microcomputer system is small, for instance, less than 16K words, the memory subsystem will usually be designed with static RAMs instead of dynamic RAMs. This is because most dynamic RAMs are organized 16K by 1 or 64K by 1. Moreover, dynamic RAMs require refresh sup-

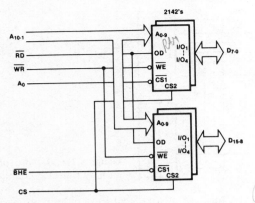

Figure 5.22 Minimum-mode static RAM data storage memory (Intel Corporation).

port circuits. This additional circuitry is not warranted if storage requirements are small.

Figure 5.22 shows how a 1K-word random access read/write memory subsystem can be constructed with 2142 static RAMs. This circuit assumes that the 8086 is configured for minimum system mode. In the circuit, we find four 2142 ICs connected to form a 1K-word data storage memory. Of course, through software the 8086 can read data from the memory either as bytes, words, or double words.

Notice that the upper two 2142 devices are connected to provide the low RAM bank. The 8086 accesses the byte storage locations in this 1K by 8 section over data bus lines D_0 through D_7. They represent odd-addressed bytes of data. On the other hand, the lower two RAMs represent the high memory bank. It corresponds to even-addressed bytes of data and are accessed over bus lines D_8 through D_{15}.

Bits A_1 through A_{10} of the address are applied in parallel to the address inputs on all four 2142s. It is this part of the address that selects the storage location that is to be accessed. The more significant address bits, which are not shown, are decoded to provide the CS_2 chip select signal. Addresses that correspond to locations in data storage memory must cause CS_2 to switch to logic 1. This selects the complete bank of RAMs for operation.

During word operations to an even-address boundary, the 8086 switches both address bit A_0 and bank high enable $\overline{BHE}$ to logic 0. Notice that these two signals are applied to the CS_1 inputs of the RAMs in the low memory bank and high memory bank, respectively. In this way, both banks are enabled for operation and both a high byte and low byte are carried over the data bus at the same time.

$\overline{WR}$ signals the devices that valid data are on the data bus during write bus cycles. When the data put on the bus by the 8086 have stabilized (valid data), $\overline{WR}$ is switched to logic 0. It is applied to the $\overline{WE}$ input of all four 2142s in parallel and causes them to take the data off the bus and store it in the addressed location.

Also notice in Fig. 5.22 that the $\overline{RD}$ output of the 8086 supplies the OD inputs of the RAMs. This signal enables the outputs of the 2142s during read bus cycles. When the 8086 switches $\overline{RD}$ to logic 0, it tells the 2142s to put the data stored in the addressed location onto the data bus.

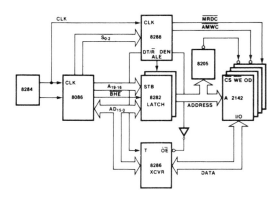

Figure 5.23   Maximum-mode static RAM data storage memory (Intel Corporation).

The read and write cycles are similar for byte data; however, the 8086 keeps either A_0 or $\overline{\text{BHE}}$ at logic 1. In this way, just the even bank or odd bank of memory is selected and a byte-wide data transfer occurs over the bus.

A maximum-mode 8086 microcomputer system with static RAM is shown in Fig. 5.23. This circuit is similar to the minimum-mode circuit we just described. The key difference is that the 8288 bus controller provides the read/write and memory control signals instead of the 8086. Notice that the advanced memory write command ($\overline{\text{AMWC}}$) output of the bus controller is used as the $\overline{\text{WE}}$ input of the 2142s. Moreover, its memory read command ($\overline{\text{MRDC}}$) output is applied to the OD inputs of the RAMs.

Finally, we find that the 8286 bus transceivers have been added to buffer the data bus. Notice that the DT/$\overline{\text{R}}$ and DEN outputs of the 8288 are applied to the T and $\overline{\text{OE}}$ inputs of the 8286, respectively. They are used to set the direction and to enable its outputs during read and write bus cycles.

5.11 128K-BYTE DYNAMIC RAM SUBSYSTEM

Today, microcomputer systems are being employed in more complex applications and with increased use of *high-level languages* such as BASIC, PL/M, C, and Pascal. Both of these conditions provide requirements for support of a large memory subsystem. At the same time, dramatic decreases in the cost of semiconductor memory have made the use of large memory subsystems more practical.

If storage requirements of the 8086 microcomputer system are 16K words or larger, the memory subsystem is usually designed using dynamic RAMs instead of static RAMs. Figure 5.24 shows a dynamic RAM subsystem for a maximum mode 8086 system. The circuit employs the 16K by 1 2118 dynamic RAM and 8202 dynamic RAM refresh controller.

Looking at the circuit in Fig. 5.24, we see that the memory subsystem is formed from 64 2118 dynamic RAMs connected to produce a 128K-byte memory subsystem. The buses of the 8086 are first demultiplexed and then applied to the memory sub-

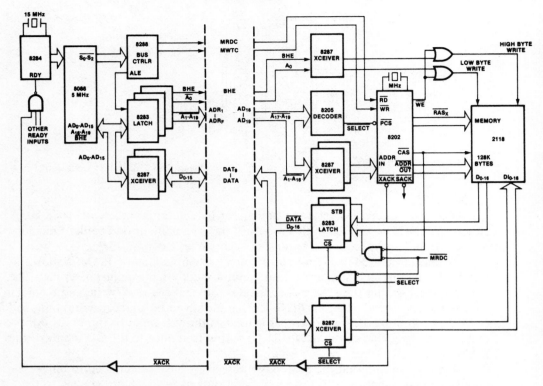

Figure 5.24   Maximum-mode dynamic RAM subsystem (Intel Corporation).

system. In the memory subsystem, additional buffering is provided by 8287 bus transceivers, 8283 latches, and an 8205 decoder.

A 17-bit address, A_0 through A_{16}, is applied to the address inputs (ADDR IN) of the 8202 refresh controller. At the same time, the address bits A_{17} through A_{19} are decoded by the 8205 1-of-8 decoder to enable the refresh controller. It does this by switching the $\overline{PCS}$ input to logic 0. The refresh controller causes the 16-bit input address to be multiplexed out as an 8-bit row address and 8-bit column address at address outputs (ADDR OUT). The appropriate $\overline{CAS}$ and $\overline{RAS}$ signals are output synchronously with the corresponding address byte. Notice that bank select signals A_0 and BHE are gated with the $\overline{WE}$ output of the 8202 to permit word or byte data transfers.

The 8288 bus controller signals whether a read or write bus cycle is in progress. In turn, it supplies the read signal MRDC and write signal MWTC to the $\overline{RD}$ and $\overline{WR}$ inputs, respectively, of the 8202. In response to these signals, the 8202 supplies the appropriate timed $\overline{WE}$, $\overline{RAS}_X$, $\overline{CAS}$, and $\overline{ADDR\ OUT}$ signals to the 128K-byte memory array.

The data outputs of the memory subsystem are interfaced to the system data bus with two 8283 latches. During memory read cycles, $\overline{SELECT}$ and $\overline{MRDC}$ are both logic 0. These signals are gated to chip select the 8283 latches. Synchronous with $\overline{\text{CAS}}$, valid read data are available at data outputs D_0 through D_{15}. The return of $\overline{\text{CAS}}$ to logic 1 completes the strobe pulse to the latches and the data output by the memory are latched on the system data bus.

During write cycles, data are input to the memory subsystem through 8287 bus transceivers. These devices are set up to just transmit data. Again the $\overline{\text{SELECT}}$ input enables the outputs of the devices such that data from the system data bus are applied to data inputs DI_0 through DI_{15} of the memory subsystem.

If the 8202 controller is busy refreshing memory, it signals this condition to the 8086 with the $\overline{\text{XACK}}$ signal. $\overline{\text{XACK}}$ is buffered and applied to the RDY input of the clock generator. In this way, wait states can be inserted into the bus cycle until the read or write cycle can be completed.

ASSIGNMENT

Section 5.2

1. Show how the double word 12345678_{16} will be stored in memory starting at address $A001_{16}$.
2. Which range of the memory address space can be used to store instructions of the program?
3. If CS contains $A000_{16}$, what is the address range of the current code segment?
4. The data segment is to be located from address $B0000_{16}$ to $BFFFF_{16}$. What value must be loaded into DS?
5. Write a sequence of instructions that will initialize CS, DS, SS, and ES so that their corresponding segments of memory start at $A0000_{16}$, $B0000_{16}$, $C0000_{16}$, and $D0000_{16}$, respectively.

Section 5.3

6. List the memory control signals together with their active logic levels that occur when a byte of data is read from memory address $B0003_{16}$. Over which data lines is the byte of data transferred?
7. List the memory control signals together with their active logic levels that occur when a word of data is written to memory address $A0000_{16}$.

Sections 5.4 and 5.5

8. When the instruction PUSH AX is executed, what address bus status code and memory bus cycle code are output by the 8086 in a maximum-mode system?

Section 5.6

9. Describe the bus activity that takes place as the 8086 writes a word of data into memory address $B0010_{16}$.
10. Explain why the READY input can be used to insert a wait state into the 8086's bus cycle.

Section 5.7

11. What is the function of the stack?

12. If the stack segment register contains $C000_{16}$ and the current value in SP is $FF00_{16}$, what is the address of the top of the stack?

Section 5.8

13. Explain the operation of the circuit in Fig. 5.19 as a word-wide read takes place from address $A0000_{16}$.

Section 5.9

14. Draw a circuit similar to that in Fig. 5.21 using four 2732 EPROMs to form an 8K-word program storage memory.

Section 5.10

15. Show how the circuit in Fig. 5.22 can be expanded to give a total of 2K words of read/write memory.

Section 5.11

16. Explain the need for the 8202 refresh controller in the circuit of Fig. 5.24.

6

Input/Output Interface of the 8086 Microprocessor

6.1 INTRODUCTION

In Chapter 5 we studied the memory interface of the 8086. Here we will study another important interface of the 8086 microcomputer system, the input/output interface. These are the topics in the order in which they are covered:

1. The input/output interface
2. I/O address space and data transfers
3. I/O instructions
4. The input and output bus cycles
5. Eight-byte-wide output ports
6. 8255A programmable peripheral interface
7. 8255A implementation of parallel I/O ports
8. Memory-mapped I/O

6.2 THE INPUT/OUTPUT INTERFACE

The *input/output interface* of the 8086 system permits it to communicate with the outside world. The way in which the 8086 deals with input/output circuitry is similar to the way in which it interfaces with memory circuitry. That is, input/output data transfers also take place over the multiplexed address/data bus. This parallel bus permits easy interface to LSI peripherals such as parallel I/O expanders and communica-

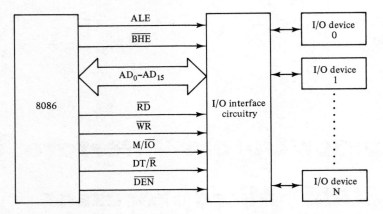

Figure 6.1 Minimum-mode 8086 system I/O interface.

tion controllers. Through these I/O interfaces, the 8086 can input or output data in bit, byte, or word formats.

Minimum-Mode Interface

Let us begin by looking at the I/O interface for a minimum-mode 8086 system. Figure 6.1 shows the minimum-mode interface. Here we find the 8086, interface circuitry, and I/O ports for devices 0 through N. The circuits in this interface section must perform functions such as select the I/O port, latch output data, sample input data, synchronize data transfers, and translate between TTL voltage levels and those required to operate the I/O devices.

The data path between the 8086 and I/O interface circuits is the multiplexed address/data bus. Unlike the memory interface, this time just the 16 least significant lines of the bus, AD_0 through AD_{15}, are in use. This interface also involves the control signals that we discussed as part of the memory interface. They are: ALE, $\overline{BHE}$, $\overline{RD}$, $\overline{WR}$, M/$\overline{IO}$, DT/$\overline{R}$, and $\overline{DEN}$.

Maximum-Mode Interface

When the 8086 system is strapped to operate in the maximum mode, the interface to the I/O circuitry changes. Figure 6.2 illustrates this configuration.

As in the maximum-mode memory interface, the 8288 bus controller produces the control signals for the I/O subsystem. The 8288 decodes bus command status codes output by the 8086 at $\overline{S}_2\overline{S}_1\overline{S}_0$. These codes tell which type of bus cycle is in progress. If the code corresponds to an I/O read bus cycle, the 8288 generates the *read I/O command output* $\overline{IORC}$ and for an I/O write cycle it generates *write I/O command outputs* $\overline{IOWC}$ and $\overline{AIOWC}$. The 8288 also produces control signals ALE, DT/$\overline{R}$, and DEN. Moreover, the address and data transfer path between 8086 and maximum-mode I/O interface remains address/data bus lines AD_0 through AD_{15}.

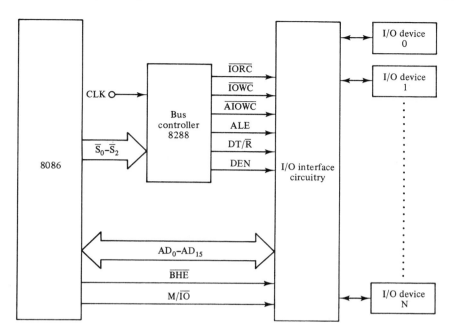

Figure 6.2 Maximum-mode 8086 system I/O interface.

In this configuration the control signals $\overline{\text{BHE}}$ and M/$\overline{\text{IO}}$ are still produced by the 8086 microprocessor.

The table in Fig. 6.3 shows the bus command status codes together with the command signals that they produce. Those for I/O bus cycles have been highlighted. The 8086 indicates that data are to be input (Read I/O port) by code $\overline{S}_2\overline{S}_1\overline{S}_0 = 001$. This input causes the bus controller to produce control output I/O read command ($\overline{\text{IORC}}$). There is one other code that represents an output bus cycle. This is the Write I/O port code $\overline{S}_2\overline{S}_1\overline{S}_0 = 010$. It produces two output command signals I/O write

Status inputs			CPU cycle	8288 command
$\overline{S}_2$	$\overline{S}_1$	$\overline{S}_0$		
0	0	0	Interrupt acknowledge	$\overline{\text{INTA}}$
0	0	1	Read I/O port	$\overline{\text{IORC}}$
0	1	0	Write I/O port	$\overline{\text{IOWC}}$, $\overline{\text{AIOWC}}$
0	1	1	Halt	None
1	0	0	Instruction fetch	$\overline{\text{MRDC}}$
1	0	1	Read memory	$\overline{\text{MRDC}}$
1	1	0	Write memory	$\overline{\text{MWTC}}$, $\overline{\text{AMWC}}$
1	1	1	Passive	None

Figure 6.3 I/O bus cycle status codes (Intel Corporation).

cycle ($\overline{\text{IOWC}}$) and advanced I/O write cycle ($\overline{\text{AIOWC}}$). These command signals are used to enable data from the I/O circuitry onto the system bus and control the direction in which data are transferred.

6.3 I/O ADDRESS SPACE AND DATA TRANSFERS

Earlier we indicated that input/output ports in the 8086 system can be either byte wide or word wide. The port that is accessed for input or output of data is selected by an *I/O address*. This address is specified as part of the instruction that performs the I/O operation.

I/O addresses are 16 bits in length and are output by the 8086 to the I/O interface over bus lines AD_0 through AD_{15}. As for memory addresses, AD_0 represents the LSB and AD_{15} the MSB. The most significant bits, A_{16} through A_{19}, of the memory address are held at the 0 logic level during the address period (T_1) of all I/O bus cycles.

The 8086 signals to external circuitry that the address on the bus is for an I/O port instead of a memory location by switching the $M/\overline{IO}$ control line to the 0 logic level. This signal is held at the 0 level during the complete input or output bus cycle. For this reason, it can be used to enable the address latch or address decoder in external I/O circuitry.

Figure 6.4 shows a map of the *I/O address space* of the 8086 system. This is an independent 64K-byte address space that is dedicated for I/O devices. Notice that its address range is from 0000_{16} through $FFFF_{16}$. The part of the map from address 0000_{16} through $00FF_{16}$ is referred to as page 0. Certain I/O instructions can only perform operations to ports in this part of the address space. Other I/O instructions can input or output data for ports anywhere in the I/O address space.

Moreover, notice that the eight ports located from address $00F8_{16}$ through $00FF_{16}$ are specified as reserved. These port addresses are reserved by Intel Corporation for use in their future hardware and software products.

Data transfers between the MPU and I/O devices are performed over the data bus. Word transfers take place over the complete data bus, D_0 through D_{15}, and can require either one or two bus cycles. To assure that just one bus cycle is required for the word data transfer, word-wide I/O ports should be aligned at even address boundaries.

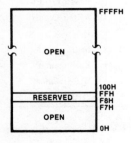

Figure 6.4 I/O address space (Intel Corporation).

On the other hand, data transfers to byte-wide I/O ports always require one bus cycle. Therefore, they can be located at either an even or an odd address. Byte data transfers to a port at an even address are performed over bus lines D_0 through D_7 and those to an odd-addressed port are performed over D_8 through D_{15}.

To input or output consecutive bytes of data to an LSI peripheral device, it should be connected such that all registers reside at either even or odd addresses. In this way, all data transfers take place over the same part of the bus. For this reason, A_0 cannot be used as a register select bit when addressing peripheral devices.

6.4 INPUT/OUTPUT INSTRUCTIONS

Input/output operations are performed by the 8086 using its *in* (IN) and *out* (OUT) instructions together with the I/O port addressing mode. There are two types of IN and OUT instructions: the *direct I/O instructions* and *variable I/O instructions*. These instructions are listed in the table of Fig. 6.5. Their mnemonics and names are provided together with a brief description of their operations.

Either of these two types of instructions can be used to transfer a byte or word of data. In the case of byte transfers, data can be input/output over the upper or lower part of the bus. This is achieved by specifying an even or odd address, for the I/O port.

All data transfers take place between I/O devices and the 8086's AL or AX register. For this reason, this method of performing I/O is known as *accumulator I/O*. Byte transfers involve the AL register and word transfers the AX register. In fact, specifying AL as the source or destination register in an I/O instruction indicates that it corresponds to a byte transfer instead of a word transfer.

In a direct I/O instruction, the address of the I/O port is specified as part of the instruction. Eight bits are provided for this direct address. For this reason, its value is limited to the address range from 0_{10} equal 0000_{16} to 255_{10} equal $00FF_{16}$. This range corresponds to page 0 in the I/O address space of Fig. 6.4.

The difference between the direct and variable I/O instructions lies in the way in which the address of the I/O port is specified. We just saw that for direct I/O instructions an 8-bit address is specified as part of the instruction. On the other hand, the variable I/O instructions use a 16-bit address that resides in the DX register within the 8086. The value in DX is not an offset. It is the actual address that is to be

Mnemonic	Meaning	Format	Operation	
IN	Input direct	IN Acc,Port	(Acc) ← (Port)	Acc = AL or AX
	Input indirect (variable)	IN Acc,DX	(Acc) ← ((DX))	
OUT	Output direct	OUT Port,Acc	(Port) ← (Acc)	
	Output indirect (variable)	OUT DX,Acc	((DX)) ← (Acc)	

Figure 6.5 Input/output instructions.

output on AD_0 through AD_{15} during the I/O bus cycle. Since this address is a full 16 bits in length, variable I/O instructions can access ports located anywhere in the 64K-byte I/O address space.

Example 6.1

Assume that two byte-size input ports at addresses AA_{16} and $A9_{16}$, respectively, are to be read and then their contents output to a word-size output port at address $B000_{16}$. Write an instruction sequence to do this.

Solution. We can read in the byte from the port at address AA_{16} into AL and then move it to AH and read in the other byte from the port at address $A9_{16}$. To write out the word in AX, we can load DX with the address $B000_{16}$ and use an output indirect instruction. This leads to the following instruction sequence:

IN	AL,AAH
MOV	AH,AL
IN	AL,A9H
MOV	DX,0B000H
OUT	DX,AX

When using either type of I/O instruction, the data must be loaded into or removed from the AL or AX register before another input or output operation can be performed. Moreover, in the case of the variable I/O instructions, the DX register must be loaded with an address. This requires execution of additional instructions.

6.5 INPUT AND OUTPUT BUS CYCLES

In Section 6.2 we found that the I/O interface signals for the minimum-mode 8086 system are essentially the same as those involved in the memory interface. In fact, the function, logic levels, and timing of all signals other than M/IO are identical to those already described for the memory interface in Chapter 5.

Waveforms for the *I/O input (I/O read) bus cycle* and *I/O output (I/O write) bus cycle* are shown in Figs. 6.6 and 6.7, respectively. Looking at the input and output bus cycle waveforms, we see that the timing of M/$\overline{IO}$ does not change. The 8086 switches it to logic 0 to indicate that an I/O bus cycle is in progress. It is maintained at the 0 logic level for the duration of the I/O bus cycle. As in memory cycles, the address (ADDRESS OUT) is output together with ALE during clock period T_1. For the input bus cycle, $\overline{DEN}$ is switched to logic 0 to signal the I/O interface circuitry when to put the data onto the bus and the 8086 reads data off the bus during period T_3.

On the other hand, for the output bus cycle in Fig. 6.7, the 8086 puts write data (DATA OUT) on the bus late in T_2 and maintains it during the rest of the bus cycle. This time $\overline{WR}$ switches to logic 0 to signal the I/O section that valid data are on the bus.

The same bus cycle requirements exist for data transfers for I/O ports as were

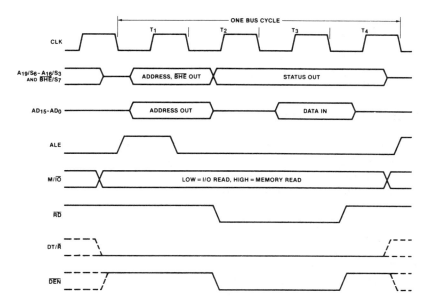

Figure 6.6 Input bus cycle (Intel Corporation).

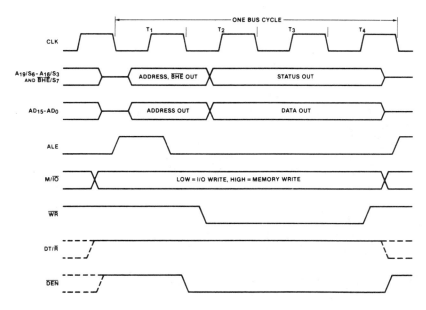

Figure 6.7 Output bus cycle (Intel Corporation).

found for memory. That is, all byte transfers and word transfers to even-addressed ports require just one bus cycle. However, two bus cycles are required to perform data transfers for odd-addressed word-wide ports. Eight bits are transferred during each of these two bus cycles.

6.6 EIGHT-BYTE-WIDE OUTPUT PORTS

Up to this point in the chapter, we have introduced the I/O interface of the 8086, the I/O address space, the I/O instructions, and I/O bus cycles. Now we will show a circuit that can be used to implement parallel output ports in an 8086 system. Figure 6.8 is such a circuit. It provides eight-byte-wide output ports that are implemented with 8282 octal latches. In this circuit, the ports are labeled PORT 0 through PORT 7. These eight ports give a total of 64 parallel output lines which are labeled O_0 through O_{63}.

Looking at the circuit, we see that the 8086's address/data bus is demultiplexed just as was done for the memory interface. Notice that two 8282 octal latches are used to form a 16-bit address latch. These devices latch the address A_0 through A_{15} synchronously with the ALE pulse. The latched address outputs are labeled A_{0L} through A_{15L}. Remember that address lines A_{16} through A_{19} are not involved in the I/O interface. For this reason they are not shown in the circuit diagram.

Actually, this circuit is designed such that the I/O ports reside at even byte addresses. This is the reason that only data bus lines D_0 through D_7 are shown connecting to the output latches. It is over these lines that the 8086 writes data into the output ports.

Address lines A_{0L} and A_{15L} provide two of the three enable inputs of the 8205 output address decoder. These signals are applied to enable inputs $\overline{E}_1$ and E_3, respectively. The decoder requires one more enable signal at its $\overline{E}_2$ input. It is supplied by $M/\overline{IO}$. These enable inputs must be $\overline{E}_1\overline{E}_2E_3$ equal to 001 to enable the decoder for operation. The condition $\overline{E}_1$ equal 0 corresponds to an even address and $\overline{E}_2$ equal 0 represents the fact that an I/O bus cycle is in progress. The third condition, E_3 equal 1, is an additional requirement that A_{15L} be at logic 1 during all data transfers for this section of parallel output ports.

Notice that the 3-bit code $A_{3L}A_{2L}A_{1L}$ is applied to select inputs ABC of the 8205 1-of-8 decoder. When the decoder is enabled, the P output corresponding to this select code switches to logic 0. Notice that logic 0 at this output enables the $\overline{WR}$ signal to the strobe (STB) input of the corresponding output latch. In this way, just one of the eight ports is selected for operation.

When valid output data are on D_0 through D_7, the 8086 switches $\overline{WR}$ to logic 0. This change in logic level causes the selected 8282 device to latch in the data from the bus. The outputs of the latches are permanently enabled by the 0 logic level at their $\overline{OE}$ inputs. Therefore, the data appear at the appropriate port outputs.

The 8286 in the circuit allows data to move from 8086 to the output ports. This

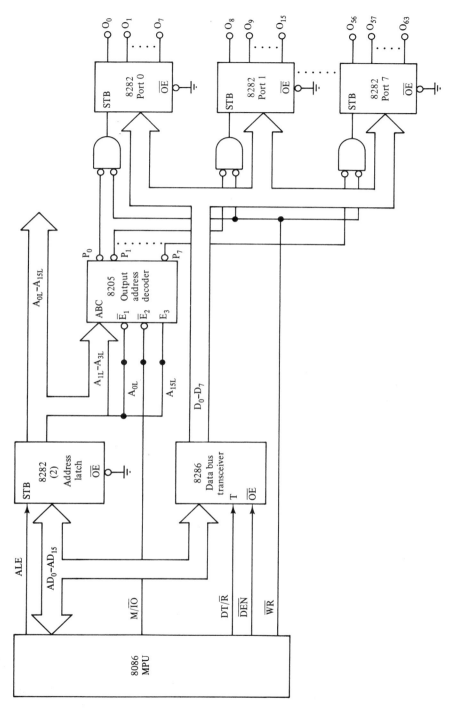

Figure 6.8 64-line output circuit.

accomplished by enabling the 8286 at its T and $\overline{OE}$ pins with the DT/$\overline{R}$ and $\overline{DEN}$ signals which are at logic 1 and 0, respectively.

Example 6.2

To which output port in Fig. 6.8 are data written when the address put on the bus during an output bus cycle is 8002_{16}?

Solution. Expressing the address in binary form, we get

$$A_{15} \cdots A_0 = A_{15L} \cdots A_{0L} = 1000000000000010_{16}$$

The important address bits are:

$$A_{15L} = 1$$
$$A_{0L} = 0$$

and

$$A_{3L}A_{2L}A_{1L} = 001$$

Moreover, whenever an output bus cycle is in progress M/$\overline{IO}$ is logic 0. Therefore, the enable inputs of the 8205 decoder are

$$\overline{E}_1 = A_{0L} = 0$$
$$\overline{E}_2 = M/\overline{IO} = 0$$
$$E_3 = A_{15L} = 1$$

These inputs enable the decoder for operation. At the same time, its select inputs are supplied with the code 001. This input causes output P_1 to switch to logic 0.

$$P_1 = 0$$

The gate at the strobe input of Port 1 has as its inputs P_1 and $\overline{WR}$. When valid data are on the bus, $\overline{WR}$ switches to logic 0. Since P_1 is also 0, the STB input of the 8282 for Port 1 switches to logic 1. This causes the data on D_0 through D_7 to be latched at outputs O_8 through O_{15} of Port 1.

6.7 8255A PROGRAMMABLE PERIPHERAL INTERFACE (PPI)

The *8255A* is an LSI peripheral designed to permit easy implementation of *parallel I/O* in the 8086 system. It provides a flexible parallel interface which includes features such as: single-bit, 4-bit, and byte-wide input and output ports; level-sensitive inputs; latched outputs; strobed inputs or outputs; and strobed bidirectional input/outputs. These features are selected under software control.

A block diagram of the 8255A is shown in Fig. 6.9(a) and its pin layout in Fig. 6.9(b). The left side of the block represents the *microprocessor interface*. It includes an *8-bit bidirectional data bus* D_0 through D_7. Over these lines, commands, status information, and data are transferred between the 8086 and 8255A. These data are transferred whenever the 8086 performs an input or output bus cycle to an address of a register within the device. Timing of the data transfers to the 8255A is controlled by the *read/write* ($\overline{RD}$ and $\overline{WR}$) *control* signals.

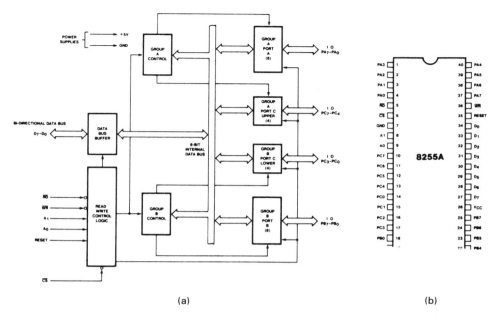

Figure 6.9 (a) Block diagram of the 8255A (Intel Corporation); (b) pin layout (Intel Corporation).

The source or destination register within the 8255A is selected by a 2-bit *register select code*. The 8086 must apply this code to the *register select inputs*, A_0 and A_1 of the 8255A. The *PORT A, PORT B*, and *PORT C registers* correspond to codes $A_1A_0 = 00$, $A_1A_0 = 01$, and $A_1A_0 = 10$, respectively.

Two other signals are shown on the microprocessor interface side of the block diagram. They are the *reset* (RESET) and *chip select* ($\overline{CS}$) inputs. $\overline{CS}$ must be logic 0 during all read or write operations to the 8255A. It enables the microprocessor interface circuitry for an input or output operation.

On the other hand, RESET is used to initialize the device. Switching it to logic 0 at power-up causes the internal registers of the 8255A to be cleared. *Initialization* configures all I/O ports for input mode of operation.

The other side of the block corresponds to three *byte-wide I/O ports*. They are called PORT A, PORT B, and PORT C and represent *I/O lines* PA_0 through PA_7, PB_0 through PB_7, and PC_0 through PC_7, respectively. These ports can be configured for input or output operation. This gives a total of 24 I/O lines.

We already mentioned that the operating characteristics of the 8255A can be configured under software control. It contains an 8-bit internal control register for this purpose. This register is represented by the *group A* and *group B control blocks* in Fig. 6.9(a). Logic 0 or 1 can be written to the bit positions in this register to configure the individual ports for input or output operation and to enable one of its three modes of operation. The control register is write only and its contents are modi-

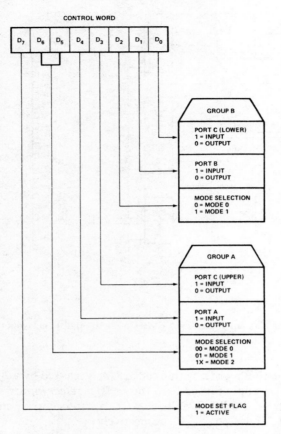

Figure 6.10 Control word bit functions (Intel Corporation).

fied under software control by initiating a write bus cycle to the 8255A with register select code $A_1A_0 = 11$.

The bits of the control register and their control functions are shown in Fig. 6.10. Here we see that bits D_0 through D_2 correspond to the group B control block in the diagram of Fig. 6.9(a). Bit D_0 configures the lower four lines of PORT C for input or output operation. Notice that logic 1 at D_0 selects input operation and logic 0 selects output operation. The next bit, D_1, configures PORT B as an 8-bit-wide input or output port. Again, logic 1 selects input operation and logic 0 selects output operation.

The D_2 bit is the mode select bit for PORT B and the lower 4 bits of PORT C. It permits selection of one of two different modes of operation called *MODE 0* and *MODE 1*. Logic 0 in bit D_2 selects MODE 0, while logic 1 selects MODE 1. These modes will be discussed in detail shortly.

The next 4 bits in the control register, D_3 through D_6, correspond to the group A control block in Fig. 6.9(a). Bits D_3 and D_4 of the control register are used to configure the operation of the upper half of PORT C and all of PORT A, respectively.

These bits work in the same way as D_0 and D_1 configure the lower half of PORT C and PORT B. However, there are now two mode select bits D_5 and D_6 instead of just one. They are used to select between three modes of operation known as *MODE 0, MODE 1,* and *MODE 2*.

The last control register bit, D_7, is the *mode set flag*. It must be at logic 1 (active) whenever the mode of operation is to be changed.

MODE 0 selects what is called *simple I/O operation*. By simple I/O, we mean that the lines of the port can be configured as level-sensitive inputs or latched outputs. To set all ports for this mode of operation, load bit D_7 of the control register with logic 1, bits $D_6D_5 = 00$, and $D_2 = 0$. Logic 1 at D_7 represents an active mode set flag. Now PORT A and PORT B can be configured as 8-bit input or output ports and PORT C can be configured for operation as two independent 4-bit input or output ports. This is done by setting or resetting bits D_4, D_3, D_1, and D_0.

For example, if $80_{16} = 10000000_2$ is written to the control register, the 1 in D_7 activates the mode set flag. MODE 0 operation is selected for all three ports because bits D_6, D_5, and D_2 are logic 0. At the same time, the 0's in D_4, D_3, D_1, and D_0 set up all port lines to work as outputs. This configuration is illustrated in Fig. 6.11(a).

By writing different binary combinations into bit locations D_4, D_3, D_1, and D_0, any one of 16 different MODE 0 I/O configurations can be obtained. The control word and I/O setup for the rest of these combinations are shown in Fig. 6.11(b) through (p).

Example 6.3

What is the mode and I/O configuration for ports A, B, and C of an 8255A after its control register is loaded with 82_{16}?

Solution.   Expressing the control register contents in binary form, we get

$$D_7D_6D_5D_4D_3D_2D_1D_0 = 10000010_2$$

Since D_7 is 1, the modes of operation of the ports are selected by the control word. The 3 least significant bits of the word configure PORT B and the lower 4 bits of PORT C. They give

$D_0 = 0$ Lower 4 bits of PORT C are outputs

$D_1 = 1$ PORT B are inputs

$D_2 = 0$ MODE 0 operation for both PORT B

and the lower 4 bits of PORT C

The next 4 bits configure the upper part of PORT C and PORT A.

$D_3 = 0$ Upper 4 bits of PORT C are outputs

$D_4 = 0$ PORT A are outputs

$D_6D_5 = 00$ MODE 0 operation for both PORT A and the upper part of PORT C

This MODE 0 I/O configuration is shown in Fig. 6.11(c).

MODE 1 operation represents what is known as *strobed I/O*. The ports of the 8255A are put into this mode of operation by setting $D_7 = 1$ to activate the mode set flag and setting $D_6 D_5 = 01$ and $D_2 = 1$.

In this way, the A and B ports are configured as two independent *byte-word I/O ports* each of which has a *4-bit control/data port* associated with it. The control/data ports are formed from the lower and upper nibbles of PORT C, respectively.

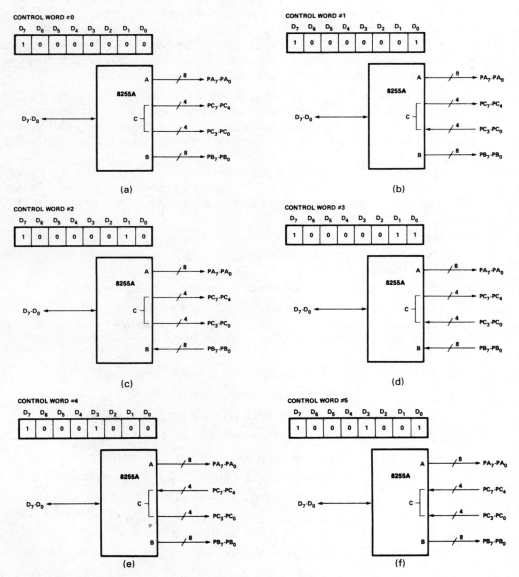

Figure 6.11 Mode 0 control words and corresponding input/output configurations (Intel Corporation).

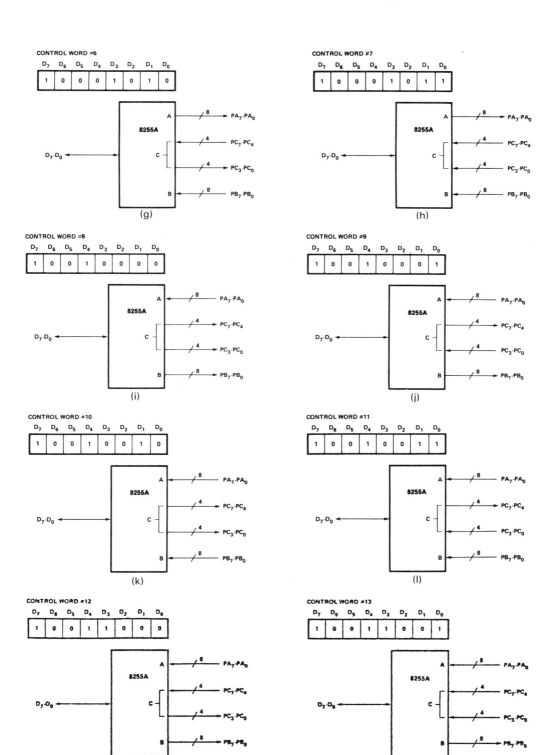

Figure 6.11 *(continued)*

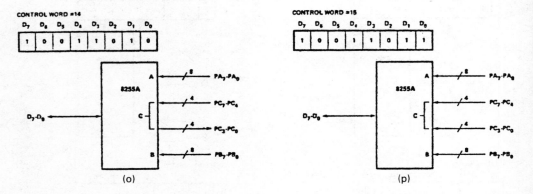

Figure 6.11   *(continued)*

When configured in this way, data applied to an input port must be strobed in with a signal produced in external hardware. Moreover, an output port is provided with handshake signals that indicate when new data are available at its outputs and when an external device has read these values.

As an example, let us assume for the moment that the control register of an 8255A is loaded with $D_7D_6D_5D_4D_3D_2D_1D_0 = 10111XXX$. This configures PORT A as a MODE 1 input port. Figure 6.12(a) shows the function of the signal lines for this example. Notice that PA_7 through PA_0 form an 8-bit input port. On the other hand, the function of the upper PORT C leads are reconfigured to provide the PORT A control/data lines. The PC_4 line becomes $\overline{STB}_A$ *(strobe input)*, which is used to strobe data at PA_7 through PA_0 into the input latch. Moreover, PC_5 becomes IBF_A *(input buffer full)*. Logic 1 at this output indicates to external circuitry that a word has already been strobed into the latch.

The third control signal is at PC_3 and is labeled $INTR_A$ *(interrupt request)*. It switches to logic 1 as long as $\overline{STB}_A = 1$, $IBF_A = 1$, and an internal signal

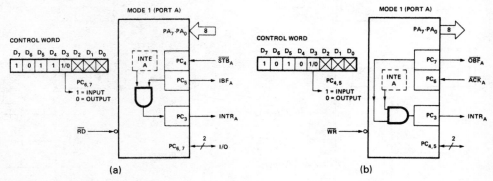

Figure 6.12   (a) Mode 1 port A input configuration (Intel Corporation); (b) mode 1 port A output configuration (Intel Corporation).

INTE$_A$ (*interrupt enable*) equals 1. INTE$_A$ is set to logic 0 or 1 under software control by using the bit set/reset feature of the 8255A. Looking at Fig. 6.12(a) we see that logic 1 in INTE$_A$ enables the logic level of IBF$_A$ to the INTR$_A$ output. This signal can be applied to an interrupt input of the 8086 to signal it that new data are available at the input port. The corresponding interrupt service routine can read the data and clear the interrupt request.

As another example, let us assume that the contents of the control register are changed to $D_7D_6D_5D_4D_3D_2D_1D_0$ = 10101XXX. This I/O configuration is shown in Fig. 6.12(b). Notice that PORT A is now configured for output operation instead of input operation. PA$_7$ through PA$_0$ are now an 8-bit output port. The control line at PC$_7$ is $\overline{OBF}_A$ (*output buffer full*). When data have been written into the output port, $\overline{OBF}_A$ switches to the 0 logic level. In this way, it signals external circuitry that new data are available at the port outputs.

Signal line PC$_6$ becomes $\overline{ACK}_A$ (*acknowledge*), which is an input. An external device can signal the 8255A that it has accepted the data provided at the output port by switching this input to logic 0. The last signal at the control port is output INTR$_A$ (*interrupt request*), which is produced at the PC$_3$ lead. This output is switched to logic 1 when the $\overline{ACK}_A$ input is active. It is used to signal the 8086 with an interrupt that indicates that an external device has accepted the data from the outputs. INTR$_A$ switches to the 1 level when $\overline{OBF}_A$ = 1, $\overline{ACK}_A$ = 0, and INTE$_A$ = 1. Again the interrupt enable (INTE$_A$) bit must be set to 1 under software control.

Example 6.4

Figure 6.13(a) and (b) show how PORT B can be configured for MODE 1 operation. Describe what happens in Fig. 6.13(a) when the $\overline{STB}_B$ input is pulsed to logic 0. Assume that INTE$_B$ is already set to 1.

Solution. As $\overline{STB}_B$ is pulsed, the byte of data at PB$_7$ through PB$_0$ are latched into the PORT B register. This causes the IBF$_B$ output to switch to 1. Since INTE$_B$ is 1, INTR$_B$ also switches to logic 1.

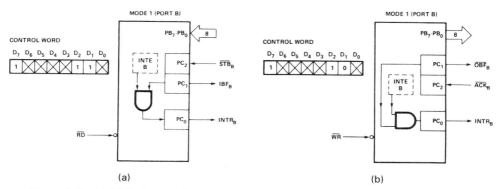

Figure 6.13   (a) Mode 1 port B input configuration (Intel Corporation); (b) mode 1 port B output configuration (Intel Corporation).

The last mode of operation, MODE 2, represents what is known as *strobed bidirectional I/O*. The key difference is that now the port works as either inputs or outputs and control signals are provided for both functions. Only PORT A can be configured to work in this way.

To set up this mode, the control register is set to $D_7D_6D_5D_4D_3D_2D_1D_0 =$ 11XXXXXX. The I/O configuration that results is shown in Fig. 6.14. Here we find that PA_7 through PA_0 operate as an *8-bit bidirectional port* instead of a unidirectional port. Its control signals are: $\overline{OBF}_A$ at PC_7, $\overline{ACK}_A$ at PC_6, $\overline{STB}_A$ at PC_4, IBF_A at PC_5, and $INTR_A$ at PC_3. Their functions are similar to those already discussed for MODE 1. One difference is that $INTR_A$ is produced by either gating $\overline{OBF}_A$ with $INTE_1$ or IBF_A with $INTE_2$.

In our discussion of MODE 1, we mentioned that the *bit set/reset* feature could be used to set the INTE bit to logic 0 or 1. This feature also allows the individual bits of PORT C to be set or reset. To do this, we write logic 0 to bit D_7 of the control register. This resets the bit set/reset flag. The logic level that is to be latched at a PORT C line is included as bit D_0 of the control word. This value is latched at the I/O line of PORT C, which corresponds to the 3-bit code at $D_3D_2D_1$.

The relationship between the set/reset control word and input/output lines is illustrated in Fig. 6.15. For instance, writing $D_7D_6D_5D_4D_3D_2D_1D_0 = 00001111_2$ into the control register of the 8255A selects bit 7 and sets it to 1. Therefore, output PC_7 at PORT C is switched to the 1 logic level.

Example 6.5

The interrupt control flag $INTE_A$ is controlled by bit set/reset of PC_6. What command code must be written to the control register of the 8255A to set its value to logic 1?

Solution. To use the set/reset feature, D_7 must be logic 0. Moreover, $INTE_A$ is to be set to logic 1; therefore, D_0 must be logic 1. Finally, to select PC_6, the code at bits $D_3D_2D_1$ must be 110. The rest of the bits are don't-care states.

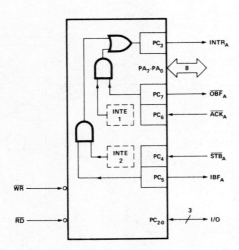

Figure 6.14 Mode 2 input/output configuration (Intel Corporation).

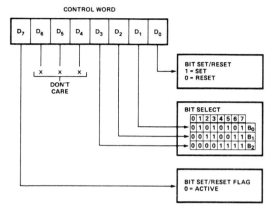

Figure 6.15 Bit set/reset format (Intel Corporation).

This gives the control word

$$D_7D_6D_5D_4D_3D_2D_1D_0 = 0XXX1101_2$$

Replacing the don't-care states with the 0 logic level, we get

$$D_7D_6D_5D_4D_3D_2D_1D_0 = 00001101_2 = 0D_{16}$$

We have just described and given examples of each of the modes of operation that can be assigned to the ports of the 8255A. In practice, the A and B ports are frequently configured with different modes. For example, Fig. 6.16(a) shows the control word and port configuration of an 8255A set up for bidirectional MODE 2 operation of PORT A and input MODE 0 operation of PORT B.

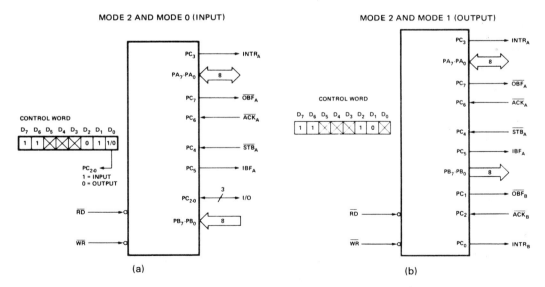

Figure 6.16 (a) Combined mode 2 and mode 0 (input) control word and I/O configuration (Intel Corporation); (b) combined mode 2 and mode 1 (output) control word and I/O configuration (Intel Corporation).

Example 6.6

What control word must be written into the control register of the 8255A such that PORT A is configured for bidirectional operation and PORT B is set up with MODE 1 outputs?

Solution.   To configure the mode of operation of the ports of the 8255A, D_7 must be 1.

$$D_7 = 1$$

PORT A is set up for bidirectional operation by making D_6 logic 1. In this case, D_5 through D_3 are don't-care states.

$$D_6 = 1$$

$$D_5 D_4 D_3 = XXX$$

MODE 1 is selected for PORT B by logic 1 in bit D_2 and output operation by logic 0 in D_1. Since MODE 1 operation has been selected, D_0 is a don't-care state.

$$D_2 = 1$$

$$D_1 = 0$$

$$D_0 = X$$

This gives the control word

$$D_7 D_6 D_5 D_4 D_3 D_2 D_1 D_0 = 11XXX10X_2$$

Assuming logic 0 for the don't-care states, we get

$$D_7 D_6 D_5 D_4 D_3 D_2 D_1 D_0 = 11000100_2 = C4_{16}$$

This configuration is shown in Fig. 6.16(b).

6.8 8255A IMPLEMENTATION OF PARALLEL I/O PORTS

The circuit in Fig. 6.17 shows how PPI devices can be connected to the bus of the 8086 to implement parallel input/output ports. This circuit configuration is for a minimum-mode 8086 system. Here we find that two groups each of up to eight 8255A devices are connected to the bus. Each group has its own 8205 address decoder. This decoder selects one of the devices at a time for input or output data transfers. The ports in the upper group are connected at odd-address boundaries and those in the lower group are at even-address boundaries. Each of these PPI devices provide up to three-byte-wide ports. In the circuit, they are labeled PORT A, PORT B, and PORT C. These ports can be individually configured as inputs or outputs through software. Therefore, each group is capable of implementing up to 192 I/O lines.

Let us look more closely at the connection of the upper port. Starting with the inputs of the 8205 address decoder, we see that its enable inputs are $\overline{E}_1 = \overline{BHE}$ and $\overline{E}_2 = M/\overline{IO}$. $\overline{BHE}$ is logic 0 whenever the 8086 outputs an odd address on the bus. Moreover, $M/\overline{IO}$ is switched to logic 0 whenever an I/O bus cycle is in progress. For this reason, the upper decoder is enabled for I/O bus cycles to an odd address in its part of the I/O address range.

When the 8205 decoder is enabled, the code at its A_0 through A_2 inputs causes one of the eight 8255A PPIs to get enabled for operation. Bits A_5 through A_3 of the I/O address are applied to these inputs of the decoder. It responds by switching the output corresponding to this 3-bit code to the 0 logic level. Decoder outputs O_0 through O_7 are applied to the chip select $(\overline{CS})$ inputs of the odd-addressed PPIs. For instance, $A_5A_4A_3 = 000$ switches output O_0 to logic 0. This enables the first 8255A, which is numbered 1 in Fig. 6.17.

At the same time that the PPI chip is selected, the 2-bit code A_2A_1 at inputs A_1A_0 of the 8255A selects the port for which data are input or output. For example, A_2A_1 equal 00 indicates that PORT A is to be accessed.

Since the upper group is located at odd-address boundaries, input/output data transfers take place over data bus lines D_8 through D_{15}. The timing of these read/write transfers are controlled by signals $\overline{RD}$ and $\overline{WR}$.

Example 6.7

What must be the address inputs of the even-addressed group of 8255As in Fig. 6.17 if PORT C of PPI 14 is to be accessed?

Solution. To enable PPI 14, the 8205 must be enabled for operation and its O_7 output switched to logic 0. This requires enable input $A_0 = 0$ and chip select code $A_5A_4A_3 = 111$.

$$A_0 = 0 \qquad \text{Enables 8205}$$

$$A_5A_4A_3 = 111 \qquad \text{Selects PPI 14}$$

PORT C of PPI 14 is selected with $A_1A_0 = 10$.

$$A_2A_1 = 10 \qquad \text{Accesses PORT C}$$

The rest of the address bits are don't-care states.

6.9 MEMORY-MAPPED I/O

I/O devices such as the 8255A can be placed in the memory address space of the 8086 system as well as in an independent I/O address space. In this case the 8086 looks at an I/O port as though it were a memory location. For this reason, the method is known as *memory-mapped I/O*. In memory-mapped systems, some of the memory address space is dedicated to I/O ports. This permits talking to I/O ports using memory-oriented instructions such as MOV instead of the IN and OUT instructions.

The disadvantages of using this method are that part of the memory address space is lost and also the memory instructions tend to execute more slowly than those specifically designed for I/O. However, these disadvantages are frequently overcome by benefits such as that a larger number of instructions and addressing modes can be used to transfer data between the 8086 and its I/O ports. Another advantage is that data can now be located in registers other than just AL or AX.

The *memory-mapped I/O interface* of a minimum mode 8086 system is essentially the same as that employed in the accumulator I/O circuit of Fig. 6.17. Figure 6.18 shows the equivalent memory-mapped circuit. Ports are still selected by an address on the address bus and byte or word data are transferred between the 8086 and I/O

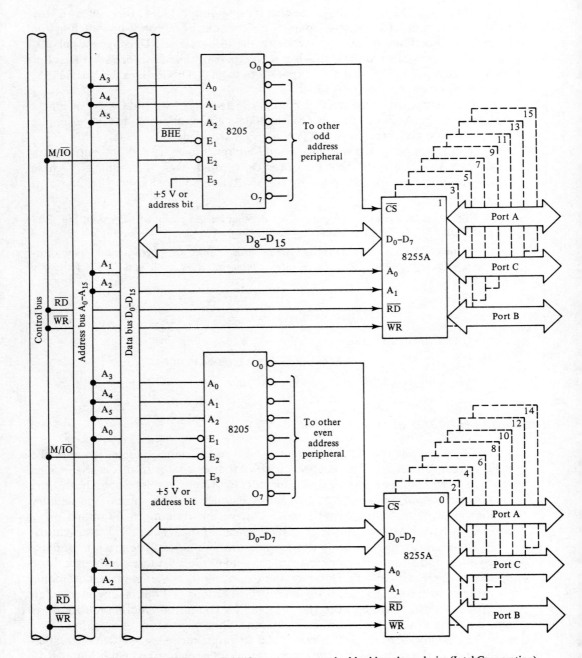

Figure 6.17   8255A parallel I/O ports at even- and odd-address boundaries (Intel Corporation).

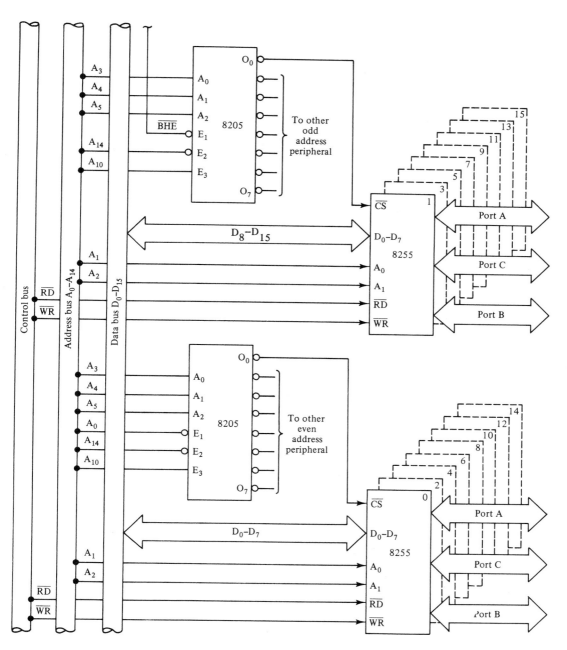

Figure 6.18   Memory-mapped 8255A I/O ports (Intel Corporation).

device over the data bus. One difference is that now the full 20-bit address is available for addressing I/O. Therefore, memory-mapped I/O devices can reside anywhere in the 1M address space of the 8086.

Another difference is that during I/O operations memory read and write bus cycles are initiated instead of I/O bus cycles. This is because we are using memory instructions, not input/output instructions, to perform the data transfers. Furthermore, $M/\overline{IO}$ stays at the 1 logic level throughout the bus cycle. This indicates that a memory operation is in progress instead of an I/O operation.

The key difference between the circuits in Figs. 6.17 and 6.18 is that $M/\overline{IO}$ is no longer used as an enable input to the 8205. Instead, it is replaced by address bits A_{14} at enable input $\overline{E}_2$ and A_{10} at E_3. The I/O circuits are accessed whenever A_{14} is equal to logic 0 and A_{10} is equal to logic 1.

Example 6.8

Which I/O port in Fig. 6.18 is selected for operation when the memory address output on the bus is 0402_{16}?

Solution. We begin by converting the address to binary form. This gives

$$A_{15} \cdots A_1 A_0 = 0000010000000010_2$$

In this address, bits $A_{14} = 0$, $A_{10} = 1$, and $A_0 = 0$. Therefore, the lower 8205 address decoder is enabled.

$$A_{14} = 0 \quad \text{Enables lower 8205 decoder}$$

$$A_{10} = 1$$

$$A_0 = 0$$

A memory-mapped I/O operation takes place to the port selected by $A_5 A_4 A_3 = 000$. This input code switches decoder output O_0 to logic 0 and chip selects PPI 0 for operation.

$$A_5 A_4 A_3 = 000 \quad \text{Selects PPI 0}$$

$$O_0 = 0$$

The port select inputs of the PPI are $A_2 A_1 = 01$. These inputs cause PORT B to be accessed.

$$A_2 A_1 = 01 \quad \text{PORT B accessed}$$

Thus the address 0402_{16} selects PORT B on PPI 0.

ASSIGNMENT

Section 6.2

1. What is the function of the 8086's address and data bus lines relative to input/output operation?

   2. In a minimum-mode 8086 system, which signal indicates to external circuitry that the current bus cycle is for the I/O interface and not the memory interface?

   3. In a maximum-mode 8086 system, how does the 8086 indicate to external circuitry that an I/O operation is in progress?

Section 6.3

   4. Can an I/O device be located at address $A0000_{16}$? Explain your answer.

Section 6.4

   5. Describe the operation initiated by the instruction IN AX,1AH.

   6. Write an instruction sequence to perform the same operation as that of the instruction in problem 5 but this time use register DX to address the I/O port.

Section 6.5

   7. Describe the sequence of events that take place at the I/O interface as the instruction of problem 5 is executed.

Section 6.6

   8. Write a sequence of instructions to output the word contents of the memory location called DATA to output ports 0 and 1 in the circuit of Fig. 6.8.

Section 6.7

   9. Describe the MODE 0, MODE 1, and MODE 2 I/O operations of the 8255A PPI.

   10. What should be the control word if ports A, B, and C are all to be configured for MODE 0 operation? Moreover, ports A and B are to be used as inputs and C as an output.

   11. Assume that the control register of an 8255A resides at memory address 0100_{16}. Write an instruction sequence to load it with the control word formed in problem 10.

Section 6.8

   12. What are the addresses of the A, B, and C ports of PPI 1 in the circuit of Fig. 6.17?

   13. Assume that PPI 1 in Fig. 6.17 is configured as defined in problem 10. Write a program that will input the data at ports A and B, add these values together, and output the sum to port C.

Section 6.9

   14. Distinguish between memory-mapped I/O and accumulator I/O.

   15. Repeat problem 13 for the circuit in Fig. 6.18.

7

Interrupt Interface of the 8086 Microprocessor

7.1 INTRODUCTION

In Chapter 6 we covered the input/output interface of the 8086 microcomputer system. Here we continue with a special input interface, the *interrupt interface*. The following topics are presented in this chapter:

1. Types of interrupts
2. Interrupt address pointer table
3. Interrupt instructions
4. Masking of interrupts
5. External hardware interrupt interface
6. External hardware interrupt sequence
7. The 8259A interrupt controller
8. 8259A minimum-mode-system interrupt interface
9. 8259A maximum-mode-system interrupt interface
10. Software interrupts
11. Nonmaskable interrupt
12. Reset interrupt
13. Internal interrupt functions

180

7.2 TYPES OF INTERRUPTS

Interrupts provide a mechanism for changing program environment. Transfer of program control is initiated by either the occurrence of an event internal to the 8086 microprocessor or an event in its external hardware. For instance, when an interrupt signal occurs indicating that an external device, such as a printer, requires service, the 8086 must suspend what it is doing in the main part of the program and pass control to a special routine that performs the function required by the device.

The section of program to which control is passed is called the *interrupt service routine*. When the 8086 terminates execution in the main program, it remembers the location where it left off and then picks up execution with the first instruction in the service routine. After this routine has run to completion, program control is returned to the point where the 8086 originally left the main body of the program.

The 8086 microcomputer is capable of implementing any combination of up to 256 interrupts. They are divided into five groups: *external hardware interrupts, software interrupts, internal interrupts*, the *nonmaskable interrupt*, and the *reset interrupt*. The function of the external hardware, software, and nonmaskable interrupts can be defined by the user. On the other hand, the internal and reset interrupts have dedicated system functions.

Hardware, software, and internal interrupts are serviced on a *priority* basis. Priority is achieved by assigning to each interrupt a *type number*. *Type 0* identifies the *highest-priority* interrupt and *type 255* the *lowest-priority* interrupt. Actually, a few of the type numbers are not available for use with software or hardware interrupts. This is because they are reserved for special interrupt functions of the 8086. In external hardware, a type number (priority level) is associated with an interrupt input lead.

The importance of priority lies in the fact that if an interrupt service routine has been initiated to perform a function at a specific priority level, only devices with higher priority can interrupt the active service routine. Lower-priority devices will have to wait until the routine is completed before their request for service can be acknowledged. For this reason, the user normally assigns tasks that must not be interrupted frequently to higher-priority levels and those that can be interrupted to lower-priority levels. An example of a high-priority service routine that should not be interrupted is that for a power failure.

Whenever the 8086 is executing instructions, it always makes a check during the last clock cycle of the current instruction to determine whether or not an interrupt is pending. If an interrupt is pending, it tests for the occurrence of the various groups based on the hierarchy that follows: internal interrupt, nonmaskable interrupt, software interrupt, and external hardware interrupt. Thus we see that internal interrupts are the *highest-priority group* and the external hardware interrupts are the *lowest-priority group*. However, if no interrupts are pending, the 8086 simply executes the next instruction in the program.

We just pointed out that once an interrupt service routine is initiated, it can be interrupted only by a function that corresponds to a higher-priority level. For example, if a level 50 external hardware interrupt is in progress, it can be interrupted by any software interrupt, the nonmaskable interrupt, all internal interrupts, or any external interrupt with type number less than 50. That is, external hardware interrupts with priority levels equal to 50 or greater are *masked out*.

7.3 INTERRUPT ADDRESS POINTER TABLE

An *address pointer table* is used to link the interrupt type numbers to the locations of their service routines in the program storage memory. Figure 7.1 shows a map of the pointer table in the memory of the 8086 microcomputer system. Looking at this table, we see that it contains 256 *address pointers (vectors)*. One pointer corresponds to each of the interrupt types 0 through 255. These address pointers identify the starting locations of their service routines in program memory.

Notice that the pointer table is located at the low-address end of the memory address space. It starts at address 00000_{16} and ends at $003FE_{16}$. This represents the first 1K bytes of memory.

Each of the 256 pointers requires two words (four bytes) of memory. These words are stored at even-address boundaries. The higher-addressed word of the two-

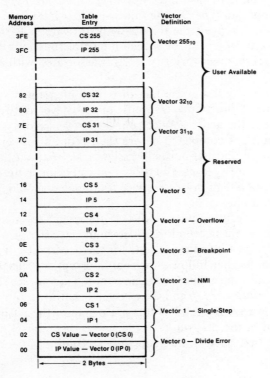

Figure 7.1 Interrupt vector table (Intel Corporation).

word vector is called the *base address*. It identifies the program memory segment in which the service routine resides. For this reason, it is loaded into the code segment (CS) register within the 8086.

The lower-addressed word of the vector is the *offset* of the first instruction of the service routine from the beginning of the code segment defined by the base address loaded into CS. This offset is loaded into the instruction pointer (IP) register. For example, the vector for type number 255, IP_{255} and CS_{255}, is stored at addresses $003FC_{16}$ and $003FE_{16}$.

Looking more closely at the table in Fig. 7.1, we find that the first five pointers have *dedicated functions*. Pointers 0, 1, 3, and 4 are required for the 8086's internal interrupts: *divide error, single step, breakpoint*, and *overflow*. Pointer 2 is used to identify the starting location of the nonmaskable interrupt's service routine. The next 27 pointers, 5 through 31, represent a *reserved portion* of the pointer table. That is, these locations can be used only for storage of interrupt vectors.

The rest of the table, the 224 pointers in the address range 00080_{16} through $003FF_{16}$, are available to the user for storage of interrupt vectors. These pointers correspond to type numbers 32 through 255 and can be employed by hardware or software interrupts. This part of memory is not reserved for pointer storage. That is, if it is not in use for storage of pointers, it can be used for storage of data.

Example 7.1

At what address should vector CS_{50} and IP_{50} be stored in memory?

Solution. Each vector requires four consecutive bytes of memory for storage. Therefore, its address can be found by multiplying the type number by 4. Since CS_{50} and IP_{50} represent the words of the type 50 interrupt pointer, we get

$$\text{Address} = 4 \times 50 = 200$$

Converting to binary form gives

$$\text{Address} = 11001000_2$$

and expressing it as a hexadecimal number results in

$$\text{Address} = C8_{16}$$

Therefore, IP_{50} is stored at $000C8_{16}$ and CS_{50} at $000CA_{16}$.

7.4 INTERRUPT INSTRUCTIONS

A number of instructions are provided in the instruction set of the 8086 for use with interrupt processing. These instructions are listed with a brief description of their functions in Fig. 7.2.

For instance, the first two instructions, which are STI and CLI, permit manipulation of the 8086's interrupt flag through software. STI stands for *set interrupt enable flag*. Execution of this instruction enables the external interrupt input (INTR) for operation. That is, it sets interrupt flag (IF). On the other hand, execution of CLI

Mnemonic	Meaning	Format	Operation	Flags Affected
CLI	Clear interrupt flag	CLI	$0 \rightarrow (IF)$	IF
STI	Set interrupt flag	STI	$1 \rightarrow (IF)$	IF
INT n	Type n software interrupt	INT n	$(Flags) \rightarrow ((SP) - 2)$ $0 \rightarrow TF, IF$ $(CS) \rightarrow ((SP) - 4)$ $(2 + 4 \cdot n) \rightarrow (CS)$ $(IP) \rightarrow ((SP) - 6)$ $(4 \cdot n) \rightarrow (IP)$	TF, IF
IRET	Interrupt return	IRET	$((SP)) \rightarrow (IP)$ $((SP) + 2) \rightarrow (CS)$ $((SP) + 4) \rightarrow (Flags)$ $(SP) + 6 \rightarrow (SP)$	All
INTO	Interrupt on overflow	INTO	INT 4 steps	TF, IF
HLT	Halt	HLT	Wait for an external interrupt or reset to occur	None
WAIT	Wait	WAIT	Wait for $\overline{TEST}$ input to go active	None

Figure 7.2 Interrupt instructions.

(*clear interrupt enable flag*) disables the external interrupt input. It does this by resetting IF.

The next instruction listed in Fig. 7.2 is the *software interrupt* instruction INT n. It is used to initiate a software vector call of a subroutine. Executing the instruction causes transfer of program control to the subroutine pointed to by the vector for type number n specified in the instruction.

For example, execution of the instruction INT 50 initiates execution of a subroutine whose starting point is identified by vector 50 in the pointer table. That is, the 8086 reads IP_{50} and CS_{50} from addresses $000C8_{16}$ and $000CA_{16}$, respectively, in memory, generates a physical address, and starts to fetch instructions from this new location in program memory.

An *interrupt return* (IRET) instruction must be included at the end of each interrupt service routine. It is required to pass control back to the point in the program where execution was terminated due to the occurrence of the interrupt. When executed, IRET causes the three words IP, CS, and flags to be popped from the stack back into the internal registers of the 8086. This restores the original program environment.

INTO is the *interrupt on overflow* instruction. This instruction must be included after arithmetic instructions that can generate an overflow condition, such as divide. It tests the overflow flag and if the flag is found to be set, a type 4 internal interrupt is initiated. This causes program control to be passed to an overflow service routine that is located at the starting address identified by the vector IP_4 at 00010_{16} and CS_4 at 00012_{16} of the pointer table.

The last two instructions associated with the interrupt interface are *halt* (HLT) and *wait* (WAIT). They produce similar responses by the 8086 and permit the operation of the 8086 to be synchronized to an event in external hardware. For instance, when HLT is executed, the 8086 suspends operation and enters the idle state. It no longer executes instructions; instead, it remains idle waiting for the occurrence of an external hardware interrupt or reset interrupt. With the occurrence of either of these two events, the 8086 resumes execution with the corresponding service routine.

If the WAIT instruction is used instead of the HLT instruction, the 8086 checks the logic level of the $\overline{\text{TEST}}$ input prior to going into the idle state. Only if $\overline{\text{TEST}}$ is at logic 1 will the MPU go into the idle state. While in the idle state, the 8086 continues to check the logic level at $\overline{\text{TEST}}$ looking for its transition to the 0 logic level. As $\overline{\text{TEST}}$ switches back to 0, execution resumes with the next sequential instruction in the program.

7.5 MASKING OF INTERRUPTS

An interrupt enable flag bit is provided within the 8086. Earlier we found that it is identified as IF. It affects only the external hardware interrupt interface, not the software or internal interrupts. The ability to initiate an external hardware interrupt at the INTR input is enabled by setting IF or masked out by resetting it. Through software, this can be done by executing the STI instruction or the CLI instruction, respectively.

During the initiation sequence of an interrupt service routine, the 8086 automatically clears IF. This masks out the occurrence of an external hardware interrupt. If necessary, the interrupt flag bit can be set with an STI instruction at the beginning of the service routine to reenable the INTR input.

7.6 EXTERNAL HARDWARE INTERRUPT INTERFACE

Up to this point in the chapter, we have introduced the interrupts of the 8086, its pointer table, interrupt instructions, and masking of interrupts. Let us now look at the *external hardware interrupt interface* of the 8086.

Minimum-System Interrupt Interface

We will begin with an 8086 microcomputer configured for the minimum system mode. The interrupt interface for this system is illustrated in Fig. 7.3. Here we see that it includes the multiplexed address/data bus and dedicated interrupt signal lines INTR and $\overline{\text{INTA}}$. Moreover, external circuitry is required to interface the interrupt inputs to the 8086's interrupt interface. This interface circuitry must identify which of the pending active interrupts has the highest priority and then pass its type number to the 8086.

In this circuit we see that the key interrupt interface signals are *interrupt request* (INTR) and *interrupt acknowledge* ($\overline{\text{INTA}}$). The logic level input at the INTR

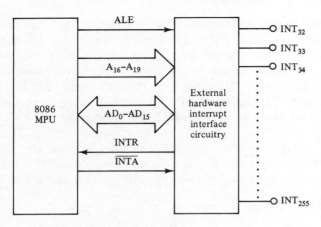

Figure 7.3 Minimum-mode 8086 system external hardware interrupt interface.

line signals the 8086 that an external device is requesting service. The 8086 samples this input during the last clock period of each instruction execution cycle. Logic 1 represents an active interrupt request. INTR is *level triggered*; therefore, its active 1 level must be maintained until tested by the 8086. If it is not maintained, the request for service may not be recognized. Moreover, the 1 at INTR must be removed before the service routine runs to completion; otherwise, the same interrupt may be acknowledged a second time.

When an interrupt request has been recognized by the 8086, it signals this fact to external circuitry. It does this with pulses to logic 0 at its INTA output. Actually, there are just two pulses produced at INTA during the *interrupt acknowledge bus cycle*. The first pulse signals external circuitry that the interrupt request has been acknowledged and to prepare to send its type number to the 8086. The second pulse tells the external circuitry to put the type number on the data bus.

Notice that the lower 16 lines of the address/data bus, AD_0 through AD_{15}, are also part of the interrupt interface. During the second cycle in the interrupt acknowledge bus cycle, external circuitry must put an 8-bit type number on bus lines AD_0 through AD_7. The 8086 reads this number off the bus to identify which external device is requesting service. It uses the type number to generate the address of the interrupt's vector in the pointer table and to read the new values of CS and IP into the corresponding internal registers. CS and IP are transferred over the full 16-bit data bus. The old values of CS, IP, and the internal flags are automatically pushed to the stack part of memory. These word-wide transfers take place over the complete data bus.

Maximum-Mode Interrupt Interface

The maximum-mode interrupt interface of the 8086 microcomputer is shown in Fig. 7.4. The primary difference between this interrupt interface and that shown for the minimum mode in Fig. 7.3 is that the 8288 bus controller has been added. In the maximum mode system, the bus controller produces the INTA and ALE signals.

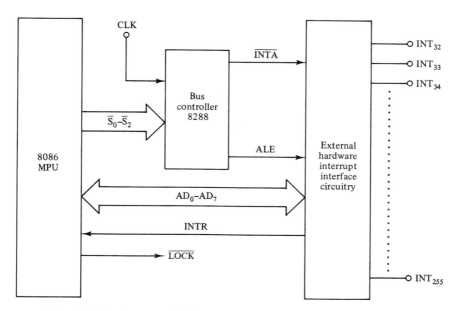

Figure 7.4 Maximum-mode 8086 system external hardware interrupt interface.

Whenever the 8086 outputs an interrupt acknowledge bus status code, the 8288 generates pulses at its $\overline{\text{INTA}}$ output to signal external circuitry that the 8086 has acknowledged an interrupt request. This interrupt acknowledge bus status code, $\overline{S}_2\overline{S}_1\overline{S}_0 = 000$, is highlighted in Fig. 7.5.

A second change in Fig. 7.4 is that the 8086 provides a new signal for the interrupt interface. This output, which is labeled $\overline{\text{LOCK}}$, is called the *bus priority lock* signal. $\overline{\text{LOCK}}$ is applied as an input to the *bus arbiter circuit*. In response to this signal, the arbitration logic assures that no other device can take over control of the system bus until the interrupt acknowledge bus cycle is completed.

Status inputs			CPU cycle	8288 command
$\overline{S}_2$	$\overline{S}_1$	$\overline{S}_0$		
0	0	0	Interrupt acknowledge	$\overline{\text{INTA}}$
0	0	1	Read I/O port	$\overline{\text{IORC}}$
0	1	0	Write I/O port	$\overline{\text{IOWC}}$, $\overline{\text{AIOWC}}$
0	1	1	Halt	None
1	0	0	Instruction fetch	$\overline{\text{MRDC}}$
1	0	1	Read memory	$\overline{\text{MRDC}}$
1	1	0	Write memory	$\overline{\text{MWTC}}$, $\overline{\text{AMWC}}$
1	1	1	Passive	None

Figure 7.5 Interrupt bus status code (Intel Corporation).

7.7 EXTERNAL HARDWARE INTERRUPT SEQUENCE

In the preceding section we showed the interrupt interfaces for the external hardware interrupts in minimum-mode and maximum-mode 8086 systems. Now we will continue by describing in detail the events that take place during the interrupt request, interrupt acknowledge bus cycle, and device service routine.

The interrupt sequence begins when an external device requests service by activating one of the interrupt inputs, INT_{32} through INT_{255} of the external interrupt interface circuit in Fig. 7.3 or Fig. 7.4. For example, the INT_{50} input could be switched to the 1 logic level. This signals that the device associated with priority level 50 wants to be serviced.

The external circuitry evaluates the priority of this input. If there is no interrupt already in progress or if this interrupt is of higher priority than that which is presently active, the external circuitry must issue a request for service to the 8086.

Let us assume that INT_{50} is the only active interrupt input. In this case, the external circuitry switches INTR to logic 1. This tells the 8086 that an interrupt is pending for service. To assure that it is recognized, the external circuitry must maintain INTR active until an interrupt acknowledge pulse is issued by the 8086.

The 8086 tests the logic level at INTR during the last clock state of the current instruction. If it is logic 1, a request for service is recognized. Before the 8086 initiates the interrupt acknowledge sequence, it checks the setting of IF. If it is logic 0, external interrupts are masked out and the request is ignored. In this case, the next sequential instruction is executed. On the other hand, if IF is at logic 1, external hardware interrupts are enabled and the service routine is to be initiated.

Let us assume that IF is set to permit interrupts to occur when INTR is tested as 1. Then the 8086 clears IF. This disables further external interrupts from requesting service. Actually, the TF flag is also cleared. This disables the single-step mode of operation if it happens to be active.

Next, the 8086 automatically pushes the contents of the flag register, CS, and IP onto the stack. This requires three write cycles to take place over the system bus. The current value of the stack pointer is decremented by 2 as each of these values is put onto the top of the stack.

The 8086 responds with two consecutive interrupt acknowledge bus cycles. These cycles are illustrated in Fig. 7.6. During T_1 of the first bus cycle, we see that a pulse is output on ALE but at the same time the address/data bus is put in the high-Z state. It stays in this state for the rest of the bus cycle. During periods T_2 and T_3, $\overline{INTA}$ is switched to logic 0. This signals external circuitry that the request for service has been granted. In response to this pulse, the logic 1 at INTR can be removed.

The signal identified as $\overline{LOCK}$ is produced only in maximum-mode systems. Notice that $\overline{LOCK}$ is switched to logic 0 during T_2 of the first INTA bus cycle and is maintained at this level until T_2 of the second INTA bus cycle. During this time, the BIU is prevented from accepting a HOLD request. Moreover, the $\overline{LOCK}$ output is used in external logic to lock other devices off the system bus, thereby assuring that the interrupt acknowledge sequence continues through to completion without interruption.

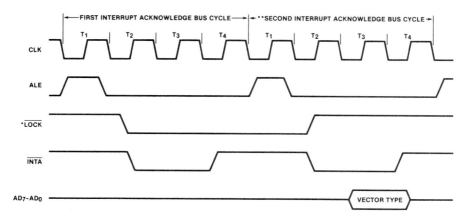

Figure 7.6 Interrupt acknowledge bus cycle (Intel Corporation).

During the second interrupt acknowledge bus cycle, a similar signal sequence occurs. However, this interrupt acknowledge pulse tells the external circuitry to put the type number of the active interrupt on the data bus. External circuitry gates one of the interrupt codes $32 = 20_{16}$ through $255 = FF_{16}$, onto data bus lines AD_0 through AD_7. This code must be valid during periods T_3 and T_4 of the second interrupt acknowledge bus cycle.

The 8086 sets up its bus control signals for an input data transfer to read the type number off the data bus. $DT/\overline{R}$ and $\overline{DEN}$ are set to logic 0 to enable the external data bus circuitry and set it for input of data. Also, $M/\overline{IO}$ is set to 0, indicating that data are to be input from the interrupt interface. During this input operation, the byte interrupt code is read off the data bus. For the case of INT_{50}, this code would be $00110010_2 = 32_{16}$. This completes the interrupt acknowledge part of the interrupt sequence.

Now the 8086 knows the type number associated with the external device that is requesting service. It must now fetch the vector that defines the starting point of its service routine from memory. The type number is internally multiplied by 4, and this result is used as the address of the first word of the interrupt vector in the pointer table.

Two read bus cycles are performed to read the two-word vector from memory. The first word, which is the lower-addressed word, is loaded into IP. The second, higher-addressed word, is loaded into CS. For instance, the vector for INT_{50} would be read from addresses $000C8_{16}$ and $000CA_{16}$.

The service routine is now initiated. That is, execution resumes with the first instruction of the service routine. It is located at the address generated from the new value in CS and IP. The service routine must include PUSH instructions to save the contents of those internal registers that it will use. Their contents are also saved in the stack.

At the end of the service routine, the original program environment must be restored. This is done by first popping the appropriate registers from the stack by executing POP instructions. Then the IRET instruction must be executed as the last instruction of the service routine. This instruction causes the old contents of the flags, CS, and IP to be popped from the stack back into the internal registers of the 8086. The original program environment has now been completely restored and execution resumes at the point in the program where it was interrupted.

7.8 THE 8259A PROGRAMMABLE INTERRUPT CONTROLLER

The 8259A is an LSI peripheral IC that is designed to simplify the implementation of the interrupt interface in an 8086 system. This device is known as a *programmable interrupt controller* or *PIC*. It is manufactured using the NMOS technology.

The operation of the PIC is programmable under software control and it can be configured for a wide variety of applications. Some of its programmable features are the ability to accept level-sensitive or edge-triggered inputs, the ability to be easily cascaded to expand from 8 to 64 interrupt inputs, and its ability to be configured to implement a wide variety of priority schemes.

Block Diagram of the 8259A

Let us begin our study of the PIC with its block diagram in Fig. 7.7(a). We just mentioned that the 8259A is treated as a peripheral in the 8086 microcomputer. Therefore, its operation must be initialized by the 8086 processor. The *host processor interface* is provided for this purpose. This interface consists of eight *data bus* lines D_0 through D_7 and control signals *read* ($\overline{RD}$), *write* ($\overline{WR}$), and *chip select* ($\overline{CS}$). The data bus is the path over which data are transferred between the 8086 and 8259A. These data can be command words, status information, or interrupt type numbers. Control input $\overline{CS}$ must be at logic 0 to enable the host processor interface. Moreover, $\overline{WR}$ and $\overline{RD}$ signal the 8259A whether data are to be written into or read from its internal registers. They also control the timing of these data transfers.

Two other signals are identified as part of the host processor interface. They are INT and $\overline{INTA}$. Together, these two signals provide the handshake mechanism by which the 8259A can signal the 8086 of a request for service and receive an acknowledgment that the request has been accepted. INT is the interrupt request output of the 8259A. It is applied directly to the INTR input of the 8086. Logic 1 is produced at this output whenever the 8259A receives a valid interrupt request.

On the other hand, $\overline{INTA}$ is an input of the 8259A. It is connected to the $\overline{INTA}$ output of the 8086. The 8086 pulses this input of the 8259A to logic 0 twice during the interrupt acknowledge bus cycle. Thereby, signaling the 8259A that the interrupt request has been acknowledged and that it should output the type number of the highest-priority active interrupt on data bus lines D_0 through D_7 such that it can be read by the 8086.

At the other side of the block in Fig. 7.7(a), we find the eight *interrupt inputs* of the PIC. They are labeled IR_0 through IR_7. It is through these inputs that external devices issue a request for service. One of the software options of the 8259A permits

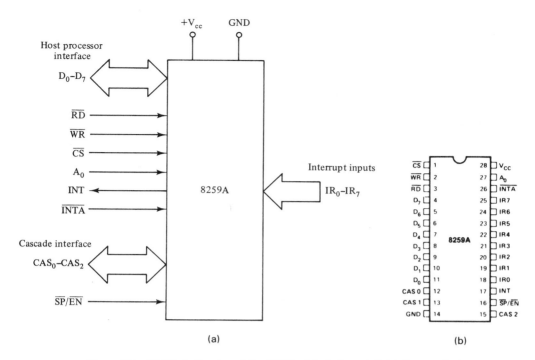

Figure 7.7   (a) Block diagram of the 8259A; (b) pin layout (Intel Corporation).

these inputs to be configured for *level-sensitive* or *edge-triggered operation.*

When configured for level-sensitive operation, logic 1 is the active level of the IR inputs. In this case, the request for service must be removed before the service routine runs to completion. Otherwise, the interrupt will be requested a second time and the service routine initiated again. Moreover, if the input returns to logic 0 before it is acknowledged by the 8086, the request for service will be missed.

Some external devices produce a short-duration pulse instead of a fixed logic level for use as an interrupt request signal. If the 8086 is busy servicing a higher-priority interrupt when the pulse is produced, the request for service could be completely missed. To overcome this problem, the edge-triggered mode of operation is used.

Inputs of the 8259A that are set up for edge-triggered operation become active on the transition from the inactive 0 logic level to the active 1 logic level. This represents what is known as a *positive edge-triggered input.* The fact that this transition has occurred at an IR line is latched internal to the 8259A. If the IR input remains at the 1 logic level even after the service routine is completed, the interrupt is not reinitiated. Instead, it is locked out. To be recognized a second time, the input must first return to the 0 logic level and then be switched back to 1. The advantage of edge-triggered operation is that if the request at the IR input is removed before the 8086 acknowledges service of the interrupt, its request is maintained latched internal to the 8259A until it can be serviced.

The last group of signals on the PIC implement what is known as the *cascade interface*. As shown in Fig. 7.7(a), it includes bidirectional *cascading bus lines* CAS_0 through CAS_2 and a multifunction control line labeled $\overline{SP/EN}$. The primary use of these signals is in cascaded systems where a number of 8259A ICs are interconnected in a master/slave configuration to expand the number of IR inputs from 8 to as high as 64.

In a cascaded system, the CAS lines of all 8259As are connected together to provide a private bus between the master and slave devices. In response to the first $\overline{INTA}$ pulse during the interrupt acknowledge bus cycle, the master PIC outputs a 3-bit code on the CAS lines. This code identifies the highest-priority slave that is to be serviced. It is this device that is to be acknowledged for service. All slaves read this code off the *private cascading bus* and compare it to their internal ID code. A match condition tells the slave that it has the highest-priority input. In response, it puts the type number of its highest-priority active input on the data bus during the second interrupt acknowledge bus cycle.

When the PIC is configured through software for the cascaded mode, the $\overline{SP/EN}$ line is used as an input. This corresponds to its $\overline{SP}$ (*slave program*) function. The logic level applied at $\overline{SP}$ tells the device whether it is to operate as a master or slave. Logic 1 at this input designates master mode and logic 0 designates slave mode.

If the PIC is configured for single mode instead of cascade mode, $\overline{SP/EN}$ takes on another function. In this case, it becomes an enable output which can be used to control the direction of data transfer through the bus transceiver that buffers the data bus.

A pin layout of the 8259A is given in Fig. 7.7(b).

Internal Architecture of the 8259A

Now that we have introduced the input/output signals of the 8259A, let us look at its internal architecture. Figure 7.8 is a block diagram of the PIC's internal circuitry. Here we find eight functional parts: the *data bus buffer, read/write logic, control logic, in-service register, interrupt request register, priority resolver, interrupt mask register*, and *cascade buffer/comparator*.

We will begin with the function of the data bus buffer and read/write logic sections. It is these parts of the 8259A that let the 8086 have access to the internal registers. Moreover, it provides the path over which interrupt type numbers are passed to the 8086. The data bus buffer is an 8-bit bidirectional three-state buffer that interfaces the internal circuitry of the 8259A to the data bus of the 8086. The direction, timing, and source or destination for data transfers through the buffer are under control of the outputs of the read/write logic block. These outputs are generated in response to control inputs $\overline{RD}$, $\overline{WR}$, A_0, and $\overline{CS}$.

The interrupt request register, in-service register, priority resolver, and interrupt mask register are the key internal blocks of the 8259A. The interrupt mask register (IMR) can be used to enable or mask out individually the interrupt request inputs. It contains 8 bits identified by M_0 through M_7. These bits correspond to interrupt

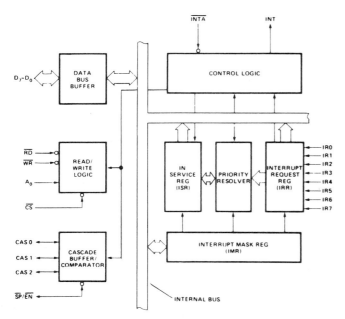

Figure 7.8 Internal architecture of the 8259A (Intel Corporation).

inputs IR_0 through IR_7, respectively. Logic 0 in a bit position enables the corresponding interrupt input and logic 1 masks it out. This register can be read from or written into under software control.

On the other hand, the interrupt request register (IRR) stores the status of the interrupt request inputs. It also contains one bit position for each of the IR inputs. The values in these bit positions reflect whether the interrupt inputs are active or inactive.

Which of the active interrupt inputs is identified as having the highest priority is determined by the priority resolver. This section can be configured to work using a number of different priority schemes through software. Following this scheme, it identifies the highest priority of the active interrupt inputs and signals the control logic that an interrupt is active. In response, the control logic causes the INT signal to be issued to the 8086.

The in-service register differs in that it stores the interrupt level that is presently being serviced. During the first $\overline{INTA}$ pulse in an interrupt acknowledge bus cycle, the level of the highest active interrupt is strobed into ISR. Loading of ISR occurs in response to output signals of the control logic section. This register cannot be written into; however, its contents may be read as status through software.

The cascade buffer/comparator section provides the interface between master and slave 8259As. As we mentioned earlier, it is this interface that permits easy expansion of the interrupt interface using a master/slave configuration. Each slave has an *ID code* that is stored in this section.

Programming the 8259A

The way in which the 8259A operates is determined by how the device is programmed. Two types of command words are provided for this purpose. They are the *initialization command words* (ICW) and the *operational command words* (OCW). ICW commands are used to load the internal control registers of the 8259A. There are four such command words and they are identified as ICW_1, ICW_2, ICW_3, and ICW_4. On the other hand, the three OCW commands permit the 8086 to initiate variations in the basic operating modes defined by the ICW commands. These three commands are called OCW_1, OCW_2, and OCW_3.

The 8086 issues commands to the 8259A by initiating output or write cycles. This can be done by executing either the OUT or MOV instruction, respectively.

LSI peripherals such as the 8259A must be located at even-word address boundaries in the 8086's address space. The address put on the system bus during the output bus cycle must be decoded with external circuitry to chip select the peripheral. When an address assigned to the 8259A is on the bus, the output of the decoder must produce logic 0 at the $\overline{CS}$ input. This signal enables the read/write logic within the PIC and data applied at D_0 through D_7 are written into the command register within the control logic section synchronously with a write strobe at $\overline{WR}$.

The interrupt request input (INTR) of the 8086 must be disabled whenever commands are being issued to the 8259A. This can be done by clearing the interrupt enable flag by executing the CLI (clear interrupt enable flag) instruction. After completion of the command sequence, the interrupt input must be reenabled. To do this, the 8086 must execute the STI (set interrupt enable flag) instruction.

The flow diagram in Fig. 7.9 shows the sequence of events that the 8086 must perform to initialize the 8259A with ICW commands. The cycle begins with the 8086 outputting initialization command word ICW_1 to the address of the 8259A.

The moment that ICW_1 is written into the control logic section of the 8259A certain internal setup conditions automatically occur. First the internal sequence logic is set up such that the 8259A will accept the remaining ICWs as designated by ICW_1. It turns out that if the least significant bit of ICW_1 is logic 1, command word ICW_4 is required in the initialization sequence. Moreover, if the next least significant bit of ICW_1 is logic 0, the command word ICW_3 is also required.

In addition to this, writing ICW_1 to the 8259A clears ISR and IMR. Also three operation command word bits, *special mask mode* (SMM) in OCW_3, *interrupt request register* (IRR) in OCW_3, and *end of interrupt* (EOI) in OCW_2, are cleared to logic 0. Furthermore, the *fully masked mode* of interrupt operation is entered with an initial priority assignment such that IR_0 is the highest-priority input and IR_7 the lowest-priority input. Finally, the edge-sensitive latches associated with the IR inputs are all cleared.

If the LSB of ICW_1 was initialized to logic 0, one additional event occurs. This is that all bits of the control register associated with ICW_4 are cleared.

In Fig. 7.9 we see that once the 8086 starts initialization of the 8259A by writing ICW_1 into the control register, it must continue the sequence by writing ICW_2 and

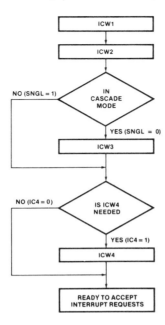

Figure 7.9 Initialization sequence of the 8259A (Intel Corporation).

then optionally ICW_3 and ICW_4 in that order. Notice that it is not possible to modify just one of the initialization command registers. Instead, all words that are required to define the device's operating mode must be output once again.

We found that all four words need not always be used to initialize the 8259A. However, for its use in the 8086 system, words ICW_1, ICW_2, and ICW_4 are always required. ICW_3 is optional and is needed only if the 8259A is to function in the cascade mode.

Initialization Command Words

Now that we have introduced the initialization sequence of the 8259A, let us look more closely at the functions controlled by each of the initialization command words. We will begin with ICW_1. Its format and bit functions are identified in Fig. 7.10(a). Notice that address bit A_0 is included as a ninth bit and it must be logic 0. This corresponds to an even address boundary.

Here we find that the logic level of the LSB D_0 of the initialization word indicates to the 8259A whether or not ICW_4 will be included in the programming sequence. As we mentioned earlier, logic 1 at D_0 (IC_4) specifies that it is needed. The next bit, D_1 (SNGL), selects between *single device* or *multidevice cascaded mode* of operation. When D_1 is set to logic 0, the internal circuitry of the 8259A is configured for cascaded mode. Selecting this state also sets up the initialization sequence such that ICW_3 must be issued as part of the initialization cycle. Bit D_2 has functions specified for it in Fig. 7.10(a). However, it can be ignored when the 8259A is being connected to the 8086 and is a don't-care state. D_3, which is labeled LTIM, defines

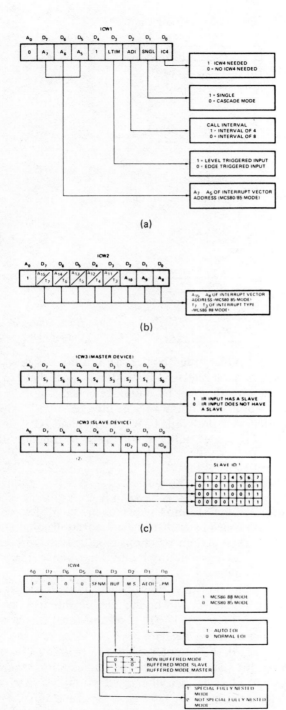

Figure 7.10 (a) ICW$_1$ format (Intel Corporation); (b) ICW$_2$ format (Intel Corporation); (c) ICW$_3$ format (Intel Corporation); (d) ICW$_4$ format (Intel Corporation).

whether the eight IR inputs operate in the level-sensitive or edge-triggered mode. Logic 1 in D_3 selects level-triggered operation and logic 0 selects edge-triggered operation. Finally, bit D_4 is fixed at the 1 logic level and the three MSBs D_5 through D_7 are not required in 8086 systems.

Example 7.2

What value should be written into ICW_1 in order to configure the 8259A such that ICW_4 is needed in the initialization sequence, the system is going to use multiple 8259As, and its inputs are to be level sensitive? Assume that all unused bits are to be logic 0. Give the result in both binary and hexadecimal form.

Solution.   Since ICW_4 is to be initialized, D_0 must be logic 1.

$$D_0 = 1$$

For cascaded mode of operation, D_1 must be 0

$$D_1 = 0$$

and for level-sensitive inputs D_3 must be 1.

$$D_3 = 1$$

Bits D_2 and D_5 through D_7 are don't-care states and are all made logic 0.

$$D_2 = D_5 = D_6 = D_7 = 0$$

Moreover, D_4 must be fixed at the 1 logic level.

$$D_4 = 1$$

This gives the complete command word

$$D_7D_6D_5D_4D_3D_2D_1D_0 = 00011001_2 = 19_{16}$$

The second initialization word, ICW_2, has a single function in the 8086 system. As shown in Fig. 7.10(b), its five most significant bits D_7 through D_3 define a fixed binary code T_7 through T_3 that is used as the most significant bits of its type number. Whenever the 8259A puts the 3-bit interrupt type number corresponding to its active input onto the bus, it is automatically combined with the value T_7 through T_3 to form an 8-bit type number. The three least significant bits of ICW_2 are not used. Notice that logic 1 must be output on A_0 when this command word is put on the bus.

Example 7.3

What should be programmed into register ICW_2 if the type numbers output on the bus by the device are to range from $F0_{16}$ through $F7_{16}$?

Solution.   To set the 8259A up such that type numbers are in the range $F0_{16}$ through $F7_{16}$, its device code bits must be

$$D_7D_6D_5D_4D_3 = 11110_2$$

The lower 3 bits are don't-care states and all can be 0s. This gives the command word

$$D_7D_6D_5D_4D_3D_2D_1D_0 = 11110000_2 = F0_{16}$$

The information of initialization command word ICW_3 is required by only those

8259As that are configured for the cascaded mode of operation. Figure 7.10(c) shows its bits. Notice that ICW_3 is used for different functions depending on whether the device is a master or slave. In the case of a master, bits D_0 through D_7 of the word are labeled S_0 through S_7. These bits correspond to IR inputs IR_0 through IR_7, respectively. They identify whether or not the corresponding IR input is supplied by either the INT output of a slave or directly by an external device. Logic 1 loaded in an S position indicates that the corresponding IR input is supplied by a slave.

On the other hand, ICW_3 for a slave is used to load the device with a 3-bit identification code $ID_2ID_1ID_0$. This number must correspond to the IR input of the master to which the slave's INT output is wired. The ID code is required within the slave so that it can be compared to the cascading code output by the master on CAS_0 through CAS_2.

Example 7.4

Assume that a master PIC is to be configured such that its IR_0 through IR_3 inputs are to accept inputs directly from external devices but IR_4 through IR_7 are to be supplied by the INT outputs of slaves. What code should be used for the initialization command word ICW_3?

Solution. For IR_0 through IR_3 to be configured to allow direct inputs from external devices, bits D_0 through D_3 of ICW_3 must be logic 0.

$$D_3D_2D_1D_0 = 0000_2$$

The other IR inputs of the master are to be supplied by INT outputs of slaves. Therefore, their control bits must be all 1.

$$D_7D_6D_5D_4 = 1111_2$$

This gives the complete command word

$$D_7D_6D_5D_4D_3D_2D_1D_0 = 11110000_2 = F0_{16}$$

The fourth control word, ICW_4, which is shown in Fig. 7.10(d), is used to configure the device for use with the 8086 and selects various features that are available in its operation. The LSB D_0, which is called uPM, must be set to logic 1 whenever the device is used together with the 8086. The next bit, D_1, is labeled AEOI for *automatic end of interrupt*. If this mode is enabled by writing logic 1 into the bit location, the EOI (*end of interrupt*) command does not have to be issued as part of the service routine.

Of the next two bits in ICW_4, BUF is used to specify whether or not the 8259A is to be used in a system where the data bus is buffered with a bidirectional bus transceiver. When buffered mode is selected, the $\overline{SP}/\overline{EN}$ line is configured as $\overline{EN}$. As indicated earlier, $\overline{EN}$ is a control output that can be used to control the direction of data transfer through the bus transceiver. It switches to logic 0 whenever data are transferred from the 8259A to the 8086.

If buffered mode is not selected, the $\overline{SP}/\overline{EN}$ line is configured to work as the master/slave mode select input. In this case, logic 1 at the $\overline{SP}$ input selects master mode operation and logic 0 selects slave mode.

Assume that the buffered mode was selected; then the $\overline{SR}$ input is no longer available to select between the master and slave modes of operation. Instead, the MS bit of ICW_4 defines whether the 8259A is a master or slave device.

Bit D_4 is used to enable or disable another operational option of the 8259A. This option is known as the *special fully nested mode*. This function is only used in conjunction with the cascaded mode. Moreover, it is enabled only for the master 8259A, not for the slaves. This is done by setting the SFNM bit to logic 1.

The 8259A is put into the fully nested mode of operation as command word ICW_1 is loaded. When an interrupt is initiated in a cascaded system that is configured in this way, the occurrence of another interrupt at the slave corresponding to the original interrupt is masked out even if it is of higher priority. This is because the bit in ISR of the master 8259A that corresponds to the slave is already set; therefore, the 8259A ignores all interrupts of equal or lower priority.

This problem is overcome by enabling the special fully nested mode of operation at the master. In this mode, the master will respond to those interrupts that are at lower or higher priority than the active level.

The last 3 bits of ICW_4, D_5 through D_7, must always be logic 0 and the word must be written to an odd-address boundary.

Operational Command Words

Once the appropriate ICW commands have been issued to the 8259A, it is ready to operate in the fully nested mode. Three operational command words are also provided for controlling the operation of the 8259A. These commands permit further modifications to be made to the operation of the interrupt interface after it has been initialized. Unlike the initialization sequence, which requires that the ICWs be output in a special sequence after power-up, the OCWs can be issued under program control whenever needed and in any order.

The first operational command word, OCW_1, is used to access the contents of the interrupt mask register (IRR). A read operation can be performed to the register to determine its present status. Moreover, write operations can be performed to set or reset its bits. This permits selective masking of the interrupt inputs. Notice in Fig. 7.11(a) that bits D_0 through D_7 of command word OCW_1 are identified as mask bits M_0 through M_7, respectively. In hardware, these bits correspond to interrupt inputs IR_0 through IR_7, respectively. Setting a bit to logic 1 masks out the associated interrupt input. On the other hand, clearing it to logic 0 enables the interrupt input.

For instance, writing $F0_{16} = 11110000_2$ into the register causes inputs IR_0 through IR_3 to be enabled and IR_4 through IR_7 to be disabled. A_0 must be logic 1 whenever the OCW_1 command is issued.

Example 7.5

What should be the OCW_1 code if interrupt inputs IR_0 through IR_3 are to be disabled and IR_4 through IR_7 enabled?

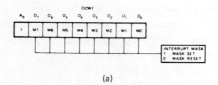

(a)

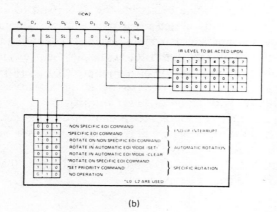

(b)

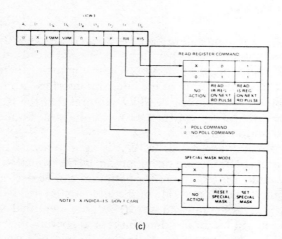

NOTE 1 X INDICATES DON'T CARE

(c)

Figure 7.11 (a) OCW_1 format (Intel Corporation); (b) OCW_2 format (Intel Corporation); (c) OCW_3 format (Intel Corporation).

Solution. For IR_0 through IR_3 to be disabled, their corresponding bits in the mask register must be made logic 1.

$$D_3D_2D_1D_0 = 1111_2$$

On the other hand, for IR_4 through IR_7 to be enabled D_4 through D_7 must be logic 0.

$$D_7D_6D_5D_4 = 0000_2$$

Therefore, the complete word for OCW_1 is

$$D_7D_6D_5D_4D_3D_2D_1D_0 = 00001111_2 = 0F_{16}$$

The second operational command word OCW_2 selects the appropriate priority scheme and assigns an IR level for those schemes that require a specific interrupt level. The format of OCW_2 is given in Fig. 7.11(b). Here we see that the three LSBs define the interrupt level. For example, using $L_2L_1L_0 = 000_2$ in these locations specifies interrupt level 0, which corresponds to input IR_0.

The other three active bits of the word D_7, D_6, and D_5 are called *rotation* (R), *specific level* (SL), and *end of interrupt* (EOI), respectively. They are used to select a priority scheme according to the table in Fig. 7.11(b). For instance, if these bits are all logic 1, the priority scheme known as *rotate on specific EOI command* is enabled. Since this scheme requires a specific interrupt, its value must be included in $L_2L_1L_0$. A_0 must be logic 0 whenever this command is issued to the 8259A.

Example 7.6

What ICW_2 must be issued to the 8259A if the priority scheme rotate on nonspecific EOI command is to be selected?

Solution.   To enable the rotate on nonspecific EOI command priority scheme, bits D_7 through D_5 must be set to 101. Since a specific level does not have to be specified, the rest of the bits in the command word can be 0. This gives OCW_2 as

$$D_7D_6D_5D_4D_3D_2D_1D_0 = 10100000_2 = A0_{16}$$

The last control word OCW_3, which is shown in Fig. 7.11(c), permits reading of the contents of the ISR or IRR registers through software, issue of the poll command, and enable/disable of the special mask mode. Bit D_1, which is called *read register* (RR), is set to 1 to initiate reading of either the in-service register (ISR) or interrupt request register (IRR). At the same time, bit D_0, which is labeled RIS, selects between ISR and IRR. Logic 0 in RIS selects IRR and logic 1 selects ISR. In response to this command, the 8259A puts the contents of the selected register on the bus, where it can be read by the 8086.

If the next bit, D_2, in OCW_3 is logic 1, a *poll command* is issued to the 8259A. The result of issuing a poll command is that the next $\overline{RD}$ pulse to the 8259A is interpreted as an interrupt acknowledge. In turn, the 8259A causes the ISR register to be loaded with the value of the highest-priority active interrupt. After this, a *poll word* is automatically put on the data bus. The 8086 must read it off the bus.

Figure 7.12 illustrates the format of the poll word. Looking at this word, we see that the MSB is labeled I for interrupt. The logic level of this bit indicates to the 8086 whether or not an interrupt input was active. Logic 1 indicates that an interrupt is active. The three LSBs $W_2W_1W_0$ identify the priority level of the highest-priority active interrupt input. This poll word can be decoded through software and when an interrupt is found to be active a branch is initiated to the starting point of its service routine. The poll command represents a software method of identifying

W0-W2 = BINARY CODE OF HIGHEST PRIORITY LEVEL REQUESTING SERVICE

I = 1 IF AN INTERRUPT OCCURRED

Figure 7.12 Poll word format (Intel Corporation).

whether or not an interrupt has occurred; therefore, the INTR input of the 8086 should be disabled.

D$_5$ and D$_6$ are the remaining bits of OCW$_3$ for which functions are defined. They are used to enable or disable the special mask mode. ESMM (*enable special mask mode*) must be logic 1 to permit changing of the status of the special mask mode with the SMM (*special mask mode*) bit. Logic 1 at SMM enables the special mask mode of operation. If the 8259A is initially configured for the fully nested mode of operation, only interrupts of higher priority are allowed to interrupt an active service routine. However, by enabling the special mask mode, interrupts of higher or lower priority are enabled, but those of equal priority remain masked out.

7.9 MINIMUM-MODE-SYSTEM AND MAXIMUM-MODE-SYSTEM INTERRUPT INTERFACES USING THE 8259A

Now that we have introduced the 8259A programmable interrupt controller, let us look at how it is used to implement the interrupt interface in the 8086 microcomputer system. The circuit in Fig. 7.13 shows three 8259A devices connected in a *master/slave configuration* to construct an interrupt interface for a minimum-mode 8086 microcomputer system.

Let us begin by tracing the path taken from the interrupt request inputs of the slaves to the interrupt request input of the 8086. A request for interrupt service is initiated at an input of a slave. This causes the INT output of the corresponding slave to switch to logic 1. Looking at the circuit, we see that the INT output of the slave PICs are applied to separate interrupt inputs on the master PIC. Then the INT output of the master is supplied directly to the interrupt request input of the 8086.

Notice that the demultiplexed address bus and data bus lines connect to all three 8259As in parallel. It is over these lines that the 8086 initializes the internal registers

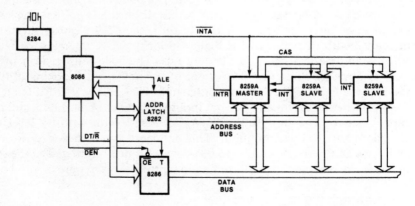

Figure 7.13 Minimum-mode interrupt interface using the 8259A (Intel Corporation).

of the 8259As, reads the contents of these registers, and reads the type number of the active interrupt during the interrupt acknowledge bus cycle. Each 8259A should reside at a unique address. In this way, during read or write cycles to the interrupt interface, the address output on the bus can be decoded to produce an enable signal to chip-select the appropriate device.

The last group of signals in the interrupt interface are the CAS bus. Notice that these lines on all three PICs are connected in parallel. It is over these lines that the master signals the slaves whether or not the interrupt request has been acknowledged.

Whenever an interrupt input is active at the master or at a slave and the priority is higher than that of an already active interrupt, the master controller switches INTR to logic 1. This signals the 8086 that an external device needs to be serviced. As long as the interrupt flag within the 8086 is set to 1, the interrupt interface is enabled and the interrupt request will be accepted. Therefore, the interrupt acknowledge bus cycle is initiated. As the first pulse is output at interrupt acknowledge (INTA), the master PIC is signaled to put the 3-bit cascade code of the device whose interrupt request is being acknowledged on the CAS bus. The slaves read this code and compare it to their internal code. In this way, the slave corresponding to the code is signaled to put the type number of its highest-priority active interrupt onto the data bus. The 8086 reads this number off the bus and then initiates a vectored transfer of control to the starting point of the corresponding service routine in program memory.

Figure 7.14 illustrates a similar interrupt interface implemented in a maximum-mode 8086 microcomputer system.

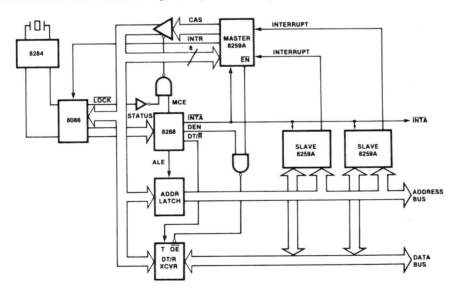

Figure 7.14 Maximum-mode interrupt interface using the 8259A (Intel Corporation).

7.10 SOFTWARE INTERRUPTS

The 8086 system is capable of implementing up to 252 software interrupts. They differ from the external hardware interrupts in that their service routines are initiated in response to the execution of a software interrupt instruction, not an event in external hardware.

The INT n instruction is used to initiate a software interrupt. Earlier in this chapter we indicated that "n" represents the type number associated with the service routine. The software interrupt service routines are vectored to, using pointers from the same memory locations as the corresponding external hardware interrupts. These locations are shown in the pointer table of Fig. 7.1. Our earlier example was INT 50. It has a type number of 50 and causes a vector in program control to the service routine whose starting address is defined by the values of IP and CS stored at addresses $00C8_{16}$ through $00CB_{16}$, respectively.

The mechanism by which a software interrupt is initiated is similar to that described for the external hardware interrupts. However, no external interrupt acknowledge bus cycles are initiated. Instead, control is passed to the start of the service routine immediately upon completion of execution of the interrupt instruction. As usual, the old flags, old CS, and old IP are automatically saved on the stack and then IF and TF are cleared.

If necessary, the contents of other internal registers can be saved on the stack by including the appropriate PUSH instructions at the beginning of the service routine. Toward the end of the service routine, POP instructions must be included to restore these registers. Finally, an IRET instruction is included to restore the original program environment.

Software interrupts are of higher priority than the external interrupts and are not masked out by IF. The software interrupts are actually *vectored subroutine calls*. A common use of these software routines is as *emulation routines* for more complex functions. For instance, INT_{50} could define a *floating-point addition instruction* and INT_{51} a *floating-point subtraction instruction*. These emulation routines are written using assembly language instructions, are assembled into machine code, and then are stored in the main memory of the 8086 microcomputer system. Other examples of their use are for *supervisor calls* from an operating system and for *testing* of external hardware interrupt service routines.

7.11 NONMASKABLE INTERRUPT

The nonmaskable interrupt (NMI) is another interrupt that is initiated from external hardware. However, it differs from the other external hardware interrupts in several ways. First, it cannot be masked out with the IF flag. Second, requests for service by this interrupt are signaled to the 8086 with the 1 logic level at its NMI input, not the INTR input. Third, the NMI input is positive edge triggered. Therefore, a request for service is latched internal to the 8086.

If the contents of the NMI latch is sampled as being active for two consecutive clock cycles, it is recognized and the nonmaskable interrupt sequence initiated. Initiation of NMI causes the current flags, current CS, and current IP to be pushed onto the stack. Moreover, the interrupt enable flag is cleared to disable all external hardware interrupts and the trap flag is cleared to disable the single-step mode of operation.

As shown in Fig. 7.1, NMI has a dedicated priority level. It automatically vectors from the type 2 vector location in the pointer table. This vector is stored in memory at word addresses 0008_{16} and $000A_{16}$.

Typically, the NMI is assigned to hardware events that must be responded to immediately. Two examples are the detection of a power failure and detection of a memory read error.

7.12 RESET INTERRUPT

The RESET interrupt input of the 8086 provides a hardware means for initializing the 8086 microcomputer. This is typically done at power-up to provide an orderly startup of the system.

Figure 7.15(a) shows that the reset interface of the 8086 includes part of the 8284 clock generator device. The 8284 contains circuitry that makes it easy to implement the hardware reset function. Notice that the $\overline{\text{RES}}$ input (pin 11) of the clock generator is attached to an *RC* circuit. The signal at $\overline{\text{RES}}$ is applied to the input of a Schmitt trigger circuit. If the voltage across the capacitor is below the 1-logic-level threshold of the Schmitt trigger, the RESET output (pin 10) stays at logic 1. This

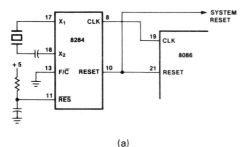

(a)

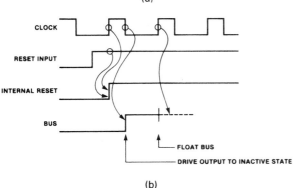

(b)

Figure 7.15   (a) Reset interface of the 8086 (Intel Corporation); (b) reset timing sequence (Intel Corporation).

output is supplied to the RESET input at pin 21 of the 8086. It can also be applied in parallel to reset inputs on LSI peripheral devices such that they are also initialized at power-on.

At power-on, $\overline{RES}$ of the 8284 is shorted to ground through the capacitor. This represents logic 0 at the input of the Schmitt trigger and RESET switches to logic 1. At the RESET input of the 8086, this signal is synchronized to the 0-to-1 edge of CLK. This is shown in the waveforms of Fig. 7.15(b). RESET must be held at logic 1 for a minimum of four clock cycles; otherwise, it will not be recognized.

The 8086 terminates operation on the 0 to 1 edge of the internal reset signal. Its bus is put in the high-Z state and the control signals are switched to their inactive states. These signal states are summarized in Fig. 7.16. Here we see that in a minimum-mode system signals AD_0 through AD_{15}, $AD_{16}/\overline{S}_3$ through $AD_{19}/\overline{S}_6$, and $\overline{BHE}/\overline{S}_7$ are immediately put in the high-Z state. On the other hand, signal lines $M/\overline{IO}$, $DT/\overline{R}$, $\overline{DEN}$, $\overline{WR}$, $\overline{RD}$, and $\overline{INTA}$ are first forced to logic 1 for one clock interval and then they are put in the high-Z state synchronously with the positive edge of the next clock pulse. Moreover, signal lines ALE and HLDA are forced to their inactive 0 logic level. The 8086 remains in this state until the RESET input is returned to logic 0.

Signals	Condition
AD_{15-0}	Three-State
A_{19-16}/S_{6-3}	Three-State
BHE/S_7	Three-State
$\overline{S2}/(M/\overline{IO})$	Driven to "1" then three-state
$\overline{S1}/(DT/\overline{R})$	Driven to "1" then three-state
$\overline{S0}/\overline{DEN}$	Driven to "1" then three-state
$LOCK/\overline{WR}$	Driven to "1" then three-state
$\overline{RD}$	Driven to "1" then three-state
$\overline{INTA}$	Driven to "1" then three-state
ALE	0
HLDA	0
$\overline{RQ}/\overline{GT0}$	1
$\overline{RQ}/\overline{GT1}$	1
QS0	0
QS1	0

Figure 7.16 Bus and control signal status during system reset (Intel Corporation).

In the maximum-mode system, the 8086 responds in a similar way. However, this time the $\overline{S}_2\overline{S}_1\overline{S}_0$ outputs, which are inputs to the 8288 bus controller, are also immediately put into the high-Z state. These inputs of the 8288 have internal pull-up resistors. Therefore, with the signal lines in the high-Z state, the input to the bus controller is $\overline{S}_2\overline{S}_1\overline{S}_0 = 111$. In response, its control outputs are set to ALE = 0, DEN = 0, DT/$\overline{R}$ = 1, MCE/$\overline{PDEN}$ = 0/1, and all of its command outputs are switched to the 1 logic level. Moreover, outputs QS_0 and QS_1 of the 8086 are both held at logic 0 and the $\overline{RQ}/\overline{GT}_0$ and $\overline{RQ}/\overline{GT}_1$ lines are held at logic 1.

When RESET returns to logic 0, the 8086 initiates its internal initialization routine. The flags are all cleared; the instruction pointer is set to 0000_{16}; the CS register is set to $FFFF_{16}$; the DS register is set to 0000_{16}; the SS register is set to 0000_{16};

CPU COMPONENT	CONTENT
Flags	Clear
Instruction Pointer	0000H
CS Register	FFFFH
DS Register	0000H
SS Register	0000H
ES Register	0000H
Queue	Empty

Figure 7.17   Internal state of the 8086 after initialization (Intel Corporation).

the ES register is set to 0000_{16}; and the queue is emptied. The table in Fig. 7.17 summarizes this state.

Since the flags were all cleared as part of initialization, the external hardware interrupts are disabled. Moreover, the code segment register contains $FFFF_{16}$ and the instruction pointer contains 0000_{16}. Therefore, execution begins after reset at $FFFF0_{16}$. This location can contain an instruction that will cause a jump to the start up program that is used to initialize the rest of the system's resources, such as I/O ports, the interrupt flag, and data memory. After system-level initialization is complete, another jump can be performed to the starting point of the microcomputer's application program.

7.13 INTERNAL INTERRUPT FUNCTIONS

Earlier we indicated that four of the 256 interrupts of the 8086 are dedicated to the internal functions: divide error, overflow error, single step, and breakpoint. They are assigned unique type numbers, as shown in Fig. 7.18. Notice that they are the highest-priority type numbers. Moreover, they are not masked out with the interrupt enable flag.

The occurrence of any one of these internal conditions is automatically detected by the 8086, and causes an interrupt of program execution and a vectored transfer of control to a corresponding service routine. During the control transfer sequence, no external bus cycles are produced. Let us now look at each of these internal functions in more detail.

Divide Error

The *divide error* function represents an error condition that can occur in the execution of the division instructions. If the quotient that results from a DIV (divide) instruction or an IDIV (integer divide) instruction is larger than the specified destination, a divide error has occurred. This condition causes automatic initiation of a type 0 interrupt and passes control to a service routine whose starting point is defined by the values of IP_0 and CS_0 at addresses 0000_{16} and 0002_{16}, respectively, in the pointer table.

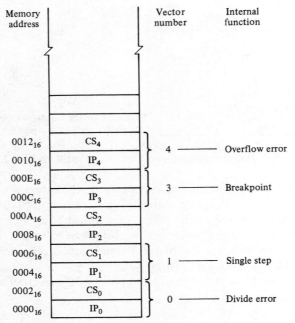

Figure 7.18 Internal interrupt vector locations.

Overflow Error

The *overflow error* is an error condition similar to that of divide error. However, it can result from the execution of any arithmetic instruction. Whenever an overflow occurs, the overflow flag gets set. In this case, the transfer of program control to a service routine is not automatic. Instead, the INTO (interrupt on overflow) instruction must be executed to test if the overflow service routine should be initiated. If the overflow flag is found to be set, a type 4 interrupt service routine is initiated. Its vector consists of IP_4 and CS_4 which are stored at 0010_{16} and 0012_{16}, respectively, in memory. The routine pointed to by this vector can be written to service the overflow condition. For instance, it could cause a message to be displayed to identify that an overflow has occurred.

Single Step

The *single-step* function relates to an operating option of the 8086. If the trap flag (TF) bit is set, the single-step mode of operation is enabled. This flag bit can be set or reset under software control.

If TF is set, the 8086 initiates a type 1 interrupt to the service routine defined by IP_1 and CS_1 at 0004_{16} and 0006_{16}, respectively, at the completion of execution of every instruction. This permits implementation of the single-step mode of operation such that the program can be executed one instruction at a time. For instance, the service routine could include a WAIT instruction. In this way, a transition to logic 0 at the $\overline{\text{TEST}}$ input of the 8086 could be used as the mechanism for stepping through a program one instruction at a time. This single-step operation can be used as a valuable software debugging tool.

Breakpoint Interrupt

The *breakpoint* function can also be used to implement a software diagnostic tool. A breakpoint interrupt is initiated by execution of the breakpoint instruction (*one-byte instruction*). This instruction can be inserted at strategic points in a program that is being debugged to cause execution to be stopped. This option can be used in a way similar to that of the single-step option. The service routine could again be put in the wait state, and resumption of execution down to the next breakpoint can be initiated by applying logic 0 to the $\overline{\text{TEST}}$ input.

ASSIGNMENT

Section 7.2

1. What are the five groups of interrupts available on the 8086 MPU?
2. What is the range of priority levels that can be assigned in an 8086 microcomputer system?

Section 7.3

3. What purpose is served by the pointer table?
4. The breakpoint service routine begins at address $AA000_{16}$ in the code segment which starts at $A0000_{16}$. Specify where and how the breakpoint vector will be stored in the pointer table.

Section 7.4

5. Explain how the CLI and STI instructions can be used to lock out external hardware interrupts during the execution of an uninterruptible subroutine.

Section 7.5

6. How can the interrupt interface be reenabled during execution of an interrupt service routine?

Section 7.6

7. Explain the function of the INTR and $\overline{\text{INTA}}$ signals in Figs. 7.3 and 7.4.

Section 7.7

8. Give an overview of the events in the order they occur during the interrupt request, interrupt acknowledge, and interrupt vector fetch cycles.

Section 7.8

9. Specify the value of ICW_1 needed to configure an 8259A as follows: ICW_4 not needed,

single device interface, and edge-triggered inputs.

10. Specify the value for ICW_2 if the type numbers produced by the 8259A are to be in the range 70_{16} through 77_{16}.

11. Specify the value of ICW_4 such that the 8259A is configured for use in an 8086 system, with normal EOI, buffered mode master, and special fully nested mode disabled.

12. Write a program that will initialize an 8259A with the initialization command words derived in problems 9, 10, and 11. Assume that the 8259A resides at address $A000_{16}$ in the memory address space.

13. Write an instruction to read OCW_1 into the AL register. Assume that the 8259A has been configured by the software of problem 12.

14. What priority scheme is enabled if OCW_2 equals 67_{16}?

15. Write an instruction sequence that when executed will toggle the state of the read register bit in OCW_3. Assume that the 8259A is located at memory address $A000_{16}$.

Section 7.9

16. How many interrupt inputs can be directly accepted by the circuit in Fig. 7.13?

Section 7.10

17. Give an overview of the context switch mechanism initiated by the instruction INT 20.

18. Show the basic structure of an interrupt service routine. Assume that the routine uses the AX, BX, CX, and DI registers.

Section 7.11

19. How does NMI differ from an external hardware interrupt?

Section 7.12

20. To what address does the reset interrupt vector?

21. Write a RESET routine that initializes the block of memory locations from address $A000_{16}$ to $A100_{16}$ to zero. The initialization routine is to start at address 1000_{16}.

Section 7.13

22. What internal interrupts are serviced by the 8086?

8

The 68000 Microprocessor

8.1 INTRODUCTION

Up to this point in the book we have studied Intel's 8086 16-bit microprocessor and its microcomputer system. We discussed its architecture, instruction set, programming, and how to interface it to memory, I/O devices, and devices that generate interrupts. Now it is time to turn our attention to Motorola's 68000 microprocessor. In this chapter we describe its general architecture. The four chapters that follow are devoted to its instruction set, programming, and hardware interfaces. The following topics are discussed in this chapter:

1. The 68000 microprocessor
2. Interface signals of the 68000
3. Internal architecture of the 68000
4. Instruction execution control

8.2 THE 68000 MICROPROCESSOR

The 68000 is a very powerful 16-bit microprocessor whose development was announced by Motorola Inc. in 1979. Since then Motorola has concentrated on bringing the device up to production, providing tools to support hardware and software development, and initiating development of a new family of LSI support peripherals. With apparent success in these areas, they have continued the growth of the product family by introducing a second microprocessor, the 68008.

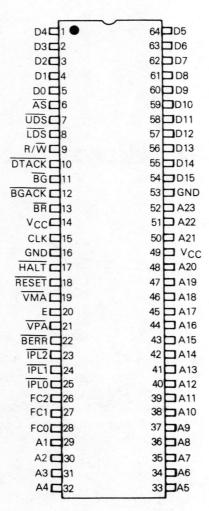

Figure 8.1 Pin layout of the 68000 microprocessor (Motorola Inc.).

Just like Intel's 8086, the 68000 is manufactured using HMOS (high-density N-channel MOS) technology. The present-day advances in circuit design, process technology, and chip fabrication techniques have enabled Motorola to implement very high performance operation and complex functions for the 68000. The circuitry within the 68000 is equivalent to approximately 68000 MOS transistors.

Unlike the 8086, the 68000 microprocessor is packaged into a 64-pin package. This package is shown together with its pin assignments in Fig. 8.1. Notice that use of the larger package eliminates the need for multifunction pins. For instance, the address bus and data bus are not multiplexed. The fact that each lead serves just one electrical function simplifies design of the external hardware interfaces in a 68000 microcomputer system.

The 68000 employs a very powerful 32-bit general-purpose internal architecture. It has 16 internal general-purpose registers that are all 32 bits in length. Eight of these registers are *data registers* and the other eight are *address registers*.

The architecture of the 68000 was planned to permit all types of data and address operations to be performed from its data registers and address registers, respectively. That is, none of its data registers have dedicated functions such as for use as an accumulator or for input/output. Therefore, instructions can be written such that their operands reside in any of the data registers or storage locations in memory. Moreover, data processed by the 68000 can be expressed in five different types. They are *bit*, *BCD (4-bit)*, *byte*, *word*, or *long word (32-bit)*.

The address registers are also designed for general use and do not have dedicated functions. For instance, if the MOVE instruction was to have its source operand located in memory instead of in one of the internal registers, any one of the address registers can be specified to contain this address.

The architecture of the 68000 also includes a number of powerful hardware and software functions. From a hardware point of view, we see that the 68000 has a large 23-bit external address bus. This gives it a much larger logical address space than the 8086. A software function that has been included in the architecture is the ability to create a *user/supervisor environment* for the 68000 microcomputer system.This feature helps the programmer to protect the software operating system and provides support for *multiprocessing* and *multitasking* applications.

8.3 INTERFACES OF THE 68000 MICROPROCESSOR

Now that we have briefly introduced the 68000 microprocessor, let us look at its electrical interfaces. From the block diagram in Fig. 8.2, we see that the signal lines can be grouped into seven interfaces: the *address/data bus, asynchronous bus control,*

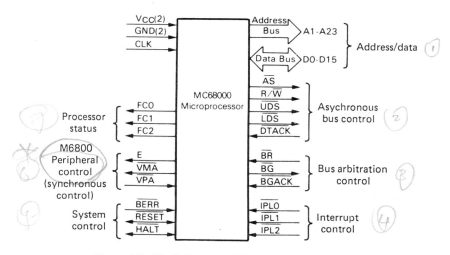

Figure 8.2   Block diagram of the 68000 (Motorola Inc.).

processor status lines, system control bus, interrupt control bus, bus arbitration control bus, and *synchronous control bus*. It is through these buses and lines that the 68000 is connected to external circuitry such as memory and input/output peripherals.

Address and Data Bus

Unlike the 8086, the 68000 has independent address and data buses. This simplifies the design of the memory and I/O interfaces because the address and data signals need not be demultiplexed with external circuitry. Another difference is that the address bus, data bus, and memory address space are used to interface to input/output devices in addition to interface to the memory subsystem. That is, all I/O devices in the 68000 microcomputer system are memory-mapped.

Earlier we indicated that the 68000 has a 23-bit *unidirectional address bus*. The function of the signals at these lines, A_{23} through A_1, is to supply addresses to the memory and input/output subsystems. A_{23} represents the most significant bit of the address and A_1 the least significant bit. Bit A_0, which is maintained internal to the 68000, indicates whether the upper or lower byte of a word is to be used when processing byte data.

The 16 *bidirectional data lines* are labeled D_{15} through D_0. They either carry read/write data between microprocessor and memory or input/output data between the microprocessor and I/O peripherals.

Asynchronous Control Bus

The control of the 68000's bus is *asynchronous*. By this we mean that once a bus cycle is initiated, it is not completed until a signal is returned from external circuitry. The signals that are provided to control address and data transfers are *address strobe* ($\overline{AS}$), *read/write* ($R/\overline{W}$), *upper data strobe* ($\overline{UDS}$), *lower data strobe* ($\overline{LDS}$), and *data transfer acknowledge* ($\overline{DTACK}$).

The 68000 must signal external circuitry when an address is available, and whether a read or write operation is to take place over the bus. It does this with the signals $\overline{AS}$ and $R/\overline{W}$, respectively. At the moment a valid address is present on the address bus, the 68000 produces the address strobe ($\overline{AS}$) control signal. The pulse to logic 0 output at $\overline{AS}$ is used to signal memory or I/O devices that an address is available.

Read/write ($R/\overline{W}$) signals which type of data transfer is to take place over the data bus. During a read or input bus cycle, when the microprocessor reads data from bus lines D_0 through D_{15}, the $R/\overline{W}$ output is switched to logic 1. Similarly, when data are written or output to memory or I/O devices, the 68000 indicates this condition by a logic 0 on this line.

Since the bus cycle is asynchronous, external circuitry must signal the 68000 when the bus cycle can be completed. Data transfer acknowledge ($\overline{DTACK}$) is an input to the microprocessor which indicates the status of the current bus cycle. During a read or input cycle, logic 0 at $\overline{\text{DTACK}}$ signals the microprocessor that valid data are on the data bus. In response, it reads and latches the data internally and completes the bus cycle. On the other hand, during a write or output operation, $\overline{\text{DTACK}}$ informs the microprocessor that the data have been written to memory or a peripheral device. Thus we see that in both cases $\overline{\text{DTACK}}$ is used to terminate the bus cycle.

Two other control outputs provided on the 68000 are upper data strobe ($\overline{\text{UDS}}$) and lower data strobe ($\overline{\text{LDS}}$). These two signals act as an extension of the address bus and signal whether a byte or word of data is being transferred over the data bus. In the case of a byte transfer, they also indicate if the data will be carried over the upper eight or lower eight data lines. Logic 0 at $\overline{\text{UDS}}$ signals that a byte of data is to be transferred across upper data lines D_{15} through D_8 and logic 0 at $\overline{\text{LDS}}$ signals that a byte of data is to be transferred over lower data lines D_7 through D_0.

Figure 8.3 shows the logic levels of $\overline{\text{UDS}}$, $\overline{\text{LDS}}$, and $R/\overline{W}$ for each type of data transfer operation. For instance, if $\overline{\text{UDS}} = 0$, $\overline{\text{LDS}} = 0$, and $R/\overline{W} = 1$, a read operation is taking place over the complete data bus.

Example 8.1

Specify the address and control signals that occur to read the lower byte from the word stored at address $001B36_{16}$.

Solution.   The address lines A_{23} through A_1 directly specify an even (upper) byte address. The odd (lower) byte address is obtained by $\overline{\text{LDS}}$ being active. Thus we get

$$A_{23}A_{22} \cdots A_1A_0 = 001B37_{16}$$
$$= 0000000000011011001101111_2$$

and

$$\overline{\text{LDS}} = 0$$
$$\overline{\text{UDS}} = 1$$

Since a byte of data is to be read,

$$R/\overline{W} = 1$$

and the data are supplied to the 68000 on the lower data lines D_0 through D_7.

$\overline{\text{UDS}}$	$\overline{\text{LDS}}$	$R/\overline{W}$	Operation
0	0	0	Word → memory/IO
0	1	0	High byte → memory/IO
1	0	0	Low byte → memory/IO
1	1	0	Invalid data
0	0	1	Word → microprocessor
0	1	1	High byte → microprocessor
1	0	1	Low byte → microprocessor
1	1	1	Invalid data

Figure 8.3   Memory access relationships for $\overline{\text{UDS}}$, $\overline{\text{LDS}}$, and $R/\overline{W}$ (Motorola Inc.).

Processor Status Bus and the Function Codes

During every bus cycle executed by the 68000, it outputs a 3-bit processor status code. These status codes are also known as *function codes* and are output on lines FC_0 through FC_2. They tell external circuitry which type of bus cycle is in progress. That is, whether data or program is being accessed and if the microprocessor is in the *user* or *supervisor state*.

The table in Fig. 8.4(a) shows the implemented function codes and also the ones that are reserved for future expansion. For instance, the code 110_2 on $FC_2FC_1FC_0$ indicates that an instruction or immediate operand acquisition bus cycle is in progress from *supervisor program memory*. Notice that 111_2 has a special function. It is the *interrupt acknowledge code*.

These codes are output by the 68000 at the beginning of each read or write cycle and remain valid until the beginning of the next read or write cycle. The timing relationship between the function code lines, the clock, and $\overline{AS}$ is shown in Fig. 8.4(b). Notice that the function code outputs are valid during the address strobe $\overline{AS}$

FC2	FC1	FC0	Cycle Type
Low	Low	Low	(Undefined, Reserved)
Low	Low	High	User Data
Low	High	Low	User Program
Low	High	High	(Undefined, Reserved)
High	Low	Low	(Undefined, Reserved)
High	Low	High	Supervisor Data
High	High	Low	Supervisor Program
High	High	High	Interrupt Acknowledge

(a)

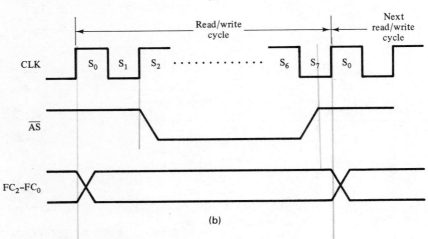

(b)

Figure 8.4 (a) Function code table (Motorola Inc.); (b) relationship between $FC_2FC_1FC_0$, CLK, and $\overline{AS}$.

pulse. Therefore, they can be combined with $\overline{\text{AS}}$ to generate device or memory select signals. As an example, the function code 001_2 can be used to gate $\overline{\text{AS}}$ to the user data section of memory.

System Control Bus

The group of control signals that are labeled as the system control bus in Fig. 8.2 are used either to control the function of the 68000 microprocessor or to indicate its operating state. There are three system control signals: *bus error* ($\overline{\text{BERR}}$), *halt* ($\overline{\text{HALT}}$), and *reset* ($\overline{\text{RESET}}$).

The control line bus error ($\overline{\text{BERR}}$) is an input that is used to inform the 68000 of a problem with the bus cycle currently in progress. For instance, it could be used to signal that the bus cycle has not been completed even after a set period of time has elapsed.

On the other hand, $\overline{\text{HALT}}$ can be used to implement a hardware mechanism for stopping the processing of the 68000. An external signal applied to the $\overline{\text{HALT}}$ input stops the microprocessor at completion of the current bus cycle. In this state all of its buses and control signals are inactive. $\overline{\text{HALT}}$ is actually a bidirectional line; that is, it has both an input and output function. When the processor stops instruction execution due to a halt condition, it informs external devices by producing an output signal at the same $\overline{\text{HALT}}$ pin.

The $\overline{\text{RESET}}$ input can be used to initiate initialization of the 68000 based on the occurrence of a signal generated in external hardware. Typically, this is done at the time of power-up. When an external reset signal is applied, the processor initiates a system initialization sequence.

The $\overline{\text{RESET}}$ line is also bidirectional, but unlike $\overline{\text{HALT}}$, its output function is initiated through software. This $\overline{\text{HALT}}$ output is used to initialize external devices such as LSI peripherals. To reset external devices connected to the $\overline{\text{RESET}}$ line, the 68000 must execute the RESET instruction. Execution of this instruction does not affect the internal state of the processor; instead, it just causes a pulse to be output at $\overline{\text{RESET}}$.

Interrupt Control Bus

In a 68000 microcomputer system, external devices request interrupt service by applying a 3-bit *interrupt request code* to the $\overline{\text{IPL}}_2$ through $\overline{\text{IPL}}_0$ inputs. This code is supplied to the microprocessor from the interrupting device to indicate its priority level. The value of $\overline{\text{IPL}}_2\overline{\text{IPL}}_1\overline{\text{IPL}}_0$ is compared to the interrupt mask value in the 68000's status register. If the encoded priority is higher than the mask, the interrupting device is serviced; otherwise, it is ignored.

Bus Arbitration Control Bus

The bus arbitration control signals provide a handshake mechanism by which control of the 68000's system bus can be transferred between devices. The device that has control of the system bus is known as the *bus master*. It controls the system address, data, and control buses. Other devices are attached to the bus but are not active. Examples of devices that can be used as masters are host processors or external devices such as *DMA controllers* or *attached processors*.

As shown in Fig. 8.2, the 68000 microprocessor has three control lines for this purpose. They are *bus request* ($\overline{BR}$), *bus grant* ($\overline{BG}$), and *bus grant acknowledge* ($\overline{BGACK}$). A device requests control of the bus by asserting the bus request ($\overline{BR}$) input. After internal synchronization, the 68000 responds by switching the bus grant ($\overline{BG}$) control output to its active low level. This means that it will give up control of the bus at completion of the current bus cycle.

At this point, the requesting device waits for the 68000 to complete its bus cycle. The fact that the bus cycle is complete is indicated by address strobe ($\overline{AS}$) and data transfer acknowledge ($\overline{DTACK}$) returning to their inactive levels. After this happens, the requesting device asserts bus grant acknowledge ($\overline{BGACK}$) and also removes bus grant request ($\overline{BR}$). The 68000 responds by removing the bus grant ($\overline{BG}$) signal. This completes the bus arbitration handshake. The requesting device has now taken over control of the bus and assumes the role of bus master. When the device has completed its function, it releases control of the bus by negating $\overline{BGACK}$ for rearbitration or return of bus mastership to the 68000.

Synchronous Control Bus

The 68000 microprocessor also has control signals that can make data transfers over its system bus occur in a synchronous fashion. There are three control signals provided for this purpose. In Fig. 8.2 we see that they are *enable* (E), *valid peripheral address* ($\overline{VPA}$), and *valid memory address* ($\overline{VMA}$). These signals provide for simple interface between, say, a 10-MHz 68000 microprocessor and 1-MHz synchronous LSI peripheral devices such as those available for use in 6800 microcomputer systems.

Let us now look at the function of each of these signals. The enable (E) output of the 68000 is used by 6800 peripherals to synchronize its data read/write operations. It is a free-running clock with a frequency equal to one-tenth of that of the 68000 clock frequency. This signal allows 1-MHz LSI peripheral ICs to be used with the 10-MHz 68000. It is applied to the $\overline{E}$ or PHI_2 input of 6800 family peripherals.

The valid peripheral address ($\overline{VPA}$) line is an input to the 68000 which is used to tell it to perform a synchronous transfer over its asynchronous system bus. When the address output on the address bus is decoded and found to correspond to an external 6800 peripheral, $\overline{VPA}$ must be switched to logic 0. This tells the microprocessor to synchronize the next data transfer with the enable (E) signal.

The valid memory address ($\overline{VMA}$) output is supplied by the 68000 in response to an active $\overline{VPA}$ input. It indicates to external circuitry that a valid address is on the address bus and that the next data transfer over the data bus will be synchronized with enable (E).

8.4 CLOCK INPUT AND WAVEFORM

Looking at Fig. 8.2, we find that the 68000 has a single *clock input* which is labeled CLK. The clock generator circuitry is not provided on the chip. Instead, the CLK signal must be generated in external circuitry and fed to the 68000. Internally, this signal is used to produce additional clock signals that synchronize the operation of the 68000's circuitry.

The 68000 is available with clock frequencies over the range from as low as 4 MHz to as high as 12.5 MHz. Figure 8.5 shows the CLK waveform. For 10-MHz operation, the cycle time (t_{CYC}) is 100 ns. The corresponding maximum pulse width low (t_{CL}) and pulse width high (t_{CH}) are both equal to 45 ns. The maximum rise and fall times of its edges, t_{Cr} and t_{Cf}, are both 10 ns. CLK is at TTL-compatible voltage levels.

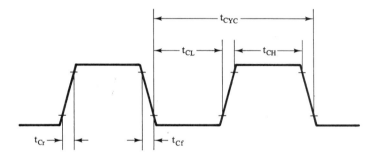

Figure 8.5   Clock waveform.

8.5 INTERNAL REGISTERS OF THE 68000 MICROPROCESSOR

Internal to the 68000 microprocessor are eighteen 32-bit registers and one 16-bit register. Figure 8.6 shows these registers. Notice that they include *eight data registers, seven address registers, two stack pointers, a program counter*, and *the status register*. The status register is the 16-bit register.

Data Registers

There are eight user-accessible data registers within the 68000. As shown in Fig. 8.6, they are called D_0 through D_7. Each register is 32 bits long and its bits are labeled 0 (least significant bit) through 31 (most significant bit). We will refer to these bits as B_0 through B_{31}, respectively.

The data registers are used to store data temporarily for use in processing. For example, they could hold the source and destination operands of an arithmetic or logic instruction. Each register can be accessed for byte operands, for word operands,

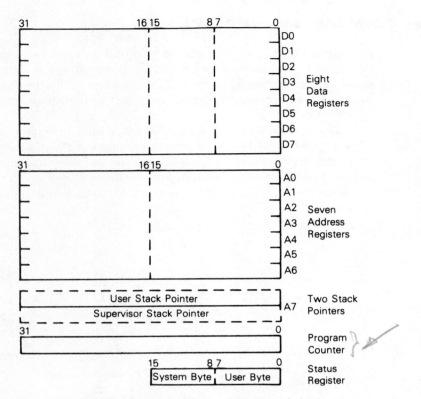

Figure 8.6 Internal registers of the 68000 (Motorola Inc.).

or for long-word operands. In Fig. 8.6 we see that byte data are always held in the 8 least significant bits of a data register: that is, B_0 through B_7. On the other hand, words of data always reside in the lower 16 bits, B_0 through B_{15}, and long words take up all 32 bits of the register.

The size of data to be used during the execution of an instruction is generally specified in the instruction. For example, a byte move instruction could be written with register D_0 as the location of the source operand and D_7 as the location of the destination operand. Executing the instruction causes the contents of bits B_0 through B_7 of D_0 to be copied into bits B_0 through B_7 of register D_7. Alternatively, the instruction could be set up to process words of data. This time, executing the instruction would cause bits B_0 through B_{15} of D_0 to be copied into B_0 through B_{15} of D_7.

The 68000 can also use the data registers as index registers. In this case the value in the register represents an offset address which when combined with the contents of another register points to the location of data in the memory subsystem.

These registers are said to be truly general purpose. That is, they do not have dedicated functions. For this reason, most instructions can perform their operations on source and destination operands that reside in any of these registers.

Address Registers

The next seven registers, which are labeled A_0 through A_6 in Fig. 8.6, are the address registers. They are also 32 bits in length. These registers are not provided for storage of data for processing. Instead, they are meant to store address information such as base addresses and pointer addresses. Moreover, they can also act as index registers.

Just like the data registers, the address registers are general purpose. That is, an instruction can reference any of them as a base or pointer address for its source or destination operands.

The values of the addresses are loaded into the address registers under software control. When used as a source register, an address register can be accessed as a long-word operand using the complete register or word operations using the lower 16 bits. On the other hand, when used as a destination register, all 32 bits are always affected.

Stack Pointers

Two other internal registers are used to hold address information. They are called the *user stack pointer* (USP) and the *supervisor stack pointer* (SSP). Only one of these two stack pointers is active at a time. For this reason, they are shown as a single register, A_7 in Fig. 8.6.

Unlike the address registers discussed earlier, these two registers have dedicated functions. The user stack pointer is active whenever the 68000 is operating in a mode known as the user state. When in this mode, the supervisor stack pointer is inactive. The address held in the user stack pointer identifies the top of the user stack in the user part of system memory. This *user stack* is the place where return addresses, register data, and other parameters are saved during operations such as the call to a subroutine.

The 68000 can be switched to a second mode, known as the supervisor state. This causes the supervisor stack pointer to become active and the user stack pointer to become inactive. The address in the supervisor stack pointer register points to the top of a second stack. It is called the *supervisor stack* and resides in the supervisor part of memory. The supervisor stack is used for the same purposes as the user stack, but it is also used by *supervisory calls* such as *software exceptions, interrupts*, and *internal exceptions*.

The address values in USP and SSP can be modified through software. However, they can be modified only when the 68000 is set to operate in the supervisor mode.

Program Counter

As with the 16-bit microprocessor we studied earlier, the program counter (PC) typically points to the next instruction to be executed. It is automatically incremented by 2 with the fetch of the instruction. In this way, it points to the next word of a multi-word instruction, an immediate source operand, or the next sequential instruction in the program. 68000 instructions can take up from one to five words of program storage memory.

An important difference between the program counter of the 68000 and that of the 8086 is its length. In Fig. 8.6 PC is shown as a 32-bit register; however, only the lower 24 bits are actually used in currently available 68000 devices. These 24 bits can generate 16M unique memory addresses for accessing bytes of data. But instructions are always stored at word boundaries. Therefore, the address space can also be considered to represent an 8M-word address space. The range of word addresses is even addresses from 000000_{16} through $FFFFFE_{16}$. In this way we see that program storage memory can reside anywhere in the 8M-word address space.

Status Register

Figure 8.6 also shows the 16-bit status register (SR) of the 68000 microprocessor. Here we see that this register is subdivided into two parts, called the *user byte* and the *system byte*.

The status register is shown in more detail in Fig. 8.7. Here we see that the bits implemented in the user byte are *flags* that indicate the processor state resulting from the execution of an instruction. The five conditions represented by the implemented bits are: *carry* (C), *overflow* (V), *zero* (Z), *negative* (N), and *extended carry* (X). Let us now look at each of these condition flags in more detail.

1. *Carry* (C): The carry flag, bit 0, is set if an add operation generates a carryout or a subtract (or compare) operation needs a borrow. Otherwise, it is reset. During shift or rotate operations, it holds the bit that is rotated or shifted out of a register or memory location.

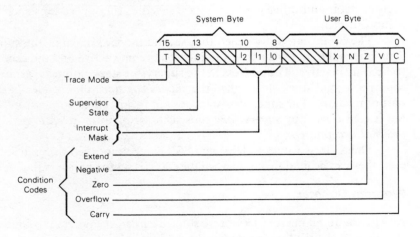

Figure 8.7   Status register (Motorola Inc.).

2. *Overflow* (V): If an arithmetic operation on signed numbers produces an incorrect result, the overflow flag (bit 1) is set; otherwise, it is reset. During an arithmetic shift operation, this flag gets set as the result of a change in the most significant bit; otherwise, it gets reset.

3. *Zero* (Z): If an operation produces a zero as its result, the zero flag (bit 2) of SR is set. A nonzero result clears Z.

4. *Negative* (N): The content of bit 3 is a copy of the most significant bit (sign bit) of the result during arithmetic, logic, shift, or rotate operations. In other words, a negative result sets the N bit and a positive result clears it.

5. *Extend* (X): During arithmetic, shift, or rotate operations, the extend flag, bit 4, receives the carry status. It is used as the carry bit in multiprecision operations.

These user bits of the status register can be tested through software to determine whether or not certain events have occurred. Typically, the occurrence of an event indicates that a change in program environment should be initiated. For instance, the overflow bit could be tested and if it is set program control is passed to an overflow service routine.

The system byte of SR contains bits that control operational options available on the 68000 microprocessor and also contains the *interrupt mask*. The implemented bits in this byte and their functions are identified in Fig. 8.7. Let us now look at these functions.

1. *Interrupt mask* ($I_2I_1I_0$): Bits 8 through 10 of SR are the interrupt mask of the 68000. This 3-bit code determines which interrupts can be serviced and which are to be ignored. Interrupting devices with priority higher than the binary value of $I_2I_1I_0$ will be accepted and those with lower or the same priority will be ignored. For example, if $I_2I_1I_0$ equals 011_2, then levels 4 through 7 are able to be active, while levels 1 through 3 are masked out.

2. *Supervisor* (S): Bit 13 of SR is used to select between the *user* and *supervisor states* of operation. A logic 1 in this bit indicates that the 68000 is operating in the supervisory state. If it is logic 0, the 68000 operates in the user state.

3. *Trace mode* (T): The T status bit is used to enable or disable *trace (single-step) mode* of operation. To activate the single-step mode, bit 15 must be set. When set in this way, the microprocessor executes an instruction, then enters the supervisor state, and vectors to a trace service routine. The service routine may pass control to a mechanism that permits initiation of execution of the next instruction or debug mode of operations for displaying the contents of the various internal registers.

The contents of the complete status register can be read at any time through software. Unimplemented bits are always read as logic 0. However, the system byte can be modified only when the 68000 is in the supervisor state.

8.6 INSTRUCTION EXECUTION CONTROL

Now that we have introduced the 68000 microprocessor, its external interfaces, and internal registers, we continue by examining how it performs the internal operations required during the execution of an instruction. Figure 8.8 shows the internal execution control architecture. It includes the *instruction register, instruction decoder, control unit*, and *execution unit*.

Let us begin by overviewing the operation of the execution control section. The instruction register accepts an instruction as it is fetched into the microprocessor for execution. Looking at this block, we see that its outputs supply the inputs of the instruction decoder. Here the instruction is decoded to determine which type of operation is to be performed. Based on the result of this decoding, it produces outputs for input to both the control unit and execution unit. The information passed to the execution unit is called *macroinstruction static* because it does not depend on timing of the execution of the instruction. For example, the registers that are to be used and the operation that is to be performed are macroinstruction static information. Moreover, the decoder supplies a *microsequence starting address* to the control unit. The control unit is responsible for sequencing the operations performed by the execu-

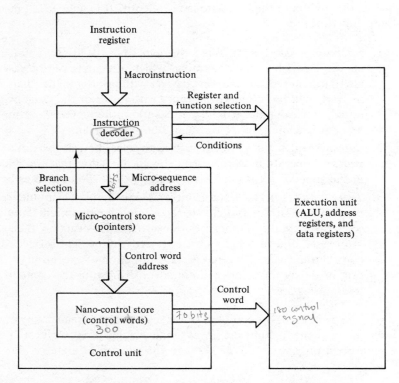

Figure 8.8 Microcoded instruction execution control.

tion unit in a way that causes it to perform the operation specified by the instruction.

The 68000 microprocessor employs a *microprogrammed control unit* similar to that used in minicomputers and mainframe computers. That is, the instructions in the instruction set of the 68000 are actually *macroinstructions* and they are emulated by the execution control unit by performing a series of lower-level micro-operations called *microinstructions.* Actually, the control unit contains a series of control words for each instruction. These series of control words are used to tell the execution unit how to perform the macro-operations. They are coded into the *control store* part of the control unit.

In this way we see that the control unit itself does not perform the operation specified by the instruction. Instead, it must interact with the instruction decoder to determine which macro-operation is to be performed, with the execution unit, which contains the data registers, address registers, and arithmetic logic unit, to perform the processing, and possibly the bus interface to control accessing of operands.

Let us now look more closely at the control unit. From Fig. 8.8 we see that the 68000 employs a two-level control store structure. The first level, which is identified as the *micro-control store*, stores a sequence of addresses for each instruction. These addresses are pointers to the micro-operations that need to be performed to emulate the macro-operation. Each address is 9 bits wide and about 625 addresses are needed to implement the complete instruction set. The second level, *nano-control store,* contains a set of about 300 control words. It is these control words that define the unique micro-operations that can be performed by the 68000's execution unit. Each control word is 70 bits in length.

During instruction execution, the macroinstruction decoder outputs to the micro-control store the starting address of the emulation routine for the instruction that is to be performed. In response, the micro-control store starts by outputting the 9-bit address of the first micro-operation that is to be performed. This address is input by the nano-control store and causes the nano-control store to output the 70-bit control word for this operation to the execution unit. This control word is further decoded within the execution unit to produce as many as 180 control signals. At completion of this first micro-operation, the micro-control store outputs the address of the next micro-operation and the nano-control store causes it to be performed. This sequence continues until the complete microcode emulation routine is performed and at its completion another instruction is input to the instruction decoder.

To improve performance, the 68000 overlaps the fetch, decode, and execution phases. For instance, when one instruction is being executed, the next one may be getting decoded, and the one following it may be getting fetched. However, many macroinstructions take more than one machine cycle to execute. For this reason, if the current instruction is not yet complete, the decode or fetch of additional instructions may not take place.

The key benefits derived from use of microcoding are decreased development time and increased flexibility. This is because the development of the instruction set is easier to manage. For instance, modification of the operation of an instruction or implementation of a new instruction does not require any hardware changes; instead, it simply requires changes of the microcode in the control store.

ASSIGNMENT

Section 8.2

1. Name the technology used to fabricate the 68000 microprocessor.
2. In what size package is the 68000 housed?
3. How many general-purpose registers does the 68000 have? What are they called? Specify the size of each register.
4. What basic data types is the 68000 able to process directly?

Section 8.3

5. How many address lines are on the 68000 IC? How many unique memory or I/O addresses can be generated using these lines?
6. How many data lines does the 68000 have?
7. What is meant by "asynchronous bus"?
8. What function is served by $\overline{DTACK}$ during read/write operations?
9. How is byte addressing accomplished by the 68000?
10. Specify the address and asynchronous bus control signals that occur to write a word of data to memory address $A000_{16}$.
11. What function code is output by the 68000 when it fetches an instruction while in the supervisor state?
12. Describe friendly the function of system control lines $\overline{BERR}$, $\overline{RESET}$, and $\overline{HALT}$.
13. How does the 68000 prioritize interrupts?
14. Why are the bus arbitration control signals provided on the 68000?
15. Why is synchronous bus operation also provided for the 68000?

Section 8.4

16. What is the duration of the clock cycle of a 68000 that is operating at 8 MHz?

Section 8.5

17. What is the difference between the functions of the 68000's address and data registers?
18. Define what is meant by a stack. Why are there two stack pointer registers?
19. What function is served by the program counter?
20. Distinguish between the user byte and the system byte of the status register.

Section 8.6

21. What is the difference between a macroinstruction and a microinstruction?
22. What is the difference in the information stored in micro-control store and the nano-control store?
23. Give a brief description of how instruction execution is implemented in a two-level microprogrammed control unit.

9

68000 Microprocessor Programming 1

9.1 INTRODUCTION

A general overview of the 68000's architecture was given in Chapter 8. In this chapter we continue our study of the 68000 with its operand addressing modes, instruction set, and software concepts. The topics covered are as follows:

1. Software model of the 68000 microprocessor
2. Operand addressing modes
3. The 68000 instruction set
4. Data transfer instructions
5. Binary and decimal arithmetic instructions
6. Logic instructions
7. Shift and rotate instructions

9.2 SOFTWARE MODEL OF THE 68000 MICROPROCESSOR

The *software model* of the 68000 microprocessor is shown in Fig. 9.1. This model specifies the resources available to the programmers for implementing their program requirements. Here we see that the 68000 is represented by eight data registers, seven address registers, two stack pointers, a program counter, and a status register. We discussed each of these registers as part of our study of the 68000's architecture in Chapter 8. From a programming point of view, it is important to understand the intended use for each of these registers, their operating capabilities, and limitations.

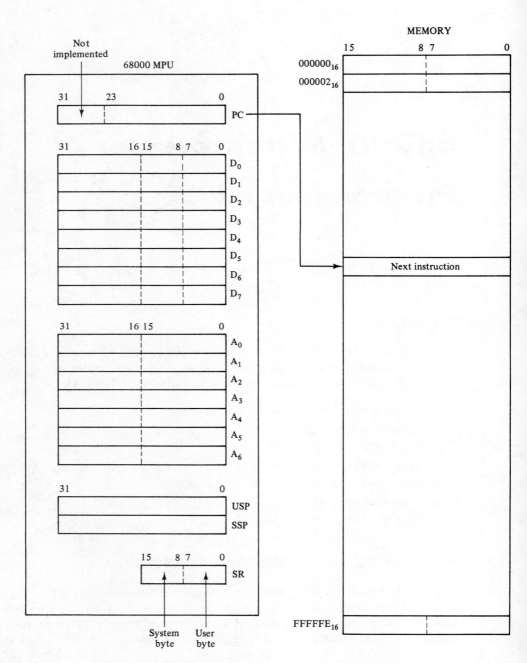

Figure 9.1 Software model of the 68000.

The program counter, status register, and stack pointer serve functions similar to those already discussed for the 8086. For this reason we concentrate here on the data registers and address register of the 68000.

Data registers D_0 through D_7 are provided for temporary storage of working data. For instance, the instruction

$$\text{ADD.W}\quad \text{D0,D1}$$

employs data registers D_0 and D_1 for storage of its source and destination operands, respectively. The sum that results from executing this instruction is saved in destination register D_1. One nice feature of the architecture of the 68000 is that its internal registers do not have dedicated functions. Instead, they can be employed in a very general way. For instance, the add instruction we just introduced could be written with any combination of these seven data registers as the locations of its source and destination operands.

These data registers also support processing of data in a variety of different data types. For example, most instructions can access the data registers for processing of byte, word, or long-word operands. A few instructions also permit processing of individual bits or data expressed as BCD numbers. The data registers can also be used as *index registers* for generating memory addresses.

Address registers A_0 through A_6 are not used to hold data for processing. Instead, they contain *address pointers* and are used to access source or destination operands that are stored in memory. For example, the instruction

$$\text{ADD.W}\quad \text{(A0),D1}$$

uses the contents of A_0 to access a source operand that resides in memory. Just as for the data registers, the 68000 permits general use of the address registers. That is, any of the seven address registers could be specified as the pointer to the location of the source operand in the addition instruction.

Also represented in the model is the 68000's *memory address space*. Here again we find a significant deviation from the architecture of the 8086. The 68000 employs a very large 16M-byte address space which has few limitation on its use. That is, program memory, data memory, and stack can be located almost at any address and are not limited in size. It may also be important for the programmer to know how memory is organized, how the various data types are stored in memory, what restrictions exist on its use, and the ways in which it can be accessed through addressing modes. Some of these topics will be discussed next.

9.3 THE OPERAND ADDRESSING MODES OF THE 68000 MICROPROCESSOR

The operands processed by the 68000 as it executes an instruction may be specified as part of the instruction in program memory, may reside in internal registers, or may be stored in data memory. The 68000 has 14 different addressing modes. They are shown in Fig. 9.2. The objective of these addressing modes is to supply different

Mode	Generation
Register Direct Addressing	
Data Register Direct	EA = Dn
Address Register Direct	EA = An
Absolute Data Addressing	
Absolute Short	EA = (Next Word)
Absolute Long	EA = (Next Two Words)
Program Counter Relative Addressing	
Relative with Offset	EA = (PC) + d_{16}
Relative with Index and Offset	EA = (PC) + (Xn) + d_8
Register Indirect Addressing	
Register Indirect	EA = (An)
Postincrement Register Indirect	EA = (An), An ← An + N
Predecrement Register Indirect	An ← An − N, EA = (An)
Register Indirect with Offset	EA = (An) + d_{16}
Indexed Register Indirect with Offset	EA = (An) + (Xn) + d_8
Immediate Data Addressing	
Immediate	DATA = Next Word(s)
Quick Immediate	Inherent Data
Implied Addressing	
Implied Register	EA = SR, USP, SP, PC

NOTES:
EA = Effective Address
An = Address Register
Dn = Data Register
Xn = Address or Data Register
    used as Index Register
SR = Status Register
PC = Program Counter
( ) = Contents of

d_8 = 8-bit Offset
   (displacement)
d_{16} = 16-bit Offset
   (displacement)
N = 1 for Byte, 2 for
   Words, and 4 for Long
   Words.
← = Replaces

Figure 9.2 Operand addressing modes of the 68000 (Motorola Inc.).

ways for the programmer to generate an *effective address* (EA) that identifies the location of an operand. In general, operands referenced by an effective address reside either in one of the 68000's internal registers or in external data memory.

Looking at Fig. 9.2, we see that the 14 addressing modes have been subdivided into six groups based on how they generate an effective address. These groups are: *register direct addressing, absolute data addressing, program counter relative addressing, register indirect addressing, immediate data addressing*, and *implied addressing*. Notice that the addressing modes in all groups other than immediate data addressing produce an effective address. Let us now look into each of these modes in detail.

Register Direct Addressing Modes

Register direct addressing mode is used when one of the data or address registers within the 68000 contains the operand that is to be processed by the instruction. In Fig. 9.2 we see that if the specified register is a data register, the addressing mode is called *data register direct addressing*. On the other hand, if an address register is used, it is known as *address register direct addressing*.

Here is an example that employs both data register direct addressing and address register direct addressing.

$$\text{MOVE.L}\quad \text{A0,D0}$$

MOVE.L is how we write the move instruction to process long-word (32-bit) data.

Notice that address register A_0 is specified to contain the source operand. This is an example of address register direct addressing. On the other hand, the destination operand uses data register direct addressing and is specified as the contents of data register D_0. In this example, neither operand is located in memory.

Execution of this instruction causes the long word in address register A_0 to be copied into data register D_0. This operation can also be expressed as

$$A0 \longrightarrow D0$$

In Fig. 9.3(a) we see that before executing the instruction A_0 contains \$76543210 and the contents of D_0 are a don't-care state. The symbol \$ stands for hexadecimal number. At the conclusion of execution of the instruction, both A_0 and D_0 contain \$76543210. This result is shown in Fig. 9.3(b).

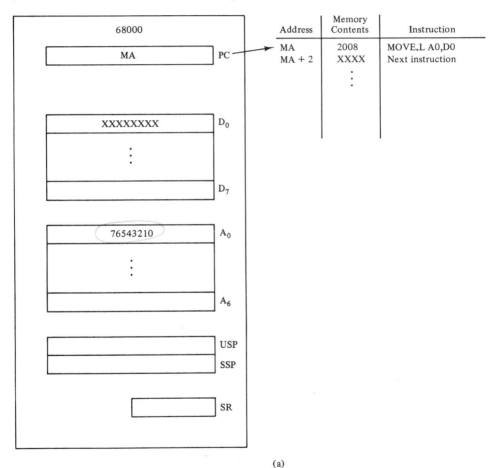

(a)

Figure 9.3   (a) Instruction using register direct addressing before execution; (b) after execution.

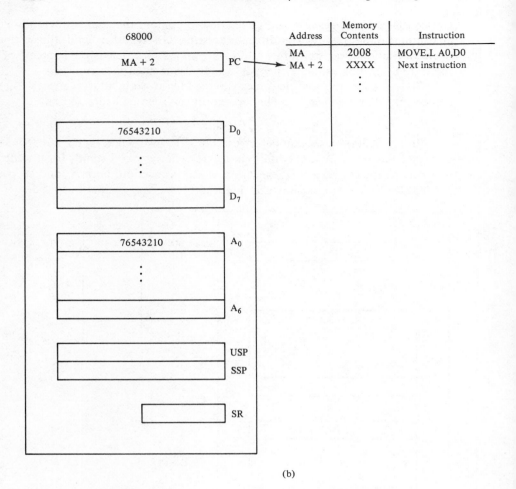

(b)

Figure 9.3 *(continued)*

Absolute Data Addressing Modes

When the effective address of an operand is included in the instruction, we are using what is called absolute data addressing mode. There are two such modes for the 68000. They are known as *absolute short addressing* and *absolute long addressing*. These addressing modes are used to access operands that reside in memory.

If an instruction uses absolute short data addressing to specify the location of an operand, a 16-bit absolute address must be included as the second word of the instruction. This word is the effective address of the storage location for the operand in memory.

As an example, let us consider the instruction

MOVE.L $1234,D0

It stands for move the long word starting at address \$1234 in memory into data register D_0. Notice that the instruction is written with \$1234 in the location for the source operand. This is the absolute address of the source operand and it is encoded by the assembler into the instruction as shown in Fig. 9.4(a). Notice that the address of the source operand is the next word after the instruction opcode in program memory.

The 68000 automatically does a sign extension based on the MSB of the absolute short address to give a 32-bit address (actually only 24 bits are used). For our example, the sign bit is 0; therefore extending it gives the address 001234_{16}. Since only 16 bits can be used in absolute short data addressing it always generates a memory address either in the range 000000_{16} through $007FFF_{16}$ or $FF8000_{16}$ through $FFFFFF_{16}$. These ranges correspond to the first 32K bytes and the last 32K bytes

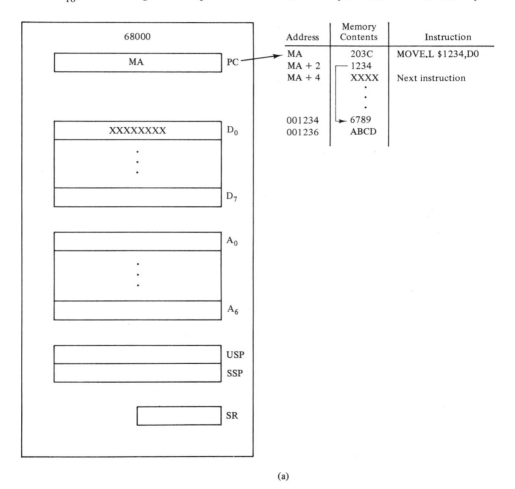

(a)

Figure 9.4 (a) Instruction using absolute data addressing before execution; (b) after execution.

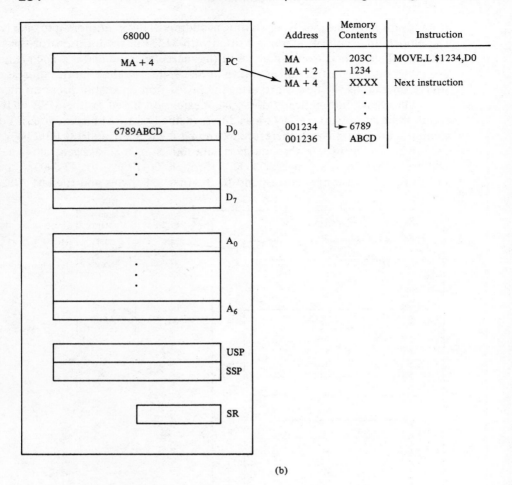

(b)

Figure 9.4 *(continued)*

of the 68000's address space, respectively. Other parts of the 68000's address space cannot be accessed with this addressing mode.

The result of executing this instruction is shown in Fig. 9.4(b). Notice that the long word starting at address 001234_{16}, which equals $6789ABCD_{16}$, is copied into D_0. Here we see that the word at the lower address, 1234_{16}, is copied into the upper 16 bits of D_0 and the word at the higher address, 1236_{16}, is copied into the lower 16 bits.

Absolute long data addressing permits use of a full 32-bit quantity as the absolute address data. This type of operand is specified in the same way except that its absolute address is written with more than four digits.

For instance, the instruction

MOVE.L $01234,D0

has the same effect as the previous instruction, but the address of the source operand is encoded by the assembler as an absolute long data address. That is, the quantity $01234 is encoded as a 32-bit number instead of a 16-bit number. This means that the instruction now takes up three words of memory instead of two.

Since all 24 bits are used, the operand specified with absolute long addressing can reside anywhere in the address space of the 68000.

Program Counter Relative Addressing Modes

It is possible to specify the location of an operand relative to the address of the instruction that is being processed. Program counter relative addressing is provided for this purpose. With it, the effective address of the operand to be accessed is calculated relative to the updated value held in program counter (PC). There are two types of program counter relative addressing: *program counter relative with offset* and *program counter relative with index and offset.*

Let us begin with program counter relative with offset addressing. In this case, a 16-bit quantity identifies the number of bytes the data to be accessed are offset from the updated value in PC. The offset, known also as the *displacement,* immediately follows the instruction word in memory. When the instruction is fetched and executed, the 68000 sign-extends the offset to 32 bits and then adds it to the updated contents of the program counter.

$$EA = PC + d16$$

The sum that results is the effective address of the operand in memory.

An example of an instruction that employs this addressing mode is as follows:

MOVE.L   TAG,D0

This means "move the long word starting at the memory location with TAG as its label into D_0." The question arises: Where is the label TAG in memory? The answer lies with the assembler. It computes the number of bytes the displacement word in the move instruction is offset from the memory location corresponding to label TAG. This offset is expressed as a signed 16-bit binary number and is encoded as the displacement word of the instruction.

Since the 16-bit quantity specifies the offset in bytes, the operand must reside within + or −32K (+32767 to −32768) bytes with respect to the updated value in PC. The second type of program counter relative addressing employs both an index and an offset. In this addressing mode, both the contents of an index register and an 8-bit displacement are combined with the updated PC to obtain the operand's memory address. That is, the effective address is given by

$$EA = PC + Xn + d8$$

The index register, which is identified by Xn, can be any of the 68000's data or address registers. The signed 8-bit displacement is specified by d_8.

Consider this instruction:

MOVE.L   TABLE(A0.L),D0

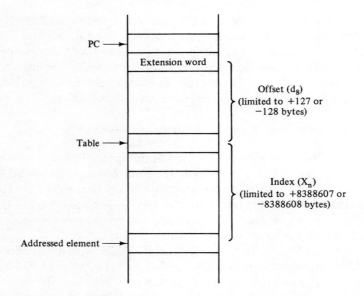

Figure 9.5 Accessing elements of a table with program counter relative with index and offset addressing.

Here the source operand is written such that TABLE represents the displacement and A_0 is the index register. This instruction says to copy the long word starting at the memory location in TABLE indexed by A_0 into D_0.

In this case the assembler computes the offset between the updated value in PC and the address of label TABLE. The value of the displacement is encoded as the least significant byte in the second word of the instruction.

The use of program counter relative addressing with offset and index to access a table in memory is illustrated in Fig. 9.5. The starting point of the table in memory is identified by the label TABLE. Since just 8 bits are provided for the offset, the table must begin within +127 or -128 bytes of the extension word of the instruction. The size of the table is determined by the index. The ability to specify up to a 32-bit index permits addressing of very long tables. Actually, the size of the data table is limited by the number of address lines on the 68000, which is 24.

Address Register Indirect Addressing Modes

Address register indirect addressing is similar to the register direct addressing we discussed earlier in that an internal register is specified when writing the instruction. However, in this case, only address registers A_0 through A_6 can be used. Moreover, the register does not represent the location of the operand; instead, it contains the effective address of the operand in memory. Notice that register indirect addressing enables the 68000 to access information that resides in external memory.

There are five different kinds of register indirect addressing supported by the

68000. As shown in Fig. 9.2, they are called: *register indirect addressing, postincrement register indirect addressing, predecrement register indirect addressing, register indirect with offset addressing,* and *indexed register indirect with offset addressing.* We shall now look at each of these types in more detail.

Register indirect is the simplest form of address register indirect addressing. When it is specified, one of the address registers contains the address of the source or destination operand. For instance, in the instruction

MOVE.L   (A0),D0

the source operand employs register indirect addressing. Notice that this type of addressing is specified by enclosing the name of the address register, which in our example is A_0, with parentheses. The destination operand is specified as D_0 using register direct addressing.

Figure 9.6 illustrates the result of using this addressing mode. In Fig. 9.6(a) we see that the contents of A_0 are $1234. Moreover, we see that the long word stored at address $1234 through $1237 is $ABCDEF89. As shown in Fig. 9.6(b), execution of the instruction causes this value to be copied into destination register D_0.

Postincrement register indirect addressing works essentially the same as the register indirect addressing we just demonstrated. However, there is one difference. This is that after the operation specified by the instruction is completed the contents of the address register are automatically incremented by 1, 2, or 4, depending on whether byte, word, or long-word data are processed. In this way, the address points to the next sequential element of data.

Our earlier example can be rewritten to use postincrement register indirect addressing. This gives

MOVE.L   (A0)+,D0

Here we see that including a + symbol after the operand specifies the postincrement operation.

If we assume that the state of the 68000 just prior to execution of this instruction is as shown in Fig. 9.7(a), the results are similar to those shown in Fig. 9.6(b) for register indirect addressing. Again $ABCDEF89 is copied into D_0. But this time the contents of A_0 are also incremented by 4 to give $1238, as shown in Fig. 9.7(b). Therefore, it points to the start of the next long word in data memory.

Predecrement register indirect addressing is the same as postdecrement register indirect addressing except that the contents of the selected address register are decremented instead of incremented. Moreover, the decrement operation takes place prior to performing the operation specified in the instruction.

For instance, in the instruction

MOVE.L   −(A0),D0

the − symbol identifies predecrement indirect addressing. If this instruction is executed with the 68000 in the state shown in Fig. 9.8(a), the address in A_0 is first decremented by 4 and equals $1230. Therefore, the contents of memory locations $1230 through $1233 are copied into D_0. This result is illustrated by Fig. 9.8(b).

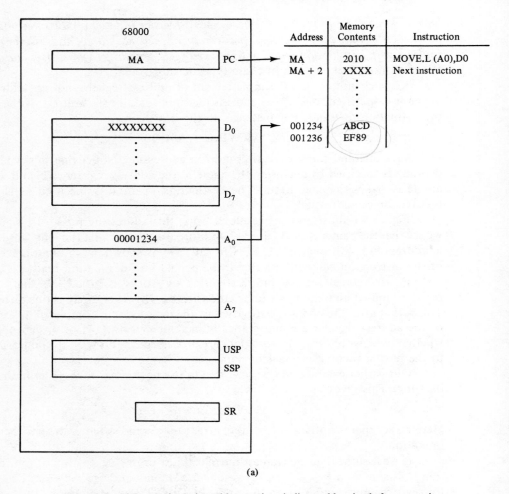

Figure 9.6   (a) Instruction using address register indirect addressing before execution;
(b) after execution.

Postincrement and predecrement indirect addressing allow a programmer to implement memory scanning operations without the need to update the address pointer with additional instructions. This type of addressing is useful for performing data processing operations such as block transfer and string searches.

In the address register indirect with offset addressing mode, a sign-extended 16-bit offset value and an address register are specified in the instruction. The effective address of the operand is generated by adding the offset to the contents of the selected address register; that is,

$$EA = An + d16$$

The value of offset d_{16} specifies the number of bytes the storage location to be ac-

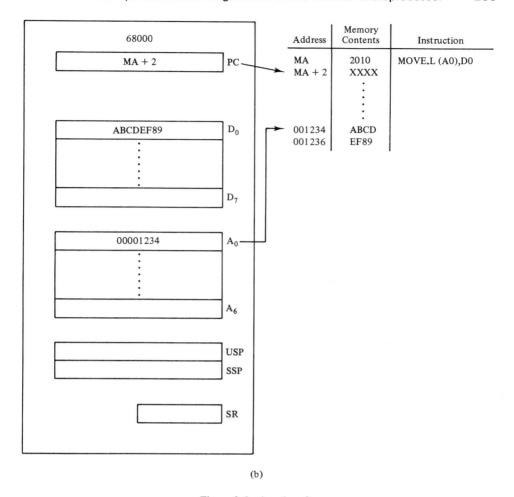

(b)

Figure 9.6   *(continued)*

cessed is offset from the address in A_n. It is encoded as the second word of the instruction.

Let us now consider the instruction

$$\text{MOVE.W}\quad 16(A0),D0$$

Here we find an offset of 16 (sixteen bytes) specified for the source operand. Execution of this instruction for the conditions in Fig. 9.9(a) produces the effective address

$$\text{EA} = 1234_{16} + 16_{10} = 1244_{16}$$

As shown in Fig. 9.9(b), the word contents of address $1244, which equals $ABCD, are copied into the least significant 16 bits of D_0.

Since the offset is a signed 16-bit integer number, the operand to be accessed

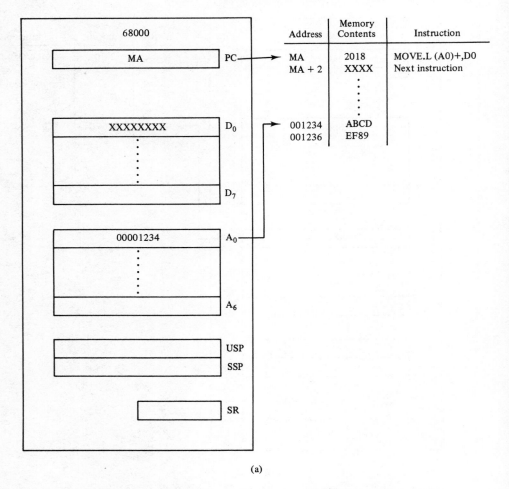

(a)

Figure 9.7 (a) Instruction using postincrement register indirect addressing before execution; (b) after execution.

must be within $+32767$ or -32768 bytes of the storage location pointed to by the contents of the address register.

The last register indirect addressing mode, indexed register indirect with offset addressing, allows specification of an address register, an offset, and an index register for formation of the effective address. The offset value is limited to a signed 8-bit quantity. On the other hand, the index register can be the contents of any of the 68000's data or address registers. The effective address is computed by adding the contents of the address register, the contents of the index register, and the offset. That is,

$$EA = An + Xn + d8$$

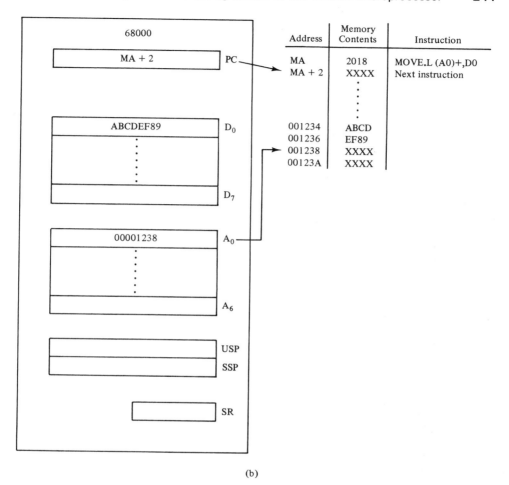

(b)

Figure 9.7 *(continued)*

Here is an instruction that uses this addressing mode for its source operand.

MOVE.W   16(A0,A1.L),D0

The offset equals 16_{10}, A_0 is the address register, and A_1 is the index register. Figure 9.10(a) shows that A_0 contains \$1234 and A_1 contains \$2344. In this case, the address of the source operand is obtained as

$$EA = A0 + A1 + 16_{10} = 1234_{16} + 2344_{16} + 10_{16}$$
$$= 3588_{16}$$

Figure 9.10(b) shows that the word contents at this memory location are $ABCD_{16}$. This value is copied into the least significant word of D_0.

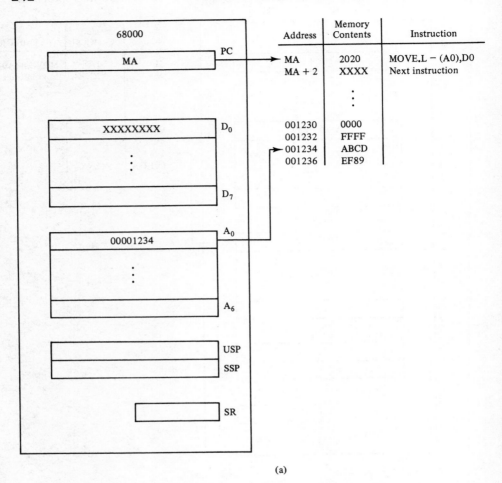

(a)

Figure 9.8   (a) Instruction using predecrement register indirect addressing before execution; (b) after execution.

Since the offset value is an 8-bit signed integer, the address offset is limited to $+127$ or -128 bytes relative to the location specified by the sum of the contents of the address register and the index register.

Address register indirect with index and offset addressing is very useful when accessing elements of an array in memory. For example, the two-dimensional array of Fig. 9.11(a), which has a size of m rows by l columns, can be stored in memory as shown in Fig. 9.11(b). Notice that the first $l + 1$ addresses, with starting address at $00F000_{16}$, contain the elements of row 0 of the array, that is, the elements located at columns 0 through l of row 0. In both figures, these are identified as $E(0,0)$ through $E(0,l)$. The elements of row 0 are followed in memory by those for rows 1 through m.

Let us look at how to access the element located at column j of row i ($E(i,j)$).

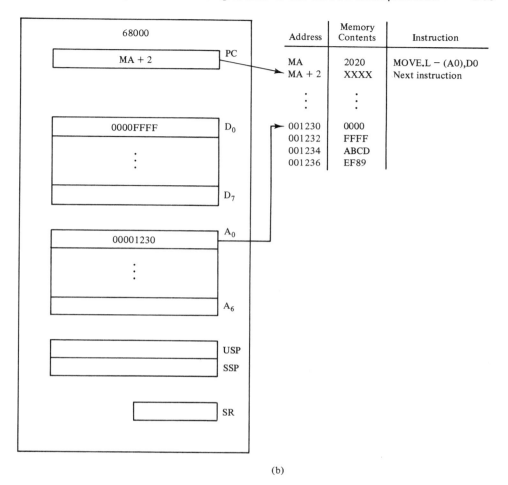

(b)

Figure 9.8 *(continued)*

In order to access this element, the first address register A_0 can be loaded with the beginning address, \$00F000, of the array in memory. In this way, it points to the first element in the first row of the array. A_1 can be used as the index register and loaded with an index number such that it points to row i in the array. Assuming that each element uses a word for storage, the value required in index register A_1 in order to access row i is computed as 2i (l + 1). Finally the offset can be used to select the appropriate column. For element j, it should be made equal to 2j. In this way the effective address computed as

$$EA = A0 + 2i\,(l + 1) + 2j$$

points to element E(i,j). Note that the 8-bit offset limits the number of columns in the array to a maximum of 128.

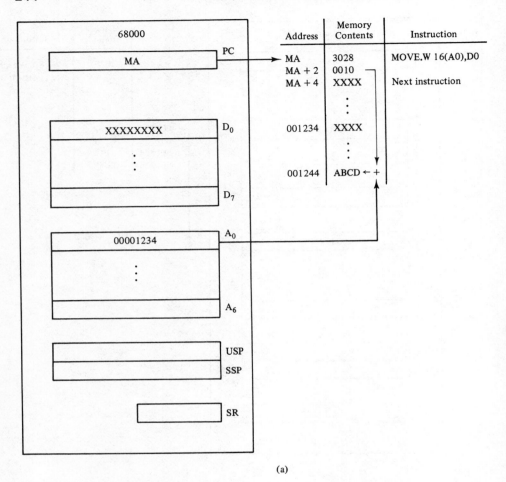

(a)

Figure 9.9 (a) Instruction using register indirect addressing with offset before execution; (b) after execution.

For instance, let us determine the effective address needed to copy the word in element $E(5,6)$ of the array in Fig. 9.11 with $m = 8$ into D_0. Assume that the array of words is stored starting at address \$00F000. First we must load registers A_0 and A_1 as follows:

$$A0 = 00F000_{16}$$
$$A1 = 2i(l + 1) = 2(5)(8 + 1) = 90_{10} = 5A_{16}$$

Then the offset is obtained by multiplying the column dimension of the array element by 2. This gives

$$d8 = 2j = 2(6) = 12_{10} = C_{16}$$

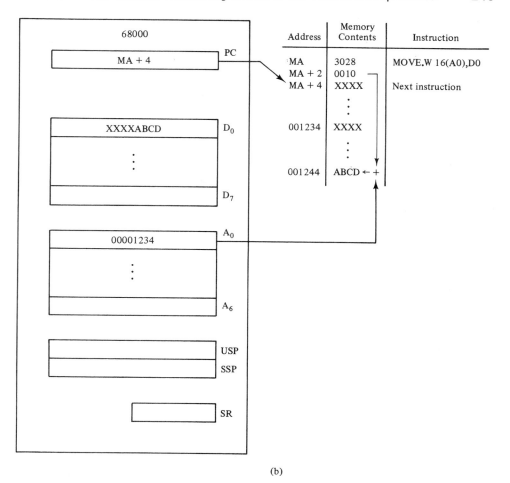

(b)

Figure 9.9   *(continued)*

Therefore, the effective address of the element is

$$EA = A0 + A1 + d8 = 00F000_{16} + 5A_{16} + C_{16}$$
$$= 00F066_{16}$$

This element can be copied into D_0 by executing the instruction

MOV.W   12(A0,A1.L),D0

Immediate Data Addressing Modes

With the immediate data addressing mode, the operand to be processed during the execution of the instruction is supplied in the instruction itself. In general, the data are encoded and stored in the word locations that follow the instruction in program

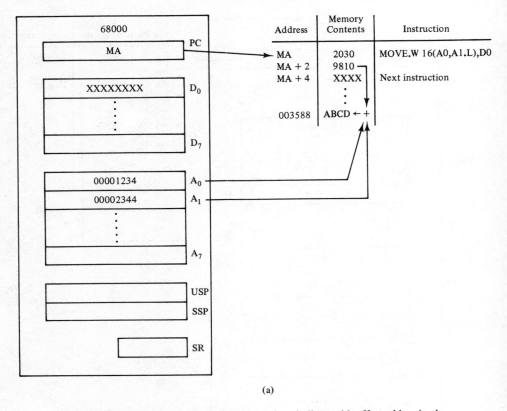

(a)

Figure 9.10 (a) Instruction using indexed register indirect with offset addressing before execution; (b) after execution.

memory. If the instruction processes bytes of data, a special form of immediate addressing can be used. This is known as *quick immediate addressing*. In this case, the data are encoded directly into the instruction's operation word. For this reason, using quick immediate addressing takes up less memory and executes faster.

Here are two examples of instructions that employ immediate data addressing for their source operands.

MOVEQ   #$C5,D0

MOVE.W   #$1234,D0

Note that the # symbol written before the operand indicates that immediate data addressing is employed. The first instruction, move quick (MOVEQ), illustrates quick immediate addressing. In this instruction, the immediate source operand is $C5_{16}$. As shown in Fig. 9.12(a), it gets encoded as $70C5, where the least significant byte of the instruction word is the immediate operand. Executing this instruction loads D_0 with the sign-extended long-word value of $C5; that is.

$$\$FFFFFFC5 \longrightarrow D0$$

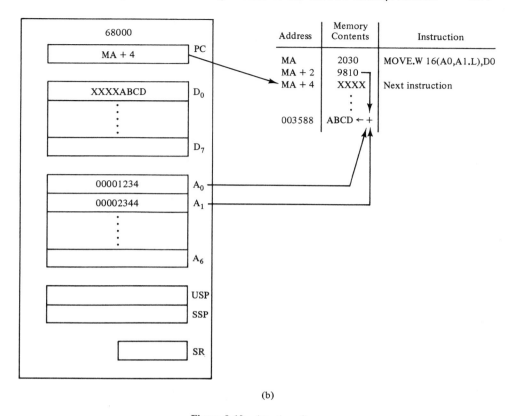

(b)

Figure 9.10   *(continued)*

Looking at the second instruction, we see that its immediate source operand is the word 1234_{16}. Figure 9.12(b) illustrates how its immediate operand gets encoded into the second word of the instruction. When the instruction is executed, sign extension is not performed; instead, the value $1234 is loaded into the least significant 16 bits of D_0. That is,

$$\$1234 \longrightarrow \text{Least significant 16 bits of } D_0$$

The most significant 16 bits of D_0 are not affected.

Implied Addressing Mode

Some of the 68000's instructions do not make direct reference to operands. Instead, inherent to their execution is an automatic reference to one or more of its internal registers. Typically, these registers are the stack pointers, the program counter, or the status register.

An example is the instruction

BSR   SUBRTN

It stands for branch to the subroutine at label SUBRTN. Both the contents of the program counter and active stack pointer are always referenced during the execution of this instruction.

Functional Addressing Categories

The addressing modes that we have discussed in this section can be divided into four categories based on the manner in which they are used. These functional categories are: *data addressing, memory addressing, control addressing,* and *alterable addressing*. The relationship between the addressing modes and these four categories is summarized by the table in Fig. 9.13.

If an addressing mode can be used to reference data operands, it is categorized as data addressing. Looking at Fig. 9.13, we see that all addressing modes other than address register direct are classified as data addressing. Address register direct is not included because it only allows access to address information.

Similarly, if an addressing mode provides the ability to reference operands in memory, it is classified as memory addressing. Notice in Fig. 9.13 that just the data register direct and address register direct addressing modes are not classified in this way. This is because their use is restricted to accessing information that resides in the internal registers of the 68000.

An addressing mode is considered control addressing if it can be used to reference an operand in memory without specification of the size of the operand. Notice in Fig. 9.13 that all direct addressing modes, indirect addressing modes with either predecrement or postincrement, and the immediate addressing modes are not included in this category.

Moreover, if an addressing mode permits reference to operands which are be-

Column\Row	0	1	. . . .	l
0	E(0, 0)	E(0, 1)	. . . .	E(0, l)
1	E(1, 0)	E(1, 1)	. . . .	E(1, l)
$\vdots$	$\vdots$	$\vdots$		$\vdots$
m	E(m, 0)	E(m, 1)	. . . .	E(m, l)

(a)

Figure 9.11   (a) An $m \times l$ two-dimensional array; (b) storage of the array in memory.

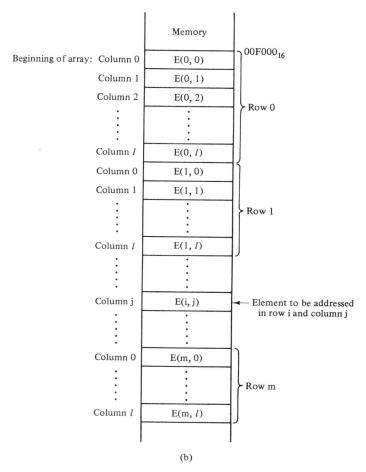

(b)

Figure 9.11   *(continued)*

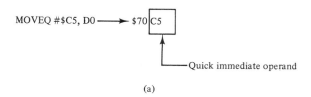

(a)

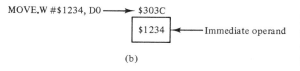

(b)

Figure 9.12   (a) Coding of a move instruction with quick immediate operand; (b) coding of a move instruction with general immediate operand.

Addressing Mode	Mode	Register	Addressing Categories				Assembler Syntax
			Data	Mem	Cont	Alter	
Data Reg Dir	000	reg no.	X	—	—	X	Dn
Addr Reg Dir	001	reg no.	—	—	—	X	An
Addr Reg Ind	010	reg no.	X	X	X	X	(An)
Addr Reg Ind w/Postinc	011	reg no.	X	X	—	X	(An)+
Addr Reg Ind w/Predec	100	reg no.	X	X	—	X	−(An)
Addr Reg Ind w/Disp	101	reg no.	X	X	X	X	d(An)
Addr Reg Ind w/Index	110	reg no.	X	X	X	X	d(An, Ri)
Absolute Short	111	000	X	X	X	X	XXX
Absolute Long	111	001	X	X	X	X	XXXXXX
Prog Ctr w/Disp	111	010	X	X	X	—	d(PC)
Prog Ctr w/Index	111	011	X	X	X	—	d(PC, Ri)
Immediate	111	100	X	X	—	—	#XXX

Figure 9.13   Effective addressing mode categories (Motorola Inc.).

ing written into, it is called an *alterable addressing mode*. That is, alterable addressing modes can be used in conjunction with destination operands. Looking at Fig. 9.13, we see that immediate data addressing is an example of an addressing mode that cannot be used to specify a destination operand. It can only be used to reference source operands.

9.4 INSTRUCTION SET

Now that we have introduced the software model of the 68000 and its addressing modes, we are ready to begin our study of its instructions. The 8086's *instruction set* has more basic instructions than that of the 68000. However, the 8086's instruction set includes a number of special-purpose instructions. An example is the XLAT (translation-table lookup) instruction.

On the other hand, Motorola Inc. has applied *orthogonality* in the design of the instruction set of the 68000. That is, instead of having a large number of instructions that include many special-purpose instructions, they have included a smaller number of general-purpose instructions. But the 68000 is equipped with more powerful addressing modes and most of the instructions can use all of the addressing modes. This makes its general instructions very versatile. Moreover, it results in fewer instruction mnemonics for the programmer to remember and less restrictions on how operands can be accessed during instruction execution.

The 68000 microprocessor provides a very powerful minicomputer-like instruction set. It has 56 basic instruction types. A summary of the instructions is shown in Fig. 9.14. These basic instruction types coupled with their variations, shown in Fig. 9.15, the 14 addressing modes, and five data types produce a large number of executable instructions at the machine code level.

For ease of learning, we will divide the instructions of the 68000's instruction set into functionally related groups. In this chapter the groups covered are: the *data movement instructions*, the *integer arithmetic instructions*, the *decimal arithmetic instructions*, the *logic instructions*, and the *shift and rotate instructions*. The rest of the instruction set will be presented in Chapter 10.

Mnemonic	Description
ABCD	Add Decimal with Extend
ADD	Add
AND	Logical And
ASL	Arithmetic Shift Left
ASR	Arithmetic Shift Right
Bcc	Branch Conditionally
BCHG	Bit Test and Change
BCLR	Bit Test and Clear
BRA	Branch Always
BSET	Bit Test and Set
BSR	Branch to Subroutine
BTST	Bit Test
CHK	Check Register Against Bounds
CLR	Clear Operand
CMP	Compare
DBcc	Test Condition, Decrement and Branch
DIVS	Signed Divide
DIVU	Unsigned Divide
EOR	Exclusive Or
EXG	Exchange Registers
EXT	Sign Extend
JMP	Jump
JSR	Jump to Subroutine
LEA	Load Effective Address
LINK	Link Stack
LSL	Logical Shift Left
LSR	Logical Shift Right
MOVE	Move
MOVEM	Move Multiple Registers
MOVEP	Move Peripheral Data
MULS	Signed Multiply
MULU	Unsigned Multiply
NBCD	Negate Decimal with Extend
NEG	Negate
NOP	No Operation
NO	Ones Complement
OR	Logical Or
PEA	Push Effective Address
RESET	Reset External Devices
ROL	Rotate Left without Extend
ROR	Rotate Right without Extend
ROXL	Rotate Left with Extend
ROXR	Rotate Right with Extend
RTE	Return from Exception
RTR	Return and Restore
RTS	Return from Subroutine
SBCD	Subtract Decimal with Extend
Scc	Set Conditional
STOP	Stop
SUB	Subtract
SWAP	Swap Data Register Halves
TAS	Test and Set Operand
TRAP	Trap
TRAPV	Trap on Overflow
TST	Test
UNLK	Unlink

Figure 9.14 Instruction set summary (Motorola Inc.).

Instruction Type	Variation	Description
ADD	ADD	Add
	ADDA	Add Address
	ADDQ	Add Quick
	ADDI	Add Immediate
	ADDX	Add with Extend
AND	AND	Logical AND
	ANDI	AND Immediate
	ANDI to CCR	AND Immediate to Condition Code
	ANDI to SR	AND Immediate to Status Register
CMP	CMP	Compare
	CMPA	Compare Address
	CMPM	Compare Memory
	CMPI	Compare Immediate
EOR	EOR	Exclusive OR
	EORI	Exclusive OR Immediate
	EORI to CCR	Exclusive Immediate to Condition Codes
	EORI to SR	Exclusive OR Immediate to Status Register
MOVE	MOVE	Move
	MOVEA	Move Address
	MOVEQ	Move Quick
	MOVE to CCR	Move to Condition Codes
	MOVE to SR	Move to Status Register
	MOVE from SR	Move from Status Register
	MOVE to USP	Move to User Stack Pointer
NEG	NEG	Negate
	NEGX	Negate with Extend
OR	OR	Logical OR
	ORI	OR Immediate
	ORI to CCR	OR Immediate to Condition Codes
	ORI to SR	OR Immediate to Status Register
SUB	SUB	Subtract
	SUBA	Subtract Address
	SUBI	Subtract Immediate
	SUBQ	Subtract Quick
	SUBX	Subtract with Extend

Figure 9.15 Variations of instruction types (Motorola Inc.).

9.5 DATA TRANSFER INSTRUCTIONS

The 68000 provides instructions to transfer data between its internal registers, between an internal register and a storage location in memory, or between two locations in memory. The basic instructions in the data transfer group are shown in Fig. 9.16. Notice that it includes the following instructions: *move* (MOVE), *move multiple* (MOVEM), *load effective address* (LEA), *exchange* (EXG), *swap* (SWAP), and *clear* (CLR).

Move Instruction—MOVE

The first of the basic data transfer instructions in Fig. 9.16 is the MOVE instruction. This instruction has the ability to perform all three of the earlier mentioned data transfer operations. That is register to register, between register and memory, or memory to memory. Looking at Fig. 9.16, we see that there are eight different forms

Mnemonic	Meaning	Type	Operand Size	Operations
MOVE	Move	MOVE EAs,EAd	8, 16, 32	(EAs) → EAd
		MOVE EA,CCR	16	(EA) → CCR
		MOVE EA,SR	16	(EA) → SR
		MOVE SR,EA	16	SR → EA
		MOVE USP,An	32	USP → An
		MOVE An,USP	32	An → USP
		MOVEA EA,An	16, 32	(EA) → An
		MOVEQ #XXX,Dn	8	#XXX → Dn
MOVEM	Move multiple	MOVEM Reg_list,EA	16, 32	Reg_list → EA
		MOVEM EA,Reg_list	16, 32	(EA) → Reg_list
LEA	Load effective address	LEA EA,An	32	EA → An
EXG	Exchange	EXG Rx,Ry	32	Rx ↔ Ry
SWAP	Swap	SWAP Dn	16	Dn 31:16 ↔ Dn 15:0
CLR	Clear	CLR EA	8, 16, 32	0 → EA

Figure 9.16 Data transfer instructions.

of this instruction. Notice that they differ in both the size of operands they process and the types of operands that they can access.

The first form of the MOVE instruction is

MOVE   EAs,EAd

It permits movement of a source operand location identified by effective address EAs into a destination location identified by effective address EAd. The source and destination operands can be located in data registers, address registers, or storage locations in memory. Moreover, this instruction can be used to process byte, word, or long-word operands.

Whenever this instruction is processing word or long-word data, the source operand can be specified using any addressing mode. However, for operation on byte data, address register direct addressing mode cannot be used. This is because the address registers can be accessed only as word or long-word operands.

For the destination operand, only the alterable addressing modes are allowed. The addressing modes in this group were identified in Fig. 9.13. In other words, program counter relative and the immediate data addressing modes cannot be used to specify the location of the destination operand. Moreover, when processing byte operands, address register direct addressing cannot be used.

Another thing that may be important to note is how the condition code bits in the user byte of the 68000's status register are affected by execution of the MOVE instruction. The condition codes affected are the negative (N) bit, the zero (Z) bit, the overflow (V) bit, and the carry (C) bit. N and Z are set or cleared based on the result of the instruction: that is, the value copied into the destination location. If the result is negative, N is set; otherwise, it is cleared. Similarly, if the result is zero, Z is set, and if it is nonzero, it is cleared. The V and C bits are always cleared.

Here is an example of the move instruction that performs a word-copy operation.

MOVE.W   D0,D1

The source operand in D_0 is specified using data register direct addressing mode. Let us assume that the contents of register D_0 are 12345678_{16}. The destination operand in D_1 is also specified using data register direct addressing mode. Execution of the instruction causes the least significant word in D_0, which equals 5678_{16}, to be copied into the lower 16 bits of D_1.

Since the result in D_1 is positive and nonzero, the condition codes are affected as follows: N = 0, Z = 0, V = 0, C = 0, and X is not affected.

The next two forms shown in Fig. 9.16 for the MOVE instruction are provided for initialization of the status register. The instruction

MOVE   EA,CCR

allows only the condition code part of the status register to be specified as the destination operand. This operand is identified by CCR. On the other hand, any of the data addressing modes can be used for the source operand. This instruction can be used to load the user byte of SR from memory or an internal register. Even though the source operand size is specified as a word, just its eight least significant bits are used to modify the condition code bits in SR.

The second instruction

MOVE   EA,SR

is used to load all 16 bits of the status register. Therefore, its execution loads both the system byte and user byte. Since this instruction updates the most significant byte in SR, it can be executed only when the 68000 is in the supervisor state (privileged instruction).

Example 9.1

What will be the result of executing the following sequence of instructions?

MOVE.W   #12,D0

MOVE   D0, SR

Assume that the 68000 is in the supervisor state.

Solution. Execution of the first instruction loads the lower word of D_0 with immediate source operand 12_{10}.

$$12_{10} = 000C_{16} = 0000000000001100_2$$

After execution of this instruction, the condition code bits of SR are as follows:

$$X = \text{unchanged}$$
$$N = 0$$
$$Z = 0$$
$$V = 0$$
$$C = 0$$

Check Fig. 8.7 for the meaning of each of these bits. The result of executing the second instruction depends on the state of the 68000. We have assumed that it is operating in the supervisor state; therefore, SR is loaded with the lower word of D_0, which is 0000000000001100_2.

$$D0 = XXXXXXXXXXXXXXXX0000000000001100_2$$

$$SR = 0000000000001100_2$$

This gives the condition codes that follow:

$$X = 0$$
$$N = 1$$
$$Z = 1$$
$$V = 0$$
$$C = 0$$

The next form of the MOVE instruction shown in Fig. 9.16 is

MOVE SR,EA

Notice that its source operand is always the contents of SR and that the destination operand is represented by the effective address EA. Therefore, this instruction permits the programmer to save the contents of the status register in an address register, data register, or a storage location in data memory. In specifying the destination operand, only those addressing modes identified in Fig. 9.13 as alterable can be used.

For example, executing the instruction

MOVE SR,D7

causes the contents of SR to be copied into data register D_7. No condition codes are affected due to the execution of this instruction.

Since this instruction reads but does not modify the contents of SR, it can be executed when the 68000 is in either the user state or supervisor state.

The move user stack pointer instructions are shown in Fig. 9.16 to be

MOVE   USP,An

and

MOVE   An,USP

Notice that the data transfer that takes place is always between the user stack pointer (USP) register and one of the address registers. For this reason these instructions are used to read and to modify the user stack pointer, respectively. Since USP is a 32-bit register, both the source and destination operands are always long words in size.

Both of the instructions are privileged and must only be executed when the 68000 is in the supervisor state.

An efficient way of loading an address register from another address register, data register, or storage location in memory is with the *move address instruction*.

In Fig. 9.16, this form of the MOVE instruction is given as

MOVEA   EA,An

This instruction allows the operand to be either 16 bits or 32 bits in length. If the source operand is specified as a word, the address word is sign-extended to give a long word before it is moved into the address register.

The source operand can be specified using any of the 68000's addressing modes. For instance, the instruction

MOVEA.L   (A0),A6

employs address register indirect addressing. Execution of this instruction causes the long-word contents of the memory location pointed to by the address in A_0 to be loaded into address register A_6. Condition codes are not affected by execution of this instruction.

The last form of the MOVE instruction we find in Fig. 9.16 is

MOVEQ   #XXX,Dn

This instruction, *move quick,* is used to load a data register efficiently with a byte-wide immediate operand. The immediate data are encoded directly into the instruction operation word. Before this byte is loaded into the data register, it is sign extended to give 32 bits.

Move Multiple Registers Instruction—MOVEM

The move multiple registers (MOVEM) instruction provides an efficient mechanism for saving the contents of the internal registers into memory or to restore their contents from memory. One use of this instruction is to initialize a group of registers from a table in memory. This operation can be done with a series of MOVE instructions or with just one MOVEM instruction.

Another operation for which it can be useful is when working with subroutines. For instance, if a subroutine is to be initiated, typically the contents of the registers that are used during its execution must be saved in memory. Moreover, after its execution is complete, their contents must be restored. In this way, when program control is returned to the main program, the registers reflect the same information that they contained prior to entry into the subroutine. Either the save or restore operation can be performed with a single MOVEM instruction.

The two forms of MOVEM are shown in Fig. 9.16. The first form,

MOVEM   Reg-list,EA

is employed to save the contents of the registers specified in *register list* (Reg-list) in memory. They are saved at consecutive addresses in memory starting at the address specified by the destination operand. Any of the control addressing modes and address register indirect with predecrement can be used in conjunction with the destination operand.

The register list can include any combination of data and address registers. Which registers are to be saved are coded into a second word of the instruction. This

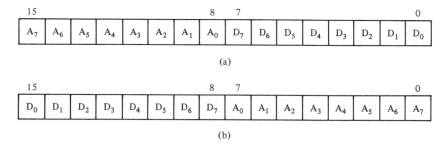

Figure 9.17   (a) Register list mask word format for control mode and postincrement addressing; (b) format for address register indirect with predecrement addressing.

word is called the *register list mask*. As shown in Fig. 9.17(a), each bit of this mask corresponds to one of the 68000's internal registers. Setting a bit to 1 indicates that the corresponding register is included in the list and 0 indicates that it is not included. Notice that data registers D_0 through D_7 correspond to bits 0 through 7 of the mask, respectively, and address registers A_0 through A_7 correspond to bits 8 through 15, respectively. When address register indirect with predecrement addressing is used, the meaning of the bits of the mask word are changed as shown in Fig. 9.17(b). The register corresponding to the first set bit is saved first, followed by the register corresponding to the next set bit and so on. The last saved register corresponds to the last set bit.

This instruction can be written to perform word or long-word data transfers. In a word operation, only the least significant word parts of the specified registers are saved in memory. In this case it requires one word of memory storage for each register. However, if long-word transfers are specified, each register needs two words of memory.

The second form of the MOVEM instruction shown in Fig. 9.16 permits the internal registers of the 68000 to be initialized or restored from memory. It is written as

$$\text{MOVEM}\quad\text{EA,Reg-list}$$

Execution of this instruction causes the word or long-word contents of the registers in Reg-list to be loaded one after the other from memory. When specifying the source operand, the starting address of the table of values to be loaded can only use the control or postincrement addressing modes.

Example 9.2

Write an instruction that will do the reverse of the instruction

$$\text{MOVEM.W}\quad\text{D0/D1/A5,\$AF00}$$

Solution.   This instruction will save the lower words of registers D_0, D_1, and A_5 in memory at word addresses $AF00_{16}$, $AF02_{16}$, and $AF04_{16}$, respectively. To restore the registers, the instruction is written as

$$\text{MOVEM.W}\quad\text{\$AF00,D0/D1/A5}$$

Figure 9.18 illustrates what happens due to the execution of these two instructions.

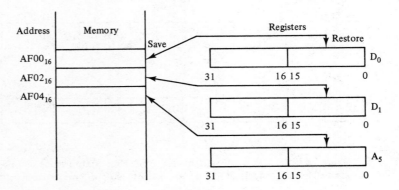

Figure 9.18 Save and restore of processor register contents as implemented with the MOVEM instructions.

Load Effective Address Instruction—LEA

Another way of loading an address register is with the load effective address (LEA) instruction. The form of this instruction is given in Fig. 9.16 as

$$LEA \quad EA,An$$

Execution of this instruction does not load the destination operand with the contents of the specified source operand. Instead, it computes an effective address based on the addressing mode used for the source operand and loads this value into the address register specified as the destination. Only the control addressing modes listed in Fig. 9.13 can be used to describe the source operand.

To understand better the operation of this instruction, let us consider an example. The instruction

$$LEA \quad 6(A1,D0),A2$$

uses address register indirect with index addressing for the source operand. Its destination is simply address register A_2. Execution of the instruction causes A_2 to be loaded with the effective address

$$A2 = A1 + D0 + 6_{10}$$

Assuming that $A_1 = 00004000_{16}$ and $D_0 = 000012AB_{16}$, the effective address that is loaded into A_2 equals

$$A2 = 00004000_{16} + 000012AB_{16} + 6_{16}$$
$$= 000052B1_{16}$$

Exchange Instruction—EXG

Earlier we showed how the MOVE instruction could be used to move the contents of one of the internal registers of the 68000 to another internal register. Another type of requirement for some applications is to exchange efficiently the contents of two registers. It is for this reason that the exchange (EXG) instruction is included in the instruction set of the 68000.

This instruction is shown in Fig. 9.16 to have the form

$$\text{EXG} \quad \text{Rx,Ry}$$

Here Rx and Ry stand for arbitrarily selected data or address registers. An example is the instruction

$$\text{EXG} \quad \text{D0,A3}$$

It will load data register D_0 with the contents of address register A_3 and A_3 with the contents of D_0. The data transfers that take place are always 32 bits long and no condition code bits are affected.

Swap Instruction—SWAP

The swap (SWAP) instruction is similar to the exchange instruction in that it has the ability to exchange two values. However, it is used to exchange the upper and lower words in a data register. The general form of SWAP is given in Fig. 9.16 as

$$\text{SWAP Dn}$$

An example is

$$\text{SWAP} \quad \text{D0}$$

When this instruction is executed, the contents of the lower 16 bits of D_0 are swapped with its upper 16 bits. The 32-bit value that results in D_0 after the swap operation is used to set or reset the condition code flags.

Clear Instruction—CLR

The CLR instruction can be used to initialize the contents of an internal register or storage location in data memory to zero. Figure 9.16 shows that the instruction is written in general as

$$\text{CLR} \quad \text{EA}$$

and that it can perform its operation on byte, word, or long-word operands. All alterable addressing modes except address register direct can be used to access the operand.

For instance, to clear the least significant 8 bits of D_0, the following instruction is executed:

$$\text{CLR.B} \quad \text{D0}$$

Whenever this instruction is executed, the Z bit of SR is set and the N, V, and C bits are cleared. Moreover, the X bit is not affected.

9.6 INTEGER ARITHMETIC INSTRUCTIONS

The instruction set of the 68000 provides instructions to perform binary arithmetic operations, such as add, subtract, multiply, and divide. These instructions can process both signed and unsigned numbers. Moreover, the data being processed can be organized as bytes, words, or long words. The instructions in this group are shown in Fig. 9.19.

The condition code bits in the SR register are set or reset as per the result of arithmetic instructions. For ADD, SUB, and NEG instructions the five condition code bits are affected as follows:

N is set if the result is negative, cleared otherwise

Z is set if the result is zero, cleared otherwise

V is set if an overflow occurs, cleared otherwise

X and C are set if carry is generated or borrow is taken, cleared otherwise

For MUL, DIV, and EXT instructions, V and C are always cleared, X not affected, and N and Z are set or cleared like that in other arithmetic instructions: ADD, SUB, and NEG.

Mnemonic	Meaning	Type	Operand Size	Operation
ADD	Add|	ADD EA, Dn	8, 16, 32	$(EA) + Dn \rightarrow Dn$
		ADD Dn, EA	8, 16, 32	$Dn + (EA) \rightarrow EA$
		ADDI #XXX, EA	8, 16, 32	$\#XXX + (EA) \rightarrow EA$
		ADDQ #XXX, EA	8, 16, 32	$\#XXX + (EA) \rightarrow EA$
		ADDX Dy, Dx	8, 16, 32	$Dy + Dx + X \rightarrow Dx$
		ADDX $^-$(Ay), $^-$(Ax)	8, 16, 32	$^-(Ay) + {}^-(Ax) + X \rightarrow (Ax)$
		ADDA EA, An	16, 32	$(EA) + An \rightarrow An$
SUB	Subtract|	SUB EA, Dn	8, 16, 32	$Dn - (EA) \rightarrow Dn$
		SUB Dn, EA	8, 16, 32	$(EA) - Dn \rightarrow EA$
		SUBI #XXX, EA	8, 16, 32	$(EA) - \#XXX \rightarrow EA$
		SUBQ #XXX, EA	8, 16, 32	$(EA) - \#XXX \rightarrow EA$
		SUBX Dy, Dx	8, 16, 32	$Dx - Dy \rightarrow Dx$
		SUBX $^-$(Ay), $^-$(Ax)	8, 16, 32	$^-(Ax) - {}^-(Ay) \rightarrow (Ax)$
		SUBA EA, An	16, 32	$An - (EA) \rightarrow An$
NEG	Negate	NEG EA, Dn	8, 16, 32	$0 - (EA) \rightarrow EA$
		NEGX EA, Dn	8, 16, 32	$0 - (EA) - X \rightarrow EA$
MUL	Multiply	MULS EA, Dn	16	$(EA) \cdot Dn \rightarrow Dn$
		MULU EA, Dn	16	$(EA) \cdot Dn \rightarrow Dn$
DIV	Divide	DIVS EA, Dn	$32 \div 16$	$Dn \div (EA) \rightarrow Dn$
		DIVU EA, Dn	$32 \div 16$	$Dn \div (EA) \rightarrow Dn$
EXT	Extend sign	EXT.W Dn	$8 \rightarrow 16$	Dn byte $\rightarrow$ Dn word
		EXT.L Dn	$16 \rightarrow 32$	Dn word $\rightarrow$ Dn long word

Figure 9.19 Integer arithmetic instructions.

Addition Instructions—ADD, ADDI, ADDQ, ADDX, and ADDA

For implementing the binary addition operation, the 68000 provides five types of add instructions. All five forms together with their permitted operand sizes are shown in Fig. 9.19. The different types of instructions are provided for dealing with different kinds of addition requirements. For instance, when addresses are manipulated, we want to operate on data in the address registers and do not want to affect the condition codes in SR. Thus for this situation a special address addition (ADDA) instruction is provided.

The first four forms of the add instruction in Fig. 9.19 are generally used to process data and the last form is for modifying addresses. Two forms of the basic *add* (ADD) instruction are shown. The first form

$$ADD\quad EA,Dn$$

adds the contents of the location specified by the effective address EA to the contents of data register D_n; that is,

$$(EA) + Dn \longrightarrow Dn$$

The source operand can be located in an internal register or a storage location in memory. Moreover, its effective address can be specified with any of the addressing modes of the 68000. The only exception is that the size of the operand cannot be specified as a byte when address register direct addressing mode is used.

For instance, the instruction

$$ADD.L\quad D0,D1$$

causes the contents of D_0 to be added to the contents of D_1. If the original contents of D_0 are $00013344 and that of D_1 are $00000FFF, the sum that is produced equals $00014343 and it is saved in D_1.

The second form is similar except that it represents the addition of the contents of a source data register to the contents of a destination operand that is identified by the effective address EA.

$$ADD\quad Dn,EA$$

$$Dn + (EA) \longrightarrow EA$$

In this case only the alterable memory addressing modes are applicable to the destination operand.

Example 9.3

Write an instruction sequence that can be used to add two long words whose locations in memory are specified by the contents of address registers A_1 and A_2, respectively.

Solution. We will use D_0 as an intermediate storage location for implementing the memory-to-memory add. The instruction sequence is

$$
\begin{array}{ll}
CLR.L & D0 \\
ADD.L & (A1),D0 \\
ADD.L & D0,(A2)
\end{array}
$$

The instruction *add immediate* (ADDI) operates similarly to the ADD instruction we just introduced. The important difference is that now the value of the source operand is always located in program memory as an immediate operand. That is, it is encoded as the second word of the instruction for byte and word operands or as a second and third word for long-word operands. The general instruction format as shown in Fig. 9.19 is

ADDI   #XXX,EA

Here #XXX stands for the immediate source operand and EA is the effective address of the destination operand. For example, the instruction

ADD.L #$0FFFF,D0

causes the value $FFFF_{16}$ to be added to the long-word contents of D_0.

The *add quick* (ADDQ) instruction of Fig. 9.19 is a special variation of the add-immediate instruction. It limits the size of the source operand to the range 1 through 8.

An example is the instruction

ADDQ #3,D1

It stands for add the number 3 to the contents of D_1. These immediate data are encoded directly into the instruction word. For this reason, ADDQ encodes in fewer bytes and executes faster than ADDI. Therefore, it is preferred when memory requirement and execution times are to be minimized. Of course, the addition that is performed cannot involve a number larger than 8 as the source operand.

The next type of addition instruction in Fig. 9.19 is the *add extend* (ADDX) instruction. It differs from the earlier instructions in that the addition it performs involves the two operands along with the extend (X) bit of SR. One form of the instruction is

ADDX   Dy,Dx

and the arithmetic operation it performs is

$$Dy + Dx + X \longrightarrow Dx$$

That is, the contents of data register Dy are added to the contents of data register Dx and extend bit X. The sum that results is placed in Dx. Notice that both operands must always be in data registers.

The other form of the ADDX instruction, as shown in Fig. 9.19, specifies its operands with predecrement address register indirect addressing. It permits access to data stored in memory.

The last form of the addition instruction in Fig. 9.19 is the *add address* (ADDA) instruction. Its form is

ADDA EA,An

and its execution results in

$$(EA) + An \longrightarrow An$$

The source operand can employ any of the addressing modes of the 68000. For this reason the source operand can reside in an internal register or storage location in memory. On the other hand, the destination is always an address register. Since the destination operand is always an address register, only word or long-word operations are permitted.

An example is

ADDA.W   D3,A3

Execution of this instruction causes the word value in D_3 to be added to the contents of A_3.

Subtract Instructions—SUB, SUBI, SUBQ, SUBX, and SUBA

Having covered the addition instructions of the 68000, let us look at the instructions provided to perform binary subtraction. As shown in Fig. 9.19, the subtraction instruction also has five basic forms. Notice that these forms are identical to those already described for the addition operation. For this reason we will present the subtraction instructions in less detail.

The general *subtraction* (SUB) instruction of the 68000 can be written in general using either the form

SUB   EA,Dn

or

SUB   Dn,EA

The first form permits the contents of an internal register or storage location in memory to be subtracted from the contents of a data register. The difference that is obtained is stored in the selected destination data register. This operation can be expressed as

$$Dn - (EA) \longrightarrow Dn$$

For instance, the instruction

SUB   D0,D1

performs a register-to-register subtraction. The difference $D_1 - D_0$ is saved in D_1.

The second SUB instruction in Fig. 9.19 performs the opposite subtraction operation. Its source operand is a data register within the 68000 and the location of the destination is specified by an effective address. Therefore, it can be a data register, address register, or storage location in data memory.

The next two subtraction instructions in Fig. 9.19, *subtract immediate* (SUBI) and *subtract quick* (SUBQ), permit an immediate operand in program memory to be subtracted from the destination operand identified by EA. The destination operand can be a data register or a storage location in data memory. These instructions operate the same as their addition counterparts except that they calculate the difference between their source and destination operands instead of their sum.

For instance,

$$\text{SUBI.W} \quad \#\$1234,\text{D0}$$

causes the value 1234_{16} to be subtracted from the contents of D_0. Assuming that D_0 initially contains $00FFFF_{16}$, the difference produced in D_0 is

$$FFFF_{16} - 1234_{16} = EDCB_{16}$$

Extend subtract (SUBX), just like ADDX, includes the extend (X) bit of SR in the subtraction. Moreover, the same source and destination operand variations are permitted as for the ADDX instruction. For example, the first form in Fig. 9.19 is

$$\text{SUBX} \quad \text{Dy,Dx}$$

and it performs the subtraction

$$\text{Dx} - \text{Dy} - \text{X} \longrightarrow \text{Dx}$$

Finally, *subtract address* (SUBA) of Fig. 9.19 is used to modify addresses in A_0 through A_6 by subtraction. For example, it can be used to subtract the contents of data register D_7 from the address in A_5 with the instruction

$$\text{SUBA} \quad \text{D7,A5}$$

Negate Instructions—NEG and NEGX

Another type of arithmetic instruction is the negate instruction. Two forms of this instruction are shown in Fig. 9.19. The negate instructions are similar to the subtract instructions in that the source operand is subtracted from a destination operand. However, in this case, the destination operand is always assumed to be zero. Subtracting any number from zero gives its negative.

The basic *negate* (NEG) instruction is used to form the negative of the specified operand. It is given in general by

$$\text{NEG} \quad \text{EA}$$

and an example is the instruction

$$\text{NEG.W} \quad \text{D0}$$

If the original contents of D_0 are $00FF_{16}$, execution of the instruction produces the result $FF01_{16}$.

Negate with extend (NEGX) differs from NEG in that it subtracts both the contents of the specified operand and the extend (X) flag from 0. That is, it performs the operation

$$0 - (\text{EA}) - \text{X} \longrightarrow \text{EA}$$

Both instructions can be written to process bytes, words, or long words of data. Moreover, the addressing modes permitted for the operand are the alterable addressing modes that were shown in Fig. 9.13.

Multiply Instructions—MULS and MULU

The 68000 provides instructions that perform the multiplication arithmetic operation on unsigned or signed numbers. Separate instructions are provided to process these two types of numbers. As shown in Fig. 9.19, they are signed multiply,

MULS EA,Dn

and unsigned multiply,

MULU EA,Dn

Both MULS and MULU have two 16-bit operands which are labeled EA and Dn. The source operand EA can be specified with any of the data addressing modes and the destination operand always uses data register direct addressing. Both the source and destination operands are treated as signed numbers when executing MULS and as unsigned numbers when executing MULU. The result, which is a 32-bit number, is placed in the destination data register.

Here is an example of the instruction needed to multiply the unsigned word number in data register D_1 by the unsigned word number in D_0.

MULU   D0,D1

At completion of execution of the instruction, the long-word product that results is in D_1.

As in most arithmetic instructions, the condition code bits of SR are updated based on the product that results. Two of the condition code bits, zero (Z) and negative (N), are affected based on the results. On the other hand, carry (C) and overflow (V) are always cleared.

Division Instructions—DIVS and DIVU

Similar to the multiplication instructions of the 68000, there is a *signed divide* (DIVS) instruction and an *unsigned divide* (DIVU) instruction. They are expressed in general as

DIVS   EA,Dn

and

DIVU   EA,Dn

The destination operand, which is the dividend, must be the contents of one of the data registers. The source operand, which is the divisor, can be accessed using any of the data addressing modes of the 68000.

Execution of either of these instructions causes the 32-bit dividend identified by the destination operand to be divided by the 16-bit divisor specified by the effective address. The 16-bit quotient that results is produced in the lower word of the destination data register and the remainder is placed in the upper word of the same register. The sign of the remainder produced by a signed division is always the same as that of the dividend.

The condition codes that are affected by the division instruction are zero (Z) and negative (N). They are set or reset based on the quotient value and its sign. Furthermore, the carry flag is always cleared. If the result turns out to be over 16 bits, the overflow condition code bit is set and the operands are not changed. Thus one should check the V flag for an overflow after executing a division instruction. An attempt to divide by zero is also automatically detected by the 68000.

Sign Extend Instruction—EXT

The 68000 provides the *sign extend* (EXT) instruction for *sign extension* of byte or word operands. As shown in Fig. 9.19, the general form of this instruction is given by

$$\text{EXT} \quad \text{Dn}$$

Note that its operand must be located in a data register. When EXT is executed, the sign bit of the operand is copied into the most significant bits of the register.

For instance, when the word value in D_1 must be extended to a long word, the instruction

$$\text{EXT.L} \quad \text{D1}$$

can be executed. It causes the value in bit 15 (the sign bit) to be copied into bits 16 through 31 of D_1.

Sign extension is required before data of unequal lengths can be involved in signed arithmetic operations. For instance, if one of the operands for an addition instruction that is written to process word data is expressed as a signed byte, it must first be extended to a signed word.

Example 9.4

Assume that data registers D_0, D_1, and D_2 contain a signed byte, a signed word, and a signed long word in 2's-complement form, respectively. Write a sequence of instructions that will produce the signed result of the operation that follows:

$$D_0 + D_1 - D_2 \longrightarrow D_0$$

Solution.   Before any addition or subtraction can be performed, we must extend each value of data to a signed long word. To convert the byte in D_0 to its equivalent long word, we must first convert it to a word and then to a long word. This is done with the following instructions:

$$\text{EXT.W} \quad \text{D0}$$

$$\text{EXT.L} \quad \text{D0}$$

Similarly, to convert the word in D_1 to a long word, we execute the instruction

$$\text{EXT.L} \quad \text{D1}$$

Since the contents of D_2 are already a signed long word, no sign extension is necessary.

To do the required arithmetic operations, we just use the appropriate arithmetic instructions. For instance, to add the contents of D_0 and D_1, we use ADD, and to sub-

EXT.W   D0
EXT.L   D0
EXT.L   D1
ADD.L   D1, D0   **Figure 9.20** Addition and subtraction of
SUB.L   D2, D0   signed numbers.

tract the contents of D_2 from this sum, we use SUB. This leads us to the following sequence of instructions.

$$ADD.L \quad D1,D0$$

$$SUB.L \quad D2,D0$$

The complete program is listed in Fig. 9.20.

9.7 DECIMAL ARITHMETIC INSTRUCTIONS

The arithmetic instructions we considered in the preceding section process data that is expressed as binary numbers. However, data are frequently provided that are coded as BCD numbers instead of as binary numbers. Traditionally, BCD-to-binary and binary-to-BCD conversion routines are used to process BCD data. However, the 68000 microprocessor has the ability to perform the add, subtract, and negate arithmetic operations directly on packed BCD numbers. Three BCD arithmetic instructions, ABCD, SBCD, and NBCD, are provided for this purpose. They provide an efficient and easy to use method for implementing BCD arithmetic. As per the result of these instructions, the condition code bits Z, C, and X are affected, whereas N and V are undefined.

Add Decimal with Extend Instruction—ABCD

Let us begin with the *add binary-coded decimal* (ABCD) instruction. In Fig. 9.21 we see its permitted operand variations, operand size, and the operation it performs. Notice that only two addressing modes can be used to specify its operands. The first form,

$$ABCD \quad Dy,Dx$$

uses data register direct addressing for both source and destination operands. Therefore, both operands must reside in internal data registers of the 68000.

Mnemonic	Meaning	Type	Operand Size	Operation
ABCD	Add BCD numbers	ABCD Dy, Dx ABCD $^-$(Ay), $^-$(Ax)	8 8	Dy + Dx + X → Dx $^-$(Ay) + $^-$(Ax) + X → (Ax)
SBCD	Subtract BCD numbers	SBCD Dy, Dx SBCD $^-$(Ay), $^-$(Ax)	8 8	Dx − Dy − X → Dx $^-$(Ax) − $^-$(Ay) − X → (Ax)
NBCD	Negate BCD numbers	NBCD EA	8	0 − (EA) − X → EA

Figure 9.21 Binary-coded-decimal arithmetic instructions.

The other form,

$$ABCD \quad -(Ay), -(Ax)$$

employs predecrement address register indirect addressing to specify both operands. Use of this addressing mode permits access of data stored in memory.

Execution of either of the ABCD instructions adds the contents of the source and destination operands together with the extend (X) bit of SR. The sum that results is saved in the destination operand location.

These instructions perform decimal addition operations; therefore, we must start with decimal operands instead of binary operands. These decimal operands are expressed in packed BCD. The sum that is produced is also a decimal number coded in packed BCD. However, the operand size is always byte wide; therefore, two BCD digits can be processed at a time.

An example is the instruction

$$ABCD \quad D0, D1$$

If D_0 initially contains the value $12_{10} = 00010010_2$, D_1 contains $37_{10} = 00110111_2$, and X is clear, execution of the instruction produces the sum

$$D0 + D1 + X = 12_{10} + 37_{10} + 0_{10}$$
$$= 49_{10}$$

At completion of the instruction, D_0 still contains 12_{10} but the contents of D_1 are changed to 49_{10}. X remains cleared because no carry results.

Condition code bits Z, X, and C are affected based on the result produced by the addition. Bits C and X are always set to the same logic level. The other two condition code bits, V and N, are undefined after execution of the instruction and do not provide any usable information.

Subtract Decimal with Extend Instruction—SBCD

The *subtract binary-coded decimal* (SBCD) instruction works similar to the ABCD instruction just discussed. Of course, in this case, the subtraction arithmetic operation is performed and not the addition operation.

As shown in Fig. 9.21, the two forms of the instruction are

$$SBCD \quad Dy, Dx$$

and

$$SBCD \quad -(Ay), -(Ax)$$

Notice that the permitted addressing modes are identical to those employed by the ABCD instruction.

An example is the instruction

$$SBCD \quad -(A0), -(A1)$$

When this instruction is executed, the byte-wide (two BCD digits) contents of the source operand and X bit of SR are subtracted from the destination operand. The difference that is produced is saved at the destination location.

In our example we are using address register indirect with predecrement addressing. Therefore, the contents of address registers A_0 and A_1 are first decremented by 1. For instance, if their original contents were $0000110F_{16}$ and $0000120F_{16}$, respectively, decrementing by 1 gives $A_0 = 0000110E_{16}$ and $A_1 = 0000120E_{16}$. These are the addresses that are used to access the operands in memory. Then the BCD data at memory location $00110E_{16}$ and (X) are subtracted from the BCD value at $00120E_{16}$. We will assume that the value stored at $00120E_{16}$ is 37_{10}, the value at $00110E_{16}$ is 12_{10}, and X is set to 1. Then the difference calculated by the instruction is

$$(00120E_{16}) - (00110E_{16}) - X = 37_{10} - 12_{10} - 1_{10}$$
$$= 24_{10}$$

This value is saved at destination address $00120E_{16}$ and the condition code bits Z, X, and C are cleared.

Negate Decimal Instruction—NBCD

The last of the decimal arithmetic instructions in Fig. 9.21 is *negate binary-coded decimal* (NBCD). It is expressed in general as

$$NBCD \quad EA$$

NBCD is effectively an SBCD instruction in which the subtrahend always equals zero. For this reason it implements the operation

$$0 - (EA) \longrightarrow EA$$

The operand identified as EA can be specified using the alterable addressing modes. One exception is the address register direct addressing, which cannot be used.

Here is an example with the operand accessed through address register indirect addressing mode with postincrement:

$$NBCD \quad (A5)+$$

The condition code bits affected by the NBCD instruction are the same as those affected by the SBCD instruction.

Example 9.5

Write a program segment that will add two four-digit packed BCD numbers that are held in registers D_0 and D_1 and place their sum in D_0. The organization of the original BCD data in the data registers is shown in Fig. 9.22(a).

Solution.   Remember that only the contents of the 8 least significant bits of a data register can be processed with the BCD instructions. Moreover, up to this point in the chapter we have not shown any direct way of exchanging the most significant byte of a word in a data register with its least significant byte. One solution to this problem is to move the contents of D_0 and D_1 to memory. This reorganizes the BCD digits at separate byte addresses, as shown in Fig. 9.22(b). To move D_0 and D_1 to memory, say D_0 to address

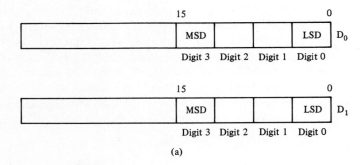

(a)

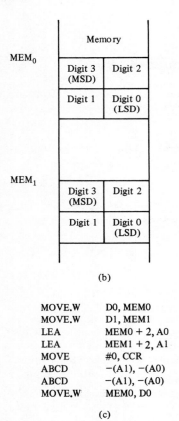

(b)

```
MOVE.W      D0, MEM0
MOVE.W      D1, MEM1
LEA         MEM0 + 2, A0
LEA         MEM1 + 2, A1
MOVE        #0, CCR
ABCD        −(A1), −(A0)
ABCD        −(A1), −(A0)
MOVE.W      MEM0, D0
```

(c)

Figure 9.22   (a) Four-digit BCD numbers in data registers D_0 and D_1; (b) storage of the BCD numbers in memory; (c) program for adding two four-digit BCD numbers.

MEM_0 and D_1 to address MEM_1, the following instructions can be used:

$$MOVE.W \quad D0,MEM0$$

$$MOVE.W \quad D1,MEM1$$

Now we can use the predecrement address register indirect form of the BCD addition instruction to perform the decimal arithmetic operations. Therefore, address registers must be loaded with pointers to the data in memory. Let us use A_0 and A_1 for this purpose. Since the predecrement mode of addressing must be used, A_0 should be loaded with $MEM_0 + 2$ and A_1 with MEM1 + 2. This is done with the instructions

$$LEA \quad MEM0+2,A0$$

$$LEA \quad MEM1+2,A1$$

Moreover, in order to use the BCD instructions, we must start with X = 0. To do this, we execute the instruction

$$MOVE \quad \#0,CCR$$

Now that the address pointers and the extend bit of SR are initialized, we are ready to perform the addition operation. Executing the instructions

$$ABCD \quad -(A1), -(A0)$$

and

$$ABCD \quad -(A1), -(A0)$$

gives the sum in MEM_0.

To put the sum into D_0, the instruction is

$$MOVE.W \quad MEM0,D0$$

The complete program is repeated in Fig. 9.22(c).

9.8 LOGIC INSTRUCTIONS

To implement logic functions, such as AND, OR, exclusive-OR, and NOT, the instruction set of the 68000 provides a group of logic instructions. The instructions in this group are shown in Fig. 9.23 together with their different forms, operand sizes, and operations. The execution of logic instructions sets the condition code bits N and Z as per the result, clears V and C, and does not affect the X bit.

AND Instructions—AND and ANDI

As shown in Fig. 9.23, there are four forms of the AND instruction. The general form, which uses the mnemonic AND, permits the contents of a data register and an operand specified by the effective address EA to be ANDed together. Let us look at the first form of the instruction

$$AND \quad EA,Dn$$

The source operand can use the data addressing modes to generate EA. Therefore,

Mnemonic	Meaning	Type	Operand Size	Operation
AND	Logical AND	AND EA,Dn	8, 16, 32	(EA) · Dn → Dn
		AND Dn,EA	8, 16, 32	Dn · (EA) → EA
		ANDI #XXX,EA	8, 16, 32	#XXX · (EA) → EA
		ANDI #XXX,CCR	8	#XXX · CCR → CCR
		ANDI #XXX,SR	16	#XXX · SR → SR
OR	Logical OR	OR EA,Dn	8, 16, 32	(EA) + Dn → Dn
		OR Dn,EA	8, 16, 32	Dn + (EA) → EA
		ORI #XXX,EA	8, 16, 32	#XXX + (EA) → EA
		ORI #XXX,CCR	8	#XXX + CCR → CCR
		ORI #XXX,SR	16	#XXX + SR → SR
EOR	Logical exclusive-OR	EOR Dn,EA	8, 16, 32	Dn ⊕ (EA) → EA
		EORI #XXX,EA	8, 16, 32	#XXX ⊕ (EA) → EA
		EORI #XXX,CCR	8	#XXX ⊕ CCR → CCR
		EORI #XXX,SR	16	#XXX ⊕ SR → SR
NOT	Logical NOT	NOT EA	8, 16, 32	$\overline{(EA)}$ → EA

Figure 9.23 Logic instructions.

the source operand can use any addressing mode except address register direct addressing. On the other hand, the destination operand can be specified only with data register direct addressing and will always be one of the eight data registers inside the 68000.

An example of the instruction, which uses register direct addressing for both the source and destination operands, is

$$\text{AND.B D0,D1}$$

Execution of this instruction causes a bit for bit AND operation to be performed on the byte contents of D_0 and D_1. The result is saved in destination register D_1.

For instance, if D_1 contains $0000ABCD_{16}$ and D_0 contains $00000F0F_{16}$, the AND operation between the least significant bytes gives

$$CD_{16} \cdot 0F_{16} = 11001101_2 \cdot 00001111_2$$
$$= 00001101_2$$
$$= 0D_{16}$$

Therefore, the new contents of D_1 are $AB0D_{16}$. Notice that the four most significant bits of the least significant byte of D_1 have been masked off.

The affected condition code bits in SR are Z, N, C, and V. The C and V bits are always cleared, but Z and N are set or reset based on the result produced in the destination register.

The second form,

$$\text{AND Dn,EA}$$

permits the contents of a source operand held in a data register to be ANDed with a destination operand identified by EA. This time the location of the destination operand can be specified using any of the alterable memory addressing modes. These addressing modes are identified in Fig. 9.13.

The next three types of the AND group are *AND immediate* (ANDI) instructions. These instructions AND an immediate source operand identified as #XXX with the contents of a specified destination operand. The immediate operand is stored as part of the instruction in program memory.

The first form,

ANDI   #XXX,EA

permits ANDing of an immediate source operand with the contents of a destination operand whose location is specified by effective address EA. This destination operand can be in a data register, address register, or storage location in data memory.

The next two forms,

ANDI   #XXX,SR

and

ANDI   #XXX,CCR

are used to AND the contents of the complete status register and the condition code byte part of SR with immediate data, respectively. The first of these two operations is privileged and can only be executed when the 68000 is in the supervisor state.

OR Instructions—OR and ORI

The OR instruction has the same five forms that we just introduced for the AND instruction. Figure 9.23 shows that they include two forms of the *general OR* instruction and three forms of the *OR immediate* (ORI) instruction.

The general OR instruction permits the OR logic operation to be performed between the contents of a data register specified using one operand and the contents of another data register, an address register, or a location in memory specified by the data addressing mode of the other operand. For example, the instruction

OR.B   (A0),D0

ORs the contents of the byte location whose effective address is the contents of A_0 with the byte contents of D_0. The result is saved in D_0. That is, it performs the logic operation

$$(EA) + D0 \longrightarrow D0$$

The OR immediate forms of the instruction allow an immediate operand to be ORed with the contents of a storage location in data memory, a data register, or the status register. An example is the instruction

ORI   #FF00,SR

Execution of this instruction causes all of the bits in the upper byte of SR to be set to 1 without changing the bits in the lower byte. Since the status register's upper byte is changed, the operation can only be performed when in the supervisor state.

Exclusive-OR Instructions—EOR and EORI

Looking at Fig. 9.23, we see that the same basic instruction forms are also provided for the *exclusive-OR* (EOR) instruction. The difference here is that they perform the exclusive-OR logic function on the contents of the source and destination operands. Let us now look at some examples. A first example of the instruction is

$$\text{EOR.L} \quad \text{A0,D0}$$

When it is executed, the operation performed is

$$\text{A0} \oplus \text{D0} \longrightarrow \text{D0}$$

Another example is

$$\text{EOR} \quad \text{\#\$0F,CCR}$$

Execution of this instruction performs the operation

$$\text{\$0F} \oplus \text{CCR} \longrightarrow \text{CCR}$$

NOT Instruction—NOT

The *NOT* instruction differs from the AND, OR, and EOR instructions we just described in that only one operand is specified. Its general form, as shown in Fig. 9.23, is

$$\text{NOT} \quad \text{EA}$$

When this instruction is executed, the contents of the specified operand are replaced by its 1's complement. To address the operand, only the alterable addressing modes can be used. However, one exception exists: it is that address register direct addressing is not permitted.

Example 9.6

Write a sequence of logic instructions that will clear the bits in register D_1 that correspond to the bits that are set in D_0.

Solution. To clear a bit that is set, it should be ANDed with logic 0. Moreover, to obtain a logic 0 from logic 1, it should be inverted. Thus if the contents of D_0 are inverted and then ANDed with D_1, the required result will be generated in D_1. The instructions that do this are

$$\text{NOT.L} \qquad \text{D0}$$

$$\text{AND.L} \qquad \text{D0,D1}$$

9.9 SHIFT AND ROTATE INSTRUCTIONS

The shift and rotate instructions of the 68000 are used to change bit positions of the data bits in an operand. These types of operations are useful to multiply or divide a given number by a power of 2, check the status of individual bits in an operand, or simply shift the position of data bits in a register or memory location.

Mnemonic	Meaning	Type	Operand Size	Operation
LSL	Logical shift left	LSL #XXX,Dy LSL Dx,Dy LSL EA	8, 16, 32 8, 16, 32 8, 16, 32	X/C ← ← 0
LSR	Logical shift right	LSR #XXX,Dy LSR Dx,Dy LSR EA	8, 16, 32 8, 16, 32 8, 16, 32	0 → → X/C
ASL	Arithmetic shift left	ASL #XXX,Dy ASL Dx,Dy ASL EA	8, 16, 32 8, 16, 32 8, 16, 32	X/C ← ← 0
ASR	Arithmetic shift right	ASR #XXX,Dy ASR Dx,Dy ASR EA	8, 16, 32 8, 16, 32 8, 16, 32	→ → X/C, MSB

Figure 9.24 Shift instructions.

Shift Instructions—LSL, LSR, ASL, and ASR

There are two kinds of shift operations: the *logical shift* and the *arithmetic shift*. Moreover, each of these two shifts can be performed in the *left direction* or *right direction*. As shown in Fig. 9.24, these variations lead to four basic shift instructions.

The two logical shift instructions are *logical shift left* (LSL) and *logical shift right* (LSR). The operation of these instructions are illustrated with diagrams in Fig. 9.24. Looking at the illustration for LSL, we see that its execution causes the bits of the operand to be shifted to the left by a specific number of bit positions. At the same time, the vacated bit positions on the least significant bit end of the operand are filled with zeros and bits are shifted out from the most significant bit end. The last bit shifted out on the left is copied in both the extend (X) and carry (C) bits of SR.

Notice in Fig. 9.24 that there are three forms of the LSL instruction. The first two forms differ in the way the shift count is specified. In the first form

$$LSL \quad \#XXX,Dy$$

the count is specified by the immediate operand #XXX. The value of this operand can be from 0 through 7. A value of zero stands for "shift left eight bit positions." In this way, we see that this form of the instruction limits the shift left to the range of from 1 to 8 bits. For instance,

$$LSL.W \quad \#5,D4$$

initiates a shift left by five bit positions for the word contents of data register D_4.

The second form

$$LSL \quad Dx,Dy$$

specifies the count as residing in data register Dx. Only the six least significant bits of this register are used for the shift count. Therefore, the shift count is extended to a range of from 1 to 63 bit positions.

Both of the forms of the LSL instruction that we have considered up to this point only have the ability to shift the bits of an operand that is held in one of the internal data registers of the 68000. The third form,

LSL　EA

permits a shift left operation to be performed on the contents of a storage location in memory. Actually, any of the data-alterable addressing modes that relate to external memory can be used to specify EA. One restriction is that the size specified for the operand must always be a word. Moreover, since no shift count is specified, execution of the instruction causes a shift left of just one bit position.

Looking at Fig. 9.24, we see that the logical shift right (LSR) instruction can be written using the same basic forms as the LSL instruction. Moreover, the operations that they perform are the exact opposite of that just described for their corresponding LSL instruction. Now data are shifted to the right instead of to the left; zeros are loaded into vacated bits from the MSB end instead of the LSB end; and the last bit shifted out from the LSB is copied into both X and C.

There are also two basic arithmetic shift instructions: *arithmetic shift left* (ASL) and *arithmetic shift right* (ASR). Their forms and operations are also shown in Fig. 9.24. Here we see that the operation performed by ASL is essentially the same as that performed by the LSL instruction. However, there is a difference in the way in which the overflow flag is handled by the two instructions. It is always 0 for the LSL instruction, but for ASL it is set to 1 if the MSB changes logic level.

On the other hand, ASR is not the same as LSR. Notice that it does not only shift the bits of its operand but also preserves its sign. The illustration of operation of ASR in Fig. 9.24 shows that vacated more significant bit positions are filled with the original value for the MSB: that is, the sign bit.

Rotate Instructions—ROL, ROR, ROXL, and ROXR

The rotate instructions of the 68000 are similar to its shift instructions in that they can be used to shift the bits of data in an operand to the left or right. However, the shift operation they perform differs in that the bits of data that are shifted out at one end are shifted back in at the other end. Hence the bits of data appear to have been rotated.

Based on the path in which bits are rotated, two kinds of rotate operations are defined. As shown in Fig. 9.25, the basic rotate operation performed by the *rotate left* (ROL) instruction or *rotate right* (ROR) instruction use a path in which bits are shifted out from one end of the operand into the carry (C) bit of SR, and at the same time they are reloaded at the other end. Notice that the path for the other two instructions, ROXL and ROXR, differs in that both C and X are loaded with the bits as they are shifted out. Moreover, bits that are reloaded at the other end pass through X.

Let us begin with the ROL instruction. Looking at the diagram of its operation in Fig. 9.25, we see that it causes the bits of the specified operand to be rotated to the left. Bits shifted out from the most significant bit position are both loaded into

Mnemonic	Meaning	Type	Operand Size	Operation
ROL	Rotate left	ROL #XXX,Dy ROL Dx,Dy ROL EA	8, 16, 32 8, 16, 32 8, 16, 32	
ROR	Rotate right	ROR #XXX,Dy ROR Dx,Dy ROR EA	8, 16, 32 8, 16, 32 8, 16, 32	
ROXL	Rotate left through extend	ROXL #XXX,Dy ROXL Dx,Dy ROXL EA	8, 16, 32 8, 16, 32 8, 16, 32	
ROXR	Rotate right through extend	ROXR #XXX,Dy ROXR Dx,Dy ROXR EA	8, 16, 32 8, 16, 32 8, 16, 32	

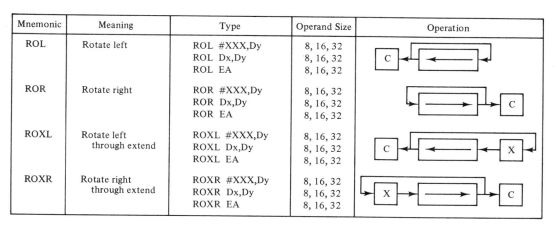

Figure 9.25   Rotate instructions.

C and the least significant bit position. The number of bit positions through which the data are to be rotated are specified as part of the instruction.

Notice that the allowed operand variations for ROL are identical to those shown in Fig. 9.24 for the shift instructions. The first form

$$\text{ROL}\quad \#XXX,Dy$$

permits an immediate operand in the range 0 to 7, to specify the count. This limits the amount of rotation to 1 to 8 bit positions. A value of 0 for XXX is actually a special case. It causes an 8-bit rotate to the left. The next form

$$\text{ROL}\quad Dx,Dy$$

uses the contents of the six least significant bits of data register Dx to specify the count. This extends the rotate range to from 1 to 63 bit positions. When either of these instructions are used, the operand that is to be processed by the rotate operation must reside in one of the data registers.

An example is the instruction

$$\text{ROL.L}\quad D0,D1$$

If D_0 contains 00000004_{16}, execution of the instruction causes the long-word contents of D_1 to be rotated four bit positions to the left. For instance, if the original contents of D_1 were $0000FFFF_{16}$, after the rotate operation is complete, the new contents of D_1 are $000FFFF0_{16}$ and C equals 0.

The last form of the rotate left instruction

$$\text{ROL}\quad EA$$

permits the operand to reside in a storage location in memory. This instruction may only be used to perform a 1-bit rotate left on a word operand.

In Fig. 9.25 we see that the rotate right (ROR) instruction is capable of performing the same operations as ROL. However, in this case, the data are rotated in the opposite direction.

As we indicated earlier, the *rotate left with extend* (ROXL) and *rotate right with extend* (ROXR) instructions essentially perform the same rotate operations as ROL and ROR, respectively. However, this time the last bit rotated out is loaded into both X and C, not just C, and bits that are reloaded at the other end pass through X. Therefore, execution of the instruction

$$\text{ROXL.L \quad D0,D1}$$

when $D_0 = 4_{16}$, $D_1 = 000FFFF0_{16}$, $C = 1$, and $X = 1$, results in $D_1 = 00FFFF08_{16}$ with $C = 0$ and $X = 0$.

Example 9.7

Implement the operation described in Example 9.5 using the rotate and decimal arithmetic instructions to add two four-digit packed BCD numbers that are held in D_0 and D_1, respectively. Place the result in D_0.

Solution.   We first start with $X = 0$ and add the two least significant digits. The instructions required to do this are

$$\text{MOVE \qquad \#0,CCR}$$

$$\text{ABCD \qquad D1,D0}$$

Let us save this result in D_2 by executing the instruction

$$\text{MOVE.B \quad D0,D2}$$

To add the most significant digits, we can rotate the words in D_1 and D_0 8 bits to the right. The instructions for this are

$$\text{ROR.W \quad \#0,D0}$$

$$\text{ROR.W \quad \#0,D1}$$

This does not change the X bit, which must be used in the addition. Now the least significant bytes in D_0 and D_1 can be added as BCD numbers by the instruction

$$\text{ABCD \quad D1,D0}$$

The result of D_0 can now be rotated to the left and the least significant result saved in D_2 can be placed back in D_0. The instructions to do this are

$$\text{ROL.W \quad \#0,D0}$$

$$\text{MOVE.B \quad D2,D0}$$

This completes the BCD addition. The entire program is shown in Fig. 9.26.

```
MOVE     #0,CCR
ABCD     D1,D0
MOVE.B   D0,D2
ROR.W    #0,D0
ROR.W    #0,D1
ABCD     D1,D0
ROL.W    #0,D0
MOVE.B   D2,D0
```

Figure 9.26   BCD addition program.

ASSIGNMENT

Section 9.2

1. Can the 68000 directly store a word of data starting at an odd address?

2. Compare a data register and an address register from a software point of view.

3. List the basic data types on which the 68000 can operate directly.

Section 9.3

4. Make a list of the addressing modes available on the 68000.

5. Identify the addressing modes for both the source and destination operands in the instructions that follow.

   (a) MOVE.W   D3,D2
   (b) MOVE.B   D3,A2
   (c) MOVE.L   D3,$ABCD
   (d) MOVE.L   XYZ,D2
   (e) MOVE.W   XYZ(D0.L),D2
   (f) MOVE.B   D3,(A2)
   (g) MOVE.L   A1,(A2) +
   (h) MOVE.L $-$(A2),D3
   (i) MOVE.W   10(A2),D3
   (j) MOVE.B   10(A2,A3.L),$A123
   (k) MOVE.W   #$ABCD,$1122

6. Compute the memory address for the source operand and/or destination operand in each of the instructions in problem 5.

7. Specify the conditions that make the following instructions equivalent.

        MOVE.L   D0,$ABCD
        MOVE.L   D0,$10(A1)
        MOVE.L   D0,$100(A2,D1.L)
        MOVE.L   D0,(A3)

Section 9.5

8. Given that D_0 = $12345678, D_1 = $ABCDEF01, and A_0 = $87654321, specify the memory contents of address $A000 to address $A002 after executing the instruction

        MOVEM.B   D0/D1/A0,$A000

9. Write an instruction that places the long-word contents of memory locations $B000, $B004, and $B008 into registers D_5, D_6, and D_7, respectively.

10. What will be the contents of D_0 and D_1 after executing the following sequence of instructions?

        MOVE.L $13579BDF,D0
        MOVE.L $02468ACE,D1
        SWAP   D0
        EXG.W   D0,D1

Section 9.6

11. Two word-wide unsigned integers are stored at the memory addresses $A000 and $B000, respectively. Write an instruction sequence that computes and stores their sum, difference, product, and quotient. Store these results at consecutive memory locations starting at address $C000 in memory. To obtain the difference, subtract the integer at $B000 from the integer at $A000. For the division, divide the integer at $A000 by the integer at $B000. Use register indirect relative addressing mode through register A_1 to store the various results.

Section 9.7

12. Two long-word BCD integers are stored at the symbolic addresses NUM1 and NUM2, respectively. Write an instruction sequence to generate their difference and store it at NUM3. The difference is to be formed by subtracting the value at NUM1 from that at NUM2. Use the predecrement indirect mode of addressing.

Section 9.8

13. Write an instruction sequence that generates a byte-size integer in the memory location identified by label RESULT. The value of the byte integer is to be calculated as follows:

$$(RESULT) = D0 \cdot NUM1 + NUM2 \cdot D0 + D1$$

Assume that all parameters are byte size.

Section 9.9

14. Implement the following operation using shift and arithmetic instructions.

$$7 \cdot D1 - 5 \cdot D2 - \frac{1}{8} D2 \rightarrow D0$$

Assume that the parameters are all long word in size.

15. Write a program that stores the long-word contents of D_0 into memory starting at address location $B001.

10

68000 Microprocessor
Programming 2

10.1 INTRODUCTION

In Chapter 9 we introduced the addressing modes and many of the instructions in the instruction set of the 68000 microprocessor. Using these instructions, we also covered some preliminary programming techniques. Here we will cover the rest of the instructions and introduce some more complex programming methods. Specifically, the following topics are presented in this chapter:

1. Compare and test instructions
2. Jump and branch instructions
3. Programs employing loops
4. Subroutines and subroutine handling instructions
5. Bit manipulation instructions

10.2 COMPARE AND TEST INSTRUCTIONS

The instruction set of the 68000 includes instructions to compare two operands or an operand with zero. The comparison is done by subtracting the source operand from the destination operand. The result of the subtraction does not modify either of the operands; instead, it is used to set or reset condition code bits (flags) in the status register. The flags affected are: negative (N), zero (Z), overflow (V), and carry (C). These flags can then be examined by other instructions to make the decision as to whether to execute one part of the program or another.

Mnemonic	Meaning	Type	Operand Size	Status Bits Affected
CMP	Compare	CMP EA,Dn	8, 16, 32	N, Z, V, C
		CMPA EA,An	16, 32	N, Z, V, C
		CMPI #XXX,EA	8, 16, 32	N, Z, V, C
		CMPM $(Ay)^+,(Ay)^+$	8, 16, 32	N, Z, V, C
TST	Test	TST EA	8, 16, 32	N, Z, V, C

Figure 10.1 Compare and test instructions.

The instructions that have the ability to compare operands are shown in Fig. 10.1. Basically two types of instructions are available: the *compare* (CMP) instruction and *test* (TST) instruction. Notice that the CMP instruction always compares two operands. On the other hand, the TST instruction compares the specified operand with zero.

Let us begin by looking in detail at the compare instruction of the 68000. Looking at Fig. 10.1, we see that there are four forms of this instruction. These forms are: *compare* (CMP), *compare address* (CMPA), *compare immediate* (CMPI), and *compare memory* (CMPM). They differ in the manner their operands are obtained for comparison.

The CMP instruction is used to compare a source operand with the contents of a data register. To specify the location of the source operand, any of the 68000's addressing modes can be used. On the other hand, the destination operand must always be one of the internal data registers. As indicated in Fig. 10.1, the specified operand size may be a byte, a word, or a long word. However, when an address register contains the source operand, byte-size comparisons cannot be made.

An example of the instruction is

$$\text{CMP.W} \quad \text{D1,D0}$$

When this instruction is executed, the word contents of D_1 are subtracted from that of D_0 and the flags are affected according to the result produced by the subtraction. For instance, if the value in D_1 is the same as that in D_0, the Z bit in SR is set and N, V, and C are all reset. Even though a subtraction is performed to determine this status, the values in D_1 and D_0 are not changed.

Compare address (CMPA) is the same as CMP except that the destination operand must reside in an address register instead of a data register. For this reason only word and long-word operands can be specified. A word source operand is sign extended to a long word before making the comparison. Here is an instruction that does a long-word comparison of the value of a long word in memory to the contents of A_0.

$$\text{CMPA.L} \quad \text{(A1),A0}$$

Notice that the address in A_1 is used to point to the long word in memory.

The next instruction, compare immediate (CMPI), is used to compare a byte, word, or long-word immediate operand to a destination operand that resides in a data register, address register, or storage location in memory. The location of the destination operand can be specified using any of the data-alterable addressing modes of the 68000. An example is the instruction

CMPI.B   #$FF,D0

The last type of compare instruction in Fig. 10.1 is compare memory (CMPM). Here both operands are located in memory and must be specified using the automatic postincrement indirect address register addressing modes. Since this instruction updates the address pointers each time it is executed, we are always ready to compare the next two pieces of data in memory. For this reason it is very useful for performing string comparisons.

Example 10.1

Determine how the condition codes will change as the following instructions are executed.

CLR.L	D0
MOVE.B	#$5A,D0
CMP.B	D0,D0
CMPI.B	#$60,D0

Solution. What happens to the condition codes as these instructions are executed is summarized in Fig. 10.2. Here we see that the first instruction clears data register D_0.

Instruction	Function	Condition Codes				
		X	N	Z	V	C
CLR.L D0	Clear D_0	X	0	1	0	0
MOVE.B #$5A,D0	Load $5A_{16}$ into D_0	X	0	0	0	0
CMP.B D0,D0	Compare D_0 with D_0	X	0	1	0	0
CMPI.B #$60,D0	Compare 60_{16} with D_0	X	1	0	0	1

Figure 10.2   Example program employing compare instructions.

This is written as a long-word instruction; therefore, all 32 bits of D_0 are cleared. That is, it is loaded with 00000000_{16}. Due to the execution of the first instruction, the Z condition code bit is set while N, V, and C are cleared.

The next instruction loads the lower byte of D_0 with the number $5A_{16}$. Since this number is positive and greater than zero, the N and Z bits of SR are cleared. Moreover, it always clears the V and C bits.

The third instruction compares the contents of D_0 with itself. Thus the Z bit is set and N, V, and C are cleared.

The last instruction compares 60_{16} with the contents of D_0. Therefore, it subtracts 60_{16} from $5A_{16}$. This subtraction yields a negative result; therefore, the N bit is set. Furthermore, to subtract a larger number from a smaller one, a borrow is required. Thus the C bit is also set. The result of subtracting the two numbers can be correctly represented as a byte. That is, no overflow has occurred. Therefore, V is reset. Moreover, the result is not zero; therefore, Z is also reset.

Test Instruction—TST

The last instruction in Fig. 10.1 is the test (TST) instruction. This instruction performs an operation that is similar to the compare instruction except that its destination operand is always assumed to be zero. The specified source operand is subtracted
from zero and based on the result, the condition code bits in SR are set or reset.
Any of the data-alterable addressing modes can be used to specify the source operand
and it can be a byte, word, or long word.

The same four condition code bits are affected by the TST instruction. But in
this case only N and Z are set or reset based on the result of the comparison. The
other two bits, V and C, are always cleared.

Set According to Condition Code Instruction—Scc

Earlier we pointed out that the condition code bits set or reset by the compare and
test instructions are examined through software to decide whether or not branching
should take place in the program. One way of using these bits is to test them directly
with the branch instructions. Another approach is to test them for a specific condition and then save a flag value representing whether the tested condition is true or
false. This flag value can then be used for program branching decisions. An instruction that performs this operation is *set according to condition* (Scc).

The form of the Scc instruction is shown in Fig. 10.3(a). The "cc" part of the
mnemonic stands for a general condition code relationship and must be replaced with
a specific relationship when writing the instruction. Figure 10.3(b) is a list of the
mnemonics and condition code relationships that can be used to replace cc. For instance, replacing cc by LE gives the instruction mnemonic SLE. This stands for *set
if less than or equal to* and tests status to determine if the logical value of

$$Z + N \cdot \overline{V} + \overline{N} \cdot V$$

is equal to 1.

Looking at Fig. 10.3(a), we see that a byte-wide destination operand is also specified in the instruction. Its location can be identified using any of the data-alterable
addressing modes. For example, an instruction could be written as

SGT D0

When this instruction is executed, it causes the condition code bits to be checked

Mnemonic	Meaning	Format	Operand Size	Operation
Scc	Set according to condition code	Scc EA	8	11111111 → EA if cc is true 00000000 → EA if cc is false

(a)

Figure 10.3 (a) Set according to condition code instruction; (b) conditional tests
of the Scc instruction.

Mnemonic	Meaning	Condition Code Relationship
SCC	Set if carry clear	$C = 0$
SCS	Set if carry set	$C = 1$
SEQ	Set if equal	$Z = 1$
SNE	Set if not equal	$Z = 0$
SMI	Set if minus	$N = 1$
SPL	Set if plus	$N = 0$
SVC	Set if overflow clear (signed)	$V = 0$
SVS	Set if overflow set (signed)	$V = 1$
SHI	Set if higher (unsigned)	$\overline{C} \cdot \overline{Z} = 1$
SLS	Set if lower or same (unsigned)	$C + Z = 1$
SGT'	Set if greater than (signed)	$NV\overline{Z} + \overline{N}\,\overline{V}\,\overline{Z} = 1$
SGE	Set if greater or equal (signed)	$NV + \overline{N}\,\overline{V} = 1$
SLT'	Set if less than	$N\overline{V} + \overline{N}V = 1$
SLE	Set if less or equal (signed)	$Z + N\overline{V} + \overline{N}V = 1$

(b)

Figure 10.3   (*continued*)

to determine if the relationship

$$N \cdot V \cdot \overline{Z} + \overline{N} \cdot \overline{V} \cdot \overline{Z} = 1$$

is satisfied. If this relationship is true, the bits of the byte part of destination register D_0 are all set. On the other hand, if the relationship is false, they are all reset.

10.3 JUMP AND BRANCH INSTRUCTIONS

For all the programs we have studied up to this point, the sequence in which the instructions were written was also the sequence in which they were executed. In other words, after execution of an instruction the program counter always points to the next sequential instruction.

For most applications, one must be able to alter the sequence in which instructions of the program execute. The changes in sequence may have to be unconditionally done or may be subject to satisfying a conditional relationship. To support these types of operations, the 68000 is equipped with jump and branch instructions.

Unconditional Jump and Branch Instructions—JMP and BRA

Unconditional changes in execution sequence are supported by both the jump and branch instructions. The first instruction in Fig. 10.4 is the *jump* (JMP) instruction. The effect of executing this instruction is to load the program counter with the contents of the effective address specified by the operand in the instruction. Therefore, program execution resumes at the location specified by the effective address.

An example of the instruction is

$$\text{JMP} \quad (\text{A0})$$

Mnemonic	Meaning	Format	Operand Size	Operation
JMP	Jump	JMP EA	– –	EA → PC
BRA	Branch always	BRA Label	8, 16	PC + d → PC

Figure 10.4 Jump and branch always instructions.

In this case, program execution is directed to the instruction at the address specified by the contents of address register A_0. Only the control addressing modes can be used to specify the operand.

A second way of initiating unconditional changes in the program execution sequence is by means of the *branch always* (BRA) instruction. The format of this instruction is also shown in Fig. 10.4. Notice that BRA differs from JMP in the manner by which the address of the next instruction to be executed is encoded. In JMP this address is specified directly by an EA operand. This permits it to reside in a data register or a storage location in memory. On the other hand, in BRA the difference between the address of the new instruction and that of the BRA instruction (displacement) is encoded following the opcode. Thus for the BRA instruction the microprocessor computes the next address by adding the displacement to the current value in PC.

The branch instruction allows the displacement d to be encoded either as an 8-bit (*short-form*) integer or 16-bit (*long-form*) integer. With an 8-bit displacement, the instruction is encoded as one word, but the branch to location must reside within + 129 or − 126 bytes of the current value in PC. On the other hand, the 16-bit displacement is encoded as a second instruction word, thereby making it a two-word instruction. This long displacement extends the range of the branch operation to + 32769 to − 32766 bytes relative to the current PC.

The programmer does not normally specify the displacement in the branch instruction. Instead, a label is written in the program to identify the branch to location. For example, the instruction

BRA   START

causes a transfer of program control to the instruction in the program with the label START. It is the duty of the assembler program to compute the actual displacement and encode it into the instruction. In this example, the displacement will be encoded as a 16-bit word. If displacement must be encoded as a byte, the instruction should be written as

BRA.S   START

JMP and BRA are called *unconditional branch* instructions. This is because the change in instruction sequence that they initiate takes place independent of any conditions in the processor status.

Conditonal Branch Instruction—Bcc

The 68000 provides a *conditional branch* instruction called *branch conditionally* (Bcc). As shown in Fig. 10.5(a), its general form is

Mnemonic	Meaning	Format	Operand Size	Operation
Bcc	Branch conditionally	Bcc Label	8, 16	(PC) + d → PC if cc is true; otherwise, next sequential instruction executes

(a)

Mnemonic	Meaning	Conditional Code Relationship
BCC	Branch if carry clear	$C = 0$
BCS	Branch if carry set	$C = 1$
BEQ	Branch if equal	$Z = 1$
BNE	Branch if not equal	$Z = 0$
BMI	Branch if minus	$N = 1$
BPL	Branch if plus	$N = 0$
BVC	Branch if overflow clear (signed)	$V = 0$
BVS	Branch if overflow set (signed)	$V = 1$
BHI	Branch if high (unsigned)	$\overline{C} \cdot \overline{Z} = 1$
BLS	Branch if less or same (unsigned)	$C + Z = 1$
BGT	Branch if greater than (signed)	$NV\overline{Z} + \overline{N}\,\overline{V}\,\overline{Z} = 1$
BGE	Branch if greater or equal (signed)	$NV + \overline{N}\,\overline{V} = 1$
BLT	Branch if less than	$N\overline{V} + \overline{N}V = 1$
BLE	Branch if less or equal (signed)	$Z + N\overline{V} + \overline{N}V = 1$

(b)

Figure 10.5   (a) Branch conditionally instruction; (b) conditional tests of the Bcc instruction.

Bcc   LABEL

Here "cc" is used to specify one of many conditional relationships. Figure 10.5(b) is a list of all the valid relationships and their mnemonics. For instance, selecting EQ we get the *branch on equal* (BEQ) instruction.

The conditional branch instruction passes control to the specified label only if the conditional relationship is true. In the example BEQ, the Z bit of SR is tested. If it is set, the branch takes place to the location specified by LABEL. If it is not set, the next sequential instruction is executed. The amount of displacement allowed with the conditional branch instruction is the same as for the branch always instruction.

Let us now consider an example. The instruction

BVS   START

means branch to the instruction identified by START if the overflow (V) bit is set. If V is not set, the instruction that follows the BVS instruction is executed. The displacement between the address of BVS plus two and the instruction with label START is computed by the assembler and encoded into the instruction as a 16-bit integer. For encoding the displacement as a byte, the instruction should be written as

BVS.S   START

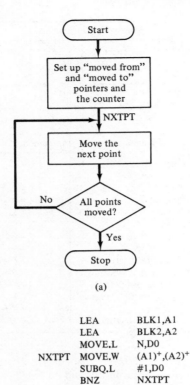

(a)

```
          LEA        BLK1,A1
          LEA        BLK2,A2
          MOVE.L     N,D0
NXTPT     MOVE.W     (A1)⁺,(A2)⁺
          SUBQ.L     #1,D0
          BNZ        NXTPT
```

(b)

Figure 10.6 (a) Block transfer flowchart; (b) program.

Example 10.2

It is required to move a set of N, 16-bit data points that are stored in a block of memory that starts at location BLK1 to a new block that starts at location BLK2. Write a program to implement this operation.

Solution.   The flowchart in Fig. 10.6(a) shows a plan for implementing the block move function. Initially, we set up two pointers, one for the beginning of BLK1 and the other for the beginning of BLK2. Address registers A_1 and A_2, respectively, can be used as these pointers. The count for the number of points to be moved is placed in D_0. This can be accomplished by the instruction sequence

$$\text{LEA} \qquad \text{BLK1,A1}$$

$$\text{LEA} \qquad \text{BLK2,A2}$$

$$\text{MOVE.L} \qquad \text{N,D0}$$

To move a word from BLK1 to BLK2, we can use a move word instruction with address register indirect addressing with postincrement mode for both its source and destination operands. Moreover, each time a data point is moved, the count in D_0 must be decreased by 1. The move instruction must be repeated if the count has not reached zero. The instructions that follow will perform these operations.

NXTPT	MOVE.W	(A1) + ,(A2) +
	SUBQ.L	#1,D0
	BNZ	NXTPT

The entire program is shown in Fig. 10.6(b).

10.4 THE TEST CONDITION, DECREMENT, AND BRANCH INSTRUCTION AND PROGRAMS INVOLVING LOOPS

The program we considered in the preceding section was an example of a *software loop*. In a software loop, a group of instructions are executed repeatedly. The repetition may be unconditional or conditional. To design a loop one can use the previously introduced compare, jump, and branch instructions. This was the approach employed in Example 10.2. However, the 68000 provides another instruction that is especially useful for handling loops. This instruction is called *test condition, decrement, and branch* (DBcc) and has the general form

DBcc   Dn,Label

Here "cc" represents the same conditions that were available for the Bcc instruction. They are listed in the table of Fig. 10.5(b). In fact, two more conditions, always true (T) and always false (F), are also available for the DBcc instructions. Dn is the data register that contains the count of how many times the loop is to be repeated, and Label identifies the location to which control is to be returned by the branch operation.

When the DBcc instruction is executed, first the condition identified by cc is tested. If it is true, no branch takes place; instead, the loop is terminated and the next sequential instruction is executed. On the other hand, if the condition is not true, the contents of the specified data register are decremented by 1. Then another test is performed. This one is on the count in Dn. If it is equal to -1, the branch does not take place because the loop operation has run to completion. In this case, execution continues with the next sequential instruction. However, if the count is not -1, program control branches to the location corresponding to Label.

An example of the instruction is as follows:

DBLE   D0,NXTPT

During the execution of this instruction, first the condition code bits of SR are tested to determine if the relationship

$$Z + N \cdot \overline{V} + \overline{N} \cdot V = 1$$

is satisfied. If true, the instruction following the DBLE instruction is executed. If false, D_0 is decremented. Next, D_0 is tested to determine if it has become -1. If it has, the next sequential instruction is executed. But if D_0 is any number other than -1, execution continues at the label NXTPT.

Example 10.3

Given N data points that are signed 16-bit numbers stored in consecutive memory locations starting at address DATA, write a program that finds their average value. The average value that results is to be stored at location AVERAGE in memory. Assume that N is in the range $0 < N < 32K$.

Solution. A flowchart that solves this problem is shown in Fig. 10.7(a). It implements an algorithm that finds the average of N data points by adding their values and then dividing the sum by N.

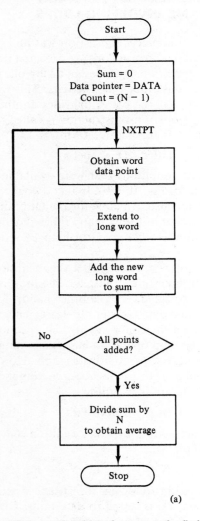

D_0 = counter
D_7 = sum
A_1 = pointer to data points
D_1 = temporary register for
        holding data point

(a)

Figure 10.7 (a) Flowchart of a program for finding the average of N signed numbers; (b) program.

```
          CLR.L      D7
          LEA        DATA,A1
          MOVE.L     #(N−1),D0
NXTPT     MOVE.W     (A1)⁺,D1
          EXT.L      D1
          ADD.L      D1,D7
          DBF        D0,NXTPT
          DIVS       #N,D7
          MOV.W      D7,AVERAGE
```

(b)   **Figure 10.7** (*continued*)

Initially we set the sum, which will reside in D_7, to 0, the address pointer in A_1 to DATA so that it points to the first data point, and the counter in D_0 equal to N − 1. Notice that the value of the count is 1 less than the number of data points to be processed. The reason for this is that we intend to use the DBcc instruction which branches out of the loop when the count in a data register becomes equal to − 1 and not 0. This initialization is performed by executing the following instructions

```
CLR.L      D7

LEA        DATA,A1

MOVE.L     #(N − 1),D0
```

To add a new data point to sum, we first move it into D_1. Since the data point is of word length, it must be sign extended to a long word before it can be added to the previous sum. Then the sign-extended data point in D_1 is added to the sum in D_7. Next the count in D_0 is decremented by 1 and checked to determine if it has become equal to − 1. A value of − 1 means that all points have been added. If it is not − 1, there are still data points to be added and we must repeat the set of instructions that add a new data point. On the other hand, if the count shows that all points have been added, we are ready to divide the sum in D_7 by N to obtain the average. This value can then be moved from D_7 to the storage location AVERAGE in memory. All this can be done by the following sequence of instructions.

```
NXTPT     MOVE.W     (A1) + ,D1

          EXT.L      D1

          ADD.L      D1,D7

          DBF        D0,NXTPT

          DIVS       #N,D7

          MOVE.W     D7,AVERAGE
```

The complete program is listed in Fig. 10.7(b).

Example 10.4

Given a four-digit BCD number located in memory location BCDNUM. Write a program to convert it to its equivalent binary number and place the result in memory location BINNUM.

Solution. Let us begin by defining an algorithm that can be used to convert a BCD number to its equivalent binary number. For the general BCD number

$$N_{BCD} = D_3D_2D_1D_0$$

its equivalent decimal number is given by the expression

$$N_{10} = 1000(D_3) + 100(D_2) + 10(D_1) + D_0$$

This expression can be reorganized to give

$$N_{10} = D_0 + 10(D_1 + 10(D_2 + 10(D_3)))$$

D_0, D_1, D_2, and D_3 in this expression stand for BCD digits and not for data registers within the 68000. This expression suggests an algorithm that can be implemented using a software loop. Notice that if we start with the MSD D_3, multiply it by 10, and then add the next MSD D_2, we will get our first temporary result. This same sequence can be performed twice more on the temporary result, first adding D_1 to the product and then adding D_0 to the product, to produce the final result.

The flowchart in Fig. 10.8(a) shows how this algorithm can be implemented on the 68000. Initialization involves setting the result, which is in D_7, to zero, setting the digit counter in D_0 to 3, and the shift counter in D_1 to 12. The BCD number at memory location BCDNUM is copied into D_2. Notice that the value of the digit counter is actually one less than the number of digits to be processed. This is due to the fact that we intend to use the DBcc instruction, which branches on the contents of a data register being equal to -1. The shift counter will be used to extract the appropriate digit from the number. This initialization can be performed with the instruction sequence that follows.

```
CLR.L      D7

MOVE.L     #3,D0

MOVE.L     #12,D1

MOVE.W     BCDNUM,D2
```

To program the conversion equation, we begin with the most significant digit of BCDNUM. To extract the MSD, the BCD number in register D_2 is first copied into register D_3 and then the contents of D_3 are shifted right logically by 12 bit positions. This places the MSD in the 4 least significant bits of register D_3. Now this digit value is added to the result in D_7. To prepare for the extraction of the next MSD, we shift the contents of register D_2 left by four bit positions. This places the next MSD in the most significant digit position so that this digit can now be treated exactly like the preceding one. The counter in register D_0 is decremented and tested; if it is not equal to -1, we repeat the process with the next digit. If we repeat, we must multiply the result by 10 before adding the value of the next digit. All this can be done by the following sequence of instructions:

```
NXTDGT     MULU       #10,D7

           MOVE.W     D2,D3

           LSR.W      D1,D3

           ADD.W      D3,D7

           LSL.W      #4,D2
```

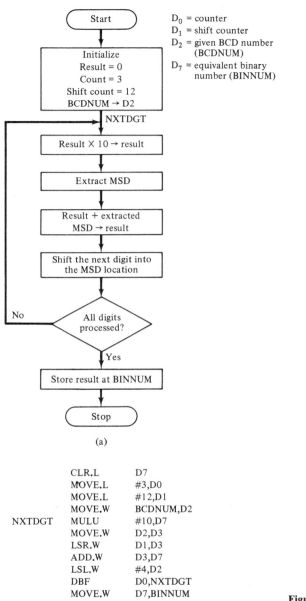

D_0 = counter
D_1 = shift counter
D_2 = given BCD number
       (BCDNUM)
D_7 = equivalent binary
       number (BINNUM)

(a)

```
           CLR.L     D7
           MOVE.L    #3,D0
           MOVE.L    #12,D1
           MOVE.W    BCDNUM,D2
NXTDGT     MULU      #10,D7
           MOVE.W    D2,D3
           LSR.W     D1,D3
           ADD.W     D3,D7
           LSL.W     #4,D2
           DBF       D0,NXTDGT
           MOVE.W    D7,BINNUM
```

(b)

Figure 10.8 (a) Flowchart for BCD-to-binary conversion routine; (b) program.

```
DBF        D0,NXTDGT

MOVE.W     D7,BINNUM
```

The entire program is shown in Fig. 10.8(b).

Example 10.5

We need to sort an array of 16-bit signed binary numbers such that they are rearranged in ascending order. Assume that the numbers of the array are stored in memory at consecutive locations from address $F400_{16}$ through $F4FE_{16}$. Write a program to perform this sort operation.

Solution. A sorting algorithm was discussed in Example 4.4. We will implement the same algorithm for the 68000 microprocessor. The flowchart for the sort algorithm is shown in Fig. 10.9(a).

The first block represents initialization of pointers PNTR1 and PNTR3. They contain addresses that point to the storage locations of the first and last elements of the array, respectively. Since registers A_1 and A_3 are used as these pointers and the addresses of the first and last elements are \$F400 and \$F4FE, respectively, the instructions used to perform the initialization are

$$\text{MOVE.L} \qquad \text{\$F400,A1}$$

$$\text{MOVE.L} \qquad \text{\$F4FE,A3}$$

Address register A_2 contains another pointer. It is called PNTR2 and points to the next element to be processed in the array. To initialize PNTR2, we can load register A_2 with the contents of A_1, which is PNTR1, and then increment this value by 2. In this way, the next word address is established for PNTR2. This is done with the instructions

$$\text{AA} \qquad \text{MOVE.L} \qquad \text{A1,A2}$$

$$\text{ADDQ.L} \qquad \text{\#2,A2}$$

As shown in the flowchart, the label AA is used to implement a branch point.

Next, starting with label BB, we first compare the two numbers. To implement the comparison, the number pointed to by PNTR2 can be copied into register D_0; next, the value pointed to by PNTR1 can be compared to it; and then a conditional branch can be made if status shows that

$$(\text{PNTR1}) \leq (\text{PNTR2})$$

The branch passes control to the point in the program identified by label CC. If the value pointed to by PNTR1 is greater than the value pointed to by PNTR2, the two values must be swapped. These operations are performed with the instructions

$$\text{BB} \qquad \text{MOVE.W} \qquad \text{(A2),D0}$$

$$\text{CMP.W} \qquad \text{(A1),D0}$$

$$\text{BLE.S} \qquad \text{CC}$$

To implement swapping of the two numbers, the number pointed to by PNTR1 is copied into the memory location pointed to by PNTR2. Next the contents of D_0 are copied to the storage location pointed to by PNTR1. This completes the swap. The corresponding instructions are

$$\text{MOVE.W} \qquad \text{(A1),(A2)}$$

$$\text{MOVE.W} \qquad \text{D0,(A1)}$$

Now pointer PNTR2 is updated by incrementing it by 2 and then it is compared to PNTR3

A_1 = $PNTR_1$ = pointer to first element
A_2 = $PNTR_2$ = pointer to next element
A_3 = $PNTR_3$ = pointer to last element

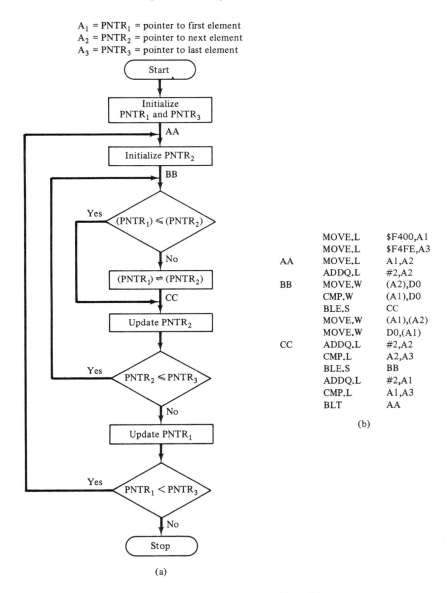

	MOVE.L	$F400,A1
	MOVE.L	$F4FE,A3
AA	MOVE.L	A1,A2
	ADDQ.L	#2,A2
BB	MOVE.W	(A2),D0
	CMP.W	(A1),D0
	BLE.S	CC
	MOVE.W	(A1),(A2)
	MOVE.W	D0,(A1)
CC	ADDQ.L	#2,A2
	CMP.L	A2,A3
	BLE.S	BB
	ADDQ.L	#2,A1
	CMP.L	A1,A3
	BLT	AA

(b)

(a)

Figure 10.9   (a) Flowchart for sort algorithm; (b) program.

to find out if the last element has been compared. If the result of this comparision shows that

$$PNTR2 \leq PNTR3$$

control is returned to the point in the program identified by BB. Otherwise, program

execution continues on to the next block in the flowchart. These operations are done
with the instructions

> CC   ADDQ.L   #2,A2
>
> CMP.L   A2,A3
>
> BLE.S   BB

When the answer to the comparison is that

$$PNTR2 > PNTR3$$

we must update PNTR1 by adding 2 and then compare it to PNTR3. If it turns out that

$$PNTR1 < PNTR3$$

we must start all over again from AA. Otherwise, the program is complete. The instructions for this part of the program are

> ADDQ.L   #2,A1
>
> CMP.L   A1,A3
>
> BLT   AA

The entire program is shown in Fig. 10.9(b).

10.5 SUBROUTINES AND SUBROUTINE-HANDLING INSTRUCTIONS

A *subroutine* is a segment of program separate from the main part of the program.
It can be called upon to execute by the main program whenever its function is needed.
The instructions provided to transfer control from the main program to a subroutine
and return control back to the main program are called *subroutine handling instructions*. Let us now examine the instructions provided for this purpose.

Subroutine Control Instructions—JSR, BSR, RTS, and RTR

The four subroutine handling instructions of the 68000 microprocessor are shown
in Fig. 10.10. These instructions include *jump to subroutine* (JSR), *branch to sub-*

Mnemonic	Meaning	Format	Operand Size	Operation
JSR	Jump to subroutine	JSR EA	32	$PC \rightarrow {}^-(SP)$ $EA \rightarrow PC$
BSR	Branch to subroutine	BSR Label	8, 16	$PC \rightarrow {}^-(SP)$ $PC + d \rightarrow PC$
RTS	Return from subroutine	RTS	—	$(SP)^+ \rightarrow PC$
RTR	Return and restore	RTR	—	$(SP)^+ \rightarrow CCR$ $(SP)^+ \rightarrow PC$

Figure 10.10 Subroutine control instructions.

routine (BSR), *return from subroutine* (RTS), and *return and restore condition codes* (RTR). These instructions provide for efficient subroutine handling and nesting.

The instructions jump to subroutine (JSR) and branch to subroutine (BSR) serve essentially the same purpose. This is to pass control to the starting point of a subroutine. As shown in Fig. 10.10, they both save the current contents of PC by pushing it to the active stack. This preserves a return address for use at completion of the subroutine. Then they pass control to the starting point of the subroutine.

These two instructions differ in how they specify the starting address of the subroutine. For the JSR instruction this address is specified as an effective address and only the control addressing modes are allowed. Therefore, the starting address can reside in a data register, address register, or in either program or data storage memory. For instance, using address register indirect addressing through register A_1, we get

$$JSR \quad (A1)$$

On the other hand, in the BSR instruction, the *displacement* between the current instruction and the first instruction of the subroutine is determined and encoded into the instruction. That is, it is stored in program storage memory. An example is

$$BSR \quad STARTSUB$$

Thus JSR provides the ability to jump to a subroutine that resides anywhere in the 16M-byte address space of the 68000. But BSR only permits branching to a subroutine that is located within the maximum allowable displacement value. The displacement can be either 8 bits for the short form of the BSR instruction or 16 bits for the long form.

The other two instructions return from subroutine (RTS) and return and restore (RTR) provide the means for returning from a subroutine back to the calling program. In Fig. 10.10 we see that executing RTS simply restores the program counter by popping the value that was saved on the active stack when the subroutine was called. The second instruction RTR restores both the condition code part of SR and PC from the stack. One of these instructions is always the last instruction of a subroutine.

Example 10.6

In a Fibonacci series, the first number is 0, the second is 1, and each subsequent number is obtained by adding the previous two numbers. For example, the first 10 numbers of the series are

$$0, 1, 1, 2, 3, 5, 8, 13, 21, 34$$

Write a program to generate the first 20 elements of a Fibonacci series. The numbers of the series are to be stored at consecutive locations in memory starting at address FIBSER. Use a subroutine to implement the part of the procedure by which the next number of the series is obtained from the previous two numbers.

Solution.   A flowchart for this program together with the assignments of various registers is shown in Fig. 10.11(a). The first part of the program initializes the registers and stores the first two numbers. The instructions used for this purpose are

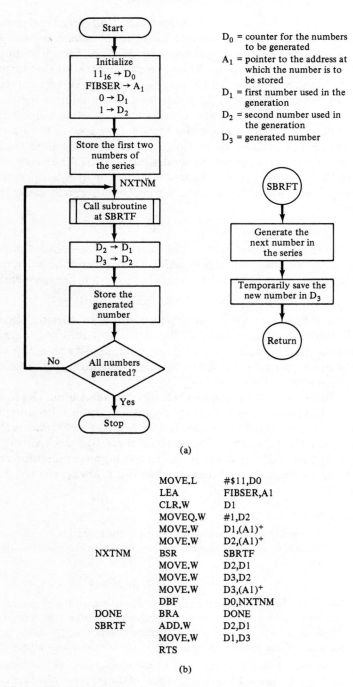

D_0 = counter for the numbers to be generated

A_1 = pointer to the address at which the number is to be stored

D_1 = first number used in the generation

D_2 = second number used in the generation

D_3 = generated number

(a)

```
        MOVE.L    #$11,D0
        LEA       FIBSER,A1
        CLR.W     D1
        MOVEQ.W   #1,D2
        MOVE.W    D1,(A1)+
        MOVE.W    D2,(A1)+
NXTNM   BSR       SBRTF
        MOVE.W    D2,D1
        MOVE.W    D3,D2
        MOVE.W    D3,(A1)+
        DBF       D0,NXTNM
DONE    BRA       DONE
SBRTF   ADD.W     D2,D1
        MOVE.W    D1,D3
        RTS
```

(b)

Figure 10.11 (a) Flowchart for the Fibonacci series program; (b) program.

```
        MOVE.L       #$11,D0

        LEA          FIBSER,A1

        CLR.W        D1

        MOVEQ.W      #1,D2

        MOVE.W       D1,(A1)+

        MOVE.W       D2,(A1)+
```

The next-to-last instruction causes 0 to be loaded into address FIBSER and increments the pointer in A_1 by 2 such that it points to the storage location of the next number in the series. Then a similar instruction is executed to load FIBSER + 2 with 1 and A_1 is again incremented.

We are now ready to call the subroutine that does the addition to form the next number in the series. Since the subroutine will be called repeatedly, the BRS instruction is identified by a label to which the program can loop back. This instruction is

```
        NXTNM     BSR.S SBRTF
```

The subroutine starts at the instruction with label SBRTF. The purpose of the subroutine is to add the contents of D_1 and D_2 so that the next number in the series is generated, temporarily save this number in D_3, and then return back to the main program. This can be done by the instruction sequence

```
    SBRTF      ADD.W        D2,D1

               MOVE.W       D1,D3

               RTS
```

At this point in the main program, we get ready for generating the next number. This is done by saving the contents of D_2 in D_1 and that of D_3 in D_2. Next we save the new number that was generated in D_3 by moving it to memory. To do this, the instructions are

```
        MOVE.W       D2,D1

        MOVE.W       D3,D2

        MOVE.W       D3,(A1)+
```

Now the count in D_0 is decremented and tested for -1. If it is not equal to -1, we loop back to the label NXTNM. However, if it is -1, we are done. The instruction for this is

```
                         DBF    D0,NXTNM
        DONE    BRA    DONE
```

The entire program is repeated in Fig. 10.11(b).

Link and Unlink Instructions—LINK and UNLK

Before the main program calls a subroutine, quite often it is necessary for the calling program to pass the values of some *variables* (*parameters*) to the subroutine. It is a common practice to push these variables onto the stack before calling the routine. Then during the execution of the subroutine, they are accessed by reading them from

Mnemonic	Meaning	Format	Operation
LINK	Link and allocate	LINK An, d	$An \rightarrow {}^-(SP)$ $SP \rightarrow An$ $SP - d \rightarrow SP$
UNLK	Unlink	UNLK An	$An \rightarrow SP$ $(SP)^+ \rightarrow An$

Figure 10.12 Link and unlink instructions.

the stack and used in computations. Two instructions are provided to allocate and deallocate a data area called a *frame* in the stack part of memory. This data area is used for local storage of parameters or other data. The two instructions, as shown in Fig. 10.12, are *link and allocate* (LINK) and *unlink* (UNLK). They make the process of passing and retrieving parameters much easier.

The LINK instruction is used at the beginning of a subroutine to create a data frame. Looking at the format of the instruction in Fig. 10.12, we see that it has two operands. The one denoted An is always an address register. The address held in A_n is known as the *frame pointer* and it points to the lowest storage location in the data frame. The other operand is an immediate operand that specifies the value of a displacement. This displacement specifies the size of the data space. Since it can be as long as 16 bits, a *frame data space* can be as large as 32K words.

An example of this instruction is

$$\text{LINK} \quad A1, - \#\$A$$

Execution of this instruction causes the current contents of A_1 to be pushed onto the active stack; then the updated contents of the active SP register are loaded into A_1; finally, A_{16} is subtracted from the new value in SP.

Figure 10.13 shows what happens by executing this instruction. First we see that pushing the contents of A_1 to the stack saves the frame pointer for the prior data frame. This is identified as "Prior frame pointer" and is stored at A_{1new}. Loading A_1 with the contents of SP establishes a frame pointer to the new data frame. Subtracting the displacement from (SP) modifies the stack pointer so that the active stack is located in memory just below the data frame. Since the displacement is A_{16}, the data frame is 10 bytes in length.

The frame pointer A_1 provides a fixed reference into the data frame and old stack. Parameters that were loaded into the stack prior to calling the subroutine can be accessed using address register indirect with displacement addressing for the operand. For example, the instruction

$$\text{MOVE.W} \quad 4(A1), D0$$

causes the word parameter stored four bytes from frame pointer A_1 to be copied into D_0. This parameter is in the old stack.

After performing the operation defined by the subroutine and just before returning to the calling program, the prior data frame must be restored. The UNLK instruction is used for this purpose. Notice in Fig. 10.12 that it causes address register

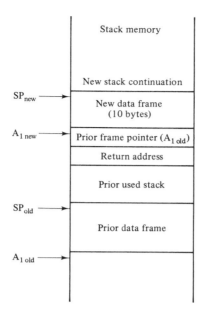

Stack memory

New stack continuation

SP_{new} ⟶   New data frame
(10 bytes)

$A_{1\ new}$ ⟶   Prior frame pointer ($A_{1\ old}$)

Return address

Prior used stack

SP_{old} ⟶

Prior data frame

$A_{1\ old}$ ⟶

Figure 10.13   Creation of a data frame with the link instruction.

A_n, which is used for the frame pointer, to be loaded into the active stack pointer register. Then the address held at the top of the stack is popped into A_n.

For our example, the unlink instruction would be

UNLK   A1

Earlier we pointed out that execution of the LINK instruction saved the old frame pointer on the stack and then created a new data frame. Executing UNLK A1 causes SP to be loaded from A_1. Looking at Fig. 10.13, we find that the stack pointer now points to the location of the prior frame pointer. Then A_1 is loaded from the stack. Therefore, the prior frame pointer is put back in A_1 and the prior stack and data frame environment is restored.

To understand this concept better, let us consider the example illustrated in Fig. 10.14. As we begin to execute the first instruction of the program segment shown in Fig. 10.14(a), we will assume that the active SP points to the top of the data frame identified in Fig. 10.14(b) as local storage area for the calling routine. Execution of the first two instructions

MOVE.W   D0, – (SP)

MOVE.W   D1, – (SP)

passes the contents of D_0 and D_1 as parameters onto the stack. Looking at Fig. 10.14(b), we see that at the completion of these two instructions SP points to the location where parameter 2 is stored.

The next instruction,

JSR   SBRT

```
              MOVE.W    D0, ⁻ (SP)       ; parameter 1 passed to stack
              MOVE.W    D1, ⁻ (SP)       ; parameter 2 passed to stack
        AA    JSR       SBRT             ; call subroutine SBRT
               .          .
               .          .
               .          .
               .          .
               .          .
               .          .

        SBRT  LINK      A0, −$8          |; FP and local storage established for called routine
               .          .
               .          .
              MOVE.W    10(A0), D5       ; parameter 1 accessed
               .          .
               .          .
              UNLK      A0               ; FP for the calling routine established
              RTS                        ; return to main program
```

(a)

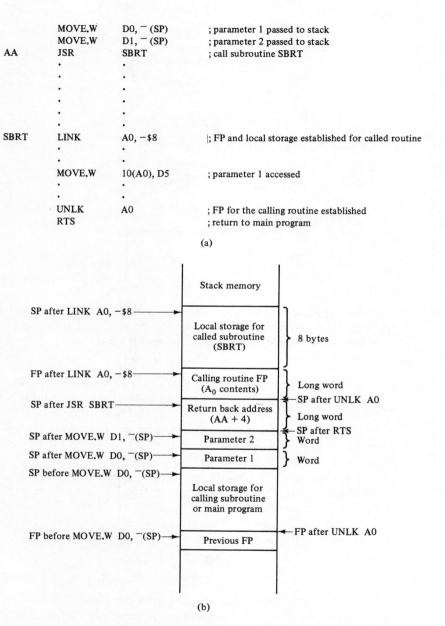

(b)

Figure 10.14   (a) Program example with LINK and UNLK instructions; (b) stack for the example program.

which has the label AA, calls the subroutine starting at label SBRT. It causes the address of the instruction that follows it to be pushed onto the stack. This return address is AA + 4 since the JSR instruction takes up four bytes of program memory. Secondly PC is loaded with the address of SBRT such that program control picks up execution from the first instruction of the subroutine.

The subroutine starts with the instruction

$$\text{LINK} \quad A0, -\#\$8$$

It causes the contents of A_0 to be saved on the stack and then loads A_0 from the active stack pointer register. This sets up a new frame pointer FP (A_0 register). Then 8 is subtracted from the value in SP. Therefore, it points to the top of the data area identified in Fig. 10.14(b) as *local storage* for the called subroutine.

As subroutine SBRT is being executed, we may need to access parameter 1. The frame pointer serves as a reference into the called routines data frame. Parameter 1 is at a displacement of 10 bytes from the frame pointer; therefore, the instruction

$$\text{MOVE.W} \quad 10(A0),D5$$

can be used to access it. Execution of this instruction copies parameter 1 into D_5.

The next instruction we see is

$$\text{UNLK} \quad A0$$

It loads SP with the contents of A_0 and then pops the contents at the top of the stack into A_0. Now A_0 once again contains the frame pointer for the calling routine and SP points to the location where the return address AA + 4 is stored.

The last instruction

$$\text{RTS}$$

loads the return address into the program counter so that execution resumes in the calling routine.

10.6 BIT-MANIPULATION INSTRUCTIONS

The bit manipulation instructions of the 68000 enable a programmer to test the logic level of a bit in either a data register or storage location in memory. The tested bit can also be set, reset, or changed during the execution of the instruction. The four bit manipulation instructions in the 68000's instruction set are shown in Fig. 10.15. They are: *test a bit* (BTST), *test a bit and set* (BSET), *test a bit and clear* (BCLR), and *test a bit and change* (BCHG).

Test a Bit Instruction—BTST

The test a bit (BTST) instruction has the ability to test any one bit in a 32-bit data register or any one bit of a byte storage location in memory. The logic state of the tested bit is inverted and copied into the Z bit of SR. That is, when the bit is tested as 1, Z is set to 0 or when the bit is tested as 0, Z is set to 1. The two valid forms

Mnemonic	Meaning	Format	Operand Size	Operation
BTST	Test a bit	BTST #XXX,EA	8, 32	$\overline{\text{EA bit}} \to \text{Z}$
		BTST Dn,EA	8, 32	
BSET	Test a bit and set	BSET #XXX,EA	8, 32	$\overline{\text{EA bit}} \to \text{Z}$
		BSET Dn,EA	8, 32	$1 \to \text{EA bit}$
BCLR	Test a bit and clear	BCLR #XXX,EA	8, 32	$\overline{\text{EA bit}} \to \text{Z}$
		BCLR Dn,EA	8, 32	$0 \to \text{EA bit}$
BCHG	Test a bit and change	BCHG #XXX,EA	8, 32	$\overline{\text{EA bit}} \to \text{Z}$
		BCHG Dn,EA	8, 32	$\overline{\text{EA bit}} \to \text{EA bit}$

Figure 10.15 Bit-manipulation instructions.

of the BTST instruction are shown in Fig. 10.15. In both forms, the destination operand, which contains the bit to be tested, is specified by an effective address.

These two forms differ in the way the number of the bit to be tested is specified. In the first form, the number of the bit is supplied as an immediate source operand that gets coded as part of the instruction in program memory. An example is the instruction

$$\text{BTST} \quad \#5,\text{D7}$$

Execution of this instruction tests bit 5 in data register D_7. The complement of the value found in this bit position is copied into Z.

The second form uses the contents of one of the data registers to specify the bit position. For instance, if D_0 contains number 5, then executing the instruction

$$\text{BTST} \quad \text{D0,D7}$$

produces the same result as the instruction that employed an immediate operand.

Other Test Bit Instructions—BSET, BCLR, and BCHG

The other instructions in Fig. 10.15, BSET, BCLR, and BCHG, operate similarly to BTST. However, they not only copy the complement of the tested bit into Z, but also set, clear, or invert the bit in the destination operand, respectively.

An example is the instruction

$$\text{BSET} \quad \#7,(\text{A1})$$

When this instruction is executed, bit 7 of the memory location pointed to by (A1) is tested. The complement of its logic level is copied into Z and then bit 7 is set to 1.

When a memory bit is addressed, BTST allows use of the data addressing modes to specify the effective address of the destination operand. The instructions BSET, BCLR, and BCHG allow the use of data-alterable addressing modes for EA.

Mnemonic	Meaning	Format	Operand Size	Operation
TAS	Test and set an operand	TAS EA	8	If destination is zero, $1 \to Z$; otherwise, $0 \to Z$ If destination is negative, $1 \to N$; otherwise, $0 \to N$ $0 \to V$ $0 \to C$ $1 \to$ most significant bit of byte addressed by EA

Figure 10.16   TAS instruction.

Test and Set Operand Instruction—TAS

Another instruction that is similar to the test bit instruction is *test and set an operand* (TAS). As shown in Fig. 10.16, TAS differs from BTST in that it tests a byte operand in a data register or storage location in memory. The test is performed by comparing the operand with zero and setting or resetting condition code bits N and Z based on the result. N is set to the logic level of the most significant bit of the operand and Z is set if the operand is zero. Second, independent of the result of the test, the

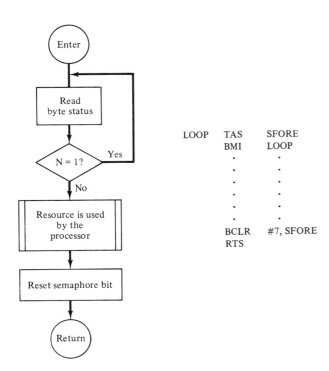

```
LOOP    TAS     SFORE
        BMI     LOOP
         .       .
         .       .
         .       .
         .       .
         .       .
         .       .
        BCLR    #7, SFORE
        RTS
```

Figure 10.17   Use of TAS for multi-processing.

most significant bit of the accessed byte is set to 1. An example is the instruction

TAS   D0

The TAS instruction is specifically designed to support *multiprocessing* and *multitasking system environments*. For instance, in a multiprocessing system, a bit called a semaphore in a byte in memory is set for resolving which processor can access a memory section reserved for a specific resource. If a processor needs to access this resource, it will first test and set the memory byte. If the resource is already in use, the test will indicate that condition and the processor can wait until it is available. Once it is done using the resource, it resets the *semaphore* bit, thus allowing access by other processors. This is illustrated in Fig. 10.17.

ASSIGNMENT

Section 10.2

1. Assuming that condition codes N, Z, V, and C are initially zero, specify their status as each of the instructions that follow is executed.

SUB.L	A0,A0
CMPI.W	#$A000,A0
TST	A0

2. Use move, shift, and logic instructions to compute the results of the logic equation

$$F = Z + N \cdot \overline{V} + \overline{N} \cdot V$$

where N, V, and Z are the condition code bits of the 68000. Store the result F at a location in memory identified as RESULT as a byte of all 1s or all 0s, depending on whether F is 1 or 0.

Section 10.3

3. Describe the difference between a JMP instruction and a BRA instruction.
4. Consider the delay loop program that follows:

	MOVE.B	#$10,D7
DLY	SUBQ.B	#1,D7
	BGT	DLY
NXT	---	---

(a) How many times does the instruction BGT DLY get executed?
(b) Change the program so that BGT DLY is executed just 17 times.
(c) Change the program so that BGT DLY is executed 2^{32} times.

Section 10.4

5. Given a number N in the range $0 < N \leq 5$, write a program that computes its factorial and saves the result in the memory location corresponding to FACT.

6. Write a program that compares the elements of two arrays, A(I) and B(I). Each array contains one hundred 16-bit integer numbers. The comparison is to be done by comparing the corresponding elements of the two arrays until either two elements are found to be unequal or all elements of the arrays have been compared and found to be equal. Assume that the arrays start at addresses $A000 and $B000, respectively. If the two arrays are found to be unequal, save the address of the first unequal element of A(I) at memory location FOUND. On the other hand, if all elements are equal, write a byte of 0s into FOUND.

7. Given an array A(I) with one hundred 16-bit signed numbers, write a program to generate two new arrays, P(J) and N(K). P(J) is to contain all the positive numbers from A(I) and N(K) is to contain all of its negative numbers. A(I) starts at address $A000 in memory and the two new arrays, P(J) and N(K), are to start at addresses $B000 and $C000, respectively.

8. Given an array A(I) of one hundred 16-bit signed integers, write a program to generate a new array, B(I), according to the following directions.

$$B(I) = A(I) \qquad \text{for I = 1, 2, 99, and 100}$$

and

$$B(I) = \text{median of } A(I-2), A(I-1), A(I), A(I+1), \text{ and } A(I+2) \qquad \text{for all}$$
$$\text{other Is}$$

Section 10.5

9. Write a subroutine that converts a given 32-bit binary number to its equivalent BCD number. The binary number is to be passed to the subroutine as a parameter in D_7 and the subroutine also returns the result in D_7.

10. Given an array A(I) of 100 signed 16-bit integer numbers, generate another array B(I) given by

$$B(I) = A(I) \qquad \text{for I = 1 and 100}$$

and

$$B(I) = \frac{1}{4}(A(I-1) + 2A(I) + A(I+1)) \qquad \text{for all other Is}$$

Use a subroutine to generate the terms of B(I). Parameters $A(I-1)$, $A(I)$, and $A(I+1)$ are to be passed to the subroutine on the stack and the subroutine returns the result B(I) on the stack.

Section 10.6

11. Write the segment of main program and show its subroutine structure to perform the following operations. The program is to repeatedly check the 3 least significant bits of D_0 and depending on their settings, executes one of three subroutines: SUBA, SUBB, or SUBC.

The subroutines are selected according to the priority that follows:

3 LSB of D0	Execute
XX1	SUBA
X10	SUBB
100	SUBC

If a subroutine is executed, before returning to the main program, the corresponding bit or bits in register D_0 are to be cleared. After returning from the subroutine, the main program continues.

11

Memory and Input/Output Interfaces of the 68000 Microprocessor

11.1 INTRODUCTION

The preceding three chapters were devoted to the architecture of the 68000, its instruction set, and programming. In this chapter we study the *memory and input/output interfaces* of this microprocessor together with the instructions that are provided to implement stack and I/O operations. In particular, the following topics are the subject of this chapter:

1. The asynchronous memory and I/O interface
2. Address space
3. Data organization
4. Dedicated and general use of memory
5. Program and data storage memory
6. Memory function codes
7. Memory and I/O read and write cycles
8. User and supervisor stacks
9. 64K-byte software refreshed dynamic RAM subsystem
10. I/O instruction—MOVEP
11. 6821 peripheral interface adapter
12. Asynchronous bus interface I/O circuitry
13. Synchronous memory and I/O interface
14. Synchronous bus I/O interface circuitry

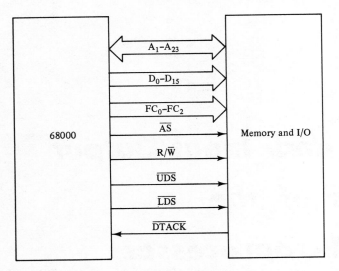

Figure 11.1 Asynchronous memory and I/O interface.

11.2 ASYNCHRONOUS MEMORY AND I/O INTERFACE

The *asynchronous memory and input/output interface* of the 68000 is shown in Fig. 11.1. It consists of the address bus, data bus, function code bus, and control bus. Unlike the 8086, the address and data buses of the 68000 are *demultiplexed*. That is, they do not share pins on the package of the IC. The advantage of this is that the interface circuitry between microprocessor and memory is simplified.

Another difference between the 8086 microcomputer and the 68000 microcomputer is that I/O devices in the 68000 system are always *memory-mapped*. By this we mean that memory and I/O do not have separate address spaces. Instead, the designer allocates a part of the memory address space to the I/O devices. Therefore, both memory and I/O are accessed in the same way through the asynchronous bus interface.

We have indicated several times that the bus between the 68000 and memory or I/O is *asynchronous*. By "asynchronous" we mean that once a bus cycle is initiated to read (input) or write (output) instructions or data, it is not completed until a response is provided by the memory or I/O subsystem. This response is an acknowledge signal that tells the 68000 that it should complete its current bus cycle. For this reason, the timing of the bus cycle in a 68000 microcomputer system can be easily matched to slow memories or I/O devices. This results in efficient use of the system bus.

11.3 ADDRESS SPACE AND DATA ORGANIZATION

Notice in Fig. 11.1 that the address bus of the 68000 consists of 23 independent address lines, which are labeled A_1 through A_{23}. The address information output on these lines selects the storage location in memory or the I/O device that is to be ac-

Word Addresses   Memory Contents

Word Addresses	Memory Contents
000000_{16}	Word 0
000002_{16}	Word 1
000004_{16}	Word 2
$\vdots$	$\vdots$
$FFFFFC_{16}$	Word 8,388,606
$FFFFFE_{16}$	Word 8,388,607

Figure 11.2   Word address space.

cessed. With this large 23-bit address, the 68000 is capable of generating 8M unique addresses. As shown in Fig. 11.2, they represent a *word address space* in the address range 000000_{16} through $FFFFFE_{16}$. Here we see that word information such as instructions, word operands, or long-word operands must always be aligned at even address boundaries.

Coupling the upper data strobe ($\overline{UDS}$) and lower data strobe ($\overline{LDS}$) control signals with this address bus gives the 68000 the ability to access bytes of data. Figure 11.3 illustrates how these two signals can be used to enable *byte-wide upper* and *lower data banks* in memory. Address lines A_1 through A_{23} are applied in parallel to both memory banks.

From an address point of view, memory can now be considered to be organized as bytes, and as shown in Fig. 11.4, bytes of data can be stored at odd or even addresses. When expressed in this way, the size of the *physical address space* is said to be 16M bytes.

The address strobe ($\overline{AS}$) control signal is output by the 68000 along with the address on A_1 through A_{23}. It is used to signal memory and I/O devices that valid address information is available on the bus.

In Fig. 11.1 we find a second bus between the 68000 and the memory or I/O device. It is the data bus and consists of the 16 bidirectional data lines D_0 through D_{15}. Data are input to the microprocessor over these lines during read (input) operations and are output by the processor over these lines during write (output) operations.

The control signals that coordinate the data transfers that take place between the 68000 and memory or I/O devices are also shown in Fig. 11.1. They are the read/write ($R/\overline{W}$) output and the data transfer acknowledge ($\overline{DTACK}$) input. The 68000 sets $R/\overline{W}$ to the appropriate logic level to tell external circuitry whether the data are being input or output by the microprocessor during the current bus cycle.

On the other hand, $\overline{DTACK}$ acknowledges that the transfer between microprocessor and memory or I/O subsystem has taken place. When the 68000 executes

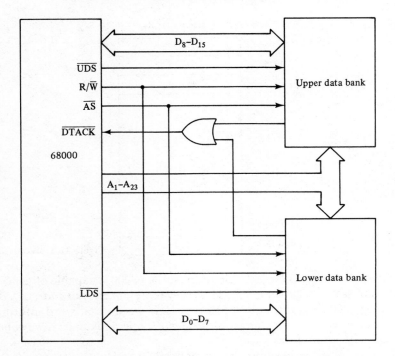

Figure 11.3 Memory organized as upper and lower data banks.

Even Byte Addresses	Memory Contents		Odd Byte Addresses
000000_{16}	Byte 0	Byte 1	000001_{16}
000002_{16}	Byte 2	Byte 3	000003_{16}
000004_{16}	Byte 4	Byte 5	000005_{16}
⋮	⋮	⋮	⋮
$FFFFFE_{16}$	Byte 16,777,214	Byte 16,777,215	$FFFFFF_{16}$

Figure 11.4 Byte address space.

a read operation, it always waits until the $\overline{\text{DTACK}}$ input goes active before completing the bus cycle. $\overline{\text{DTACK}}$ is asserted by the memory or I/O device when the data it has put on the bus are valid. In response to $\overline{\text{DTACK}}$ equal to 0, the 68000 latches in the data from the bus and completes the read cycle. During a write operation, $\overline{\text{DTACK}}$ indicates to the 68000 that data have been written; therefore, it terminates the bus cycle.

Remember that most of the instructions in the instruction set of the 68000 have the ability to process operands expressed in *byte, word,* or *long-word formats.* Let us now look at how data expressed in these forms are stored in memory. From Fig. 11.5(a), we see that within a byte of data bit 0 represents the least significant bit and

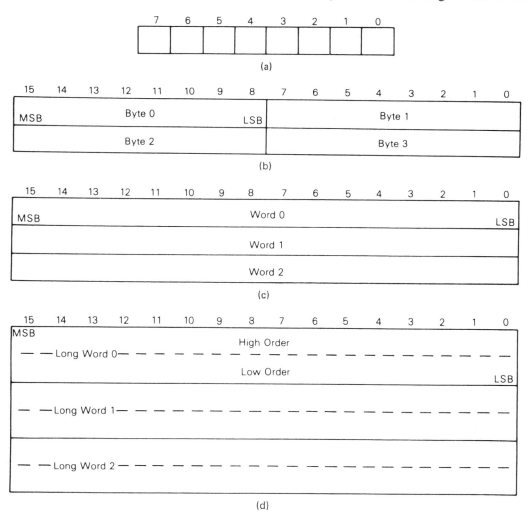

Figure 11.5 Data organization in memory (Motorola Inc.).

bit 7 represents the most significant bit. Next, Fig. 11.5(b) shows that two bytes of data can be stored at each word address. Notice that even-addressed bytes such as byte 0 and byte 2 are stored in most significant byte locations and odd-addressed bytes such as byte 1 and byte 3 are stored in least significant byte locations. Figure 11.5(c) and (d) show that a word is simply stored at each word address and that a long word is stored at two consecutive word addresses.

Looking at the memory subsystem hardware configuration in Fig. 11.3, we see that for an addressed word storage location the upper 8 bits of the word are in the upper data bank. This is the even byte and it is transferred between memory and microprocessor over data bus lines D_8 through D_{15}. The lower 8 bits of the word, the odd byte, are in the lower data bank. They are transferred between microprocessor and memory over D_0 through D_7.

For a word transfer to take place over the bus, both $\overline{UDS}$ and $\overline{LDS}$ must be active at the same time. Therefore, they are both switched to the 0 logic level. Moreover, the direction in which data are transferred is identified by the logic level of $R/\overline{W}$. For instance, if the word of data is to be written into memory, $R/\overline{W}$ is set to logic 0. $\overline{UDS}$ and $\overline{LDS}$ can also be set to access just the upper byte or lower byte of data. In this case, either $\overline{UDS}$ or $\overline{LDS}$ remains at its inactive 1 logic level.

Figure 11.6 summarizes the types of data transfers that can take place over the data bus and the corresponding control signal logic levels. For example, when an even byte is read from the high memory bank $\overline{UDS} = 0$, $\overline{LDS} = 1$, $R/\overline{W} = 1$ and data are transferred from memory to the 68000 over data lines D_8 through D_{15}.

$\overline{UDS}$	$\overline{LDS}$	$R/\overline{W}$	D8-D15	D0-D7
High	High	—	No valid data	No valid data
Low	Low	High	Valid data bits 8-15	Valid data bits 0-7
High	Low	High	No valid data	Valid data bits 0-7
Low	High	High	Valid data bits 8-15	No valid data
Low	Low	Low	Valid data bits 8-15	Valid data bits 0-7
High	Low	Low	Valid data bits 0-7	Valid data bits 0-7
Low	High	Low	Valid data bits 8-15	Valid data bits 8-15

Figure 11.6 Relationship between bus control signals and data bus transfers (Motorola Inc.).

11.4 DEDICATED AND GENERAL USE MEMORY

Now that we have introduced the memory interface of the 68000, its address space, and data organization, let us continue by looking at which parts of the address space have dedicated uses and which parts are for general use. In Fig. 11.7 we see that the lower end of the address space has a *dedicated function*. That is, the word storage locations over the address range from 000000_{16} to $0003FE_{16}$ are allocated for stor-

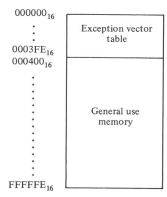

Figure 11.7   Memory map.

age of an address vector table. As shown, it contains the 68000's exception vector table. Each vector address is 24 bits long and takes up two words of memory. An example of 68000 exceptions are its hardware interrupts. The exception processing capability of the 68000 is the subject of Chapter 12.

From the *memory map* in Fig. 11.7 we see that the rest of the address space is for *general use*. Therefore, it can be used to store instructions of the program, data operands, or address information.

11.5 PROGRAM AND DATA STORAGE MEMORY AND THE FUNCTION CODES

In the preceding section we showed how the memory address space of the 68000 is partitioned into a dedicated use area and a general use area. Another way of partitioning the memory subsystem in a 68000 microcomputer system is in terms of *program and data storage memory*. In general, the program segment of memory contains the opcodes of the instructions in the program, direct addresses of operands, and data of immediate source operands. It can be implemented with ROM or RAM.

On the other hand, the data segment is generally implemented with RAM. This is because it contains data operands that are to be processed by the instructions. Therefore, it must be able to be read from or written into.

During all bus cycles to memory, the 68000 outputs bus status codes to indicate whether it is accessing program or data memory. The bus status code is known as the *function code* and is output on function code bus lines FC_0 through FC_2. The table in Fig. 11.8 lists all function codes output by the 68000 and the corresponding type of bus cycle. Notice that program and data memory accesses are further categorized based on whether they occur when the 68000 is in the user state or supervisor state. For instance, an instruction acquisition bus cycle performed when the 68000 is in the user state is accompanied by the function code $FC_2 FC_1 FC_0 = 010$, but the same type of access in the supervisor state is accompanied by $FC_2 FC_1 FC_0 = 110$.

One use of the function codes is to partition the memory subsystem hardware. This can be done by decoding the function codes in external logic to produce enable

Function code output			Reference class
FC_2	FC_1	FC_0	
0	0	0	(Unassigned)
0	0	1	User data
0	1	0	User program
0	1	1	(Unassigned)
1	0	0	(Unassigned)
1	0	1	Supervisor data
1	1	0	Supervisor program
1	1	1	Interrupt acknowledge

Figure 11.8 Memory function codes (Motorola Inc.).

signals for the *user program segment, user data segment, supervisor program segment*, and *supervisor data segment*.

One approach is illustrated in Fig. 11.9. Here the memory subsystem has been partitioned into a user memory segment and a supervisor memory segment. Looking at Fig. 11.8, we see that the logic level of function code line FC_2 indicates whether the 68000 is in the user or supervisor state. Notice that in this circuit FC_2 is gated with address strobe $\overline{AS}$ to produce select input $\overline{S}_1$ for the supervisor memory bank. In this way, the 68000 can access either the user or supervisor memory banks when it is in the supervisor state, but when it is in the user state the supervisor memory bank is locked out.

Another approach would be to partition the memory subsystem such that it has an independent 16M-byte program memory segment and a 16M-byte data memory segment. This expands the address space to 32M bytes in a segmented fashion.

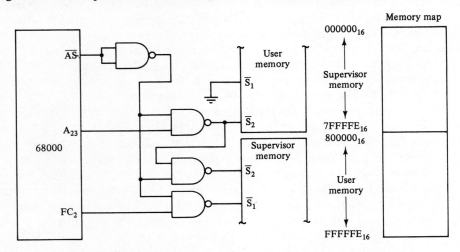

Figure 11.9 Partitioning memory into user and supervisor segments (Motorola Inc.).

11.6 MEMORY AND I/O READ CYCLE TIMING

To read a word or byte from an input device or memory, the signal lines that are used are address lines A_1 through A_{23}, data lines D_0 through D_{15}, and asynchronous control lines: address strobe ($\overline{AS}$), upper and lower data strobes ($\overline{UDS}$ and $\overline{LDS}$), read/write ($R/\overline{W}$), and data transfer acknowledge ($\overline{DTACK}$). Figure 11.10(a) is a

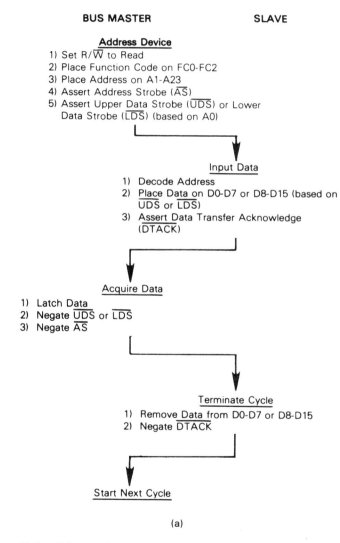

(a)

Figure 11.10   (a) Byte read cycle flowchart (Motorola Inc.); (b) upper byte read timing diagram.

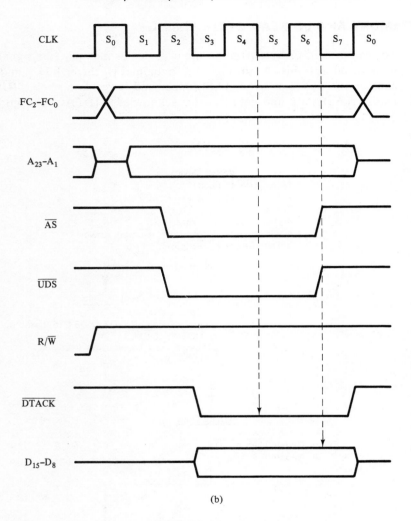

(b)

Figure 11.10 *(continued)*

flowchart that shows the sequence of events that takes place in order to read a byte of data from the memory subsystem in Fig. 11.3. A timing diagram for an upper bank *read bus cycle* is shown in Fig. 11.10(b).

From the timing diagram, we see that a read cycle can be completed in as few as four clock cycles. Each clock cycle consists of a high and low state for a total of eight states. They are labeled S_0 through S_7 in the timing diagram. With the 100-ns clock cycle of the 10-MHz 68000, this gives a minimum read bus cycle time of 400 ns.

In Fig. 11.10(a) we see that the read bus cycle begins with R/$\overline{\text{W}}$ being switched to logic 1. As shown in Fig. 11.10(b), this happens at the leading edge of state S_0.

During S_0, a function code $FC_2FC_1FC_0$ is output and address lines A_1 through A_{23} are put in the high-Z state. Next the address is output during the S_1 state followed by address strobe $\overline{AS}$ and the appropriate data strobes during S_2. In our example, we are to read only the upper byte; therefore, $\overline{UDS}$ is switched to its active 0 logic level. The address phase of the bus cycle is now complete.

Next the memory or I/O subsystem must decode the address and put the selected data on bus lines D_8 through D_{15}. This must happen during S_3. Then in S_4 it must assert $\overline{DTACK}$ by switching it to logic 0. This signals the 68000 that valid data are on the bus and that the bus cycle should be continued through to completion.

$\overline{DTACK}$ is tested by the 68000 during S_5. If it is active (logic 0), data are read off the bus at the end of S_6. During S_7, the 68000 returns $\overline{AS}$ and $\overline{UDS}$ to their inactive logic levels and the address bus and data lines to the high-Z state. Moreover, the memory or I/O subsystem must return $\overline{DTACK}$ to the 1 level before another bus cycle can be initiated.

If the 68000 finds $\overline{DTACK}$ not asserted, it inserts wait clock cycles until it goes low to indicate that valid data are on the data bus.

Accesses of byte or word data require execution of one bus cycle by the 68000. On the other hand, long-word accesses require two words of data to be transferred over the bus. Therefore, they take two bus cycles.

11.7 MEMORY AND I/O WRITE CYCLE TIMING

To write a word or a byte of data to memory or an I/O device, the same basic interface signals we identified for the read operation are used. The flowchart and timing diagram for a bus cycle that writes a word of data are shown in Fig. 11.11(a) and (b), respectively. Here we see that a minimum of five clock cycles, which equals 10 states S_0 through S_9, are required to perform a *write bus cycle*. At 10 MHz this takes 500 ns.

Looking at Fig. 11.11(a), we see that the bus cycle begins with a function code being output on the FC bus during S_0. The address lines that are floating during S_0 are asserted with a valid address during S_1 and $\overline{AS}$ and $R/\overline{W}$ go active during S_2. This time, $R/\overline{W}$ is set to 0 to indicate that a write operation is to take place and data are output on the complete bus D_0 through D_{15} during S_3.

Selection of byte or word data is made by the 68000 asserting the data strobe signals. For a word access, both $\overline{UDS}$ and $\overline{LDS}$ are switched to their active 0 logic level. This is done during the S_4 state.

Up to this point, the 68000 has output the address of the storage location and put the data on the bus. External circuitry must now decode the address to select the memory location or I/O device. Then the data, which were put on the bus during S_3, are written into the enabled device during S_4. After the write of data has been completed, the memory or I/O device must inform the 68000 of this condition by pulling $\overline{DTACK}$ to its active 0 logic level. $\overline{DTACK}$ is tested by the 68000 at the be-

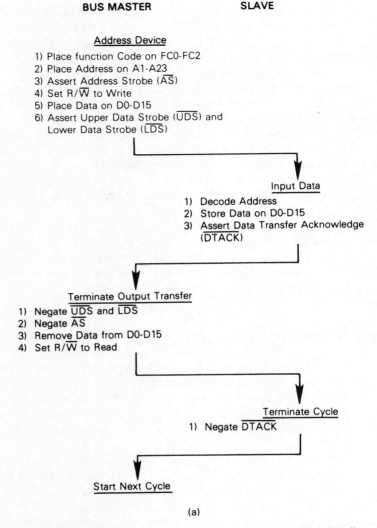

BUS MASTER   **SLAVE**

<u>Address Device</u>
1) Place function Code on FC0-FC2
2) Place Address on A1-A23
3) Assert Address Strobe ($\overline{AS}$)
4) Set R/$\overline{W}$ to Write
5) Place Data on D0-D15
6) Assert Upper Data Strobe ($\overline{UDS}$) and
   Lower Data Strobe ($\overline{LDS}$)

<u>Input Data</u>
1) Decode Address
2) Store Data on D0-D15
3) Assert Data Transfer Acknowledge
   ($\overline{DTACK}$)

<u>Terminate Output Transfer</u>
1) Negate $\overline{UDS}$ and $\overline{LDS}$
2) Negate $\overline{AS}$
3) Remove Data from D0-D15
4) Set R/$\overline{W}$ to Read

<u>Terminate Cycle</u>
1) Negate $\overline{DTACK}$

<u>Start Next Cycle</u>

(a)

Figure 11.11 (a) Word write cycle flowchart (Motorola Inc.); (b) timing diagram.

ginning of S_7 and if it is not asserted, wait clock cycles are inserted between the S_6 and S_7 states. This extends the duration of the write cycle. However, if $\overline{DTACK}$ is found to be at its active 0 level, $\overline{UDS}$, $\overline{LDS}$, and $\overline{AS}$ are returned to their inactive 1 logic levels at the beginning of the S_9 state. Furthermore, at the end of S_9, the address and data lines are returned to the high-Z state and R/$\overline{W}$ is switched to 1.

Before the S_0 state of the next bus cycle, $\overline{DTACK}$ must be returned to logic 1. However, this is done by the memory or I/O subsystem, not the 68000.

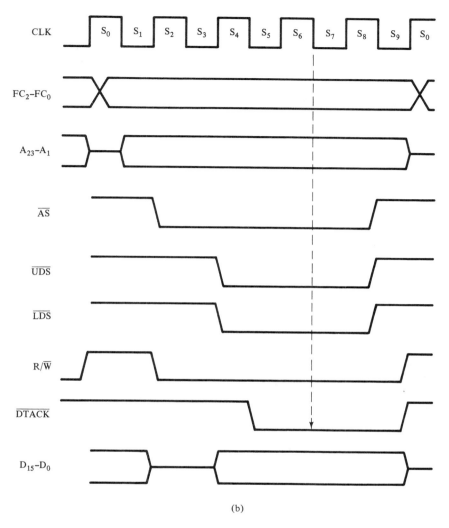

(b)

Figure 11.11 *(continued)*

11.8 THE USER AND SUPERVISOR STACKS

Just like the 8086 microprocessor, the 68000 employs a stack-oriented architecture. But the 68000 has two internal stack pointer registers instead of one like the 8086. In Chapter 8 we indicated that these stack pointers are called the user stack pointer (USP) and supervisor stack pointer (SSP). As shown in Fig. 11.12, the addresses held in these registers point to the top storage locations in their respective stacks: that is, their tops of stacks. The storage locations identified as bottom of stack represent

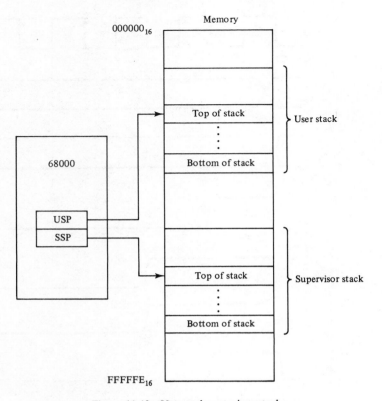

Figure 11.12 User and supervisor stacks.

the locations pointed to by the initial values loaded into the stack pointers. When the stacks are empty, the stack pointers point to this location. The *user stack* is active whenever the 68000 is in the user state and the *supervisor stack* is active whenever it is in the supervisor state. Both stacks can be located in memory anywhere in the address space of the 68000, and they are not limited in size.

During exception processing or subroutine calls, the contents of certain internal registers of the 68000 are saved on the stack. For instance, when exception processing is initiated for a hardware interrupt, the current contents of the program counter (PC) and status register (SR) are automatically pushed to the stack. In this way, they are temporarily saved.

Additional stack operations are usually performed as part of the exception processing service routine or subroutine. These are push operations that save the contents of registers that are to be used within the service routine on the stack. For instance, instructions in a hardware interrupt service routine can cause the contents of data registers D_0, D_1, and D_2 to be pushed to the user stack. One way of doing this is with the instruction sequence

$$\text{MOVE.W} \quad \text{D2}, -(\text{USP})$$

$$\text{MOVE.W} \quad \text{D1}, -(\text{USP})$$

$$\text{MOVE.W} \quad \text{D0}, -(\text{USP})$$

These examples all push word data to the user stack. Byte data can also be pushed to the stack. However, each byte also consumes one word of stack. The byte of data is stored in the most significant byte location of the word storage location and the least significant byte is not affected.

At the completion of processing of the exception routine, the saved contents of internal registers can be restored by popping them from the stack. When pushing or popping a number of registers, the move multiple (MOVEM) instruction can be used to efficiently perform the operation. For example, the instruction

$$\text{MOVEM} \quad (\text{USP}) +, \text{D0}/\text{D1}/\text{D2}$$

would restore the contents of D_0, D_1, and D_2 from the user stack.

Moreover, the return instructions for exception processing and subroutines cause automatic reloading of some internal registers. An example is the *return from exception* (RTE) instruction. It causes the contents of both PC and SR to be restored from the top of the stack.

11.9 64K-BYTE SOFTWARE-REFRESHED DYNAMIC RAM SUBSYSTEM

The circuit diagram in Fig. 11.13 shows one way of implementing a dynamic RAM subsystem for a 68000 microcomputer system. This circuit is designed to provide 64K bytes of memory which are mapped into the address range 008000_{16} through $017FFF_{16}$ of the 68000's address space.

Because of the large memory support capability of the 68000, it is essential to buffer all of the memory interface signals. This is done by the leftmost group of circuits in Fig. 11.13. For example, two 74245 devices are used to buffer the bidirectional data bus lines D_0 through D_{15} and two 74LS244 devices are used to buffer address lines A_1 through A_{16}. These buffers increase the drive capability of the address and data buses over that supplied directly by the lines of the 68000.

Let us next look at the storage array of the memory subsystem. It is located at the right of the circuit diagram and employs thirty-two 16K by 1 dynamic RAMs. The type of memory device used is the MCM4116. The circuit is set up to implement a structure similar to that shown in Fig. 11.3. The upper 16 devices form a 32K-byte upper data bank. This bank is used to store even-addressed bytes of data and they are transferred between microprocessor and memory over data bus lines D_8 through D_{15}. The lower 16 devices form a 32K-byte lower data bank. It stores odd bytes of data which are carried between 68000 and memory over data lines D_0 through D_7.

Since dynamic RAMs are in use instead of static RAMs, the address output

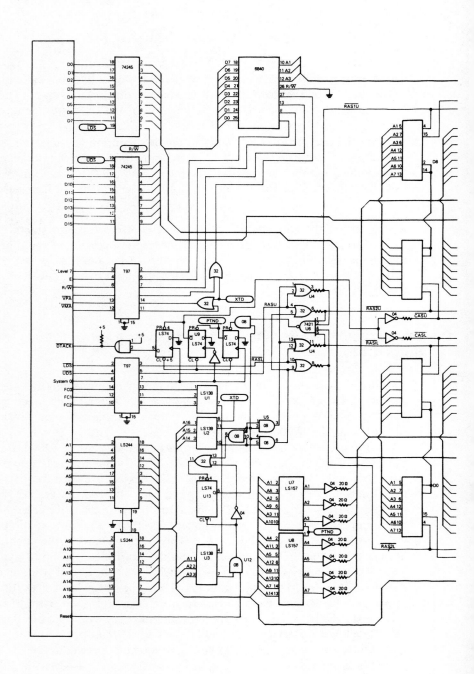

324

Figure 11.13 Software-refreshed dynamic RAM subsystem (Motorola Inc.).

by the 68000 on A_1 through A_{14} must be multiplexed into separate row and column addresses before it can be applied to the memory devices. In Fig. 11.13 we see that these address lines are input to two 74LS157 multiplexers which produce 7-bit row and column addresses at their outputs, A_1 through A_7. The timing of the address output on these lines is determined by the PTND output of a 74LS74 flip-flop in IC U_9.

Both bank and byte/word selection is performed through the generation of $\overline{RAS}$ signals. Notice that the control logic implemented with ICs U_2, U_4, U_5, and U_9 produces four RAS signals. They are denoted as RAS_{1U}, RAS_{2U}, RAS_{1L}, and $\overline{RAS_{2L}}$. Also, two $\overline{CAS}$ signals, $\overline{CAS_U}$ and $\overline{CAS_L}$, are produced by this section. The inputs from which the row select and column select signals are derived are address bits A_{14} through A_{16}, upper and lower data select $\overline{UDS}$ and $\overline{LDS}$, and the system clock SYSTEM 0.

For example, to perform a word access from the group 1 RAMs, both $\overline{LDS}$ and $\overline{UDS}$ are logic 0. This makes both the $\overline{RAS_L}$ and $\overline{RAS_U}$ signals active. At the same time, the address code $A_{16}A_{15}A_{14}$ is decoded by ICs U_2 and U_5 to enable both $\overline{RAS_{1U}}$ and $\overline{RAS_{1L}}$ to the memory array. These signals are synchronized to the output of the row address from the multiplexer. A short time later the $\overline{CAS_U}$ and $\overline{CAS_L}$ signals are produced. They are synchronized to the output of the column address from the multiplexer.

Notice that the data acknowledge ($\overline{DTACK}$) signal is also produced by this section of control logic. It is buffered and then sent to the 68000.

This memory subsystem employs *software refresh* and not *hardware refresh*. The 6840 device is provided for this purpose. It contains a timer that is set up to initiate an interrupt to the 68000 every 1.9 ms. This interrupt has a priority level of 7 and execution of its service routine performs the software-refresh function. The advantage of software refresh is that the interface hardware is simplified. However, it also has a disadvantage—the software and time overhead required to perform the refresh operation.

11.10 AN I/O INSTRUCTION—MOVEP

The 68000 microprocessor has one instruction that is specifically designed for communicating with LSI peripherals that interface over an 8-bit data bus. It is the *move peripheral data* (MOVEP) instruction. An example of an LSI peripheral that can be used in the 68000 microcomputer system is the *6821 peripheral interface adapter* (PIA). Internal to this device is a group of byte-wide interface registers. When the device is built into the microcomputer system, these registers will all reside at either odd addresses or even addresses. This poses a problem if we attempt to make multibyte transfers by specifying word or long-word data operands. For instance, a MOVE instruction for word data would cause the two bytes to be transfered to consecutive byte addresses, one of which is even and the other is odd. This problem is overcome with the MOVEP instruction.

The general formats of the instruction are

MOVEP   Dn,d(An)

and

MOVEP   d(An),Dn

The first form of the instruction is for output of data. It copies the contents of a source operand that is in data register Dn to the location at the effective address specified by the destination operand. Notice that the destination operand must always be specified using address register indirect with displacement addressing.

As an example, let us write an instruction that will transfer a word of data that is in D_0 to two consecutive output ports. Assume that the contents of A_0 are 16000_{16} and it is a pointer to the first of a group of eight byte-wide registers in an LSI peripheral. These registers are at consecutive even addresses. That is, register 0 is at address 16000_{16}, register 1 at 16002_{16}, and so on. We want to transfer data to the last two of these registers, registers 6 and 7. The displacement of register 6 from the address in A_0 is C_{16}; therefore, the instruction is

MOVEP.W   D0,12(A0)

Execution of this instruction causes the bytes of the word contents of D_0 to be output to two consecutive even-byte addresses. The most significant byte is output to the effective destination address, which is $1600C_{16}$. This is register 6. Then the address is incremented by 2 to give $1600E_{16}$ and the second byte is output to register 7. The pointer address in A_0 remains unchanged.

A MOVEP instruction that employs long-word operands operates in a similar way except that it would output four bytes to consecutive odd or even addresses. As an example, let us assume that four byte-wide input ports are located at odd-byte addresses 16001_{16}, 16003_{16}, 16005_{16}, and 16007_{16}. The data at these 32 input lines can be read into a data register by executing a single MOVEP instruction. If A_1 contains a pointer to the first input port, the long word of data can be input to D_1 with the instruction

MOVEP.L   0(A1),D1

11.11 THE 6821 PERIPHERAL INTERFACE ADAPTER

In the 68000 microcomputer system, parallel input/output ports can be implemented with the 6821 peripheral interface adapter. The 6821 is one of the simpler LSI peripherals designed for implementing parallel input/output. It has two byte-wide ports called A and B. Each line at both of these ports can be independently configured as an input or output.

Figure 11.14 is a block diagram that shows the internal architecture of the 6821 device. Here we find six programmable registers. They include an *output register* (OR), *data direction register* (DDR), and *control register* (CR) for each of the I/O ports. Let us overview the function of each of these registers before going on.

All input/output data transfers between the microprocessor and PIA take place

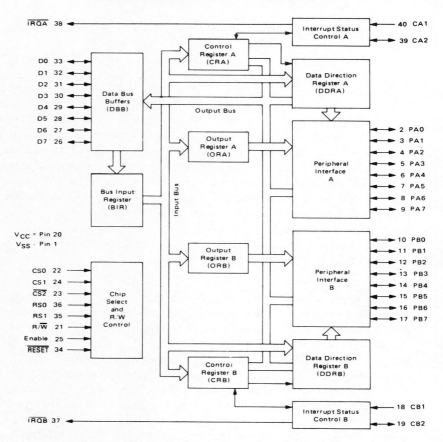

Figure 11.14   Block diagram of the 6821 (Motorola Inc.).

through the output data registers. These registers are 8 bits wide and their bits correspond to the I/O port lines. For example, to set the logic level of an output line at port A to logic 1, we simply write logic 1 into the corresponding bit in port A's output register.

Each I/O line of the 6821 also has a bit corresponding to it in the A or B data direction register. The logic level of this bit decides whether the corresponding line works as an input or an output. Logic 0 in a bit position selects input mode of operation for the corresponding I/O line and logic 1 selects output operation. For instance, port A can be configured as a byte-wide output port by initializing its data direction register with the value FF_{16}.

The control register (CR) serves three main functions. First it is used to configure the operation of *control inputs* CA_1, CA_2, CB_1, and CB_2. A second function is that it can be read by the 68000 to identify control status. However, its third function is what we are interested in right now. This is how it is used to select between the DDR and OR registers when they are loaded or read by the 68000. In Fig. 11.15

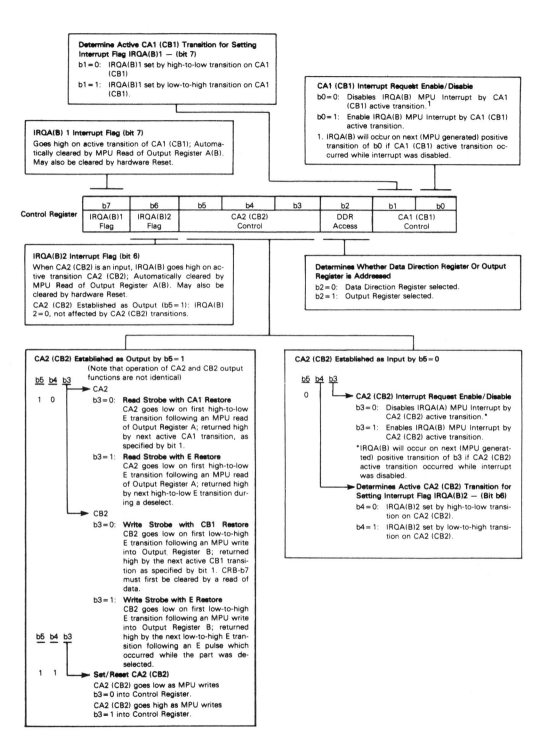

Figure 11.15 Control register bit functions (Motorola Inc.).

we see that the logic level of bit b2 in CR selects DDR when it is zero and OR when it is 1.

Looking at Fig. 11.14, we find that the microprocessor interface of the 6821 is shown on the left. The key signals here are the eight *data bus lines* D_0 through D_7. It is over these lines that the 68000 can initialize the registers of the 6821, write commands to the control registers, read status from the control registers, and read from or write into the peripheral data registers. The direction in which data are to be transferred is signaled to the 6821 by the logic level of $R/\overline{W}$. For example, logic 0 on $R/\overline{W}$ indicates that data are to be written into one of its registers.

Even though the 6821 has six addressable registers, only two *register select lines* have been provided. They are labeled RS_0 and RS_1. The table in Fig. 11.16 shows

| RS1 | RS0 | Control Register Bit | | Location Selected |
		CRA-2	CRB-2	
0	0	1	X	Peripheral Register A
0	0	0	X	Data Direction Register A
0	1	X	X	Control Register A
1	0	X	1	Peripheral Register B
1	0	X	0	Data Direction Register B
1	1	X	X	Control Register B

X = Don't Care

Figure 11.16 User-accessible register selection (Motorola Inc.).

how they are used together with bit b_2 of the control registers to select the internal registers. Notice that if both RS_1 and RS_0 are logic 0, the data direction register and output register for port A are selected. As we pointed out earlier, the setting of b_2 in the A control register selects between the two registers. For instance, if this bit is logic 0, the data transfer takes place between the microprocessor and the DDR for port A. In this way we see that bit 2 in control register A must be set to select the appropriate register before initiating the data transfer.

As part of the microprocessor interface, there are also three *chip select inputs*. They are labeled CS_0, CS_1, and $\overline{CS_2}$ and must be 1, 1, and 0, respectively, to enable the microprocessor interface.

At the right side of the 6821 block diagram in Fig. 11.14, we find the A and B byte-wide I/O ports. The individual I/O lines at these ports are labeled PA_0 through PA_7 and PB_0 through PB_7, respectively.

Two more lines are associated with each I/O port. They are control lines. For instance, looking at the A port, we find control lines CA_1 and CA_2. Notice that CA_1 is a dedicated output, but CA_2 is bidirectional and can be configured to operate as an input or an output. The mode of operation of these control lines are determined by the settings of the bits in port A's control register.

These control lines permit the user of the 6821 to implement a variety of different *I/O handshake mechanisms*. For example, port A could be configured for a *strobed mode* of operation. If this is the case, a pulse is output at CA_2 whenever new data are available at PA_0 through PA_7. Moreover, the 6821 can be configured such that the pulse at CA_2 is automatically produced by the 6821 or is generated under software control from the 68000. In the *automatic mode*, the pulse that is output is of a fixed duration. But if the pulse is initiated by the 68000, it can be set to any duration.

11.12 DUAL 16-BIT PORTS FOR THE 68000 MICROCOMPUTER USING 6821s

The circuit in Fig. 11.17 shows how 6821 PIAs can be used to implement a parallel I/O interface for a 68000 microcomputer system. At the left of the circuit diagram, we find the asynchronous interface bus signals. Included are address lines A_1 through A_{16}, data lines D_0 through D_{15}, and control signals $\overline{AS}$, R/$\overline{W}$, and $\overline{DTACK}$.

In order to construct two 16-bit ports, we use two 6821 ICs, U_{14} and U_{15}. The A ports on the two 6821 ICs are cascaded to make a word-wide output port. On the other hand, the B ports on the two devices are cascaded to make a word-wide input port.

This circuit has been designed such that the registers in the PIAs reside in the address range 18000_{16} through 18007_{16}. The chart in Fig. 11.18(a) shows the address for each register. Notice that the data direction registers corresponding to the bytes of the 16-byte output port are at addresses 18000_{16} and 18001_{16}. Those of the 16-bit input port are at 18004_{16} and 18005_{16}.

The address decoding for selecting between the two chips and their internal registers is shown in Fig. 11.18(b). Notice that bits A_1 and A_2 of the address are applied to register select inputs RS_0 and RS_1, respectively. Moreover, A_3 and A_4 are applied to the CS_1 and CS_0 chip select inputs of both 6821 devices. The rest of the address lines, A_5 to A_{16}, and $\overline{AS}$ are decoded by gates U_{9A}, U_{9B}, U_{10E}, U_{11A}, and U_{11B}. Their output is synchronized with a 2-MHz externally generated clock signal by flip-flops U_{13A} and U_{13B}. The output of this circuit is the third chip select signal, $\overline{CS_2}$, for the PIAs.

The data bus lines are simply buffered and then applied to both PIAs in parallel. Notice that the upper PIA device is coupled to the 68000 over the lower eight data bus lines and the lower PIA by the upper eight data lines. Therefore, as shown in Fig. 11.18(a), the registers of the upper device reside at odd byte addresses and those of the lower device are at even byte addresses.

To use the B ports on the two 6821 devices as inputs, their B port DDRs must be initialized with all zeros. These two registers are located at addresses 18004_{16} and 18005_{16}, respectively. However, to select these DDRs, bit 2 in the corresponding control registers must be loaded with logic 0. These control registers are located at addresses 18006_{16} and 18007_{16}. Thus to configure the B ports as inputs, we can execute the following instruction sequence:

```
MOVE.W   #$0000,$18006    SELECT DATA-DIRECTION REGISTERS B
MOVE.W   #$0000,$18004    PORT B IS INPUT-PORT
```

Execution of these instructions loads the word-wide memory locations at addresses 18006_{16} and 18004_{16} with 0000_{16}.

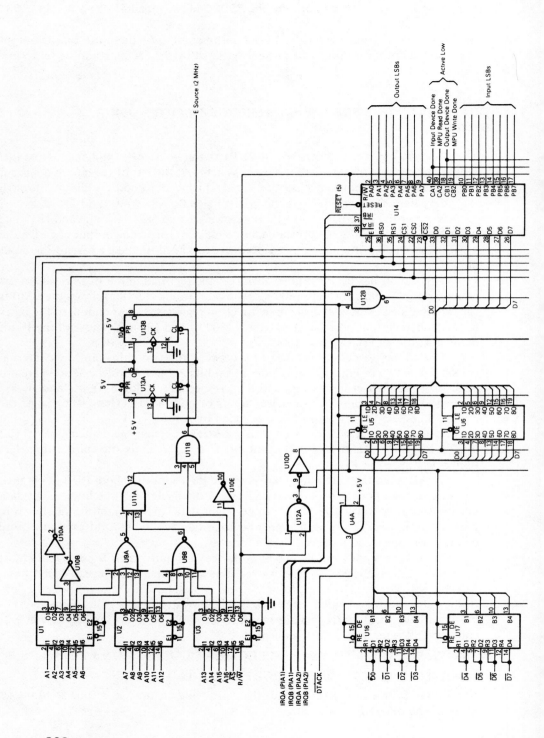

332

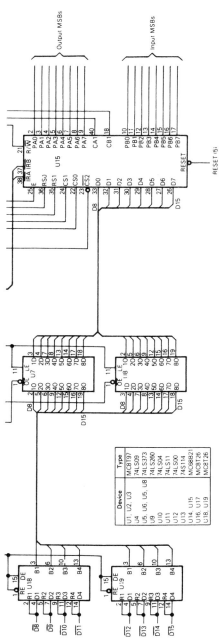

Figure 11.17 Dual 16-bit I/O ports using the 6821 (Motorola Inc.).

333

18000	Peripheral Data/DDRA	(U15)
18001	Peripheral Data/DDRA	(U14)
18002	CRA	(U15)
18003	CRA	(U14)
18004	Peripheral Data/DDRB	(U15)
18005	Peripheral Data/DDRB	(U14)
18006	CRB	(U15)
18007	CRB	(U14)

(a)

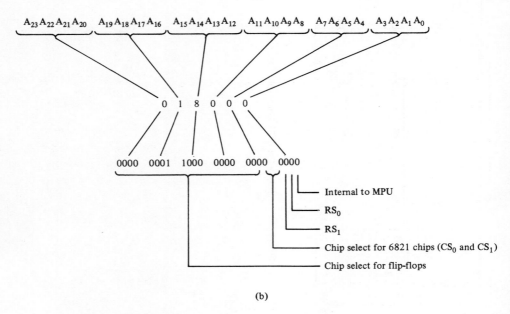

(b)

Figure 11.18   (a) 6821 register address map (Motorola Inc.); (b) address decoding for port selection.

To configure the A ports on the two chips, we first select the DDRs for port A by clearing bit 2 in their control registers. These CRs are located at addresses 18002_{16} and 18003_{16}. The DDRs are located at 18000_{16} and 18001_{16}. To configure the A ports as outputs, we must load their DDRs with all 1s. This gives the following instruction sequence:

MOVE.W   #$0000,$18002   SELECT DATA-DIRECTION REGISTERS A

MOVE.W   #$FFFF,$18000   PORT A IS OUTPUT-PORT

Now to use the ports for inputting or outputting of data, we must select the data registers. To select the two data registers for port A, we must load their control registers so that bit 2 is logic 1. A similar configuration is needed for port B. To do this, the following instructions can be executed:

MOVE.W   #$0404,$18002   SELECT DATA REGISTERS A

MOVE.W   #$0404,$18006   SELECT DATA REGISTERS B

Now the two ports are ready to perform I/O operations.

As an example of how data are input and output, let us show how to read a 16-bit word from the input port, increment it by 1, and output the new value to the output port. This can be accomplished by the following instructions:

MOVE.W $18004,D1

ADDQ.W   #1,D1

MOVE.W   D1,$18000

The first instruction moves the contents of the input port to D_1. Then we increment the value in D_1 by 1. Finally, the third instruction outputs the value in D_1 to the output port.

11.13 SYNCHRONOUS MEMORY AND I/O INTERFACE

Up to this point in the chapter, we have been considering the asynchronous bus interface of the 68000 microprocessor. However, the 68000 also provides a *synchronous bus interface*. This capability is provided primarily for interface with slower 8-bit LSI peripherals such as those in the 6800 family. The synchronous interface is shown in Fig. 11.19. This interface looks quite similar to the asynchronous interface of Fig. 11.1. It includes the complete address bus A_1 through A_{23}, the 16-bit data bus D_0 through D_{15}, and control signals $\overline{UDS}$, $\overline{LDS}$, $\overline{AS}$, and R/W. Notice that $\overline{DTACK}$ is not part of this interface. Instead, it is replaced by three synchronous bus control

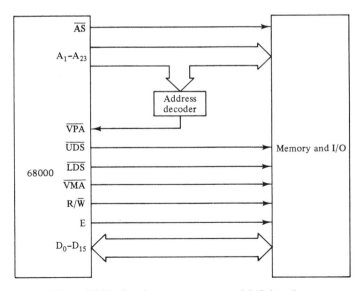

Figure 11.19 Synchronous memory and I/O interface.

signals. They are valid peripheral address ($\overline{\text{VPA}}$), valid memory address ($\overline{\text{VMA}}$), and enable (E).

Let us look briefly at the function of each of these control signals. $\overline{\text{VPA}}$ is an input to the 68000. It must be switched to the 0 logic level to tell the 68000 to perform a synchronous bus cycle. As shown in Fig. 11.19, external decoder circuitry is supplied in the interface to detect that the address on the bus is in the address space of the synchronous peripherals. On the other hand, $\overline{\text{VMA}}$ is an output produced by the 68000 only during synchronous bus cycles. It signals that a valid address is on the bus.

E is an enable clock that is produced within the 68000. It is at a rate equal to 1/10 that of the system clock. For instance, in a 10-Mz 68000 microcomputer system, E is at 1 MHz. The duty cycle of this signal is such that the pulse is at the 1 logic level for four clock states and at the 0 logic level for six clock states. This signal is applied to the E clock input of 6800 LSI peripherals.

Synchronous Bus Cycle

A flowchart of the 68000's *synchronous bus cycle* is shown in Fig. 11.20(a). Moreover, a general timing diagram for the key interface signals involved in a synchronous read/write operation is shown in Fig. 11.20(b). Notice that the waveforms of the FC, R/$\overline{\text{W}}$, $\overline{\text{UDS}}$, and $\overline{\text{LDS}}$ signals are not shown. They have the same function and timing as in the asynchronous bus cycle.

The synchronous bus cycle starts out just like an asynchronous bus cycle with a function code being output on the FC bus during state S_0. It is followed by the address on A_1 through A_{23} during S_1. When the address is stable in S_2, $\overline{\text{AS}}$ is switched to the 0 logic level. At this time R/$\overline{\text{W}}$ is set to 0 if a write cycle is in progress; otherwise, it stays at the 1 logic level. Moreover, if a write operation is in progress, the data are output on D_0 through D_{15} and it is maintained valid during the rest of the bus cycle.

By the end of S_4, external circuitry must have decoded the address on the bus. At this time it asserts $\overline{\text{VPA}}$ by switching it to the 0 logic level. In response to this, the 68000 begins to assert wait states to extend the bus cycle. At the end of the next clock state, the $\overline{\text{VMA}}$ output is switched to the 0 level. This signals external circuitry that an address is on the bus. The peripheral transfers the data after E is active. For a read cycle, the MPU reads the data when E goes low. The data transfer cycle is terminated by the processor by negating control signals $\overline{\text{VMA}}$, $\overline{\text{AS}}$, $\overline{\text{UDS}}$, and $\overline{\text{LDS}}$.

Interfacing the 6821 PIA to the Synchronous Interface Bus

The circuit diagram of Fig. 11.17 illustrates how 6821 PIAs are interfaced to the 68000's asynchronous bus. This circuit can be easily modified so that the LSI peripherals work off a synchronous bus cycle instead of an asynchronous bus cycle. Figure 11.21 shows a simple circuit that makes this modification. First the ICs U_{11A}, U_{12B}, U_{13A}, and U_{13B} are removed from the circuit of Fig. 11.17. This is because $\overline{\text{DTACK}}$ is not required to support the synchronous bus. Moreover, the E output of the 68000 now gets directly connected to the E inputs of both 6821 devices in parallel.

Looking at Fig. 11.21, we see that the chip select (CS) output at pin 6 of U_{11B} gets connected to one input of the 74LS00 NAND gate. The other input of this gate is supplied by the $\overline{VMA}$ output of the 68000 after it is inverted. The output of the NAND gate goes to the $\overline{CS_2}$ input of both 6821 devices in parallel. In this way, we see that the 6821s get chip-selected only when one of their addresses is on the bus

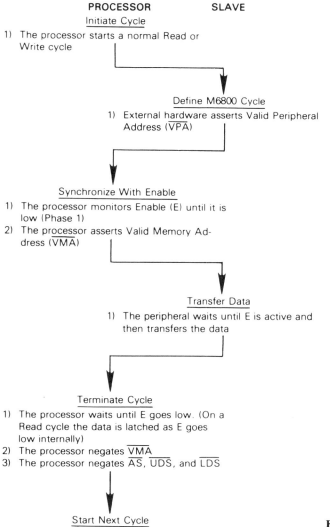

PROCESSOR   **SLAVE**

Initiate Cycle

1) The processor starts a normal Read or Write cycle

Define M6800 Cycle

1) External hardware asserts Valid Peripheral Address ($\overline{VPA}$)

Synchronize With Enable

1) The processor monitors Enable (E) until it is low (Phase 1)
2) The processor asserts Valid Memory Address ($\overline{VMA}$)

Transfer Data

1) The peripheral waits until E is active and then transfers the data

Terminate Cycle

1) The processor waits until E goes low. (On a Read cycle the data is latched as E goes low internally)
2) The processor negates $\overline{VMA}$
3) The processor negates $\overline{AS}$, $\overline{UDS}$, and $\overline{LDS}$

Start Next Cycle

(a)

Figure 11.20 (a) Synchronous bus cycle flowchart (Motorola Inc.); (b) timing diagram (Motorola Inc.).

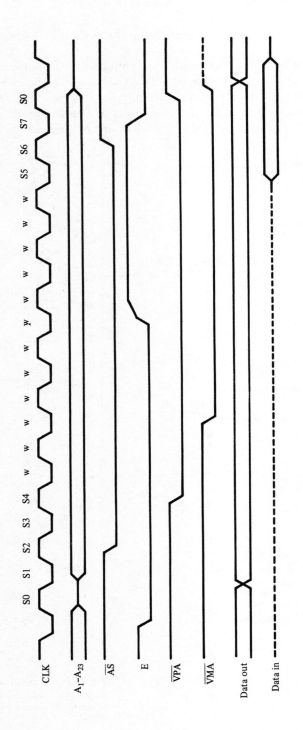

Figure 11.20 *(continued)*

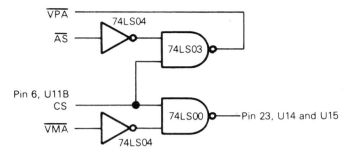

Figure 11.21 Conversion circuit for implementing synchronous bus cycle (Motorola Inc.).

and the 68000 has signaled that a valid address is on the bus during a synchronous bus cycle.

The upper NAND gate in this circuit also has CS as one of its inputs and $\overline{\text{AS}}$ as the other. Therefore, it detects when an address corresponding to one of the LSI peripherals is on the bus. When this condition occurs, it switches $\overline{\text{VPA}}$ to logic 0, thereby signaling to the processor that a synchronous bus cycle should be performed.

ASSIGNMENT

Section 11.2

1. Does the 68000 employ separate memory and I/O address spaces?

Section 11.3

2. Can an instruction access word data that starts at an odd memory address?
3. Write a sequence of instructions to store the long-word contents of D_0 in memory starting at address $A001.

Section 11.4

4. In which address range can interrupt service routine vectors be stored?

Section 11.5

5. What function code would be anticipated on the FC lines when the result of an ADD instruction is being written to the destination location in memory? Assume that the 68000 is in the user state.
6. Why would a user/supervisor system environment be employed?
7. Draw a circuit similar to the one in Fig. 11.9 in which a 16M-byte memory address space is implemented as four 4M-byte blocks: the user program memory, user data memory, supervisor program memory, and supervisor data memory. The supervisor is to have access to all memory areas.

Section 11.6

8. Give an overview of the sequence of events that occur when an instruction word is read from address $A000.

Section 11.7

9. Give an overview of the sequence of events that occur when a byte of data is written to address $A001.

Section 11.8

10. Write a single instruction to push the long-word contents of registers A_0, A_1, and A_2 onto the supervisor stack.

11. Restore the contents of the registers saved in problem 10 by individually popping them from the stack.

Section 11.9

12. Give an overview of the operation of the circuit in Fig. 11.13 for an upper byte access from the group 2 RAMs.

Section 11.10

13. Write an instruction sequence that will output the long-word contents of D_0 to four-byte-wide output ports starting at address $16000. The output ports are located at consecutive even addresses.

14. Write an instruction that will input a word of data from two byte-wide input ports and store it in D_1. Assume that the input ports are located at consecutive odd addresses which are displaced by 10 bytes in the positive direction from an input address pointer held in register A_1.

Section 11.11

15. Referring to the table in Fig. 11.15, give an overview of each of the different modes of I/O operation for which a byte-wide port on the 6821 can be configured.

Section 11.12

16. For the circuit in Fig. 11.17 and the address map in Fig. 11.18(a), write instructions that do the following:
   (a) Configure the B port of both U_{14} and U_{15} as output ports.
   (b) Configure the A port of both U_{14} and U_{15} as input ports.
   (c) Configure the B output ports such that they produce a fixed duration strobe pulse at their CB_2 output and select its data output register.
   (d) Configure the A input ports such that they initiate an interrupt request through their CA_1 inputs; the interrupt is to be initiated by a high-to-low transition at CA_1; and the output register is to be selected.

17. Write a program that moves five bytes of data from a table in memory starting at address $A000 to the B port of U_{14} in the circuit of Fig. 11.17. Assume that the B port is configured as defined in problem 16(c).

Section 11.13

18. What is meant by synchronous bus operation for the 68000?
19. How does the synchronous bus cycle of Fig. 11.20(a) differ from the asynchronous bus cycle in Fig. 11.10(a)?

12

Exception Processing of the 68000 Microprocessor

12.1 INTRODUCTION

This chapter concludes our study of the 68000 microprocessor and its microcomputer system. Here we will consider its exception processing capability and external hardware interrupt interface. The topics covered are as follows:

1. Types of exceptions
2. Exception vector table
3. Exception group priorities
4. External hardware interrupt interface
5. External interrupt priorities and the interrupt mask
6. General interrupt processing sequence
7. General interrupt interface circuit
8. Autovector interrupt mechanism
9. Autovector interrupt interface circuit
10. Exception instructions
11. Bus error
12. Reset
13. Internal exception functions

12.2 TYPES OF EXCEPTIONS

For the 68000 microcomputer system, Motorola, Inc. has defined the concept of *exception processing*. Exception processing is similar to the interrupt processing we studied for the 8086. Just like the interrupt capabilities of the 8086, the exception mechanism allows the 68000 to respond quickly to special internal or external events. Based on the occurrence of this type of event, the main program is terminated and a context switch is initiated to a new program environment. This new program environment, the exception service routine, is a segment of program designed to service the requesting condition. At completion of exception processing, program control can be returned to the point at which the exception occurred in the main program.

The 68000 has a broad variety of methods by which exception processing can be initiated. They include the *external exception functions, hardware reset,* and *user-defined external interrupts*, which are similar to those provided on the 8086. In this group, there is one interrupt that is unique to the 68000. It is the *bus error exception*. Furthermore, the 68000 has a number of instructions that can initiate exception processing. Some examples of these instructions are TRAP, TRAPV, and CHK. The 68000 also has extensive internal exception capability. It includes exceptions for internal error conditions (*address error, illegal/unimplemented opcodes*, and *privilege violation*) and internal functions (*trace* and *spurious interrupt*).

12.3 EXCEPTION VECTOR TABLE

Each of the exception functions that is performed by the 68000 has a number called the *vector number* assigned to it. For external interrupts, the interrupting device supplies the vector number to the 68000. On the other hand, for other types of interrupts, the vector number is generated within the microprocessor. The 68000 converts the vector number to the address of a corresponding long-word storage location in memory. Held at this memory location is a 24-bit address known as the *vector address* of the exception. It defines the starting point of the service routine in program storage memory. Figure 12.1 shows the format in which the address vector is stored in memory. As shown, it takes up two word locations. The lower addressed word is the high word of the new program counter and the higher addressed word is the low word of PC. Only the 8 LSBs of the high word are used.

The vector addresses are stored in a part of the 68000's memory system known

Figure 12.1 Exception vector organization (Motorola Inc.).

as the *exception vector table*. As shown in Fig. 12.2, the vector table contains up to 256 vectors, which are labeled with vector numbers 0 through 255. Notice that the table must reside in the address range 000000_{16} through $0003FE_{16}$, which is the first 1024 bytes of the 68000's 16M-byte address space. All vectors other than vector 0 must reside in supervisor data memory. Vector 0, which is assigned to the hardware reset function, must be stored in supervisor program memory.

The hexadecimal address at which each vector is located in memory is also provided in the table of Fig. 12.2. The address of the most significant word of any vec-

Vector	Address			Assignment
Number(s)	Dec	Hex	Space	
0	0	000	SP	Reset: Initial SSP
—	4	004	SP	Reset: Initial PC
2	8	008	SD	Bus Error
3	12	00C	SD	Address Error
4	16	010	SD	Illegal Instruction
5	20	014	SD	Zero Divide
6	24	018	SD	CHK Instruction
7	28	01C	SD	TRAPV Instruction
8	32	020	SD	Privilege Violation
9	36	024	SD	Trace
10	40	028	SD	Line 1010 Emulator
11	44	02C	SD	Line 1111 Emulator
12*	48	030	SD	(Unassigned, reserved)
13*	52	034	SD	(Unassigned, reserved)
14*	56	038	SD	(Unassigned, reserved)
15	60	03C	SD	Uninitialized Interrupt Vector
16-23*	64	04C	SD	(Unassigned, reserved)
	95	05F		—
24	96	060	SD	Spurious Interrupt
25	100	064	SD	Level 1 Interrupt Autovector
26	104	068	SD	Level 2 Interrupt Autovector
27	108	06C	SD	Level 3 Interrupt Autovector
28	112	070	SD	Level 4 Interrupt Autovector
29	116	074	SD	Level 5 Interrupt Autovector
30	120	078	SD	Level 6 Interrupt Autovector
31	124	07C	SD	Level 7 Interrupt Autovector
32-47	128	080	SD	TRAP Instruction Vectors
	191	0BF		—
48-63*	192	0C0	SD	(Unassigned, reserved)
	255	0FF		—
64-255	256	100	SD	User Interrupt Vectors
	1023	3FF		—

Figure 12.2 Vector table (Motorola Inc.).

tor can be determined by multiplying its vector number by 4. For instance, vector 8 is stored starting at address $4_{10} \times 8_{10} = 32_{10} = 000020_{16}$.

All of the low-numbered vectors serve special functions of the 68000 microcomputer system. Examples are the *bus error exception vector* at address 000008_{16}, *address error exception vector* at $00000C_{16}$, *CHK instruction vector* at 000018_{16}, and *spurious interrupt vector* at 000060_{16}. Within this group we also find a small number of reserved vector locations.

The next group, vectors 25 through 31 at addresses 000064_{16} through $00007C_{16}$, is dedicated to what are known as the *autovector interrupts*. They are followed by the *trap instruction vectors* in the address range 000080_{16} through $0000BF_{16}$ and some more reserved vector locations. The last 192 vectors, which are said to be user definable, are used for the external hardware interrupts.

Since the addresses that are held in this table are defined by the programmer, the corresponding exception service routines can reside anywhere in the 68000's 16M-byte address space.

Example 12.1

At what address is the vector for TRAP #5 stored in memory? If the service routine for this exception is to start at address 010200_{16}, what will be the stored vector?

Solution.   The TRAP #5 instruction corresponds to vector number 37. Therefore, its address is calculated as

$$4_{10} \times 37_{10} = 148_{10} = 000094_{16}$$

The vector address 010200_{16} is broken into two words for storage in memory. These words are

$$\text{Most significant word} = 0001_{16}$$

$$\text{Least significant word} = 0200_{16}$$

They get stored as

$$0001_{16} \quad \text{at address } 000094_{16}$$

$$0200_{16} \quad \text{at address } 000096_{16}$$

12.4 EXCEPTION PRIORITIES

Just like the other 16-bit microprocessor we studied, exception processing of the 68000 is handled on a *priority* basis. Remember that *priority level* of an exception or interrupt function determines whether or not its operation can be interrupted by another exception. In general, the 68000 will acknowledge a request for service by an exception only if there is no other exception already in progress or if the requesting function is at a higher-priority level then the active exception.

Figure 12.3 shows that the exception functions are divided into three basic priority groups and then assigned additional priority levels within these groups. Here *group 0* represents the highest-priority group. It includes the exception functions of external events such as reset and bus error, as well as the internal address error detection condi-

Group	Exception	Processing
0	Reset Bus Error Address Error	Exception processing begins within two clock cycles.
1	Trace Interrupt Illegal Privilege	Exception processing begins before the next instruction
2	TRAP, TRAPV, CHK, Zero Divide	Exception processing is started by normal instruction execution

Figure 12.3 Exception priority groups (Motorola Inc.).

tion. Within group 0, reset has the highest priority. It is followed by bus error and address error in that order.

Exception functions from group 0 always override an active exception from *group 1* or *group 2*. Moreover, a group 0 function does not wait for completion of execution of the current instruction; instead, it is initiated at the completion of the current bus cycle.

The next-to-highest priority group, group 1, includes the external hardware interrupts and internal functions: trace, illegal/unimplemented opcode, and privilege violation. In this group, trace has the highest priority and it is followed in order of descending priority by external interrupts, illegal/unimplemented instruction, and privilege violation.

In all four cases in group 1, exception processing is initiated with the completion of the current instruction. If a group 1 exception is in progress, its service routine can be interrupted only by a group 0 exception or another exception from group 1 with higher priority. For instance, if an interrupt service routine is in progress when an illegal instruction is detected, the interrupt service routine will run to completion before service is initiated for the illegal opcode.

Group 2 is the lowest-priority group and its exceptions will be interrupted by any group 0 or group 1 exception request. This group includes the software exception functions, TRAP, TRAPV, CHK, and divide by zero. These exceptions differ from those in the other groups in that they are initiated through execution of an instruction. Therefore, there are no individual priority levels within group 2.

Let us assume that a TRAP exception is in progress when an external device requests service using an interrupt input. In this case the hardware interrupt is of higher priority. Therefore, the trap routine is suspended and execution resumes with the first instruction of the interrupt service routine.

12.5 EXTERNAL HARDWARE INTERRUPTS

The first type of 68000 exception that we shall consider in detail is the *external hardware interrupts*. The external hardware interrupt interface can be considered to be a special-purpose input interface. It allows the 68000 to respond quickly and efficiently to events that occur in its external hardware. Through it, external devices can signal the 68000 whenever they need to be serviced. For this reason, the processor does not have to dedicate any of its processing time for checking to determine which of the external devices needs service. For example, the occurrence of a power failure is typically detected by an external power failure detection circuit and signaled to the microprocessor as an interrupt.

The General Interrupt Interface

Figure 12.4 shows the *general interrupt interface* of the 68000. Here we have shown the signals that are involved in the interface and see that some circuitry is required to interface external devices to the interrupt request inputs of the 68000. Notice that as many as 192 unique devices could apply interrupt requests to the 68000. However, few applications require this many.

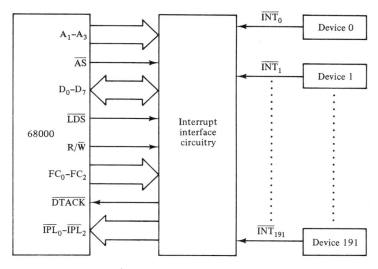

Figure 12.4   General interrupt interface.

Let us now look just briefly at the function of each of the signals involved in the interrupt interface. First we find that three address lines, A_1 through A_3, are in use. They carry an interrupt priority number that is output during the interrupt acknowledge bus cycle. The logic level of $\overline{AS}$ signals external circuitry when this code is available at $A_3A_2A_1$. Accompanying this priority-level number is the *interrupt acknowledge* (IACK) *function code* at outputs FC_2 through FC_0.

During the interrupt acknowledge bus cycle, external circuitry must return an 8-bit vector number to the 68000. Data bus lines D_0 through D_7 are used to input this vector number. The external device signals that the code is available on the bus with the data transfer acknowledge ($\overline{DTACK}$) signal. $R/\overline{W}$ and $\overline{LDS}$ control the direction and timing of data transfer over the bus.

External devices must issue a request for service to the 68000. The external *inter-*

rupt request inputs of the 68000 are labeled $\overline{IPL}_2$, $\overline{IPL}_1$, and $\overline{IPL}_0$. 000_2 at these inputs represents no interrupt request. On the other hand, a nonzero input represents an active interrupt request.

External Hardware Interrupt Priorities

The external hardware interrupts of the 68000 have another priority scheme within their group 1 priority assignment. The number of priority levels that can be assigned is determined by the number of interrupt inputs. As shown in Fig. 12.5, for three interrupt inputs we get seven independent priority levels. They are identified as 1 through 7 and correspond to interrupt codes $\overline{IPL}_2\overline{IPL}_1\overline{IPL}_0$ equal 001_2 through 111_2, respectively. Here 7 represents the highest priority level and 1 the lowest priority level.

    The external interrupt circuitry can be designed to allow a large number of devices to respond at each of these interrupt levels. It is for this reason that we have identified 192 external devices in Fig. 12.4. Any number of these 192 devices can be assigned to any one of the interrupt levels. Moreover, additional external priority logic circuitry can be added to prioritize the interrupts into 192 unique priority levels.

Priority Level	Interrupt Code		
	$\overline{IPL}_2$	$\overline{IPL}_1$	$\overline{IPL}_0$
None	0	0	0
1	0	0	1
2	0	1	0
3	0	1	1
4	1	0	0
5	1	0	1
6	1	1	0
7	1	1	1

Figure 12.5   External interrupt priorities.

Interrupt Mask

Bits 8 through 10 in the system byte of the status register are used as a mask for the external hardware interrupts. Figure 12.6 shows that these bits are labeled I_0 through I_2, respectively. Only active interrupts with a priority level higher than the current value of the mask are enabled for operation. Those of equal or lower priority level are masked out.

    When the 68000 is reset at power-up, the mask is automatically set to 111_2. This disables interrupts from occurring. For the interrupt interface to be enabled, the mask must be modified to a lower priority level through software. For instance, it could be set to 000_2. This would enable all interrupts for operation.

    Whenever a higher-priority interrupt occurs, the mask is automatically changed so that equal- or lower-priority interrupts are masked out. For instance, with initiation of a level 5 interrupt it is changed to 101_2. This masks out from level 5 down through 1.

    The level 7 interrupt request code is not actually masked out with the interrupt

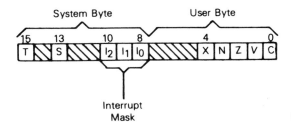

Interrupt
Mask

Figure 12.6 Interrupt mask bits in the status register (Motorola Inc.).

mask. Even if the mask is set to 111_2, it remains enabled. For this reason, it can be used to implement a nonmaskable interrupt for the 68000 microcomputer system.

12.6 GENERAL INTERRUPT PROCESSING SEQUENCE

Whenever the code at interrupt inputs $\overline{IPL}_2\overline{IPL}_1\overline{IPL}_0$ is nonzero, an external device is requesting service. It is said that an interrupt is *pending*. At the completion of the current instruction, the 68000 compares this code to the contents of the interrupt mask, $I_2I_1I_0$ in bits 10 through 8 of the status register. If the priority level of the active request is higher than that in the mask, the request for service is accepted. Otherwise, execution continues with the next instruction in the currently active exception processing service routine.

Upon accepting the exception service request, the 68000 initiates a sequence by which it passes control to the service routine located at the address specified by the interrupt's vector number. First, the contents of the status register are temporarily saved. Next, the S-bit, bit 13, of the status register is set to 1 and the T-bit, bit 15, is cleared to 0. They enable the supervisor mode of operation and disable the trace function, respectively. Then interrupt mask $I_2I_1I_0$ is set to the priority level of the interrupt request just granted.

Now the 68000 initiates an *interrupt acknowledge (IACK) bus cycle*. The sequence of events that occur during this bus cycle are summarized in Fig. 12.7(a) and are shown by waveforms in Fig. 12.7(b). Here we see that it first signals external devices that service has been granted. It does this by putting the interrupt code of the device to which service was granted on address bus lines A_1 through A_3 and makes control signals $R/\overline{W} = 1$, $\overline{As} = 0$, and $\overline{LDS} = 0$. When $R/\overline{W} = \overline{LDS} = 0$, a byte of data will be transferred over data bus lines D_0 through D_7. At the same time, it outputs the interrupt acknowledge function code. This code is $FC_2FC_1FC_0$ equal to 111. In this way it tells the external circuitry which priority-level interrupt is being processed.

In response to the interrupt acknowledge function code, the external device that corresponds to the interrupt code on A_1 through A_3 must put an 8-bit vector number on data bus lines D_0 through D_7. Then it must switch $\overline{DTACK}$ to logic 0 to signal the 68000 that the vector number is available on the bus. The 68000 reads the vector number off the bus and then returns both $\overline{LDS}$ and $\overline{AS}$ to logic 1.

It is this 8-bit code that tells the 68000 which of the devices associated with

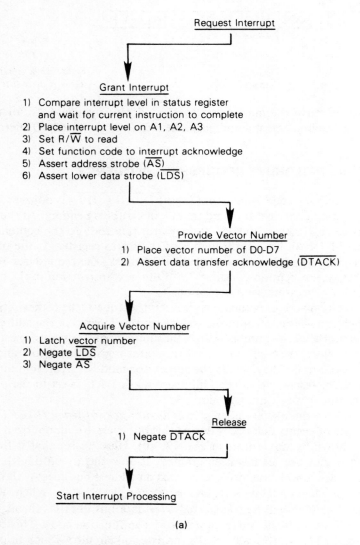

PROCESSOR   INTERRUPTING DEVICE

Request Interrupt

Grant Interrupt
1) Compare interrupt level in status register
   and wait for current instruction to complete
2) Place interrupt level on A1, A2, A3
3) Set R/$\overline{W}$ to read
4) Set function code to interrupt acknowledge
5) Assert address strobe ($\overline{AS}$)
6) Assert lower data strobe ($\overline{LDS}$)

Provide Vector Number
1) Place vector number of D0-D7
2) Assert data transfer acknowledge ($\overline{DTACK}$)

Acquire Vector Number
1) Latch vector number
2) Negate $\overline{LDS}$
3) Negate $\overline{AS}$

Release
1) Negate $\overline{DTACK}$

Start Interrupt Processing

(a)

Figure 12.7   (a) IACK bus cycle flowchart (Motorola Inc.); (b) IACK bus cycle waveforms (Motorola Inc.).

the active interrupt level is requesting service. Notice in Fig. 12.2 that not all of the
256 vectors in the table are to be used with the user-defined external hardware interrupts. Only the 192 vectors from vector 64 through 255 should be used for this purpose.

Finally, the interrupt acknowledge bus cycle is completed when the external device returns $\overline{DTACK}$ to the 1 logic level.

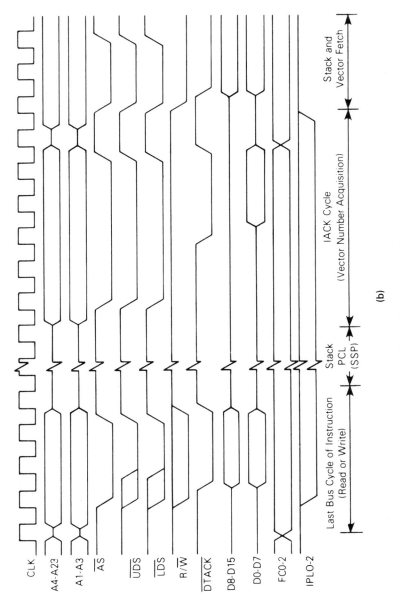

Figure 12.7 *(continued)*

Next, the 68000 pushes the current contents of its program counter onto the top of the supervisor stack. Since PC is 24 bits long, it requires two words of stack and takes two write bus cycles. Then the contents of the old status register, which were saved earlier, are also pushed to the supervisor stack. It takes just one word of memory and is accomplished with one write cycle.

Now the address of the interrupt's vector, which the 68000 calculates from the interrupt vector number, is put on the address bus. The value at this address in the vector table is read over the data bus and loaded into PC. It takes two read bus cycles to fetch the complete vector. During the first bus cycle, the most significant word is carried over the bus and during the second bus cycle, the least significant word. The 68000 now has the new address at which it begins executing the routine that services the interrupt.

Figure 12.8 shows how the 68000 internally generates a *vector address* from an 8-bit *vector number*. As shown in Fig. 12.8(a), the vector number was read off of the lower eight data bus lines, D_0 through D_7. First, the 68000 multiplies the vector number by 4. This is done by performing a shift left by two bit positions. Then it fills the upper 14 bits with 0s to form a 24-bit address. This gives the address shown in Fig. 12.8(b), which points to the vector in the table.

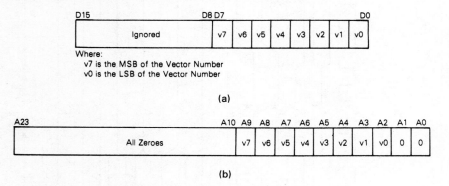

(a)

(b)

Figure 12.8   (a) Vector for address generator (Motorola Inc.); (b) generated address (Motorola Inc.).

12.7 GENERAL INTERRUPT INTERFACE OF THE 68000

The block diagram of Fig. 12.9 illustrates the type of circuitry needed to support a general interrupt interface for the 68000 microcomputer system. This circuit has 192 interrupt request inputs, which are labeled IRQ_0 through IRQ_{191}. These inputs are synchronized by latching them into an *interrupt latch circuit*.

The 192 outputs of the interrupt latch circuit are applied to inputs of the *interrupt absolute priority encoder circuit*. Here they are prioritized and encoded to produce an 8-bit output code which identifies the highest-priority active interrupt request. These codes are in the range IRQ_0 equal $00000000_2 = 0_{10}$ to IRQ_{191} equal $10111111_{16} = 191_{10}$.

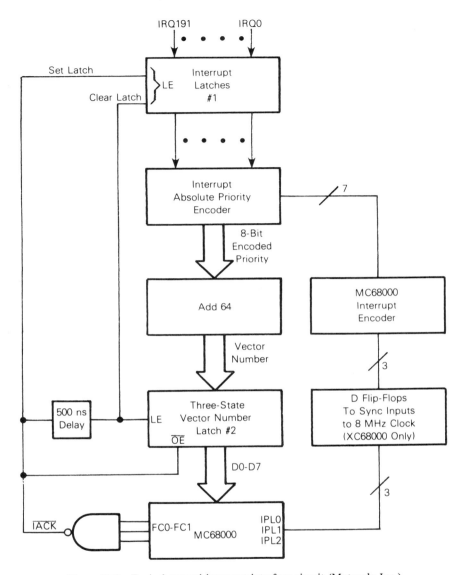

Figure 12.9 Typical general interrupt interface circuit (Motorola Inc.).

Remember that in the vector table of Fig. 12.2, the vectors assigned to the user-defined external interrupts are in the range 64 through 255, not 0 to 191. For this reason, the priority codes that are produced by the *encoder circuit* must be displaced by 64 before they are applied to the data bus of the 68000 during the IACK bus cycle. The circuit labeled *add 64* is provided for this purpose. It simply adds 64 to the 8-bit code at its input.

The output of the add 64 circuit, which is the correct vector number, is latched into the *three-state output vector number latch circuit*. Notice that the outputs of this latch are enabled by $\overline{\text{IACK}}$. In this way, the vector number is put on data bus lines D_0 through D_7 only during the interrupt acknowledge bus cycle. At all other times, the outputs of the latch are in the high-Z state.

Up to this point, we have just described the part of the interrupt interface circuit that is used to generate the vector number. But at the same time, another circuit path, which includes the *interrupt encoder* and *synchronization flip-flops*, must produce an interrupt request to the 68000.

Notice that the *interrupt absolute priority encoder circuit* outputs a 7-bit code in addition to the 8-bit priority code. The 7-bit code is input to the interrupt encoder circuit. In this code, just one bit is set to 0 and it identifies the priority level of the interrupt request. In response, the encoder produces a 3-bit request code for this priority level at its output. This code is latched onto the $\overline{\text{IPL}}_2$ through $\overline{\text{IPL}}_0$ inputs of the 68000, where it represents an interrupt request.

12.8 AUTOVECTOR INTERRUPT MECHANISM

In 68000 microcomputer systems that do not require more than seven interrupt inputs, a modified interrupt interface configuration can be used. This interface decreases the amount of external support circuits and at the same time shortens the response time from interrupt request to initiation of the service routine. This simplified interrupt mechanism uses what is known as the *autovector mode* of operation.

The *autovector interrupt interface* is shown in Fig. 12.10. It simplifies the interface requirements between external devices and the 68000. In this case, external hard-

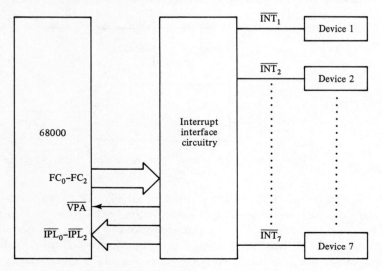

Figure 12.10   Autovector interrupt interface.

ware need just recognize the IACK function code at $FC_2FC_1FC_0$ and respond by switching $\overline{VPA}$ to logic 0. This signals the 68000 to follow its *autovector interrupt sequence*.

When using autovector exception processing, the source of the interrupt vector is determined in a different way. Instead of external circuitry supplying an 8-bit vector number on D_7 through D_0, the 68000 generates the vector address internally from the interrupt request code $\overline{IPL_2}\,\overline{IPL_1}\,\overline{IPL_0}$ and the address of the service routine is fetched from the autovector section of the vector table in Fig. 12.2. In this way, we see that the interrupt acknowledge sequence is shortened. This is the reason that the response time between interrupt request and entry of the service routine is decreased.

As an example, assume that autovector interrupt request code 101_2 is applied to $\overline{IPL_2}$ through $\overline{IPL_0}$. Looking at the table in Fig. 12.2, we see that vector 29 is fetched from addresses 000074_{16} and 000076_{16} and loaded into the PC of the 68000.

12.9 AUTOVECTOR INTERFACE SUPPORT CIRCUIT

Now that we have introduced the autovector interrupt mechanism of the 68000, let us look at a simple circuit that can be used to implement the external hardware interface.

The circuit of Fig. 12.11 can be used to implement the autovector interface in a 68000 microcomputer system. Here we find the seven interrupt request inputs identified as level 1 through level 7. The logic levels at these inputs are latched into the 74LS273 octal latch synchronously with the CLK signal from the 68000. This latch is provided to synchronize the application of interrupt inputs to the priority encoder.

Interrupt requests must be prioritized and encoded into a 3-bit interrupt request code for input to the 68000. This is done by the 74LS348 8-line to 3-line priority encoder. Notice that the inputs of this device are active low, with input 7 corresponding to the highest-priority input and 0 to the lowest-priority input. The binary code corresponding to the highest-priority active input is always output at $A_2A_1A_0$. This interrupt code is latched in a 74LS175 latch and its outputs applied to the $\overline{IPL_2}$ through $\overline{IPL_0}$ inputs of the 68000.

In addition to this interrupt request code interface circuit, another circuit is required to support the autovector interrupt interface. This circuit is required to detect the IACK code when it is output by the 68000 and in response assert the $\overline{VPA}$ signal. Typically, this is done by the function decoder circuit of the 68000 microcomputer system. Alternatively, a single three-input NAND gate can be used.

12.10 EXCEPTION INSTRUCTIONS

The instruction set of the 68000 includes a number of instructions that use the exception processing mechanism. They differ from the hardware-initiated exceptions that we have covered up to this point in that they are initiated as the result of the 68000

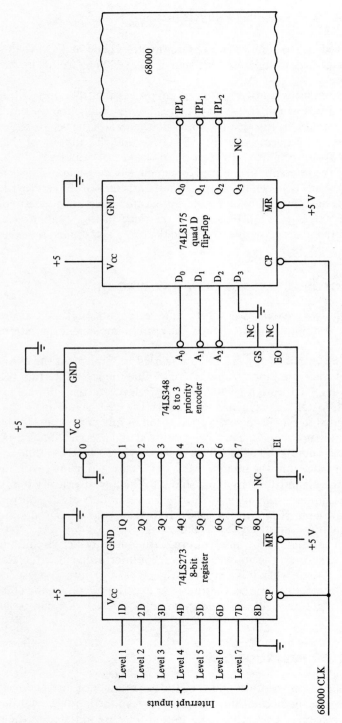

Figure 12.11 Typical autovector interrupt interface circuit (Motorola Inc.)

executing an instruction. Some of these instructions make a conditional test to determine whether or not to initiate exception processing.

There are five such instructions. They are *trap* (TRAP), *trap on overflow* (TRAPV), *check register against bounds* (CHK), *signed divide* (DIVS), and *unsigned divide* (DIVU). The operation of these instructions is summarized in Fig. 12.12. Let us now look at the exception processing of each of these instructions in more detail.

Instruction	Condition	Operation
TRAP #n	None	Trap sequence using trap vector n
TRAPV	V = 1	Trap sequence using TRAPV vector
CHK EA,Dn	Dn < 0 or Dn > (EA)	Trap sequence using CHK vector
DIVS EA,Dn DIVU EA,Dn	(EA) = 0	Trap sequence using zero divide vector
RTE		Return from exception routine to the program in which exception occurred

Figure 12.12 Exception instructions.

Trap Instruction—TRAP

The TRAP instruction can be considered to be the software interrupt instruction of the 68000. It permits the programmer to perform a vectored call of an exception service routine. We can call this routine the trap service routine and it is typically used to perform vectored subroutine calls such as *supervisory calls*.

The trap instruction is simply written as

$$\text{TRAP} \quad \#n$$

Here n represents the *trap vector number* that is to be used to locate the starting point of the exception processing routine in program memory. Looking at the vector table in Fig. 12.2, we see that the 24-bit starting addresses for the trap instructions are located at addresses in the range 000080_{16} through $0000BE_{16}$. This gives a total of 32 words of memory allocated to storage of trap vectors. Since each vector requires two words of memory, there is room for 16 vectors, which correspond to instructions TRAP #0 through TRAP #15.

For instance, the most significant word of the vector for TRAP #0 is held at 000080_{16} and its least significant word at 000082_{16}. Execution of the TRAP #0 instruction causes the 24-bit value stored at these locations to be loaded into the PC of the 68000. Therefore, program execution resumes with the first instruction of the TRAP #0 service routine.

Let us look more closely at the series of events that takes place to pass control to the exception service routine of a trap instruction. After the 68000 executes the trap instruction, it first saves the current contents of its status register in a temporary holding register. Then the S-bit of SR is set. This enables the supervisor system environment. Next, bit T of SR is cleared to disable the trace mode of operation.

Now the 68000 preserves the current program environment such that it can be reentered at completion of exception processing. It does this by pushing the current contents of PC onto the supervisor stack. This value of PC points to the instruction following the TRAP instruction that just initiated exception processing. Then the status word is pushed onto the supervisor stack.

We are now ready to enter the exception service routine. The address of the trap vector is automatically calculated by the 68000 from the trap number. The trap vector is read from this location and loaded into PC. Execution picks up with the first instruction of the service routine.

Notice that just the old PC and SR are automatically saved on the supervisor stack by the exception-processing mechanism. Frequently, the exception service routine will require use of the 68000's data or address registers. For this reason, their contents may also be saved on the stack. The 68000 does not have PUSH or POP instructions for this purpose. Instead, its MOVE instruction is used to perform these types of operations. For example, the instruction

$$\text{MOVE.L} \quad \text{D0}, -(\text{SP})$$

will effectively push the 32-bit contents of D_0 onto the top of the supervisor stack. Typically, this is done with the first few instructions of the service routine.

Just as for interrupts, the return mechanism of the TRAP instruction is the return from exception (RTE) instruction. Execution of this instruction at the end of the service routine causes the saved values of PC and SR to be popped from the supervisor stack. Prior to executing the RTE instruction, the contents of any additional registers saved on the stack must also be popped back into the 68000. Again, this can be done with the MOVE instruction. For example,

$$\text{MOVE.L} \quad (\text{SP}) + , \text{D0}$$

causes the 32-bit value at the top of the stack to effectively be popped into register D_0.

TRAPV, CHK, and DIVU/DIVS Instructions

The rest of the exception instructions initiate a trap to an exception service routine only upon detection of an abnormal processing condition. For instance, the trap on overflow (TRAPV) instruction checks overflow bit V, bit 1 of the status register, to determine whether or not an overflow has resulted from execution of the previous instruction. If V is found to be set, an overflow has occurred and exception processing is initiated with an overflow service routine. In this case control is passed to the overflow service routine pointed to by the TRAPV vector at addresses $00001C_{16}$ and $00001E_{16}$ of the vector table. On the other hand, if V is not set, execution continues with the next sequential instruction in the program.

The check register against boundaries (CHK) instruction, as its name implies, can determine if the contents of a data register lie within a set of minimum/maximum values. The minimum value (boundary) is always 0000_{16}. On the other hand, the maximum value (boundary), $MMMM_{16}$, is specified as a source operand and can reside in an internal register or a location in external memory.

An example is the instruction

$$\text{CHK   \#\$5A,D0}$$

Here register D_0 contains the parameter under test and \$5A is the maximum boundary. If during execution of the instruction, the contents of D_0 are found to be within the range 0000_{16} to the value \$5A, the parameter is within bounds and exception processing is not initiated. On the other hand, if it is negative or greater than \$5A, it is out of bounds and exception processing is initiated. The change in program environment is to the address defined by vector 6 at 000018_{16} and $00001A_{16}$ in the vector table.

The last two exception instructions, DIVU and DIVS, cause a trap to a service routine if the division they perform involves a divisor equal to zero. This divide-by-zero exception is initiated through the vector at addresses 000014_{16} and 000016_{16}.

12.11 BUS ERROR

It is possible with the asynchronous bus of the 68000 to get into a situation where a bus cycle is not completed. This would be due to the fact that the data acknowledge ($\overline{\text{DTACK}}$) signal is not received by the 68000. If this happens, execution of the current instruction would not be completed; instead, the MPU would be hung up at the instruction. This represents what is known as a *bus error* condition.

To resolve this problem, bus error exception capability is provided on the 68000. This exception provides a means to assure that bus cycles initiated by the 68000 are carried through to completion. The bus error condition is not detected automatically by the 68000 itself; instead, it must be detected with external circuitry and signaled to the 68000. External logic would do this by switching the $\overline{\text{BERR}}$ (bus error) input of the 68000 to logic 0. In fact, $\overline{\text{BERR}}$ and $\overline{\text{HALT}}$ can be used together to automatically rerun bus cycles that result in a bus error.

Remember that earlier we indicated that the only higher-priority exception than the bus error function is reset. Therefore, the bus error exception takes precedence and occurs as long as the reset exception is not already in progress. Moreover, we found that it did not wait for the completion of the current instruction before it is initiated. This is also important because when a bus error occurs, execution of the instruction that is in progress would not be completed.

When $\overline{\text{BERR}}$ is switched to the 0 level, the MPU aborts the current bus cycle and initiates exception processing. A change in program environment is initiated to a service routine for the bus error condition. The location of this service routine is defined by vector 2 in the table of Fig. 12.2. Execution of the service routine can attempt to correct the bus error by rerunning the bus cycle or signal its occurrence by displaying or printing the address at which the error occurred and the type of bus cycle that was in progress.

An example of a type of circuit that can be used to determine whether or not bus cycles are completed is a *watchdog timer*. This timer can be started as each bus cycle is initiated and then observe the 68000's bus control signals to assure that the cycle is completed before a maximum period of time has elapsed. If the timer times out before the bus cycle is finished, the circuit sets $\overline{BERR}$ to logic 0 signaling the 68000 of the bus error condition.

The sequence of events by which the 68000 passes control to the bus error exception service routine is almost the same as that described earlier for the TRAP instruction. For this reason, we will just look at how they differ.

The only difference between the two exception-processing control transfer sequences is that several additional parameters are pushed to the supervisor stack in the case of a bus error. Figure 12.13 shows this information and the order in which they are put onto the stack. Notice that, again, SR and PC are pushed to the stack. But this time they are followed by the first word of the instruction that was in progress when the bus error occurred, the address used in the bus cycle that resulted in the bus error, and a special *access-type error word*.

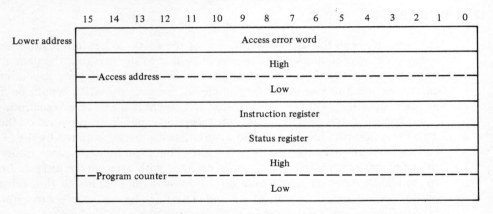

Figure 12.13   Information pushed to the stack during a bus error exception (Motorola Inc.).

In Fig. 12.14 we have shown the implemented bits of the error word and their meanings. Just 5 bits are in use. Bit 4 identifies whether the bus cycle that was aborted due to the bus error condition was a read or a write cycle. It is reset if the bus cycle was for a write operation and is set if it was for a read operation.

The next bit, bit 3, indicates whether the bus cycle was related to normal instruction execution or exception processing. Logic 0 represents instruction execution and logic 1 means exception processing. The 68000 considers the occurrence of a bus error for any group 2 exception, that is, during the execution of an exception instruction, to be a normal instruction execution bus error. For this reason, bit 3 is set to logic 0 for this type of occurrence.

The last 3 bits are used to store the code, $FC_2FC_1FC_0$, that was output on the function code bus during the bus error cycle. This code tells what type of memory

Figure 12.14   Access error word (Motorola Inc.).

reference was in process when the bus error took place, that is, whether user or supervisor memory was being accessed or if it was an interrupt acknowledge reference.

The bus error service routine can access this bus error information in the stack. In this way, it can identify the type of error made and initiate an appropriate response in an attempt to recover from the condition or simply signal that the error condition has occurred.

Example 12.2

If the access-type error word pushed to the stack as the result of a bus error condition is 0005_{16}, what type of bus cycle was in progress when the error occurred?

Solution.   To identify how the bus error bits are set, let us first express the error word in binary form. This gives

$$0005_{16} = 0000000000000101_2$$

Looking at bit 4, we see that it is set to 0. This stands for a write cycle. Bit 3 is also 0 and means that a normal instruction was being executed when the error took place. Finally, the function code that was output for the bus cycle was 101_2 or 5_{10}. This represents an access of supervisor data memory. Thus the bus error occurred when the 68000 was writing to supervisor data memory.

12.12 RESET EXCEPTION

Typically, a microcomputer system must be reset either at power-up or to recover from a system failure condition. An example of a system failure that may require a reset to be performed is the bus error condition we discussed in the preceding section. A reset will cause the microcomputer to be initialized.

The $\overline{\text{RESET}}$ line is provided on the 68000 for initiating initialization. Actually, $\overline{\text{RESET}}$ is a bidirectional line that provides for 68000 initialization when a reset signal is applied to it by the external hardware, and system initialization when the 68000 applies a reset signal to external hardware. Let us look first at its operation for 68000 initialization.

A reset exception at power-up is initiated by switching the $\overline{\text{RESET}}$ input of the 68000 to the 0 logic level. It must be maintained at this level for a minimum of 100 ms. Earlier we indicated that reset is the highest-priority exception function. Therefore, its exception processing sequence is always initiated and cannot be interrupted by any of the other exception functions.

The reset exception processing sequence begins just like other exception processing sequences, with the S-bit of the status register being set and the T-bit being cleared. This puts the 68000 in the supervisor mode and disables its trace function. But this is where the similarity ends. Next, the interrupt mask bits of the status register, bits

8 through 10, are all set to 1. This makes the interrupt mask equal 7, which is the highest-priority level, and masks out all external interrupts other than level 7 (non-maskable interrupt), preventing them from being serviced.

It is at this point in the control transfer sequence of an exception that the contents of the status register and program counter should be pushed to the stack. However, when the MPU is being reinitialized, control would never be returned to the program environment that existed prior to the reset. Therefore, the reset sequence does not save these values on the stack. Instead, it initiates automatic loading of the internal supervisor stack pointer (SSP) register and program counter from supervisor program memory and supervisor data memory, respectively.

First, the SSP register is loaded with vector 0 at addresses 000000_{16} and 000002_{16}. This defines a supervisor stack in supervisor data memory. Next, PC is loaded with vector 1 at addresses 000004_{16} and 000006_{16} and then execution begins with the first instruction of the reset exception service routine.

The reset exception service routine is normally a power-up routine for the microcomputer system. It is used to initialize all of the system's resources. For instance, it could clear the MPU's internal data and address registers, load its user stack pointer (USP) register, and modify the contents of the system byte of the status register to enable interrupts.

The output function of $\overline{RESET}$ is initiated through software by the RESET instruction. When a RESET instruction is executed by the 68000, its internal registers are not affected; instead, the $\overline{RESET}$ line is set to act as an output and a pulse is generated. The pulse produced at $\overline{RESET}$ is to the 0 logic level and has a duration of 124 clock periods. This pulse can be applied to the reset, clear, or preset inputs of external devices, such as LSI peripherals or flip-flops, to initialize their operation.

The reset instruction can be included as part of the power-up service routine. In this way, external devices can be initialized and then their internal registers loaded to configure their mode of operation.

12.13 INTERNAL EXCEPTION FUNCTIONS

Just like the 8086 microprocessor, the 68000 has a number of internally initiated exception functions. In fact, it has four such functions: address error, privilege violation, trace, and illegal/unimplemented opcode detection. We will look next at each of these internal exception functions in detail.

Address Error Exception

In Chapter 11 we discussed how data are organized in the memory of a 68000 microcomputer system. At that time, we pointed out that instructions, words of data, and long words of data all must always reside at even-address boundaries. However, software can be written that incorrectly attempts to access one of these types of information from an odd-address boundary. It is to detect and correct for this error condition that the address error feature is provided on the 68000.

Address error detection does not have to be done with external circuitry, as we saw earlier for bus error detection. Instead, this capability is built within the 68000 as an internal exception function. Whenever an attempt is made to read or write word-wide data from an odd-address boundary, the 68000 automatically recognizes the memory access as an address error condition. Upon detection, the exception processing sequence is initiated and control is passed to the address error exception service routine. This routine can attempt to correct the error condition, or if correction is not possible, its occurrence can be signaled in some way. For instance, the address and type of access could be displayed on a panel of LEDs.

The control transfer sequence that takes place for address error exceptions is identical to that performed for the bus error condition. As mentioned in Section 12.11, the information pushed to the stack includes the contents of SR and PC, the first word of the current instruction, the address that was in error, and an access-type error word. The format of the access-type error word saved on the stack during an address error exception is identical to that shown for the bus error in Fig. 12.14. One difference is that vector 3 instead of vector 2 is used to locate the service routine. As shown in Fig. 12.2, this vector resides at addresses $00000C_{16}$ and $00000E_{16}$ of the vector table.

Privilege Violation Exception

In earlier chapters we found that the 68000 has the ability to easily implement a *user/supervisor microcomputer system environment* and that the state of operation can be selected under software control. The importance of this capability lies in that it permits certain system resources to be accessible only by the supervisor. In this way it provides a level of security in the system design.

Another internal exception feature of the 68000 that we have not yet considered gives it the ability to identify when a user attempts to use a supervisor resource. These illegal accesses are referred to as *privilege state violations*.

Remember that the S-bit in the system byte of the status register determines whether the 68000 is in the user state or the supervisor state. For instance, when S is set to logic 0, the user state of operation is selected. The user state is the lower security level. Switching S to logic 1 under software control puts the microprocessor at the higher security level or supervisor state.

When in the supervisor state, the 68000 can execute all of the instructions of its instruction set. However, when in the user mode, certain instructions are considered privileged and cannot be executed. For example, instructions that AND, OR, or exclusive-OR an immediate word operand with the contents of the status register are not permitted. Any attempt to execute one of these privileged instructions, while in the user state, results in a privileged state violation exception. The privilege violation exception service routine can signal the occurrence of the violation and provide a means of recovery.

Figure 12.2 shows that the privilege mode violation uses vector 8 at addresses 000020_{16} and 000022_{16} of the vector table.

Trace Exception

The 68000 has a trace option that allows for implementation of the single-step mode of operation. Just like the privileged state, this option can be enabled or disabled under software control by toggling a bit in the status register. Trace is controlled by the T-bit in the system byte of SR. Trace is turned on by setting T and turned off by clearing it to 0.

When *trace mode* is enabled, the 68000 initiates a trace exception through vector 9 at completion of execution of each instruction. This exception routine can pass control to a monitor that allows examination of the MPU's internal registers or external memory. This type of information is necessary for debugging software. The monitor can also be used to initiate execution of the next instruction. In this way, the instructions of the program can be stepped through one after the other and their operations verified.

Illegal/Unimplemented Instructions

The last internal exception function of the 68000 is its *illegal/unimplemented instruction detection* capability. This feature of the 68000 permits it to detect automatically whether or not the opcode fetched as an instruction corresponds to one of the instructions in the instruction set. If it does not, execution is not attempted; instead, the opcode is identified as being illegal and exception processing is initiated. This *illegal opcode detection mechanism* permits the 68000 to detect errors in its instruction stream.

Occurrence of an illegal opcode initiates a change of program context through the illegal instruction vector, vector 4 in the table of Fig. 12.2. The exception service routine that gets initiated can signal the occurrence of the error condition.

The *unimplemented instruction* concept is an extension of the illegal instruction detection mechanism by which the instruction set of the 68000 can be expanded. It lets us use two ranges of unused opcodes to define new instructions. They correspond to all opcodes of the form $FXXX_{16}$ and $AXXX_{16}$. Here the X's stand for don't-care digits and can be any hexadecimal numbers.

Whenever an opcode of the form $FXXX_{16}$ is detected by the 68000, control is passed to an exception-processing routine through vector 11 at addresses $00002C_{16}$ and $00002E_{16}$ of the exception vector table. The service routine pointed to by this vector should be an *emulation routine* for the new instruction. For example, floating-point arithmetic or double-precision arithmetic emulation routines could be implemented. The emulation routine is written and debugged in assembly language and then stored in main memory as machine code. To use the new instruction in a program, we just insert this opcode, $FXXX_{16}$, as an instruction statement.

As shown in Fig. 12.2, the other unimplemented instruction opcode, $AXXX_{16}$, vectors out of addresses 000028_{16} and $00002A_{16}$.

ASSIGNMENT

Section 12.2

1. What are the different types of exceptions available on the 68000?

Section 12.3

2. Where in memory must the exception vector table be stored?
3. The illegal instruction exception service routine starts at address $B000. Show where and how its vector will be stored in the exception vector table.

Section 12.4

4. If the service routine for TRAPV is in progress when an external interrupt occurs, what happens?

Section 12.5

5. What is the highest priority level for external hardware interrupts?
6. If the interrupt mask value is 5 when the 68000 receives an external hardware interrupt request with code 100_2, will the request be acknowledged or ignored?
7. Write an instruction to load the interrupt mask with the value 011_2 without changing any of the other bits in the status register. Assume that the 68000 is in the supervisor state.

Section 12.6

8. Give an overview of the events that take place during the IACK bus cycle.

Section 12.7

9. Overview the response of the circuit in Fig. 12.9 to an active IRQ_{60} input.

Sections 12.8 and 12.9

10. Overview the operation of the autovector interrupt interface circuit in Fig. 12.11 when a level 2 request for service is received.

Section 12.10

11. Show the general structure of a TRAP service routine. Assume that the service routine uses registers D_0, D_1, and A_2.
12. Write an instruction sequence that will check the index of an array. The index is stored in memory location INDEX and the upper bound of the array is stored at UBD.

Section 12.11

13. What is a bus error in the 68000 microcomputer system?
14. Explain how a bus error condition is handled by the 68000.

Section 12.12

15. Write a reset service routine that will clear the data registers, address registers, and set the supervisor stack pointer to $FFFFFE. Then branch to $A000, where the application program begins.

Section 12.13

16. What internal exceptions are implemented in the 68000?
17. Explain what is meant by an address error exception.
18. What happens when the unused opcode $F100_{16}$ is encountered during instruction execution?

Bibliography

BRYCE, HEATHER, Microprogramming Makes the MC68000 a Processor for the Future, *Electronic Design 22*, Oct. 25, 1979.

CIARCIA, STEVEN, The Intel 8086, *Byte*, Nov. 1979.

DAVIS, REX, *Prioritized Individually Vectored Interrupts for Multiple Peripheral Systems with the 68000*. Austin, TX: Motorola Inc., 1981.

GRADEN, DUANE, *Software Refreshed Memory Card for the MC68000 (AN-816)*. Austin, TX: Motorola Inc., 1981.

INTEL CORPORATION, *Component Data Catalog*. Santa Clara, CA: Intel Corporation, 1980.

INTEL CORPORATION, *iAPX86,88 User's Manual*. Santa Clara, CA: Intel Corporation, July 1981.

INTEL CORPORATION, *MCS-86$_{tm}$ User's Manual*. Santa Clara, CA: Intel Corporation, Feb. 1979.

INTEL CORPORATION, *Peripheral Design Handbook*. Santa Clara, CA: Intel Corporation, Apr. 1978.

KANE, GERRY, DOUG HAWKINS, AND LANCE LEVENTHAL, *68000 Assembly Language Programming*. Berkeley, CA: Osborne/McGraw-Hill, 1981.

LEMAIR, IAN, AND ROBERT NOBIS, *Electronic Design 18,* Sept. 1, 1978.

MCKENZIE, JAMES, *Dual 16-Bit Ports for the MC68000 Using Two MC6821s (AN-810)*. Austin, TX: Motorola Inc., 1981.

MORSE, STEPHEN P., *The 8086 Primer*. Rochelle Park, NJ: Hayden Book Company, Inc., 1978.

MOTOROLA INC., *MC68000 16-Bit Microprocessor User's Manual*, 3rd ed. Englewood Cliffs, NJ: Prentice-Hall, Inc., 1982.

RECTOR, RUSSELL, AND GEORGE ALEXY, *The 8086 Book*. Berkeley, CA: Osborne/McGraw-Hill, 1980.

SCANLON, LEO J., *The 68000: Principles and Programming*. Indianapolis, IN: Howard W. Sams & Company, Inc., Publishers, 1981.

STARNES, THOMAS W., Compact Instructions Give the MC68000 Power While Simplifying Its Operation, *Electronic Design 20*, Sept. 27, 1979.

STARNES, THOMAS W., Handling Exceptions Gracefully Enhances Software Reliability, *Electronics*, Sept. 11, 1980.

STARNES, THOMAS W., Powerful Instructions and Flexible Registers of the MC68000 Make Programming Easy, *Electronic Design 9*, Apr. 26, 1980.

STRITTNER, SKIP, AND TOM GUNTER, A Microprocessor Architecture for a Changing World: The Motorola 68000, *Computer*, Feb. 1979.

STRITTNER, SKIP, AND NICK TREDENNICK, Microprogrammed Implementation of a Single Chip Microprocessor, *Proceedings, 11th Annual Microprogramming Workshop*, Dec. 1978.

TRIEBEL, WALTER A., *Integrated Digital Electronics*. Englewood Cliffs, NJ: Prentice-Hall, Inc., 1979.

TRIEBEL, WALTER A., AND ALFRED E. CHU, *Handbook of Semiconductor and Bubble Memories*. Englewood Cliffs, NJ: Prentice-Hall, Inc., 1982.

Answers to Selected Odd-Numbered Problems

Chapter 1

Section 1.2

1. Computer program.

Section 1.3

5. A computer that has been tailored to meet the needs of a specific application.

Section 1.4

7. Secondary storage is for long-term storage of data that are not in use. On the other hand, the data that are currently being processed are held temporarily in primary storage memory.

Section 1.5

9. Program storage memory is the part of the memory subsystem that contains the program that is executed by the microcomputer. On the other hand, the data that are processed during execution of the program are held in the data storage part of memory.

Section 1.6

11. 4-bit, 8-bit, 16-bit, and 32-bit.

Chapter 2

Section 2.2

1. High-density N-channel MOS (HMOS).
3. 1M byte.

Section 2.3

5. Logic 1 at the MN/$\overline{\text{MX}}$ input selects the minimum mode and logic 0 at this input selects the maximum mode.

Section 2.4

7. Address bus width equals 20 bits and data bus width equals 16 bits.
9. $\overline{\text{INTA}}$ output.

Section 2.5

11. HOLD, HOLDA, $\overline{\text{WR}}$, M/$\overline{\text{IO}}$, DT/$\overline{\text{R}}$, $\overline{\text{DEN}}$, ALE, and $\overline{\text{INTA}}$ in minimum mode are $\overline{\text{RQ}/\text{GT}_0}$, $\overline{\text{RQ}/\text{GT}_1}$, $\overline{\text{LOCK}}$, $\overline{\text{S}}_2$-$\overline{\text{S}}_0$, QS_0, and QS_1, respectively, in the maximum mode.
13. The 8289 implements the Multibus arbitration protocol that permits multiple processors to reside on the 8086's system bus.
15. $\overline{\text{RQ}/\text{GT}_0}$, $\overline{\text{RQ}/\text{GT}_1}$.

Section 2.6

17. The BIU is used to prefetch instructions from memory and store them in its queue and perform bus cycles to access data operands. The EU reads instructions from the queue and performs the operations defined in the instructions.

Section 2.7

21. Pointer registers are SP and BP and the index registers are SI and DI. The pointer and index registers generally contain memory addresses, whereas the general-purpose registers generally contain data for operations or data that result from an operation.
23. Status flags monitor (record) the processor status that results from the execution of an instruction. On the other hand, the control flags control processor operations or the execution of instructions.

CF = carryout/borrow-in or no carryout/no borrow-in for the MSB during an arithmetic instruction

PF = result produced by executing an instruction; has even or odd parity

AF = carryout/borrow-in or no carryout/no borrow-in between the high and low nibble in the lower byte of a word; result of an arithmetic instruction

ZF = result produced by executing an instruction is zero or nonzero

SF = result produced by executing an instruction is positive or negative

OF = an overflow or nonoverflow condition has occurred during the execution of the arithmetic instruction

TF = enables/disables single-step mode of operation

IF = enables/disables external maskable interrupts

DF = determines whether the string count increments or decrements

Section 2.8

25. $V_{Hmin} = 3.9$ V and $V_{Hmax} = V_{cc} + 1$ V; $V_{Lmin} = -0.5$ V and $V_{Lmax} = 0.6$ V.

Section 2.9

27. Idle states are performed if the queue is full and the EU does not require the BIU to read or write operands from memory. On the other hand, wait states are initiated in response to slow memory or I/O devices which make the CPU wait for the READY signal to be returned before the processor can proceed to complete the current bus cycle.

Chapter 3

Section 3.2

1. Yes, the 8086 can directly store a word of data starting at an odd-address boundary.

3. Code segment (CS) register, data segment (DS) register, stack segment (SS) register, and extra segment (ES) register.

Section 3.4

7. Register addressing mode, immediate addressing mode, direct addressing mode, register indirect addressing mode, based addressing mode, indexed addressing mode, based indexed addressing mode, string addressing mode, and I/O port addressing mode.

9.

	Destination operand	Source operand
(a)	AL	BL
(b)	AX	FF_{16} (immediate value)
(c)	$PA = (DS)0_{16} + (SI)_{16}$	AX
(d)	SI	$PA = (DS)0_{16} + (DI)_{16}$
(e)	$PA = (DS)0_{16} + (BX)_{16} + XYZ_{16}$	CX
(f)	$PA = (DS)0_{16} + (SI)_{16} + XYZ_{16}$	AH
(g)	$PA = (DS)0_{16} + (BX)_{16} + (DI)_{16} + XYZ_{16}$	AL

Section 3.6

11. MOV   CX,BX
MOV   BX,AX
MOV   AX,CX

Section 3.7

13. MOV   DS,0H   ; INITIALIZE DATA SEGMENT
MOV   SI,0A000H
MOV   AX,[SI]
MOV   BX,0C000H   ; POINTER FOR RESULTS
MOV   DI,0B000H
MOV   DX,[DI]
ADD   DX,AX
MOV   [BX],DX   ; SAVE THE SUM

```
SUB     DX,AX           ; RESTORE NUMBER
SUB     DX,AX
ADD     BX,2H
MOV     [BX],DX         ; SAVE THE DIFFERENCE
ADD     DX,AX           ;RESTORE NUMBER
MUL     DX
ADD     BX,2H
MOV     [BX],AX         ; SAVE LS PART OF PRODUCT
ADD     BX,2H
MOV     [BX],DX         ; SAVE MS PART OF PRODUCT
MOV     AX,[SI]         ; RESTORE NUMBER
DIV     [DI]
ADD     BX,2H
MOV     [BX],AX         ; SAVE QUOTIENT
ADD     BX,2H
MOV     [BX],DX         ; SAVE THE REMAINDER
```

Section 3.8

```
15.  NOT     NUM2
     MOV     CL,AL
     AND     AL,NUM2
     OR      AL,BL
     AND     CL,NUM1
     OR      AL,CL
```

Section 3.10

```
17.  MOV     BL,AL
     MOV     CL,5
     SHR     BX,CL
     AND     BX,1
```

Chapter 4

Section 4.2

```
1.  CLI
    LAHF
    MOV DS, 0H
    MOV BX, 0A000H
    MOV [BX],AH
    CLC
```

Section 4.3

3.

Instruction	ZF	CF
Initial state	0	0
MOV BX,1111H	0	0
MOV AX,0BBBBH	0	0
CMP BX,AX	0	1

Section 4.4

```
5.              MOV     AL,1H
                MOV     CL,0H
                MOV     DL,N
      NXT:      CMP     CL,DL
                JE      DONE
                INC     CL
                MUL     CL
                JMP     NXT
      DONE:     MOV     FACT,AL
```

```
7.              MOV     CX,100
                MOV     DS,0H
                MOV     BX,0A000H
                MOV     SI,0B000H
                MOV     DI,0C000H
      AGAIN:    MOV     AX,[BX]
                CMP     AX,0H
                JGE     POSTV
      NEGTV:    MOV     [DI],AX
                INC     DI
                INC     DI
                JMP     NXT
      POSTV:    MOV     [SI],AX
                INC     SI
                INC     SI
      NXT:      DEC     CX
                JNZ     AGAIN
```

Section 4.6

```
13.             MOV     AL,1H
                MOV     CX,N
                JCXZ    DONE      ; N = 0 CASE
                LOOPZ   DONE      ; N = 1 CASE
                INC     CX        ; RESTORE N
      AGAIN:    MUL     CL
                LOOP    AGAIN
      DONE:     MOV     FACT,AL
```

Chapter 5

Section 5.2

1.

Address	Contents
A001	78
A002	56
A003	34
A004	12

3. $A0000_{16}$ through $AFFFF_{16}$.

5.
MOV	DX,0A000H
MOV	CS,DX
MOV	DX,0B000H
MOV	DS,DX
MOV	DX,0C000H
MOV	SS,DX
MOV	DX,0D000H
MOV	ES,DX

Section 5.3

7. $\overline{BHE} = 0$, $A_0 = 0$, $\overline{WR} = 0$, $M/\overline{IO} = 1$, $DT/\overline{R} = 1$, $\overline{DEN} = 0$.

Section 5.6

9. During T_1 the 8086 outputs address $B0010_{16}$ on the address bus; asserts $\overline{BHE}$; and asserts ALE. The address for the memory must be latched external to the 8086 using ALE to gate the latch device. The 8086 also asserts the M and DT signals at this time. During T_2, $\overline{WR}$ is inserted and then the 8086 puts the data word onto the data bus. These data remain valid until the end of T_4 and should be written into memory with the rising edge of $\overline{WR}$ early in the T_4 cycle.

Section 5.7

11. Stack is the area of memory used to temporarily store data (parameters) that are to be passed to subroutines and information, such as the contents of IP and CS, that is needed to return from a called subroutine to the calling program.

Section 5.8

13. During T_1 of the bus cycle, the 8086 supplies the address $A0000_{16}$ to the 8282 data latches. It also outputs logic 0 on $\overline{BHE}$ and a pulse to logic 1 on ALE. This pulse is used to latch the address and $\overline{BHE}$ into the latches. Also during T_1, the 8086 sets the DT/$\overline{R}$ line to logic 0. This specifies a read cycle and when applied to the 8286 devices configures them to transfer data from their ports B to ports A. The data to be read from memory are available at the B ports. During T_2, the 8086 switches $\overline{DEN}$ to logic 0, which enables the 8286 devices to transfer data, and during T_3 it reads the word of data on its 16 data lines.

Section 5.10

15. 2K-word read/write memory subsystem (see figure on page 375).

Chapter 6

Section 6.2

1. The address bus carries the address of the I/O port and the data bus carries the data that are transferred between CPU and the I/O port.

3. When in the maximum mode, the 8086 outputs status code $\overline{S}_2\overline{S}_1\overline{S}_0 = 001$ or 010 to inform external circuitry that an I/O operation is in progress.

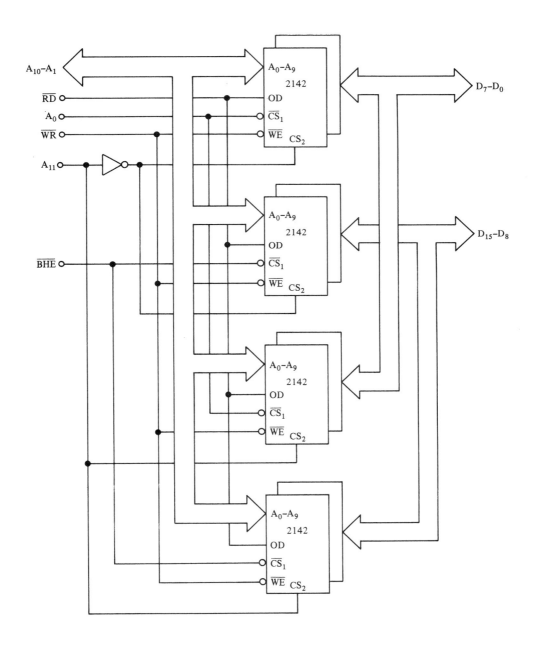

Section 6.4

5. Execution of this input instruction causes the accumulator AX to be loaded with the contents of the word-wide input port at address $1A_{16}$.

Section 6.5

7. During T_1 of the bus cycle, the 8086 outputs address $A000_{16}$ on the address bus. Then it sets $M/\overline{IO}$ to logic 0 to signal that the address on the bus is an I/O address instead of a memory address. Finally, ALE goes active to latch the address in external circuitry. During T_2, $\overline{RD}$ goes active, logic 0, to signal that an input cycle is to be performed. Then $\overline{DEN}$ is switched to logic 0 to enable the data from the input port at address $A000_{16}$ onto the data bus, and status is output. In the T_3 part of the bus cycle, the 8086 reads the data off the bus and puts them into the AX register. This is followed by $\overline{RD}$ and $\overline{DEN}$ being returned to their inactive 1 level in T_4 to complete the bus cycle.

Section 6.7

11. MOV DS, 0H
    MOV AL,092H
    MOV BX,0100H
    MOV [BX],AL

Section 6.8

13. IN   AL,01H   ; READ PORT A
    MOV   BL,AL   ; SAVE IN BL
    IN   AL,03H   ; READ PORT B
    ADD   AL,BL   ; ADD THE TWO NUMBERS
    OUT   05H,AL   ; OUTPUT TO PORT C

Section 6.9

15. MOV   CX,0401H
    MOV   AL,[CX]
    MOV   BL,AL
    MOV   CX,0403H
    MOV   AL,[CX]
    ADD   AL,BL
    MOV   CX,0405H
    MOV   [CX],AL

Chapter 7

Section 7.2

1. External hardware interrupts, software interrupts, internal interrupts, nonmaskable interrupt, and reset interrupt.

Section 7.3

3. The pointer table contains the starting memory addresses of the service routines for the various interrupts.

Section 7.4

5.
```
        .
        .
        .
   CLI       ;Entry point of noninterruptible service routine and disable interrupts
        .
        .
        .
        .
        .
   STI       ;Reenable interrupts
   IRET      ;Return to main part of program
        .
        .
```

Section 7.6

7. INTR is the interrupt request signal that must be applied to the 8086 MPU by external interrupt interface circuitry to request service for an interrupt driven device. In a minimum-mode system, the MPU signals external devices that the request for service has been granted by outputting a pulse to logic 0 on the interrupt acknowledge ($\overline{\text{INTA}}$) line. In a maximum-mode 8086 system, an interrupt acknowledge bus status code is output on $\overline{S}_0$ through $\overline{S}_2$ and this code is decoded by the 8288 bus controller to produce the $\overline{\text{INTA}}$ signal.

Section 7.8

9. $D_0 = 0$ ICW_4 not needed
$D_1 = 1$ Single device
$D_3 = 0$ Edge triggered
and assuming all other bits are logic 0 gives
$ICW_1 = 00000010_2 = 02_{16}$

11. $D_0 = 1$ Use with the 8086
$D_1 = 0$ Normal end of interrupt
$D_3 D_2 = 11$ Buffered mode master
$D_4 = 0$ Disable special fully nested mode
and assuming that the rest of the bits are 0, we get
$ICW_4 = 00001101_2 = 0D_{16}$

Section 7.10

17. INT 20 is a software interrupt whose service routine starts at the address defined by the values IP and CS stored at memory locations 80_{16} and 82_{16}, respectively. When the instruction is executed, first the old values of CS and IP are saved on the top of the stack. Then the IF and TF flags are cleared to 0. Next, IP and CS are loaded from addresses 80_{16} and 82_{16}, respectively. Finally, execution resumes with the first instruction of the service routine.

Section 7.11

19. NMI differs from the external hardware interrupts in three ways:
a. NMI is not masked out with the IF flag.
b. The NMI interrupt is initiated from the NMI input lead while external hardware interrupts are initiated from the INTR input.
c. The NMI input is edge triggered instead of level sensitive. Therefore, its occurrence is internally latched into the 8086 as it is switched to the 1 logic level.

Section 7.12

21.

```
        PUSHF
        PUSH    DS
        PUSH    CX
        PUSH    DI
        MOV     DS,0
        MOV     CX,100H
        MOV     DI,0A000H
NXT:    MOV     [DI], 0
        INC     DI
        DEC     CX
        JNZ     NXT
        POP     DI
        POP     CX
        POP     DS
        POPF
        IRET
```

Chapter 8

Section 8.2

1. High-density N-channel MOS (HMOS).
3. 16 general-purpose registers, 8 data registers D_0 through D_7 and 8 address registers A_0 through A_7, and all are 32 bits in length.

Section 8.3

5. 23 address lines A_1 through A_{23}, 2^{23} unique addresses.
7. For an asynchronous bus, once the bus cycle is initiated, it is not completed until external circuitry returns a signal to the processor.
9. The address lines A_1 through A_{23} present a word address and the upper and lower bytes of that word are accessed using the $\overline{UDS}$ and $\overline{LDS}$ signals.
11. $FC_2 FC_1 FC_1 = 110$.
13. The code value applied at the interrupt priority inputs is compared to the internal mask. If its value is more than that in the mask, the interrupt is serviced; otherwise, it is ignored.
15. To provide interface signals so that low-speed 6800 synchronous peripheral devices can be used with the high-speed 68000 CPU.

Section 8.5

17. In general, the address registers are meant for use in storing memory addresses such as pointers, while the data registers are to be used to store data that are to be processed by the CPU. However, their functions can be interchanged according to the need.

19. The program counter provides the address of the next instruction to be executed.

Section 8.6

21. Macroinstructions are the basic assembly language instructions defined by the instruction set of the 68000. Microinstructions are the internal machine instructions which are executed by the CPU in order to perform the function defined by a macroinstruction.

Chapter 9

Section 9.2

1. No, all words of data must be at even-address boundaries.
3. Bit, byte, word, long word, and BCD.

Section 9.3

5. Instruction		Source Addressing Mode	Destination Addressing Mode
(a)	MOVE.W D3,D2	Data register direct	Data register direct
(b)	MOVE.B D3,A2	Data register direct	Address register direct
(c)	MOVE.B D3,$ABCD	Data register direct	Absolute short
(d)	MOVE.L XYZ,D2	Immediate/absolute	Data register direct
(e)	MOVE.W XYZ(A0.L),D2	Register indirect with offset	Data register direct
(f)	MOVE.B D3,(A2)	Data register direct	Register indirect
(g)	MOVE.L A1,(A2)+	Address register direct	Postincrement register indirect
(h)	MOVE.L −(A2),D3	Predecrement register indirect	Data register direct
(i)	MOVE.W 10(A2),D3	Register indirect with offset	Data register direct
(j)	MOVE.B 10(A2,A3.L),$A123	Indexed register indirect with offset	Absolute short
(k)	MOVE.W #$ABCD,$1122	Immediate	Absolute short

7. $ABCD = $10 + A1 = $100 + A2 + D1 = A3.

Section 9.5

9. MOVEM $B000,D5/D6/D7

Section 9.6

11. MOVE.L   #$C000,A1
      MOVE.L $A000,D0
      ADD.L $B000,D0

```
MOVE.L    D0,(A1)
MOVE.L    $A000,D0
SUB.L     $B000,D0
MOVE.L    D0,4(A1)
MOVE.L    $A000,D0
MULU      $B000,D0
MOVE.L    D0,8(A1)
MOVE.L    $A000,D0
DIVU      $B000,D0
MOVE.W    D0,12(A1)        ; QUOTIENT
```

Section 9.8

13.
```
MOVE.B    D0,D7
AND.B     NUM1,D7
MOVE.B    NUM2,D6
NOT.B     D6
AND.B     D0,D6
OR.B      D1,D6
OR.B      D6,D7
MOVE.B    D7,RESULT
```

Section 9.9

15.
```
MOVE.B    D0,$B001
ROR.L     #8,D0
MOVE.W    D0,$B002
ROR.L     #8,D0
ROR.L     #8,D0
MOVE.B    D0,$B004
ROR.L     #8,D0
```

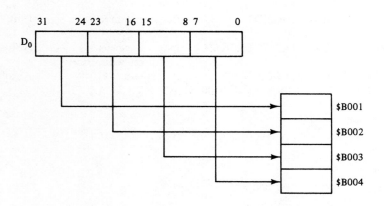

Chapter 10

Section 10.2

1.

Instruction	N	Z	V	C
Initial value	0	0	0	0
SUB.L A0,A0	0	1	0	0
CMPI.W #$A000,A0	0	0	0	1
TST A0	0	1	0	0

Section 10.3

3. The JMP instruction encodes the address of the location to which the jump is to take place into the instruction. On the other hand, the BRA instruction encodes the displacement, the number of bytes, of the "branch to address" from the BRA instruction, into the instruction word. Therefore, BRA both encodes in fewer bytes and executes faster than JMP.

Section 10.4

5.

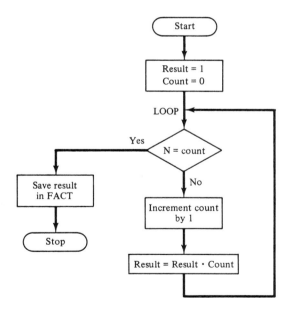

```
        MOVEQ   #1,D7
        CLR.W   D6
LOOP:   CMP.B   N,D6
        BEQ     DONE
```

```
              ADDQ.W    #1,D6
              MULU      D6,D7
              BRA       LOOP
     DONE:    MOVE.L    D7,FACT
```
7.

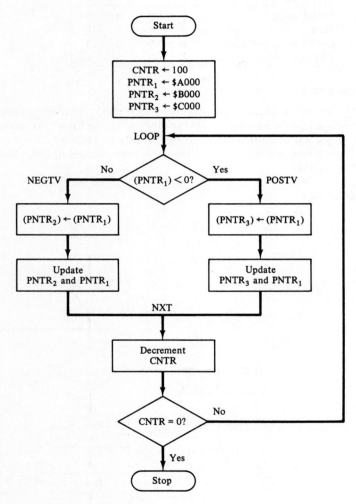

```
              MOVE.B    #100,D7
              MOVE.L    $A000,A6
              MOVE.L    $B000,A5
              MOVE.L    $C000,A4
     LOOP:    CMPI.W    #0,(A6)
              BMI       NEGTV
```

```
POSTV:    MOVE.W    (A6)+,(A5)+
          BRA       NXT
NEGTV:    MOVE.W    (A6)+,(A4)+
NXT:      SUBI      #1,D7
          BNE       LOOP
DONE:     BRA       DONE
```

Section 10.6

```
11. AGAIN:    BTST.B    #0,D0
              BNE       SUBA
              BTST.B    #1,D0
              BNE       SUBB
              BTST.B    #2,D0
              BNE       SUBC
              BRA       AGAIN
    SUBA:     •         •
              •         •
              •         •
              EORI.B    #1,D0
              RTS
    SUBB:     •         •
              •         •
              •         •
              EORI.B    #2,D0
              RTS
    SUBC:     •         •
              •         •
              •         •
              EORI.B    #4,D0
              RTS
```

Chapter 11

Section 11.2

1. No, both memory and I/O are located in the same address space.

Section 11.3

3. See Problem 15, Section 9.9.

Section 11.5

5. $FC_2FC_1FC_0 = 001$.

7.

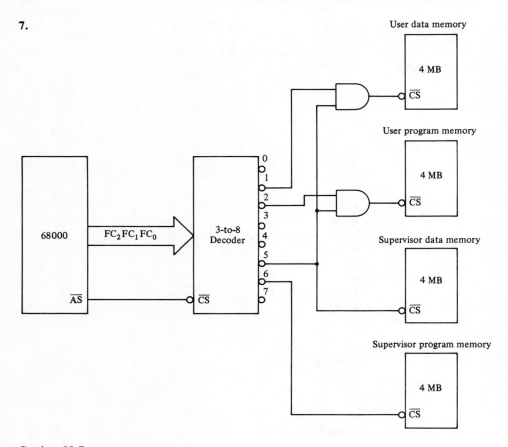

Section 11.7

9. (a) 68000 outputs $FC_2FC_1FC_0$ = 001 in user mode or 101 in supervisor mode.
   (b) 68000 places address \$A001 on A_{23} through A_1.
   (c) 68000 asserts $\overline{AS}$ (logic 0).
   (d) 68000 sets R/$\overline{W}$ to logic 0.
   (e) 68000 places the byte of data on D_7 through D_0.
   (f) 68000 asserts $\overline{LDS}$ (logic 0).
   (g) Memory interface decodes the address and enables memory devices.
   (h) Memory stores data available at D_7 through D_0 in \$A001 using $\overline{LDS}$.
   (i) Memory interface asserts $\overline{DTACK}$ (logic 0).
   (j) 68000 negates $\overline{LDS}$ and $\overline{AS}$ (logic 1).
   (k) 68000 removes data from D_7 through D_0.
   (l) 68000 returns R/$\overline{W}$ to logic 1.
   (m) Memory interface negates $\overline{DTACK}$ (logic 1).

Section 11.8

11. MOVE.L   (SSP)+,A2

```
MOVE.L    (SSP)+,A1
MOVE.L    (SSP)+,A0
```

Section 11.10

13.
```
MOVE.L    #$16000,A0
MOVEP.L   D0,0(A0)
```

Chapter 12

Section 12.2

1. External exceptions: reset, interrupts, and bus error.
Internal exceptions: instructions (TRAP, TRAPV, CHK, DIVS, DIVU), privilege violation, trace, illegal address, illegal instruction, and unimplemented instruction.

Section 12.3

3.

Vector Address	Contents
$10	$0
$12	$B000

Section 12.5

5. 7

7. ORI #$0300,SR

Section 12.10

11.

Save registers D_0, D_1, and A_2
Service routine body
Restore registers D_0, D_1, and A_2
Return to calling program

Section 12.11

13. "Bus error" means that an error has occurred during the execution of a bus cycle. For instance, external circuitry has detected a parity error or a watchdog timer has timed out before $\overline{\text{DTACK}}$ was asserted.

Section 12.12

15. CLR.L   D0

```
CLR.L     D1
  .         .
  .         .
  .         .
CLR.L     D7
CLR.L     A0
CLR.L     A1
  .         .
  .         .
  .         .
CLR.L     A6
MOVE.L    $FFFFFE,SSP
BRA       $A000
```

Section 12.13

17. An attempt is made to access a word or long word that resides at an odd-numbered address.

Index